**Keep this book. You will
need it and use it throughout
your career.**

About the American Hotel & Lodging Association (AH&LA)

Founded in 1910, AH&LA is the trade association representing the lodging industry in the United States. AH&LA is a federation of state lodging associations throughout the United States with 11,000 lodging properties worldwide as members. The association offers its members assistance with governmental affairs representation, communications, marketing, hospitality operations, training and education, technology issues, and more. For information, call 202-289-3100.

LODGING, the management magazine of AH&LA, is a "living textbook" for hospitality students that provides timely features, industry news, and vital lodging information.

About the American Hotel & Lodging Educational Institute (AHLEI)

An affiliate of AH&LA, the Educational Institute is the world's largest source of quality training and educational materials for the lodging industry. AHLEI develops textbooks and courses that are used in more than 1,200 colleges and universities worldwide, and also offers courses to individuals through its Distance Learning program. Hotels worldwide rely on AHLEI for training resources that focus on every aspect of lodging operations. Industry-tested videos, CD-ROMs, seminars, and skills guides prepare employees at every skill level. AHLEI also offers professional certification for the industry's top performers. For information about AHLEI's products and services, call 800-349-0299 or 407-999-8100.

About the American Hotel & Lodging Educational Foundation (AH&LEF)

An affiliate of AH&LA, the American Hotel & Lodging Educational Foundation provides financial support that enhances the stability, prosperity, and growth of the lodging industry through educational and research programs. AH&LEF has awarded millions of dollars in scholarship funds for students pursuing higher education in hospitality management. AH&LEF has also funded research projects on topics important to the industry, including occupational safety and health, turnover and diversity, and best practices in the U.S. lodging industry. For more information, go to www.ahlef.org.

HOTEL and RESTAURANT ACCOUNTING

Educational Institute Books

HOTEL and RESTAURANT ACCOUNTING

Seventh Edition

Raymond Cote

AMERICAN HOTEL & LODGING
EDUCATIONAL INSTITUTE

Disclaimer

This publication is designed to provide accurate and authoritative information in regard to the subject matter covered. It is sold with the understanding that the publisher is not engaged in rendering legal, accounting, or other professional service. If legal advice or other expert assistance is required, the services of a competent professional person should be sought.
—From the Declaration of Principles jointly adopted by the American Bar Association and a Committee of Publishers and Associations

The author, Raymond Cote, is solely responsible for the contents of this publication. All views expressed herein are solely those of the author and do not necessarily reflect the views of the American Hotel & Lodging Educational Institute (AHLEI) or the American Hotel & Lodging Association (AH&LA).

Nothing contained in this publication shall constitute a standard, an endorsement, or a recommendation of AHLEI or AH&LA. AHLEI and AH&LA disclaim any liability with respect to the use of any information, procedure, or product, or reliance thereon by any member of the hospitality industry.

Contents

About the Author

Raymond Cote

FOLLOWING AN accomplished business career, Raymond Cote became an educator and achieved the rank of full professor at a major hospitality university in the United States. For 18 years, Professor Cote taught undergraduate and graduate courses in hospitality accounting, hospitality financial management, taxation, and advanced accounting subjects. His teaching experience includes setting up hospitality accounting courses in the United States and abroad for an international hospitality college.

In the private sector, he has held the positions of vice president, controller, MIS director, and chief accountant for a major food and lodging corporation. As an entrepreneur, he was president of several business conglomerates consisting of a food and beverage operation, retail and service companies, and a consulting/certified public accounting firm.

Professor Cote is a graduate of the undergraduate and graduate schools of Suffolk University and Burdett College, both located in Boston, Massachusetts. His professional credentials have included Certified Public Accountant (CPA), Certified Computer Professional (CCP), Enrolled Agent (EA) authorized to practice before the Internal Revenue Service, and an Accreditation in Accountancy by the American Council for Accountancy. He held civic and professional positions as President of a Chamber of Commerce and Vice President and Director of Education for the Florida Accountants Association.

Professor Cote has written hospitality accounting textbooks and supporting material for the Educational Institute: *Hotel and Restaurant Accounting*, now in its seventh edition, and *Accounting for Hospitality Managers,* now in its fifth edition. Previous works include another text, *College Business Math* (1984–1988, PAR, Inc.), and numerous training and procedures manuals for private industry.

Preface

HOTEL AND RESTAURANT ACCOUNTING delivers an all-inclusive learning package. Most chapters close with a relevant case study. All chapters feature key terms definitions, review questions, and problems for students to work. Each chapter has been reviewed for its contemporary substance, applicability to the hospitality industry, and conformance with the distinct uniform system of accounts for hotels, stand-alone restaurants, and fast-food operations. Some major changes in this seventh edition include the following:

- Chapter 1 has been reorganized and revised to include new topics such as the concept of fair value and the necessity for accounting.

- Chapter 2's new topics include the feasibility study and purchasing a franchise. The discussions of Subchapter C corporations, Subchapter S corporations, and limited liability companies have been completely revised and updated.

- Chapter 10 has been extensively revised and updated. It presents and explains the hotel income statements issued to stockholders and to internal users. The new internal summary operating statement is in accordance with recommendations in the tenth revised edition of the *Uniform System of Accounts for the Lodging Industry*. In addition, the chapter discusses the statement of gaming operations for hotel casinos.

- Chapter 11, a new chapter, explores various depreciation and amortization methods.

- Chapter 17, also new, discusses business math topics for hospitality managers, such as the calculation of simple interest, cash discounts, and compound, present, and annuity values.

Also available are accompanying materials to complement the text. An instructor's guide containing the solutions to the chapter problems is available to faculty. A supplementary student exercise workbook is available for purchase as well. A corresponding solutions manual is available to instructors.

Author's Website Information

The author owns and frequently updates a website at www.raymondcote.com. The site features hospitality news and other special accounting and hospitality reports.

Author's Gratitude for Exceptional Attention and Service

- *Hotel and Restaurant Accounting* owes its existence to the greatest customers in the world. Thank you.

- Managing Editor Tim Eaton and the editorial staff do a remarkable job in producing this text. No matter how busy Tim is, he is always available for advice and assistance.

- VP of Customer Service Mari Behrendt and her staff, no matter how busy they are, provide courteous, proficient, and speedy responses to my inquiries and to those of my customers.

I dedicate this work to the cherished memory of my mother and father, Alice and Raymond Cote, with love, honor, and gratitude.

Chapter 1 Outline

The Necessity for Accounting
Why Study Accounting?
What Is Business Accounting?
    Fundamental Purpose
    Bookkeeping
    Accounting
    The "Bean Counter" Myth
Why Financial Statements Are Necessary
    The Elements Necessary to Assemble
        Financial Statements
The Corporate Accounting Department
Business Transactions
The Accounting Equation
Financial Statements
    Consolidated Financial Statements
Accounting Income vs. Taxable Income
The Accounting Profession
The Certified Public Accountant
    Audit and Attest Function
Influence of Government and Professional
    Organizations
    Securities and Exchange Commission
    Internal Revenue Service
    American Institute of Certified Public
        Accountants
    Financial Accounting Standards Board
    Hospitality Financial & Technology
        Professionals
    American Hotel & Lodging Association
    American Hotel & Lodging
        Educational Institute
    National Restaurant Association
Generally Accepted Accounting Principles
    Unit of Measurement
    Historical Cost
    Going-Concern
    Conservatism
    Objectivity
    Time Period
    Realization
    Matching
    Materiality
    Consistency
    Full Disclosure
    Fair Value

Competencies

1. Explain why it is essential that hospitality owners and managers thoroughly understand accounting and why hospitality students should study it. (pp. 3–5)

2. Describe business accounting and its purpose, and explain why financial statements are necessary. (pp. 5–7)

3. Describe management and other positions in the corporate accounting department, and explain the differences between financial accounting and managerial accounting. (p. 8)

4. Describe how business transactions are recorded in a double-entry accounting system. (pp. 8–11)

5. Identify the fundamental accounting equation and the five account classifications, and describe the basic financial statements. (pp. 11–13)

6. Explain the differences between accounting income and taxable income. (pp. 13–14)

7. Describe the various types of specialized accounting positions and responsibilities available in private and public accounting. (pp. 14–16)

8. Identify various government and professional organizations and how they influence hospitality accounting. (pp. 16–18)

9. Identify the generally accepted accounting principles discussed in the chapter, and explain each one's purpose. (pp. 19–23)

1

Accounting: A Management Resource

THIS CHAPTER BEGINS A JOURNEY into the world of business. If a business is to succeed, its owners and managers require more than business skill. Successful business management demands an awareness and understanding of the many components of a business. A successful business owner or manager needs instant, critical, and reliable information to understand the business's current financial condition and to forecast its financial prosperity. Accounting provides that information.

Accounting is often referred to as the language of business. Executives, investors, bankers, creditors, and government officials use this language in their day-to-day activities to effectively communicate in today's business world; these individuals must have a fundamental grasp of the theory and practice of accounting.

Accounting, like any other profession, has its own technical symbols, terminology, and principles. These elements form the vocabulary used to convey financial information, especially that information presented in the form of financial statements.

Many of those presently employed within the hospitality industry and many students new to the field of hospitality sometimes feel that the language of business is understood only by specialists who seem to thrive on number crunching. This misconception arises from unfamiliarity with the fundamental purpose of accounting and the logic that lies behind basic accounting activities.

This introductory chapter dispels many misconceptions about basic accounting activities, while providing answers to such questions as:

1. What are the purposes of business accounting and bookkeeping?
2. Why are financial statements necessary?
3. Why should hospitality students study accounting?
4. What is a corporate accounting department?
5. What is a business transaction?
6. What is the significance and meaning of the accounting equation?
7. What are the two most common financial statements?
8. What is a consolidated financial statement?
9. Why is accounting income different from taxable income?
10. What is a certified public accountant?

11. Which governmental agencies and private associations influence the standards and profession of accounting?

12. What are the generally accepted accounting principles?

The Necessity for Accounting

The hospitality business is a challenging one; location, the economy, weather, energy costs, continuously changing guest attitudes, and the quality of management all affect its success. A large number of businesses fail because management lacks financial knowledge and planning skills. Good management, provided by those who have acquired the proper education and planning skills, helps ensure a business's survival because it can adapt to the many challenges it faces.

A flourishing hospitality business owes its success to its management, staff, and guests. Profits are essential to the survival and growth of any business. Accounting provides information to owners and managers so they can make prudent, intelligent business decisions. While management does not produce financial information, every business owner or manager must be able to read financial information, process its meaning, and make essential decisions that will affect the owner's future and the future of employees. Management's ability to understand and interpret financial results is crucial to the survival of any business. This is applicable to food and beverage operations because of small unit sales per guest, often referred to as *the average check*. Lodging operation owners and managers are concerned with *fixed costs* (those costs that exist regardless of guest traffic).

Simply stated, it is essential that hospitality business owners and managers acquire a thorough understanding of accounting.

Why Study Accounting?

Your professional career will require you to make economic decisions, all of which require financial information. Accounting is the function that provides financial data. Your career might not require you to prepare financial data, but you will use this information. For this reason, you need to know how the data is processed and how the reports are prepared so that you better understand the information on the financial statements. With this knowledge, you can make intelligent economic decisions and succeed in this extremely competitive business environment.

Knowledge of the basic theory and practice of accounting is a valuable tool with which to achieve success not only in the hospitality industry but in the management of your personal finances as well. However, students planning careers in the hospitality industry often tend to neglect the accounting aspects of their field of study. Some believe that they will be able to pick up the essentials of accounting once they are out of school and on the job. But, once hired, many find that day-to-day responsibilities confine them to specific areas of a property's operation. Increased specialization within the hospitality industry at times creates a situation in which relatively few, outside of those actually employed in accounting departments, have opportunities to learn the theory and practice of accounting at a level required by the demands of today's business world.

Most colleges and universities require accounting as part of a business curriculum because the future managers of any type of business need to grasp the essentials of accounting in order to make sound business decisions. Managers need to understand how basic decisions regarding operational matters (such as replacing equipment or changing policy regarding the extension of credit to customers) will affect the financial statements of the business.

Managers and supervisors working in the hospitality industry recognize the importance of understanding the basic theory and practice of accounting. In the highly competitive field of hospitality, successful careers often depend on an ability to make daily operating decisions based upon analyses of financial information. To achieve satisfactory profit objectives for their areas of responsibility, managers must thoroughly understand how the accounting system accumulates and processes financial information. The increasing use of computers to record accounting information and to prepare financial statements has not diminished the need to master this business language.

Some individuals are reluctant to learn the fundamentals of accounting because they mistakenly believe that accounting is numbers oriented, requiring a sophisticated background in mathematics. Accounting theory and practice is not based on complicated mathematics; it is based on *logic* and emphasizes basic terminology, fundamental concepts, and relatively straightforward procedures. Applying the logic of accounting requires only the most basic math skills: addition, subtraction, multiplication, and division. Once individuals master accounting terminology, concepts, and procedures, accounting practices are not so difficult to understand.

What Is Business Accounting?

Though there are many fanciful and technical definitions of accounting, all fall short in conveying in understandable terms what it is that accounting exactly does. This chapter does not repeat or attempt to add yet another academic definition that is difficult, if not impossible, to understand. Rather, it attempts to clarify just what accounting is.

Fundamental Purpose

The fundamental purpose of **accounting** is to provide accurate, useful, and timely financial information. This information may take the form of financial statements, forecasts, budgets, and many types of reports that can be used to measure the financial position and operating performance of a hospitality business.

A full and comprehensible sense of the accounting profession is captured in the following practical, workable, and unsophisticated definition:

> Accounting involves recording business transactions, analyzing business records and reports, and producing reliable information.

The American Institute of Certified Public Accountants provides a definition of accounting based on the **accounting function**:

> Its function is to provide quantitative information, primarily financial in nature, about economic entities that is intended to be useful in making economic decisions.[1]

Bookkeeping

Bookkeeping is the initial phase of accounting and is only part of the overall function of accounting. Accountants supervise bookkeepers, whose primary function is to record business transactions in the accounting records. An accountant analyzes the accounting records for accuracy and compliance with accepted accounting practices and company rules. After the accounting records are judged satisfactory, the financial statements are prepared.

Accounting

It is impossible to produce a full description of the profession of accounting in a single statement, because the field is varied and extensive. This chapter attempts to clarify the issue by examining the different tasks an accountant performs, analyzing a corporate accounting department, and describing the specialization of an independent certified public accountant.

Accounting data is used to produce several different kinds of reports, such as formal financial statements, one-line messages (that is, cash balance, receivables), graphs, and statistical data. Exhibit 1 shows how accounting data is used to depict what happens to the U.S. lodging industry dollar.

The "Bean Counter" Myth

When companies cut jobs or expenses, the blame is often placed on the "bean counters," an incorrect and undeserved reference to accountants. Accountants are not responsible for staff cuts. They process and report information produced from real business transactions; accountants do not fabricate drops in sales or profits, they merely report actual conditions. Nor do accountants make decisions to eliminate jobs or reduce expenses; such actions are not within their purview. The management of a company makes any decisions to cut jobs and expenses.

Why Financial Statements Are Necessary

Managers need timely and accurate financial information to make intelligent decisions if their businesses are to succeed; the alternative—failure—is unacceptable. Investors need financial statements to analyze the quality of a potential investment or current stock holding. Banks need financial statements to decide whether to loan money. Creditors need financial statements to identify any risk involved in doing business with customers on an open line of credit.

The users of financial statements are sometimes referred to as *external users* and *internal users*. External users are those outside of the business, such as investors, banks, and suppliers. Internal users are the management of the company, such as the board of directors, the president and other officers, and the managers of the business.

The Elements Necessary to Assemble Financial Statements

Business transactions consist of sales, purchases, payroll, and numerous other financial transactions that are required in business operations. These business

Exhibit 1   U.S. Lodging Industry Dollar

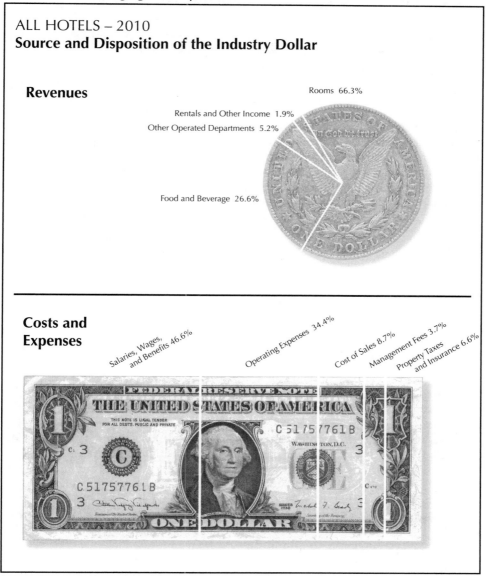

ALL HOTELS – 2010
Source and Disposition of the Industry Dollar

Revenues

Rooms 66.3%

Rentals and Other Income 1.9%

Other Operated Departments 5.2%

Food and Beverage 26.6%

Costs and Expenses

Salaries, Wages, and Benefits 46.6%

Operating Expenses 34.4%

Cost of Sales 8.7%

Management Fees 3.7%

Property Taxes and Insurance 6.6%

Source: *Trends in the Hotel Industry—USA Edition 2011* (San Francisco: PKF Consulting, 2011).

transactions are represented by documents such as register tapes, bank deposits, invoices, checks, and loans. The information from these documents is recorded in accounting records that are then sorted, summarized, and compiled into financial statements. Financial statements are customarily prepared on a monthly basis.

The Corporate Accounting Department ──────────

With the availability of inexpensive computers to small businesses, the clerical function of accounting has changed. Because the records are maintained in computerized files, bookkeepers no longer have to perform the tedious process of manually recording to individual bookkeeping records and computing a balance for each record. Accountants no longer prepare manual listings of individual records with balances (called *trial balances*) because the balances are computer-generated.

However, as useful as the computer has become, there still are processes that require human intervention. Bookkeepers must still determine how a business transaction is to be recorded, and the accountant must continue to analyze those records. Even though computers can easily print the financial statements, the accountant must carefully review them for accuracy. Because computers have taken over much of the number crunching, accountants have become analyzers, financial interpreters, and consultants.

The management structure of the accounting function (in descending order) is typically:

- Chief financial officer (CFO)
- Vice president of finance
- Treasurer
- Controller
- Chief accountant
- Accounting supervisor

Bookkeepers and various levels of skilled accountants form the staff of the accounting department. The departments of larger companies separate the duties of the staff into two divisions of responsibility: financial accounting and managerial accounting.

Financial accounting is concerned primarily with recording and accumulating accounting information to be used in the preparation of financial statements for external users. Financial accounting involves the basic accounting processes of recording, classifying, and summarizing business transactions. It also includes accounting for assets, liabilities, equity, revenue, and expenses.

Managerial accounting is concerned primarily with recording and accumulating information so that financial statements and reports can be prepared for internal users. Managerial accounting provides various management levels of a hospitality organization with detailed information, such as performance reports that compare the actual results of operations with budget plans.[2]

Business Transactions ──────────

Business transactions initiate the accounting process. A **business transaction** can be defined as the exchange of merchandise, property, or services for cash or a promise to pay. Specific accounts are set up to record the results of business transactions that involve promises to pay.

Exhibit 2   Cash, Payables, and Receivables Transaction

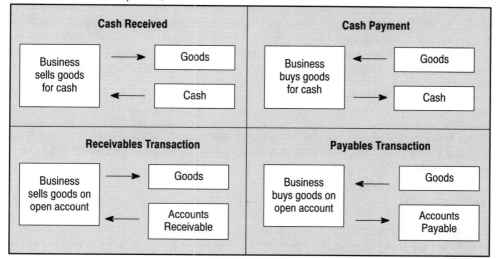

For example, if a restaurant buys merchandise or supplies on open account, this promise to pay is classified as an **account payable.** If a guest purchases food and beverage items from the restaurant on open account, the guest's promise to pay is classified as an **account receivable.** Exhibit 2 shows the effect on cash and receivables when goods are sold and the effect on cash and payables when goods are purchased.

Promises to pay may also involve the use of legal documents. If, in order to purchase certain equipment, a restaurant obtains funds by signing a promissory note, the liability is classified as a note payable. If realty (land or buildings) is involved, the liability is classified as a **mortgage payable.**

A business transaction creates events that affect two or more bookkeeping accounts in the accounting records. The following examples present very basic business transactions, describe the events created by those transactions, and identify the bookkeeping accounts that are affected by those events.

Example #1. When a guest enjoys a dinner at a restaurant and pays for the meal with cash, the business transaction that occurs is the exchange of food and services for cash. This business transaction creates the following events that affect the restaurant:

1. The cash received increases the assets of the restaurant.
2. A sale is made, thus increasing the sales volume (revenue).

These events affect the following bookkeeping accounts:

1. Cash
2. Food Sales

Example #2. When a guest enjoys a dinner at a restaurant and pays for the meal by charging the amount of the guest check to an open account maintained for him or her by the restaurant (no credit card is involved), the business transaction that occurs is similar to the previous example. However, in this case, food and services are exchanged not for cash, but for a promise to pay. The change in the method of payment does not affect the basic events created by the business transaction:

1. The guest's promise to pay increases the assets of the restaurant.

2. A sale is made, thus increasing the sales volume (revenue).

However, the change in the method of payment *does* change one of the accounts affected by the events. The promise to pay and the sale affect the following bookkeeping accounts:

1. Accounts Receivable

2. Food Sales

Example #3. When a restaurant buys food provisions on open account from a supplier, the business transaction that occurs is also an exchange of food and services for a promise to pay. However, the events created by this transaction that affect the restaurant are as follows:

1. The increase in food provisions increases the assets of the restaurant.

2. The restaurant's promise to pay increases the liabilities of the restaurant.

The bookkeeping accounts affected by these events are as follows:

1. Food Inventory

2. Accounts Payable

Every business transaction affects two or more bookkeeping accounts. This **double-entry system** of accounting, which is prevalent in recording business transactions, takes its name from the fact that equal dollar amounts of debits and credits are entered for each business transaction. If more than two bookkeeping accounts are affected by a transaction, the sum of the debit amounts must equal the sum of the credit amounts.

The double-entry system does not relate to addition and subtraction, and should not be confused with the misconception that for every *plus* there must be a *minus*. Pluses and minuses do not have any application in the recording of business transactions.

Business transactions are recorded in terms of whether their associated events increase or decrease the affected business accounts. Increases are not necessarily offset by decreases, or vice versa. One type of business transaction may increase all affected accounts; another type of transaction may decrease all affected accounts; yet another type may produce a combination of increases and decreases.

Most people know that accountants are concerned with debits and credits, which, indeed, play an important role in accounting. To apply debits and credits correctly, however, it is first necessary to learn the different types of accounts and understand the increase/decrease effect of business transactions.

Exhibit 3   The Accounting Equation

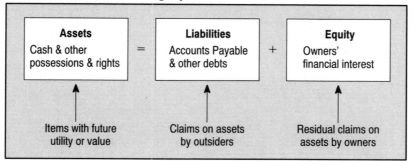

It is a mistaken conclusion that a debit will add and a credit will subtract. Such an error will make it difficult to comprehend debits and credits.

The foundation for debits and credits is the increase/decrease effect that is based on the types of accounts affected by a particular business transaction. It is more important to understand the effect and content of business transactions than to learn how to record them in an accounting format. This approach enables the student to analyze how a business transaction affects the bookkeeping accounts.

The Accounting Equation

All bookkeeping accounts in any accounting system for all businesses consist of the following five classifications:

- Assets
- Liabilities
- Equity
- Revenue
- Expenses

Understanding accounting can be simplified if one takes the time and effort to learn these five account classifications and the types of accounts that compose these classifications.

These five classifications also play an important part in the logic of accounting and its system of checks and balances. One such factor is the **accounting equation,** which is stated as follows:

$$\text{Assets} = \text{Liabilities} + \text{Equity}$$

Assets are cash, possessions, and purchased rights; **liabilities** are the debts of the business; and **equity** represents the owner's financial interest in the business. Exhibit 3 illustrates the relationship of these three account classifications. Exhibit 4 shows the accounting equation for a company that has assets of $100,000, liabilities of $60,000, and equity of $40,000.

Exhibit 4   Accounting Equation with Amounts

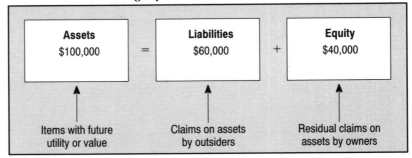

The accounting equation becomes more important to a business manager or creditor if its intent is viewed as a financial equation. From a finance perspective, assets are the sum total of any company, liabilities are a claim on those assets by creditors (outsiders), and equity is the leftover (residual) claim on those assets by owners.

At this point, the question might arise, "What happened to the other two classifications, revenue and expenses?" Disregarding accounting technicalities for the present, the result of revenue and expense accounts produces a profit or loss that is transferred to an account in the equity classification in the accounting process. Thus, while there are five account classifications, the accounting equation is still correctly stated as:

$$\text{Assets} = \text{Liabilities} + \text{Equity}$$

Its abbreviated form is stated thus:

$$A = L + EQ$$

Financial Statements

The numerous business transactions are recorded into bookkeeping accounts. These accounts are then analyzed and summarized to prepare important financial statements. Two common, easily recognized financial statements are the *balance sheet* and the *income statement*. The balance sheet can also be referred to as the *statement of financial position,* and the income statement is often called the *statement of operations,* especially in reports prepared by certified public accountants.

The balance sheet shows the assets, liabilities, and equity of the business. The income statement shows revenue (sales) and expenses and the resulting profit or loss. Both statements are fairly standard to every business. They are critical for profitability planning and business survival in the highly competitive hospitality industry. Exhibit 5 lists the three major sections of the balance sheet and the income statement. Each major section on the balance sheet and income statement features an itemized list of the appropriate bookkeeping accounts together with the relevant financial information.

Exhibit 5   Major Sections of the Balance Sheet and the Income Statement

Balance Sheet	Income Statement
Assets	Revenue
Liabilities	Expenses
Equity	Net income (loss)

Consolidated Financial Statements

Sometimes a corporation will have control over other corporations through stock ownership of those companies. Based on its control, the controlling corporation may have to include the results of its controlled companies and affiliates in its financial statements. Such combined financial statements are called *consolidated financial statements*.

Consolidated financial statements report the financial results as if they represent a single business entity. Assets and liabilities for the controlling company and all of its affiliates are reported on one balance sheet, revenues and expenses are reported on one income statement, and cash flows are reported on one statement of cash flows.

Accounting Income vs. Taxable Income

Differences arise because the objectives of financial accounting are not the same as the objectives that may lie behind the Internal Revenue Code (IRC).

The objectives of financial accounting are:

- To provide accurate, timely, and relevant information to help users of financial information make economic, financial, and operational decisions regarding the business.

- To satisfy the common interests of the many users of financial statements, rather than satisfy the specific interests of any single group.

- To select from various accounting alternatives those methods that will fairly present the financial condition of the business and the results of business operations.

These objectives focus solely on the interests and needs of internal and external users of financial information. The overall objective is to ensure that the results of business transactions are fairly presented in the financial statements of a business.

The objectives of the IRC, on the other hand, are guided by large-scale political, economic, and social concerns. Some major objectives of the IRC could be the following:

- To influence change in the economy

- To promote policies that are in the public interest

- To achieve social objectives

These political, economic, and social objectives can powerfully influence business activities. For example, governmental economic policy may lower taxes during an economic recession in an attempt to increase consumer demand for products and services, which eventually may increase production and decrease unemployment. Or governmental economic policy may raise taxes during a period of high inflation in an attempt to decrease consumer spending and eventually reduce spiraling prices. Political policy may direct legislators to grant tax credits during an energy crisis in an attempt to stimulate purchases of energy-saving equipment. Social policy may legislate tax incentives for private businesses to hire the elderly, the disabled, or individuals from disadvantaged social groups.

An important practical result of the difference in objectives is that the method of accounting for revenue and expenses under accounting principles differs from procedures dictated by income tax law. Consequently, the income shown on a business's financial statements *(income before income taxes)* may not be the same figure that appears as *taxable income* on the business's income tax return.

Differences among depreciation methods used for financial reporting and tax reporting are not uncommon. This allowable practice will result in a temporary difference between the income before income taxes reported on the financial statement, and the income reported on the income tax return, as shown in the following hypothetical comparison:

	Financial Statement	Tax Return
Sales	$100,000	$100,000
Depreciation	20,000	30,000
Other expenses	60,000	60,000
Income before income taxes	$ 20,000	$ 10,000
	↑	↑
	Accounting Income	Taxable Income

The Accounting Profession

One reason it is difficult to give a simple definition of accounting is that the field encompasses many different disciplines requiring various levels of education and experience. Accountants can be employed in any of a number of broadly defined specialties, namely not-for-profit accounting, public accounting, and private accounting.

Not-for-profit accountants serve such organizations as schools, hospitals, and government agencies.

Public accountants provide services such as taxation accounting, management consulting, and auditing of financial statements. The qualifications and work of the certified public accountant are discussed later in this chapter.

Private accountants are employed by a business enterprise. The following is just a small representation of the many and varied types of specialized accounting positions in a corporate accounting department:

- Budgeting and forecasting
- Cost accounting
- Tax accounting
- Internal auditing
- Accounting systems design

Budgeting and forecasting deals with estimating (forecasting) a company's future performance in the form of a plan called the budget. Accountants who work in this area develop forecasts, and then compare the predicted results with actual results to determine any variances from the forecast. These accountants also analyze the variances and their causes and report them to management for any corrective action.

Cost accounting relates to the recording, classification, allocation, and reporting of current and prospective costs. Cost accountants determine costs in relation to products and services offered by a hospitality business and in relation to the operation of individual departments within the property. One of the primary purposes of cost accounting is to assist management in controlling expenses.

Tax accounting is the discipline of preparing and filing tax forms required by various government agencies. A significant part of the tax accountant's work involves tax planning to minimize the amount of taxes that must be paid by a business. Although the emphasis of tax accounting lies in minimizing income tax payments at the federal, state, and local levels, this branch of accounting also involves other areas, such as sales, excise, payroll, and property taxes.

Internal auditing focuses on the review of company operations to determine compliance with management policies. Internal auditors also review accounting records to determine whether these records have been processed according to proper accounting procedures. Another important responsibility is the internal auditor's design and review of internal control policies and systems.

Internal auditing in the private sector should not be confused with the audit and the attest function performed by independent certified public accountants. Internal auditors are employees of a company, but generally do not report to the company's chief accounting officer; this arrangement allows them to maintain their independence. Usually they report to the company's board of directors or an audit committee.

Accounting systems design focuses primarily on the information system of a hospitality organization. This information system includes accounting and other areas as well, such as reservations. As more and more hospitality operations become computerized, accounting systems experts will necessarily become electronic data processing specialists, such as computer programmers and systems analysts.

The Certified Public Accountant

A **certified public accountant (CPA)** is an individual who has met educational and experience requirements prescribed by state licensing laws and who has passed the national Uniform CPA Examination.

To qualify for certification, the applicant must meet rigid academic standards. Many states now require an applicant to have 150 credit hours of college education to qualify just to sit for the exam. In addition, a certain number of these hours must be in accounting and business courses as specified by the state's board of accountancy.

The CPA examination is a multiple-day examination covering topics such as financial accounting and reporting, auditing, and business law. The financial accounting area includes federal income taxes, managerial accounting, and governmental accounting. The examination not only tests an applicant's problem-solving skills and knowledge of theory, it also evaluates the individual's writing skills by means of essay questions.

Passing the CPA exam is only the beginning. Before being licensed to practice, an individual may be required to complete an internship period under the supervision of experienced CPAs. But the process doesn't end there. Once a CPA is licensed, both the state licensing board and the American Institute of Certified Public Accountants require that a program of continuing professional education be maintained under standards established by these organizations.

Audit and Attest Function

An audit is a comprehensive investigation conducted by an independent CPA of a company's records and financial statements. An independent CPA is one who is neither employed by that company nor related to any officer of the company. The investigation involves an examination of the financial records and evidential matter, confirmation of receivables and payables, and observation of the physical inventory.

The objective of an audit is the **attest function**, which involves issuing an **opinion**. The word *opinion* in accounting has a very special meaning. Included in a letter accompanying the financial statements, this opinion expresses a conclusion on the reliability and fairness of the statements and states whether the financial statements were prepared in accordance with generally accepted accounting principles.

Influence of Government and Professional Organizations –

A number of government and private organizations influence the field of accounting. Even though all have similar interests and seek timely and reliable financial information, each has specialized interests demanded by the accounting profession. Bankers, investors, stockholders, trade organizations, government agencies, and business enterprises influence the practice of accounting in the public, private, and government sectors. The accountant working in the hospitality field is deluged by regulations and recommended guidelines from government agencies, professional organizations, and accounting organizations such as the following:

- The Securities and Exchange Commission

- The Internal Revenue Service

- The American Institute of Certified Public Accountants

- The Financial Accounting Standards Board
- Hospitality Financial & Technology Professionals
- The American Hotel & Lodging Association (AH&LA)
- American Hotel & Lodging Educational Institute
- The National Restaurant Association

Securities and Exchange Commission

The **Securities and Exchange Commission (SEC)** is concerned primarily with promoting disclosure of important information, enforcing securities laws, and protecting investors by maintaining the integrity of the securities markets. The SEC requires public companies to disclose meaningful financial and other information to the public. The SEC also oversees other key participants in the securities world, including stock exchanges, broker-dealers, investment advisers, mutual funds managers, and public utility holding companies.

The SEC's effectiveness derives from its enforcement authority. The SEC can bring civil enforcement actions against individuals and companies that break securities laws. Typical infractions include insider trading, accounting fraud, and providing false or misleading information about securities and the companies that issue them. In addition to being the primary overseer and regulator of the U.S. securities markets, the SEC works closely with many other entities, including Congress, other federal departments and agencies, the stock exchanges, state securities regulators, and various private sector organizations.

Internal Revenue Service

The **Internal Revenue Service (IRS)**, an agency of the U.S. Department of the Treasury, is responsible for enforcing the internal revenue laws and intervening when necessary. Revenues are collected through individual income taxes; corporation taxes; excise, estate, and gift taxes; and social security/retirement taxes. The IRS is structured into functional areas such as collection of taxes, investigation of violations of internal revenue laws, legal enforcement, taxpayer services, returns processing, compliance, information systems, and criminal investigation.

Congress enacts the tax laws. After a statute is enacted, the IRS issues regulations to help interpret and apply the law. The **Internal Revenue Code (IRC)** is a codification of the tax laws and regulations. The taxation of income is a major consideration for individuals, investors, business management, and the accounting profession.

American Institute of Certified Public Accountants

The **American Institute of Certified Public Accountants (AICPA)** is the national professional organization for all certified public accountants. Its mission is to provide members with the resources, information, and leadership that will enable them to provide valuable, professional services to the public, employers, and clients. In fulfilling its mission, the AICPA works with state CPA organizations and assigns priority to those areas where public reliance on CPA skills is most significant.

To achieve its mission, the AICPA promotes and protects the CPA designation and seeks the highest possible level of uniform certification and licensing standards. It establishes professional standards and helps members to improve their professional conduct, performance, and expertise. The AICPA monitors the performance of its members in enforcing current standards and requirements.

Financial Accounting Standards Board

The mission of the **Financial Accounting Standards Board (FASB)** is to establish and improve standards of financial accounting and reporting for the guidance and education of the public, including issuers, auditors, and users of financial information. The FASB is the designated organization in the private sector for establishing standards of financial accounting and reporting. Those standards govern the preparation of financial reports and are officially recognized as authoritative by the SEC.

Hospitality Financial & Technology Professionals

The **Hospitality Financial & Technology Professionals (HFTP)** is the society for financial and MIS professionals in the hospitality industry. HFTP offers numerous training sessions on hospitality accounting and technology, as well as professional development seminars for clubs, gaming, and other areas of special interest.

American Hotel & Lodging Association

The **American Hotel & Lodging Association (AH&LA)**, formerly the American Hotel & Motel Association (AH&MA), is the largest national trade association for the U.S. hotel and lodging industry. AH&LA provides its members with resources to operate more efficiently and more profitably; these resources cover the lodging, hospitality, and travel and tourism fields. Educational resources are produced by the organization's Educational Institute.

American Hotel & Lodging Educational Institute

The **American Hotel & Lodging Educational Institute** (**AHLEI,** or simply EI) is the world's leading provider of industry-tested, research-driven training resources for the hospitality field. EI succeeds in meeting its education and training mission by publishing videos, textbooks, courseware, seminars, multi-media CD-ROM programs, and self-paced learning courses on the Internet to reach all levels of hospitality personnel. EI is the certifying body for hospitality industry personnel. EI's academic division develops course materials for two-year and four-year hospitality schools worldwide and offers distance-learning programs of college-level hospitality courses on a home-study basis via the Internet and by mail. In addition to publishing world-leading hospitality textbooks, EI publishes the *Uniform System of Accounts for the Lodging Industry.*

National Restaurant Association

The **National Restaurant Association (NRA)** is the leading business association for the restaurant industry. The NRA and its Educational Foundation share a mission to represent, educate, and promote the rapidly growing food and beverage industry.

Generally Accepted Accounting Principles

Almost every profession has guidelines and rules to ensure that members carry out their responsibilities in accordance with accepted quality standards. Professional accounting standards have evolved from commonly adopted practices and in response to changes in the business environment. These accounting standards are known within the profession as **generally accepted accounting principles,** commonly referred to by the acronym GAAP. GAAPs encompass not only standards, but also conventions and principles from which specific technical rules and procedures are developed.

These GAAPs have received substantial authoritative support and approval from professional accounting associations such as AICPA and HFTP, from the FASB through its Statements on Financial Accounting Standards (SFAS), and from government agencies such as the SEC. Additionally, the AICPA publishes Statements of Position and industry practice and audit guides.

The application of these GAAPs ensures that consistent accounting procedures are followed in recording the events created by business transactions and in preparing financial statements. This consistency makes it possible for internal and external users of financial statements to make reasonable judgments regarding the overall financial condition of a business and the success of business operations from period to period.

Unit of Measurement

Since the value exchanged in a business transaction is expressed in monetary terms, the prevailing monetary unit is used to record the results of business transactions. For businesses in the United States, the common unit of measurement is the U.S. dollar.

A common **unit of measurement** permits the users of accounting data to make meaningful comparisons between current and past business transactions. Imagine the difficulties that would arise if the accounting records of a hospitality operation recorded food purchases in terms of the British pound and food sales in terms of the U.S. dollar!

Historical Cost

The principle of **historical cost** states that the value of merchandise or services obtained through business transactions should be recorded in terms of actual costs, not current market values.

For example, assume that a truck having a market value of $15,000 is purchased from a distressed seller for $12,800. The amount recorded as the cost of the truck is $12,800. As long as the truck is owned, the value (cost) shown in the accounting records and on the financial statements will be $12,800.

Going-Concern

The principle of **going-concern**, also known as *continuity of the business unit,* states that financial statements should be prepared under the assumption that the business will continue indefinitely and thus carry out its commitments. Normally, a business is assumed to be a going-concern unless there is objective evidence to the contrary.

The going-concern assumption can be used to defend the use of historical costs in the presentation of financial statements. Since there is no evidence of liquidation of the business in the near future, the use of liquidating or market values would not be appropriate unless the principle of conservatism applies.

Conservatism

The principle of **conservatism** serves to guide the decisions of accountants in areas that involve estimates and other areas that may call for professional judgment. However, it is important to stress that this principle is applied only when there is uncertainty in reporting factual results of business transactions.

The FASB states that assets and income should be fairly presented and not overstated. This does not in any way suggest that income or assets should be deliberately understated. The purpose of the principle of conservatism is to provide the accountant with a practical alternative for situations that involve doubt. When doubt is involved, the solution or method that will not overstate assets or income should be selected.

For example, if a hotel is the plaintiff in a lawsuit and its legal counsel indicates that the case will be won and estimates the amount that may be awarded to the hotel, the amount is not recorded until a judgment is rendered.

Other examples involve the valuation of inventories, marketable securities, and accounts receivable. Determining the net realizable value of these items requires professional judgment. Following the principle of conservatism, inventories and marketable securities are presented in the financial statements at either cost or market value, whichever is lower. Accounts receivable are presented along with an offsetting account (a contra account) that provides for accounts that are judged to be uncollectible, as follows:

Accounts Receivable	$255,000
Less: Allowance for Doubtful Accounts	5,000
Accounts Receivable (Net)	$250,000

Objectivity

The principle of **objectivity** states that all business transactions must be supported by objective evidence proving that the transactions did in fact occur. Obtaining objective evidence is not always a simple matter. For example, a canceled check serves as objective evidence that cash was paid. However, it is not evidence of the reason for which the check was issued. An invoice or other form of independent evidence is necessary to prove the reason for the expenditure.

When independent evidence is not available to document the results of a business transaction, estimates must be made. In these cases, the choice of the best estimate should be guided by the principle of objectivity. Consider the case of the owner of a restaurant who contributes equipment, purchased several years before for personal use, to the business in exchange for 100 shares of company stock. Let's further assume that there is no known market value of the restaurant corporation's stock. Ambiguity arises as the owner believes that the equipment is worth $1,200, while the catalog used by the owner when the equipment was purchased several years ago shows the cost to have been $1,400, and an appraiser estimates the current value of the equipment at $850. In this case, the principle of objectivity determines the amount to record. The most objective estimate of the current value of the equipment is the appraiser's estimate of $850.

Time Period

The **time period** principle, also known as the *periodicity assumption,* recognizes that users of financial statements need timely information for decision-making purposes. Therefore, accountants are charged with preparing more than just annual financial statements.

The accounting departments of many hospitality operations prepare financial statements not only on an annual basis, but quarterly and monthly as well. Financial statements that are prepared during the business year are referred to as *interim financial statements.* Because accountants may not have all the information at hand to complete accurate interim financial statements, they must often proceed on the basis of assumptions and make estimates based on their professional judgment.

Realization

The **realization** principle states that revenue resulting from business transactions should be recorded only when a sale has been made *and* earned. The simplest example of the principle of realization involves a customer paying cash for services rendered. When a hotel receives cash from a guest served in the dining room, a sale has been made and earned. The results of the transaction are recorded in the proper accounts.

What about the guest served in the dining room who charges the bill to an open account maintained by the hotel? In this case, even though cash is not received at the time of performance, a sale has been made *and* earned. The revenue and the account receivable are recorded at the time of the sale. However, according to the principle of realization, if a hotel receives cash for services and the services have not yet been provided (that is, the cash has not yet been earned), the transaction cannot be classified as a sale. For example, if a hotel receives an advance deposit of $500 for a wedding banquet to be held two months in the future, the cash received must be recorded—but the event cannot be classified as a sale. This is because the business has not yet earned the revenue; services have not been performed or delivered. In this case, receiving cash creates a liability account called Unearned Revenue. The full amount of the advance deposit is recorded in this account.

Matching

The **matching** principle states that all expenses must be recorded in the same accounting period as the revenue they helped to generate. When expenses are matched with the revenue they helped to produce, external and internal users of financial statements and reports are able to make better judgments regarding the financial position and operating performance of the hospitality business. Two accounting methods—cash accounting and accrual accounting—are used to determine when to record the results of a business transaction.

Cash Accounting. The **cash accounting** method records the results of business transactions only when cash is received or paid out. Small businesses usually follow cash accounting procedures in their day-to-day bookkeeping activities. However, financial statements that are prepared solely on a cash accounting basis may not necessarily comply with GAAP. If expenses are recorded on the basis of cash disbursements, expenses will not necessarily match the revenue they helped to generate. This may occur for any number of reasons.

For example, assume that each month begins a new accounting period for a particular restaurant. During each month, the restaurant follows the principle of realization and records revenue only as sales are made and earned. The restaurant also records expenses only as cash payments (which include payments by check) are made to various suppliers and vendors. This cash accounting method will not ensure that expenses will match the revenue generated during the month because many expenses will be incurred during each month but not paid until the following month. Such expenses include utility bills, laundry bills, and telephone bills that the restaurant may not even receive until the first week of the following month.

The IRS generally will accept financial statements prepared on a cash accounting basis only if the business does not sell inventory products and meets other criteria. Since food and beverage operations sell inventory products, these operations must use the accrual method.

Accrual Accounting. To conform to the matching principle, most hospitality operations use the accrual method of accounting. The **accrual accounting** method adjusts the accounting records by recording expenses that are incurred during an accounting period but that (for any number of reasons) are not actually paid until the following period. Once the adjusting entries have been recorded, financial statements and reports for the accounting period will provide a reasonable basis for evaluating the financial position and operating performance of the hospitality business.

Materiality

The principle of **materiality** states that material events must be accounted for according to accounting rules; however, insignificant events may be treated in an expeditious manner. Decisions concerning the materiality of events vary. Most of these decisions call for professional judgment on the part of the accountant.

In general, an event (or information) is material depending on its magnitude and the surrounding circumstances. The general criterion is based on whether, in the judgment of a reasonable person, that person would be affected by its omission. Information is material if it can make a difference in the decision process of a reasonable user of the financial statements. For example, a pending lawsuit for $150 against a million-dollar corporation would not be considered a material item.

Consistency

Several accounting methods are available to determine certain values that are used as accounting data. For example, there are various methods for determining inventory values and for depreciating fixed assets. The choice of which method to use is the responsibility of high-level management officials of the hospitality operation.

The principle of **consistency** states that once an accounting method has been adopted, it should be consistently followed from period to period. Consistent application of accounting methods and principles across accounting periods ensures that accounting information is comparable. When circumstances warrant a change in the method of accounting for a specific kind of transaction, the change must be reported along with an explanation of how this change affects other items shown on the operation's financial statements.

Full Disclosure

The **full disclosure** principle states that the financial statements of a hospitality operation should be accompanied by explanatory notes. These notes should describe all significant accounting policies adopted by the operation and should also report all significant conditions or events that materially affect the interpretation of information presented in the financial statements.

Commonly required disclosures include, but are not limited to, policies regarding the accounting method used to depreciate fixed assets and the methods used to determine the value of inventory and marketable securities. Commonly disclosed items that affect the interpretation of information reported in financial statements include, but are not limited to, changes in accounting methods, extraordinary items of income or expense, and significant long-term commitments. Exhibit 6 presents examples of the types of disclosures that may be included in notes accompanying the financial statements of a hospitality property.

Fair Value

The principle of **fair value** applies to valuation of assets and liabilities under current market conditions in transactions other than in liquidation. The fair value of an asset is the amount at which it can be bought or sold; the fair value of a liability is the amount at which the liability can be settled. Fair value is estimated as follows:

- A quoted market price, if available, provides the best evidential evaluation.
- If a quoted market price is not obtainable, an estimate based on the best available information is acceptable.

Endnotes

1. Statements of the Accounting Principles Board, No. 4, "Basic Concepts and Accounting Principles Underlying Financial Statements of Business Enterprises" (New York: American Institute of Certified Public Accountants, 1970), par. 40.

2. Raymond Cote, *Accounting for Hospitality Managers*, 5th ed. (Lansing, Mich.: American Hotel & Lodging Educational Institute, 2007).

Exhibit 6   Types of Disclosure and Examples

Types of Disclosure	Example
Accounting methods used	Straight-line method of depreciation
Change in accounting methods	A change from depreciating a fixed asset using the straight-line method to using the double declining balance method
Contingent liability	A lawsuit against the company for alleged failure to provide adequate security for a guest who suffered personal injury
Events occurring subsequent to the financial statement date	A fire destroys significant uninsured assets of the hotel company one week after the end of the year
Unusual and nonrecurring items	A hotel firm in Michigan suffers significant losses due to an earthquake

 **Key Terms**

accounting—The process and function of recording business transactions, analyzing business records and reports, and producing reliable information. The accounting profession comprises varied fields of specialization.

accounting equation—Assets = liabilities + equity. It plays an important role in the logic of accounting and its system of checks and balances.

accounting function—The system of providing quantitative information, primarily financial, about economic entities; it is useful in making economic decisions.

accounting systems design—The architecture of a hospitality organization's information system, it includes not only accounting, but other functional areas, such as reservations.

account payable—The amount owed to a supplier for purchases on open account.

account receivable—The amount due from customers for sales of goods and services on open account.

accrual accounting—An accounting method that adjusts the accounting records through the recording of expenses that are incurred during an accounting period but that are not actually paid until the following period.

American Hotel & Lodging Association (AH&LA)—A trade association for the U.S. lodging industry; formerly called the American Hotel & Motel Association.

American Hotel & Lodging Educational Institute (AHLEI)—A world leader in the publication of texts, courses, and other educational materials for the hospitality industry.

American Institute of Certified Public Accountants (AICPA)—The national professional organization for CPAs.

assets—A business's total of cash, possessions, and purchased rights.

attest function—The result of comprehensive investigation by an independent CPA, called an audit. The attest function involves issuing a professional auditor's opinion.

bookkeeping—The initial phase of accounting; its primary function is to record business transactions.

budgeting and forecasting—Estimating a company's future performance in the form of a plan called the budget.

business transaction—The exchange of merchandise, property, or services for cash or a promise to pay.

cash accounting—An accounting method that records the results of business transactions only when cash is received or paid out.

certified public accountant (CPA)—A designation for an accounting professional who has passed a national exam and also has qualifying academic and experience credentials.

conservatism—An accounting principle that serves to guide the decisions of accountants in areas that involve estimates and other areas that may call for professional judgment.

consistency—A GAAP that states that, once an accounting method has been adopted, it should be consistently followed from period to period.

cost accounting—The recording, classification, allocation, and reporting of current and prospective costs.

double-entry system—A bookkeeping system in which every business transaction affects two or more accounts and total debits must equal total credits.

equity—An owner's financial interest in a business. It represents the assets remaining after liability claims have been satisfied.

financial accounting—A branch of accounting concerned with preparation of financial statements for external users.

Financial Accounting Standards Board (FASB)—An organization having the authority to enact and enforce accounting standards.

full disclosure—A GAAP that states that the financial statements of a hospitality operation should be accompanied by explanatory notes.

generally accepted accounting principles (GAAP)—The conventions from which specific technical rules and procedures for accounting are developed.

going-concern—A GAAP that states that financial statements should be prepared under the assumption that the business will continue indefinitely and thus carry out its commitments.

Hospitality Financial & Technology Professionals (HFTP)—A society for financial and MIS professionals in the hospitality industry.

historical cost—A GAAP that states that the value of merchandise or services obtained through business transactions should be recorded in terms of actual costs, not current market values.

internal auditing—A review of a company's operations to determine compliance with management policies.

Internal Revenue Code (IRC)—A codification of the U.S. tax laws and regulation.

Internal Revenue Service (IRS)—A government agency that has the authority to enforce tax regulations and collect income tax revenues.

liabilities—The total debts of an operation.

managerial accounting—A branch of accounting concerned with the preparation of financial information for internal users.

matching—A GAAP that states that all expenses must be recorded in the same accounting period as the revenue they helped to generate.

materiality—A GAAP that states that material events must be accounted for according to accounting rules, but insignificant events may be treated expeditiously. Decisions regarding the materiality of an event or information call for the accountant's professional judgment.

mortgage payable—A liability related to realty (land and buildings).

National Restaurant Association (NRA)—The leading business association for the restaurant industry.

objectivity—A GAAP that states that all business transactions must be supported by objective evidence proving that the transactions did in fact occur.

opinion—The result of an audit and attest procedure. The auditor's opinion is stated in a letter accompanying the financial statements and expresses a conclusion on the reliability and fairness of the statements.

realization—A GAAP that states that revenue resulting from business transactions should be recorded only when a sale has been made *and* earned.

Securities and Exchange Commission (SEC)—A government agency that has the authority to enact and enforce laws relating to the securities markets.

tax accounting—The discipline of preparing and filing tax forms required by various government agencies.

time period—A GAAP that recognizes that users of financial statements need timely information for decision-making purposes. Therefore, accountants prepare more than just annual financial statements.

unit of measurement—This GAAP lets users of accounting data make meaningful comparisons between current and past business transactions, since the prevailing monetary unit is used to record the results of business transactions. In the United States, the common unit of measurement is the U.S. dollar.

 **Review Questions** ——————————————————

1. Why is it essential that business owners and managers possess a thorough education in and knowledge of accounting?

2. What is the fundamental purpose of accounting?

3. What is the definition of accounting based on its function?

4. What is the difference between accounting and bookkeeping?

5. Why are financial statements necessary?

6. What are some examples of external and internal users of financial statements?

7. How is financial accounting different from managerial accounting?

8. What is the definition of a business transaction?

9. What are the definitions of the terms *accounts receivable* and *accounts payable*?

10. What is the accounting term for Cash, Buildings, and Equipment that a business owns?

11. What is the accounting term for Accounts Payable and other debt of a business?

12. Which are the two most common financial statements? What is their typical content?

13. What is a consolidated financial statement?

14. What is the attest function as performed by a certified public accountant?

15. How do generally accepted accounting principles serve the accounting profession?

16. What are the 12 generally accepted accounting principles presented in this chapter? Identify and describe them.

 Internet Sites ————————————————————————————————

For more information, visit the following Internet sites. Remember that Internet addresses can change without notice. If the site is no longer there, you can use a search engine to look for additional sites.

Accounting Dictionary and Terminology Guides
www.accountz.com/glossary.html

American Hotel & Lodging Association (AH&LA)
www.ahla.com

American Institute of Certified Public Accountants
www.aicpa.org

Association of Chartered Certified Accountants (ACCA)
www.accaglobal.com/

Canadian Institute of Chartered Accountants
www.cica.ca/

Canadian Restaurant and Food Services Association
www.crfa.ca/

European Commission on Accounting
http://ec.europa.eu/internal_market/
   accounting/index_en.htm

Financial Accounting Standards Board
www.fasb.org

*Generally Accepted Accounting
   Principles (GAAP)*
www.fasab.gov/accepted.html

*Hospitality Financial & Technology
   Professionals*
www.hftp.org

Internal Revenue Service
www.irs.gov

*Introduction to the Government of
   Canada–Business Services*
canada.gc.ca/main_e.html

National Restaurant Association
www.restaurant.org

*U.S. Securities and Exchange
   Commission (SEC)*
www.sec.gov/

 **Problems**

Problem 1

Decide whether each of the following statements is true or false.

1. The receipt of cash or payment of cash must be present for a business transaction to occur.
2. Accounting and bookkeeping are identical.
3. A check is not evidence of a business transaction because it shows only that cash was paid; it is not evidence of the reason for the payment.
4. Financial accounting is primarily concerned with external users.
5. Managerial accounting is primarily concerned with internal users.
6. The five classifications of accounts are assets, liabilities, equity, revenue, and expenses.
7. The accounting equation can also be viewed as a financial equation.
8. The FASB is a hospitality trade association.
9. A building that cost $60,000 is now appraised for $85,000. The appraised value will appear on the financial statements.
10. The concept of materiality is difficult to quantify because an amount that is significant for one company may not be material for another company.

Problem 2

A restaurant's cash register shows sales of $1,400 for the day. Of this amount, $600 was cash sales. The restaurant does not accept any credit cards. What amount represents the sales to be recorded to Accounts Receivable?

Problem 3

Land and a building were purchased by a restaurant for $225,000. The down payment was $75,000, and the balance was financed by a mortgage. What amount will be recorded to Mortgage Payable?

Problem 4

A restaurant makes the following food purchases, which will go directly to the stockroom: Vendor A for $50 cash and Vendor B for $450 on Accounts Payable. What total amount will be recorded to Food Inventory?

Problem 5

A hospitality corporation is preparing its annual reports. The accounting records show sales of $250,000, and expenses, excluding depreciation, at $175,000. The company elects to use different depreciation methods for financial and tax reporting purposes. Depreciation for accounting purposes is $40,000, and for tax purposes the depreciation expense is $65,000. Compute the income before income taxes on the financial statements and the taxable income on the income tax return.

Problem 6

A guest books a banquet to be held six months from today. The price of the banquet is $9,000, and the guest pays 10% of that amount today. What amount will be recorded as a sale today?

Problem 7

A lodging operation purchases a parcel of land with cash. What bookkeeping accounts are affected?

Problem 8

A restaurant purchases land and buildings with a cash down payment and the balance financed by a mortgage. What bookkeeping accounts are affected?

Problem 9

Match the following situations with the accounting principle that best applies. In some cases, more than one principle may apply.

A.	Unit of Measurement	G.	Realization
B.	Historical Cost	H.	Matching
C.	Going-Concern	I.	Materiality
D.	Conservatism	J.	Consistency
E.	Objectivity	K.	Full Disclosure
F.	Time Period	L.	Fair Value

1. A large hotel corporation is preparing its year-end financial statements. Management has informed the certified public accountant that in two months it will begin closing 15 of its hotel properties. The accountant will provide information of this future event on the current year-end financial statements because of the _____ principle and the _____ principle.

2. A hotel purchases a van for $5,000 from a distressed rental agency. Due to the _____ principle, it is recorded at $5,000, even though the hotel could resell it for $6,500.

3. A motel receives an advance deposit of $150 for reserving guestrooms and meeting-room space. This transaction cannot be classified as a sale because of the _____ principle.

4. A resort hotel has used the straight-line method to depreciate its recreation equipment. This year it decides to use another type of depreciation method on these same assets. This violates the _____ principle.

5. A medium-size hotel with an extensive food and beverage operation records business transactions on a cash accounting basis. This violates the _____ principle.

Problem 10

A company has assets of $150,000. The liabilities of the company total $45,000. What amount is the owner's equity?

Ethics Case

Tom Daring had been employed by a national CPA firm for the last several years. Recently, Tom was discharged for failing to pass the CPA exam after several attempts. The CPA firm was satisfied with his performance, but company policy prohibited the retention of anyone who could not be licensed as a CPA.

Tom holds a degree in accounting and was an honors graduate from a well-known university. For several months he has been searching for employment in private industry where the CPA designation is not always a requirement. He has been to dozens of unsuccessful interviews. He was fully qualified for these positions, but other applicants who are CPAs were selected to fill the openings.

To improve his chances of finding employment, Tom has decided to declare that he is a CPA on his résumé.

1. Identify the stakeholders in this case. (Stakeholders are those parties who are affected beneficially or negatively.)

2. Describe the legal and moral issues involved in this case.

3. Assume that Tom has been hired by a new employer who is unaware that Tom has falsified his CPA credential. Tom's performance is outstanding, and he has contributed many profit-improving suggestions. Now Tom is being considered for promotion. Should he continue to deceive his employer?

Chapter 2 Outline

Feasibility Study
Legal Business Structure
    Proprietorship
    Partnership
    Corporation
    Limited Liability Company
Taxation of Business Income
    Proprietorship
    Partnership
    Corporation
    Limited Liability Company
Buying a Franchise

Competencies

1. Describe a feasibility study, and explain its purpose and its basic contents. (pp. 33–34)

2. Describe the major forms of business organization and the advantages and disadvantages of each. (pp. 34–41)

3. Outline the taxation of business income for the major forms of business organization. (pp. 41–44)

4. Explain what hospitality entrepreneurs should know before deciding to operate a franchise. (pp. 44–45)

2

Business Formation: Important Decisions

THE TERM *VENTURE* is frequently used to refer to the start-up of a new business. A venture may be initially funded by the owner or a group of investors. Many new business ventures fail within the first one to three years because of lack of funds, incompetent management, unsatisfactory location, or a combination of these, as well as other reasons, such as failure to prepare an initial feasibility study.

Whether or not to incorporate the business is a critical decision. No one legal structure fits all businesses. The best choice isn't always obvious. Each business form has different personal legal and tax liabilities. The prudent entrepreneur gets guidance from a lawyer and an accountant because the legal and income tax consequences can be complex and costly.

Most hospitality business ventures choose the corporate form of business organization. Incorporating creates a legal entity and a *corporate veil* that generally protects the owner's personal assets from any claims made against the business. However, this protection has limitations that will be explained in this chapter.

A business plan with a feasibility study is essential for a new or existing business. A good business plan describes in detail the business's mission and its goals, and states how these goals will be achieved. Business plans are required of those applying for business loans or seeking investors. An in-depth version of a business plan is beyond the scope of this chapter. However, the next section briefly summarizes the feasibility study. The Internet Sites section at the end of the chapter provides key links to such vital information.

Students, entrepreneurs, managers, and executives must have the answers to such questions as the following:

1. What is a feasibility study?
2. Which type of business form should be selected: Proprietorship? Partnership? Corporation? LLC?
3. What are the legal advantages and limitations of each business form?
4. If the business is incorporated, what is the difference between a Subchapter S corporation and a Subchapter C corporation?
5. What is the federal income tax impact on each business form?
6. What is a franchise?

Feasibility Study

One of the first things an entrepreneur must do before making a down payment on, starting up, or purchasing a hospitality business is prepare a **feasibility study**. The study should be prepared with expert consultants such as an attorney, accountant, or a hospitality consulting firm.

A feasibility study is a preliminary study of a proposed project, such as a business start-up, purchase, or expansion of an existing business. Its purpose is to determine the likelihood of success. The feasibility study can take many forms and be either lengthy or condensed. The study uses the present time to predict the future and may reach a positive or negative conclusion. A positive conclusion does not guarantee success due to many unpredictable variables. Despite this limitation, it is far better to have research results in hand rather than rely on mere hope or guesswork that a business will succeed.

The content of a feasibility study will vary with the type of business planned and with the study's intended readers. If bank financing is required, the study must have more depth and content. A full analysis of a feasibility study is beyond the scope of this chapter.[1] Basically, a feasibility study should, at a minimum, contain the following:

- Business description
- Market research
- Business location evaluation
- Competition analysis
- Equipment requirements
- Estimated income statement

Legal Business Structure

The legal structure of a business must be chosen before business operations begin. The legal business structure refers to the statutory form of business organization, set up in accordance with state and federal provisions. A permissible business organization can take the form of a proprietorship, partnership, corporation, or limited liability company. Making the right decision on the type of business organization is of vital importance, because each form of business organization differently affects the following:

- Start-up costs
- Personal asset risk
- Governmental regulation
- Accounting and legal fees
- Independence of owner
- Choice of business year
- Income taxes
- Complexity of the accounting system

Choosing a business organization is not simple, because each form has unique advantages and disadvantages that can affect profits. In most cases, the choice of an inappropriate legal form of business organization can be expensive and difficult to correct.

Many individuals select the corporate form of business because someone carelessly makes a hasty statement that it is the best legal form of business organization. In fact, it may be the most inflexible and expensive form of business. The predominant reason for selecting the corporate form is the exaggerated claim of *no personal liability*. This is a misleading claim, because (1) the government can hold owners of a corporation personally liable for unpaid income and payroll taxes, and (2) any business form can be protected by liability insurance.

It is essential that the hospitality student become familiar with the various legal forms of business. The decision of which legal form of business to choose requires the assistance of a lawyer and accountant, because legal, accounting, and governmental regulations have a bearing on this issue and are complex to decipher.

The following legal forms of business organization will be examined in this section:

- Proprietorship
- Partnership
- Corporation
- Limited liability company

Proprietorship

In a **proprietorship** business form, the business is not legally incorporated, and the business is owned by a single self-employed individual. A significant advantage of this unincorporated form of business is that it is the easiest, quickest, and least expensive form of business to legally establish.

Exhibit 1 compares the distinguishing features of a proprietorship to those of a partnership and a corporation. A significant disadvantage is that the owner has unlimited personal liability for any debts or uninsured claims against the business because, from a legal perspective, the owner and business are the same party and are inseparable. However, from an accounting point of view, the business and owner are separate entities; therefore, the financial statements of the business cannot include the owner's assets or liabilities.

No Wages for the Owner. A self-employed individual (owner of a proprietorship) cannot be legally paid a salary or wage from the business, because the law interprets the owner and business as one and the same legal entity. A self-employed individual can withdraw funds at his or her pleasure, providing that such funds are available in the business. These withdrawals are not deductible business expenses. The owner does not pay any income tax on these withdrawals.

No Income Taxes for the Business. The business does not directly pay income taxes. Since the business and owner are legally viewed as one entity, the profits of the business are declared on the owner's *personal* income tax return (IRS Form

Exhibit 1   Legal Forms of Business Organization

	Human Resources			Initial Funding			Government Regulation	Revenue	
	Management Control	Personnel and Expertise	Continuity/ Transferability	Requirements and Costs	Ability to Raise Capital	Losses/Debts		Profits	Growth Potential
Proprietorship	One owner in total control	Depends mainly on owner's skills; hard to obtain quality employees	Ends on death of owner; free to sell or transfer	Costs are lowest (filing fee required if business held under name other than owner's)	Limited—all equity (funding) must come from proprietor; loans based on credit-worthiness of owner	Owner liable for all debts	Little regulation; few records needed	All profits to owner	Limited options —reinvest profits, obtain loans on owner's line-of-credit
Partnership	Divided among two or more partners; decisions made by majority or prearranged agreement (limited partner cannot manage the business)	Depends mainly on partners' skills; hard to find suitable employees	Ends on death of partner (unless otherwise agreed in writing); transfer conditions vary with agreement	Costs low, general partnership agreement optional but recommended (limited means that agreement stating liabilities and responsibilities of each partner is required)	Limited to resources of each of the partners and the ability of each to acquire loans and/or investors	Partners liable for all debts (limited partner has restricted liability and involvement per partnership agreement)	Subject to limited regulation; few records needed; articles of partnership should be drawn up	Divided among partners	Limited options —reinvest profits, obtain loans on owners' lines-of-credit
Corporation	Corporation acts as one person, but Board of Directors holds legal, formal control; working control held by those who manage the business day-to-day	Allows for flexible management; easier to secure quality employees with the necessary expertise	Continues with overlapping; most flexible in terms of transfer of interest (i.e., ownership) from one shareholder to another	Costs are highest; legal forms, documents, professional fees required	Greatest equity potential—can sell new stock; loans based on corporate financial strength and expertise, thus providing larger borrowing base	Corporation liable for all debts (i.e., shareholders are liable only for amount invested; are liable for more only if personal guarantees were given)	Extensive record-keeping required; must have articles of incorporation, by-laws and filing fees	Retained in corporation; shareholders receive dividends	Flexible—can reinvest profits (at discretion of Board of Directors); sell additional shares; obtain loans on corporate credit

Source: *Minding Your Own Small Business: An Introductory Curriculum*, Department of Health, Education, and Welfare 1979. Contract Number 300-7000330.

1040, Schedule C). Because the owner pays an income tax on the profits of the business, his or her withdrawals are not taxed.

Partnership

A **partnership** has many similarities to a proprietorship, except for the number of owners (see Exhibit 1). In a partnership, the business form is not legally incorporated, and the business is owned by two or more individuals. This type of unincorporated business carries many risks: each partner is responsible for the debts of and claims against the business, and each partner is responsible for the business actions of the other partner(s).

A partnership is a very complex form of business and should not be organized without a formal document called a *partnership agreement* that specifies the allocation of profits or losses and other items, such as the responsibilities and the investment of each partner. Because of the risks involved, legal and accounting services prior to the formation of a partnership are vital.

Similarities to Proprietorship. The partnership form of business is arguably the most difficult to comprehend. The legal, accounting, and tax issues are substantial even for the experienced professional. The following list of similarities between a partnership and a proprietorship helps to clarify the issue:

- Neither form is legally incorporated.
- Both incur unlimited liability for partners (except for limited partners, described below).
- Income taxes of the business are paid by the proprietor or each of the partners.
- Partners are not paid a salary or wage.

While the partnership does not pay income taxes, it files an information return (IRS Form 1065). This return shows the income or loss of the partnership allocated to each partner on the basis of the partnership agreement. Each partner then reports his or her share of the income or loss on IRS Form 1040, using Schedule E.

General vs. Limited Partners. Every partnership must have at least one **general partner** responsible for the management and control of the business. A partnership may have any number of **limited partners,** who do not and legally may not participate in the active management of the business. General partners have unlimited personal liability, while limited partners enjoy the freedom of not being personally liable for the acts of the general partners or any debts or claims against the business.

Corporation

A **corporation** is distinguished by the facts that the business form is legally incorporated and the business is owned by one or more individuals, as shown in Exhibit 1.

The owners of a corporation are called shareholders or stockholders. From a legal, tax, and accounting perspective, the owners of a corporation and the business are *not* related; each is a separate entity. The following is a list of some of the characteristics of a corporation:

- It is legally incorporated.
- The assets are owned by the business, not the shareholders.
- Shareholders have only limited liability.
- Income taxes are paid by the corporation (except for Subchapter S corporations, discussed later in this chapter).
- The owners may be paid a salary or wage.

Articles of Incorporation. Unlike many nations, the United States does not have a single, national law governing the formation and governance of corporations. Although there are federal laws relating to taxation, disclosure, and trading of securities, the formation of corporations is left to state law. Forming a corporation involves an incorporation process that is a legal procedure performed by filing *articles of incorporation* with the secretary of corporation's office in the state in which the corporation's home office is located. Each state has its own incorporation laws. In general, the articles of incorporation (also called the *certificate of incorporation*) identify the incorporator and describe the corporation and its stock. The incorporator need not be an expected owner or officer of the corporation.

The appendix at the end of the chapter presents the filing instructions and articles of incorporation for the state of North Carolina. This is a representative sample; space does not permit the inclusion of forms used by other states. If you would like to see similar information for another state, an Internet search that includes "secretary of state" and the name of the state in question will get you started in finding the desired information.

Description of Corporation. The secretary of corporation's office must approve the corporate name to avoid duplication with other corporations in that state. The articles of incorporation must state the business purpose of the corporation. Stating a single purpose such as "food and beverage operation" may limit future business activities. To avoid filing an amendment to the articles of incorporation (incurring legal and state fees), a broader definition of the corporation's business is generally used. For example, the nature or purpose of the business might be stated as "the corporation may engage in any lawful act or activity for which corporations may be incorporated under the general corporation law."

Authorized Stock. The kind of stock and number of shares the corporation might intend to issue must be stated in the articles of incorporation. One should not confuse stock authorized and **stock issued**. The number of shares of stock the corporation may legally issue (sell) is its **authorized stock;** the shares actually issued later are called stock *issued*. A corporation is not required to sell all of its authorized stock. The state incorporation fees are generally based on the number of authorized shares, the number being in a range such as 1 to 1,000 and progressing to larger number ranges. If the corporation later requires more authorized shares, a simple amendment to the articles of incorporation is all that is required. Describing the authorized stock also involves terms like par value, capital stock, common stock, and preferred stock.

Par value. Some states base their incorporation fees on **par value** per share or a combination of par value and number of authorized shares. Par value is one of the most misunderstood terms regarding corporate stock. For common stock, par is typically a small amount that has nothing to do with the stock's market price. For preferred stock, par is the basis on which dividend payments are calculated.

Par value is a legal term and its relevance generally is that corporate stock cannot be originally issued below its par value per share. Corporations generally select a low par value of one cent, five cents, or ten cents. For example, the par value of Wendy's common stock is ten cents per share, which has no relationship to its market value. To give corporations greater flexibility, many states allow the use of *no-par value* stock.

Capital stock. The term **capital stock** does not designate any one type of stock; instead, the term represents a generic reference to all types of stock. Corporations may issue a single class of stock or multiple classes of stock, as the certificate of incorporation provides. Stock may be voting or non-voting, and shares of one class may be given a greater or lesser number of votes per share than shares of another class. Ownership of stock is generally evidenced by a stock certificate such as that shown in Exhibit 2; however, it is not necessary to issue a stock certificate. A corporation may plan to issue common stock and preferred stock. Generally, common stock must be issued because it gives shareholders a voting privilege.

Common stock. Common stock is one type of capital stock. Common stock stands last in line for dividends and proceeds in the event of liquidation. The advantage of **common stock** is that it generally gives the stockholders a voting privilege. This voting right gives stockholders the decisive power to *elect* a board of directors who set corporate policy. The board of directors then *appoints* the officers of the corporation to carry out these policies. This line of command and hierarchy is illustrated in Exhibit 3.

Common stock is attractive because of its potential for significant increase in its market value. There are many success stories of stockholders who became wealthy individuals because they bought IBM, Microsoft, Wal-Mart, or any of a number of other growth companies.

Preferred stock. Preferred stock is another type of capital stock. The advantages of **preferred stock** are that preferred stockholders receive dividends before the common stockholders, and, in the event of liquidation, the preferred stockholders receive liquidating dividends before the common stockholders. However, in the event of liquidation, creditors receive liquidation proceeds first, and preferred and common stockholders receive them last; this leftover claim is referred to as a **residual claim**. The following are disadvantages of preferred stock:

- The annual dividend (usually paid on a quarterly basis) is fixed for the life of the stock.

- The market value of preferred stock does not enjoy the potential growth value of common stock.

- The right to vote often is not granted to preferred stockholders.

- Preferred stock may be **callable preferred stock**, meaning that the company can repurchase it at a predetermined price.

Exhibit 2 Stock Certificate

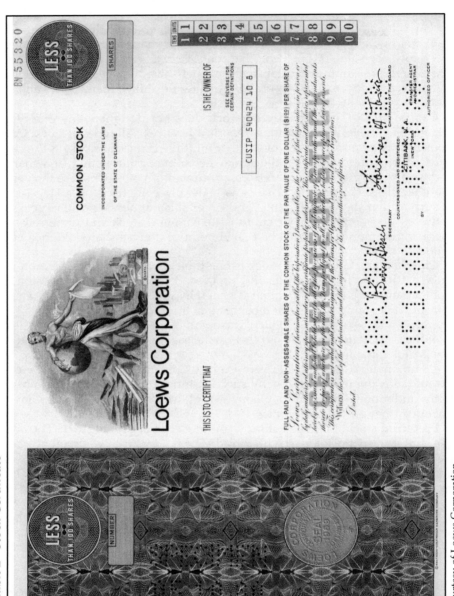

Courtesy of Loews Corporation

Exhibit 3   Organization Chart for a Corporation

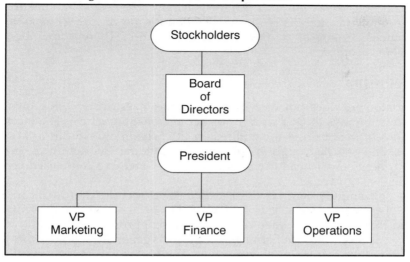

To overcome some of these disadvantages, preferred stock may be issued as **convertible preferred stock**, which allows the stockholder to convert the preferred stock to common stock at a predetermined exchange ratio.

Limited Liability Company

All states now have enacted **limited liability company** (LLC) statutes. An LLC is a separate legal entity formed by filing articles of organization with the secretary of state. The LLC is a relatively new form of business entity; it is neither a partnership nor a corporation, but it combines the major advantages of both forms of doing business. For example, the members of an LLC may enjoy the limited liability of a corporation but yet be taxed as a partnership.

Taxation of Business Income

The taxation of business income is a complex process requiring the expertise of a qualified tax preparer. It is important to retain the services of a qualified professional during the initial business-planning phase, because the legal form of business organization has a major impact on the taxation of business income. A certified public accountant (CPA) or enrolled agent (EA) authorized to practice before the Internal Revenue Service (IRS) has demonstrated knowledge in the field of taxation by virtue of having completed professional examinations.

The federal government and most states tax business income. A few cities also tax business income. The income tax is computed on **taxable income** multiplied by an applicable tax rate. Taxable income is the result of business sales and all other taxable revenue minus deductible business expenses allowed by tax law. Taxable income and accounting income may not be identical, because of the difference between income tax accounting rules and generally accepted accounting principles.

The following analysis of income taxation for the various forms of business organizations pertains only to federal income taxation. There is no uniformity of state income taxation.

Proprietorship

A proprietorship does not directly pay income taxes. Instead, the owner of a proprietorship pays the tax with his or her personal tax return. The income and deductions of the business are entered on IRS Schedule C—Profit or Loss From Business, and attached to Form 1040—U.S. Individual Tax Return. A qualifying small business may instead use Schedule C-EZ, which is a condensed version of Schedule C.

The **self-employment tax** (SE tax) is a social security and Medicare tax for owners of proprietorships. It is similar to the social security and Medicare tax withheld from the pay of wage earners. Because a proprietor does not withhold these taxes from employees' earnings, the SE tax is generally at double the rate that would be withheld from employee wages. The SE tax is computed on IRS Form SE—Self-Employment Tax, which is also attached to Form 1040.

Partnership

A partnership does not directly pay income taxes, but it does file Form 1065—U.S. Return of Partnership Income (which is an information return) with the IRS. Each partner receives notice of his or her share of taxable income from the partnership. This income is reported on Schedule E—Supplemental Income and Loss, and is attached to Form 1040. Each partner is also liable for any self-employment tax.

Corporation

A corporation is a business form of organization that has legally filed the articles of incorporation in a particular state. A corporation is legally and completely separate from its owners. However, from a federal and state income tax perspective, the taxation of a corporation has two possible treatments depending on whether it elects to be taxed as one of the following:

- Subchapter C corporation
- Subchapter S corporation

Subchapter C Corporation. A **Subchapter C corporation** pays federal and state income taxes on its profit. C corporations generally distribute these profits to their shareholders. These distributions are called dividends and are taxable income to shareholders on their personal tax returns. In essence, a C corporation's earnings are taxed twice. In contrast, the earnings of a Subchapter S corporation are taxed only once, as explained in the next section.

The advantage of a C corporate structure is the fact that, unlike S corporations, it has no limits to the number of shareholders and no restrictions on who can be an owner. Most publicly traded companies are incorporated.

Subchapter S Corporation. A **Subchapter S corporation** is a corporation that has met the Subchapter S requirements of the IRC and has made a proper election to be taxed as a Subchapter S (Sub S) corporation. To become an S corporation, the corporation must submit Form 2553, "Election by a Small Business Corporation," signed by all the shareholders.

The primary benefit is that the Sub S corporation's net profit (or net loss) directly associated with the business is not taxed to the corporation; instead it is allocated to its stockholders. The Sub S stockholders, in turn, have to include that allocation on their individual tax returns, whether or not they have actually received cash. The distributed income or loss (and other specified items) are reported on Schedule E, Supplemental Income and Loss, and is attached to the taxpayer's form 1040.

In effect, a Sub S corporation and its shareholders have only one layer of income tax. This allows an S corporation to avoid double taxation on its corporate income. Recall that Subchapter C corporations pay taxes on their profit and then the corporate stockholders pay personal income taxes when those same profits are later paid out to them in the form of dividends.

To qualify for S corporation status, the corporation must meet the following requirements:

- Be a domestic corporation
- Have only allowable shareholders, defined as individuals, certain trusts, and estates
- May not have the following as shareholders: partnerships, corporations, or non-resident alien shareholders
- Have no more than 100 shareholders
- Have one class of stock
- Not be an ineligible corporation (that is, certain financial institutions, insurance companies, and domestic international sales corporations)

Limited Liability Company

A limited liability company (LLC) is a particular form of business organization allowed by state statute. In essence, an LLC is:

- Similar to a corporation: owners have limited personal liability for the debts and actions of the LLC.
- Similar to a partnership: it is has pass-through taxation (its taxable income or loss is passed through to its owners).

An LLC combines the major advantages of the corporate and partnership legal forms of business: it is taxed as a partnership but its owners enjoy the limited liability typical of corporate shareholders. Owners of an LLC are called members. Members may include individuals, corporations, other LLCs, and foreign entities. No limitations are imposed on the number of members an LCC can have.

The LLC must file its *articles of organization* (some states use the term *certificate of formation* or *certificate of organization*) with its state's LLC filing office. Most states permit *single member* LLCs, those having only one owner. Each state has different rules governing the formation of an LLC. LLCs are subject to filing annual reports, paying the annual report fees, and perhaps paying a franchise tax. A few types of businesses generally cannot be formed as LLCs, such as, but not limited to, banks and insurance companies.

Although many states do not require a formal operating agreement, it is advisable to have one to avoid member misunderstandings and disputes. The operating agreement might specify, for example, its profit-sharing formula, operating method, accounting and financial matters, and other important issues.

Buying a Franchise

A **franchise** is a marketing right granting the use of the name, trademark, and marketing of branded services or products. The **franchisor** grants this right by contract (called a *franchise agreement*) to the **franchisee** (the business operator/owner).

A franchise right might require an initial one-time purchase fee, a continuing royalty based on sales, and perhaps ongoing assessments for the franchisor's national and regional advertising costs.

Among major reasons to buy a franchise are the following:

- The business gets a business name that is easily recognized and acclaimed by consumers.

- The franchisor provides a proven business system, including training and business advice.

- The franchisor may provide support through periodic newsletters, a toll-free telephone number, a website, and scheduled workshops or seminars.

- The business will perhaps enjoy a greater chance of success.

The decision to franchise must also consider possible shortcomings, such as the following:

- The initial cost

- Continuing franchise fees (called *royalty payments*)

- Perhaps a loss of freedom in making operating and marketing decisions

- Franchisor restrictions on the goods and services the franchise sells

Renewal of Franchise Agreement. Franchise agreements generally are made for a specified period of time. At the end of the contract period, the franchisor may decline to renew. If the franchisor renews the contract, the franchisor might revise the original terms and conditions. For example, the franchisor might increase royalty payments, require renovations, and impose new sales restrictions.

Franchise Termination. In addition to the limited time factor, a franchisor can end the franchise agreement for a variety of reasons, such as the following:

- The franchisee's failure to pay royalties

- The franchise's performance falling short of standards

- Violations of sales restrictions
- A contract breach by the franchisee

Endnote

1. More information on feasibility studies is available in Raymond Cote, *Accounting for Hospitality Managers,* 5th ed. (Lansing, Mich.: American Hotel & Lodging Educational Institute, 2007).

Key Terms

authorized stock—The kind of stock and number of shares a corporation is allowed to issue as described in its articles of incorporation.

callable preferred stock—A preferred stock that the issuer has the right to buy from shareholders at a predetermined price.

capital stock—A term representing the classes of stock, namely common and preferred.

common stock—A type of capital stock with voting privileges.

convertible preferred stock—A preferred stock that gives stockholders the right to convert it to common stock at a predetermined exchange ratio.

corporation—An incorporated business owned by one or more individuals.

feasibility study—A preliminary study made before a business is started or purchased. Its purpose is to determine the likelihood of business success.

franchise—A marketing right granting the use of the name, trademark, and marketing of branded services or products.

franchisee—The owner of a franchise conveyed by a franchisor.

franchisor—A company that grants a franchise right by contract called a *franchise agreement* to the franchisee.

general partner—A partner with authority in the management of a partnership. General partners have personal liability.

limited liability company—A form of business organization that may be taxed as a partnership but enjoys the limited liability of a corporation.

limited partner—A partner with no management authority and no personal liability.

partnership—A business form owned by two or more individuals and not incorporated.

par value—For common stock, typically a small amount that has nothing to do with the stock's market price. For preferred stock, it is the basis on which dividend payments are calculated. Its relevance is that corporate stock cannot be originally issued below its par value per share.

preferred stock—A type of capital stock preferred as to dividends but whose owners generally do not have voting privileges.

proprietorship—A business form owned by one individual and not incorporated.

residual claim—A leftover claim, being last in line for any proceeds from a business liquidation.

self-employment tax—A combination of social security and Medicare taxes payable by self-employed individuals such as owners of proprietorships and partnerships.

stock issued—The actual number of shares issued by a corporation from its authorized stock.

Subchapter C corporation—A corporation taxed under Subchapter C of the Internal Revenue Code that pays federal and state income taxes on its profits. It generally distributes profits (called dividends) to shareholders, who must report the profits as taxable income on their personal tax returns. Essentially, a C corporation's earnings are taxed twice.

Subchapter S corporation—A corporation taxed under Subchapter S of the Internal Revenue Code that passes its taxable income (or loss) to its shareholders, who in turn must include the allocation on their individual tax returns.

taxable income—Sales plus other taxable revenue minus deductible business expenses.

 Review Questions ───────────────────────────────

1. What is the most significant advantage of a proprietorship?

2. What is the most significant disadvantage of a proprietorship?

3. What is the difference between a general partner and a limited partner?

4. What is the difference between authorized stock and issued stock?

5. What is capital stock?

6. What is taxable income?

7. What is the self-employment tax?

8. What is the legal difference between a Subchapter C corporation and a Subchapter S corporation?

9. What is the difference in federal income tax treatment between a Subchapter C corporation and a Subchapter S corporation?

10. What are the major differences between a general partner and limited partner in the partnership form of business organization?

11. What is an LLC? How is it taxed?

12. What is a feasibility study? What is its purpose?

13. What is the minimum content of a feasibility study?

14. What is the definition of *franchise, franchisor,* and *franchisee?*

15. What are the advantages and disadvantages of having a franchised operation?

Internet Sites

For more information, visit the following Internet sites. Remember that Internet addresses can change without notice. If the site is no longer there, you can use a search engine to look for additional sites.

Canada: Legal Business Structures
www.cra-arc.gc.ca/tx/bsnss/tpcs/
   crprtns/menu-eng.html
www.inc.com/choosing-the-right-
   legal-structure

Canada: Revenue Agency
www.cra-arc.gc.ca/

Canada: Starting a Business
www.canadabusiness.ca/eng/125/

Global: Taxation Around the World
http://en.wikipedia.org/wiki/
   Tax_rates_around_the_world

India: Doing Business in India
www.indianembassy.org/doing-
   business-in-india.php

Malaysia: Company Law Basics
http://syarikat.tripod.com/basic.html

Sri Lanka: Incorporation Information
www.drc.gov.lk/App/ComReg.
   nsf?Open

*United States: Forms of Business
   Ownership*
www.mslawyer.com/businesr.htm
http://asbtdc.ualr.edu/business-
   information/1005-legal-forms-
   ownership.asp

United States: Internal Revenue Service
www.irs.gov/

*United States: Mistakes to Avoid When
   Incorporating*
http://findarticles.com/p/articles/
   mi_m1563/is_n2_v12/ai_15035422/

*United States: Secretary of State Sites/All
   States*
www.aicpa.org/Research/External
   Links/Pages/GovernmentStates
   SecretariesofStateLinks.aspx

Writing a Business Plan
www.sba.gov/category/naviga-
   tion-structure/starting-manag-
   ing-business/starting-business/
   writing-business-plan
www.bplans.com/sample_business_
   plans.cfm

Problems

Problem 1

Which of the following apply/applies to a proprietorship?

Limited liability of owner	_____
In accounting, owner and business are separate	_____
By law, owner and business are not separate	_____
Owner can be paid a wage or salary	_____
Income tax on business profits are paid by the owner	_____
Owner must pay income tax on withdrawal of $90,000	_____
Business profit is reported on Form 1040, Schedule C	_____
Owner pays a self-employment tax on business profit	_____

Problem 2

An incorporator files articles of incorporation with the state's secretary of state office. The stock entries on the form are 50,000 shares of common stock and 10,000 shares of preferred stock. What is the number of shares for each of the following items?

Capital stock   _____

Common stock authorized   _____

Preferred stock authorized   _____

Common stock issued   _____

Preferred stock issued   _____

Problem 3

A corporation has the following business results: Sales $100,000; nontaxable dividend income $20,000; rental income $10,000; business expenses of $60,000. What is its taxable income?

Problem 4

Which of the following will pay income tax on the profits of a business?

Corporation qualified under Subchapter C   _____

Corporation qualified under Subchapter S   _____

General partner   _____

Limited partner   _____

Proprietorship   _____

Problem 5

Decide whether each of the following statements is true or false.

1. A well-prepared and in-depth feasibility study ensures success for a business.
2. The owner of a proprietorship is legally entitled to a fair wage.
3. A proprietorship may have one or more owners.
4. A partnership is a legally incorporated business.
5. A partnership pays its own tax on its own profits.
6. A corporation may have an unlimited number of partners.
7. The shareholders of an S corporation are liable for its debts.
8. Preferred stock is not a capital stock.
9. An LLC is not a separate legal entity.
10. An LLC is formed under federal statute.

Ethics Case

Finer Foods, Inc., is applying for a bank loan of $250,000. Fred Helendona is the president and only shareholder of the corporation. The corporation is very profitable, and the loan will be used for expansion of facilities to accommodate customer demand.

The real estate (land and building) is not owned by the corporation; it is leased from Fred Helendona, who owns it as an individual. This rental arrangement is not unusual and was recommended by Fred's accountant before the business was started.

Because the corporation does not own any real estate, its balance sheet appears weak when its assets are compared to its liabilities. As company president, Fred instructs the accountant to enter the value of the real estate on the company's balance sheet in order to improve its assets picture. This balance sheet will be used to apply for the bank loan.

1. Identify the stakeholders in this case.

2. Comment on the legal and accounting issues involved in this deception.

3. What other alternative is available to the president to help the company get a bank loan?

Chapter Appendix:

Sample Filing Instructions and Articles of Incorporation

This appendix contains the filing instructions and the articles of incorporation necessary to form a corporation in the state of North Carolina.

Guidelines to Incorporating in North Carolina

- The corporation must have one or more shareholders
- The fee for incorporation is $125
- After the Articles of Incorporation have been filed, a certified copy will be provided
- An attorney is not required; however, the Corporations Division can only act in an administrative capacity—it cannot offer any legal advice or opinion

After filing the Articles of Incorporation, the Department of the Secretary of State suggests several more steps before a corporation can begin:

- Hold an organizational meeting
- Elect directors
- Appoint the officers
- Adopt a set of corporate by-laws
- Issue shares of stock
- Adopt banking resolutions
- Fix dates for the start and end of each corporate fiscal year
- Approve any other agreements or contracts deemed desirable
- Get tax identification numbers from the North Carolina Department of Revenue and the IRS
- Check with the Business License Information Office to see if your corporation needs a license to operate
- Purchase a company seal
- Contact county and local agencies to see what regulations and restrictions may apply to the business

Instructions for Filing

ARTICLES OF INCORPORATION
(Form B-01)

Item 1   Enter the complete corporate name which must include a corporate ending required by N.C.G.S. §55D-20-01(a) (corporation, company, limited, incorporated, corp., co., ltd., or inc.).

Item 2   Enter the number of shares the corporation will have the authority to issue.

Item 3   Check (a) or (b), whichever is applicable. If (b) is checked, add an attachment that includes the description of the designations, preferences, limitations, and relative rights of the shares.

Item 4   Enter the complete street address of the registered office and the county in which it is located.

Item 5   Enter the complete mailing address of the registered agent only if mail is not delivered to the street address stated in Item 3 or if you prefer to receive mail at a P. O. Box or Drawer.

Item 6   Enter the name of the registered agent. The registered agent must be either an individual who resides in North Carolina; a domestic business corporation, nonprofit corporation, or limited liability company whose business office is identical with the registered office; or a foreign corporation, nonprofit corporation or limited liability company authorized to transact business in North Carolina whose business office is identical with the registered office.

Item 7   Select item "a" if the corporation has a principal office. Enter the complete street address of the principal office and the county in which it is located. If mail is not delivered to the street address of the principal office or if you prefer to receive mail at a P.O. Box or Drawer, enter the complete mailing address of the principal office.

Select item "b" if the corporation does not have a principal office.

Item 8   See form.

Item 9   Enter the name and address of each incorporator. Only one incorporator is required in order to file.

Item 10   The document will be effective on the date and at the time of filing, unless a delayed date or an effective time (on the day of filing) is specified. If a delayed effective date is specified without a time, the document will be effective at 11:59:59 p.m. on the day specified. If a delayed effective date is specified with a time, the document will be effective on the day and time so specified. A delayed effective date may be specified up to and including the 90th day after the day of filing.

Date and Execution

Enter the date the document was executed.
In the blanks provided enter:

- The name of the entity executing the Articles of Incorporation; if an individual, leave blank.
- The signature of the incorporator or representative of the incorporating entity.
- The name of the incorporator or name and title of the above signed representative

ATTENTION: Corporations wishing to render a professional service as defined in N.C.G.S. §55b-2(6) shall contact the appropriate North Carolina licensing board to determine whether compliance with additional licensing requirements may be mandated by law.

CORPORATIONS DIVISION   P. O. BOX 29622   RALEIGH, NC 27626-0622
(Revised January, 2002)   *(Form B-01)*

State of North Carolina
Department of the Secretary of State

ARTICLES OF INCORPORATION

Pursuant to §55-2-02 of the General Statutes of North Carolina, the undersigned does hereby submit these Articles of Incorporation for the purpose of forming a business corporation.

1.   The name of the corporation is: _____

2.   The number of shares the corporation is authorized to issue is: _____

3.   These shares shall be: *(check either a or b)*

    a. ☐   all of one class, designated as common stock; or

    b. ☐   divided into classes or series within a class as provided in the attached schedule, with the information required by N.C.G.S. Section 55-6-01.

4.   The street address and county of the initial registered office of the corporation is:

    Number and Street _____

    City_____State _____Zip Code_____County_____

5.   The mailing address, *if different from the street address,* of the initial registered office is:

    Number and Street _____

    City_____State _____Zip Code_____County_____

6.   The name of the initial registered agent is: _____

7.   Principal office information: (*must select either a or b.*)

    a. ☐   The corporation has a principal office.

    The street address and county of the principal office of the corporation is:

    Number and Street _____

    City_____State _____Zip Code_____County_____

    The mailing address, *if different from the street address*, of the principal office of the corporation is:

    Number and Street _____

    City_____State _____Zip Code_____County_____

    b. ☐   The corporation does not have a principal office.

CORPORATIONS DIVISION   P. O. BOX 29622   RALEIGH, NC 27626-0622
(Revised January, 2002)   *(Form B-01)*

8. Any other provisions, which the corporation elects to include, are attached.

9. The name and address of each incorporator is as follows:

_____

_____

_____

_____

_____

10. These articles will be effective upon filing, unless a date and/or time is specified:

_____

_____

_____

This the _____ day of _____ 20 _____

_____

Signature

_____

Type or Print Name and Title

NOTES:
1.   **Filing fee is $125. This document must be filed with the Secretary of State.**
CORPORATIONS DIVISION   P. O. BOX 29622   RALEIGH, NC 27626-0622
(Revised January, 2002)   *(Form B-01)*

Chapter 3 Outline

Basic Financial Statements
Statement of Income
    Revenue
    Cost of Sales
    Gross Profit
    Operating Expenses
    Income Before Fixed Charges and
       Income Taxes
    Fixed Charges
    Income Before Income Taxes
    Income Taxes
    Net Income (or Loss)
Equity Statements
    Statement of Owner's Equity
    Statement of Retained Earnings
Balance Sheet
    Current Assets
    Property and Equipment
    Other Assets
    Current Liabilities
    Long-Term Liabilities
    Equity Section
Statement of Cash Flows
    Operating Activities
    Investing Activities
    Financing Activities

Competencies

1. Identify the major financial statements and explain when they are issued. (pp. 55–56)

2. Describe the purpose and the contents of the statement of income, statement of owner's equity, statement of retained earnings, balance sheet, and statement of cash flows. (pp. 56–70)

3

Survey of Financial Statements

THE PURPOSE OF FINANCIAL STATEMENTS is to present in monetary terms what a business has accomplished, its financial well-being, and the sources and uses of its cash during the period examined. The income statement presents what a company has accomplished, the balance sheet shows its well-being, and the statement of cash flows explains where cash came from and how the cash was spent.

Statements are important to stockholders, investors, managers, creditors, and other interested parties who need to evaluate a company's financial accomplishment. A company may have the best product or services, but it cannot stay in business unless it is properly managed, achieves a status of profitability, and is able to pay its bills. While financial statements by nature are historical, professional analysis can render an opinion as to the outlook for a company.

This chapter provides the reader with a comparison of statements issued for both a corporation and a proprietorship, using the same financial data. The chapter answers such questions as:

1. What are annual and interim financial statements?
2. What is the purpose and content of the statement of income?
3. What is the purpose and content of the statement of owner's equity?
4. What is the purpose and content of the statement of retained earnings?
5. What is the purpose and content of the balance sheet?
6. What is the purpose and content of the statement of cash flows?

Basic Financial Statements

The basic financial statements prepared by hospitality businesses are the statement of income, the equity statement (the name of which varies by business form), the balance sheet, and the statement of cash flows. These four statements present independent information, yet have a relationship to each other. For example, the income (or loss) from the income statement is transferred to the equity statement; the result of the equity statement is carried over to the balance sheet; the statement of cash flows is prepared from information on the income statement and balance sheet.

Annual financial statements are issued at the end of a company's business year, also called a fiscal year. A **fiscal year** might be a calendar year or a year consisting of 12 consecutive months starting in any month other than January. It is customary for companies whose stock is publicly traded to issue an elegant packet containing the financial statements, a president's letter to stockholders, and glossy pictures of products, people, and services. Managers, stockholders, investors, creditors, and other interested parties are eager to obtain the annual statements of businesses so that they can properly examine and evaluate the companies' performances.

The Internet site of any company whose stock is publicly traded should provide a link to the company's annual financial statements, as well as links to other corporate information.

The best-run companies also issue monthly financial statements to management. Those companies whose stock is publicly traded also issue quarterly financial statements to their stockholders. Such statements issued during the business year are called **interim financial statements**.

Statement of Income

The **statement of income** shows revenue and expenses and provides information about the *results of operations* for a stated period of time. This is the financial statement that shows if a business operated at a profit or loss for the period of time covered by the statement. The time period may be one month or longer, but does not exceed one business year. Since the owners of proprietorships or partnerships pay personal income taxes on the net income from their operations, their fiscal years generally begin on the first of January. However, the fiscal year of certain corporate forms of business organization may be any 12 consecutive months.

Since the statement of income reveals the results of operations for a period of time, it is an important measure of management's effectiveness and efficiency. Understanding how the statement is used to evaluate management is the key to understanding the logic behind the sequence of categories that appears on the statement. The major categories that appear on the statement of income are:

- Revenue
- Cost of Sales
- Gross Profit
- Operating Expenses
- Fixed Charges
- Net Income (or Loss)

The following sections discuss these categories in some detail and provide a brief explanation of the line items appearing within them. Exhibits 1 and 2 point out the differences between statements of income prepared for proprietorships and those prepared for corporations.

Revenue

Revenue results when products and services are sold to guests. The total revenue figure on the statement of income indicates the actual dollar amount that guests have been billed for products and services offered by the hospitality property.

Exhibit 1   Statement of Income for a Proprietorship

Deb's Steakhouse
Statement of Income
For the Year Ended December 31, 20X2

REVENUE

Food Sales	$120,000	
Liquor Sales	50,000	
Total Revenue		$170,000

COST OF SALES

Food	42,000	
Liquor	11,000	
Total Cost of Sales		53,000

GROSS PROFIT   117,000

OPERATING EXPENSES

Salaries and Wages	36,000	
Employee Benefits	6,900	
China, Glassware, and Silverware	300	
Kitchen Fuel	900	
Laundry and Dry Cleaning	2,100	
Credit Card Fees	1,500	
Operating Supplies	5,000	
Advertising	2,000	
Utilities	3,800	
Repairs and Maintenance	1,900	
Total Operating Expenses		60,400

INCOME BEFORE FIXED CHARGES   56,600

FIXED CHARGES

Rent	6,000	
Property Taxes	1,500	
Insurance	3,600	
Interest Expense	3,000	
Depreciation and Amortization	5,500	
Total Fixed Charges		19,600

NET INCOME $ 37,000

Note: The net income figure is transferred to the
      Statement of Owner's Equity illustrated in
      Exhibit 3

Exhibit 2   Statement of Income for a Corporation

Deb's Steakhouse, Inc.
Statement of Income
For the Year Ended December 31, 20X2

REVENUE

Food Sales	$120,000	
Liquor Sales	50,000	
Total Revenue		$170,000

COST OF SALES

Food	42,000	
Liquor	11,000	
Total Cost of Sales		53,000

GROSS PROFIT | | 117,000

OPERATING EXPENSES

Salaries and Wages	55,000	
Employee Benefits	7,900	
China, Glassware, and Silverware	300	
Kitchen Fuel	900	
Laundry and Dry Cleaning	2,100	
Credit Card Fees	1,500	
Operating Supplies	5,000	
Advertising	2,000	
Utilities	3,800	
Repairs and Maintenance	1,900	
Total Operating Expenses		80,400

INCOME BEFORE FIXED CHARGES AND INCOME TAXES | | 36,600

FIXED CHARGES

Rent	6,000	
Property Taxes	1,500	
Insurance	3,600	
Interest Expense	3,000	
Depreciation and Amortization	5,500	
Total Fixed Charges		19,600

INCOME BEFORE INCOME TAXES | | 17,000

INCOME TAXES | | 2,000

NET INCOME | | $ 15,000

Note: The net income figure is transferred to the Statement of
       Retained Earnings illustrated in Exhibit 4

Revenue is *not* income. Revenue appears at the top of the statement of income; net income (or loss) appears at the bottom. Income results when total revenue exceeds total expenses. A loss results when total expenses exceed total revenue.

Exhibits 1 and 2 show the total revenue figure for Deb's Steakhouse at $170,000. Note that revenue generated by food sales ($120,000) is listed separately from revenue generated by beverage sales ($50,000). Distinguishing the major sources of revenue allows management to identify the separate contributions of the food operation and the beverage operation to the establishment's total gross profit.

Cost of Sales

The **cost of sales** section of the statement of income shows the cost of merchandise used in the selling process; it does not contain any cost for labor or employee meals. Since the revenue appearing on the income statement for Deb's Steakhouse resulted from sales of food and beverages to guests, the cost of sales figure ($53,000) represents *the cost of food and beverage merchandise served to guests*. Cost of sales can also be called *cost of goods sold*.

Gross Profit

Gross profit is calculated by subtracting cost of sales from net revenue (net sales). Gross profit is sometimes referred to as *gross margin* or *gross margin on sales*.

Gross profit is an intermediate income amount from which operating expenses and fixed charges are deducted to arrive at net income. Gross profit must be large enough to cover all of these expenses for the business to earn a net income.

Operating Expenses

The **operating expenses** section of the statement of income lists expenses that are most directly influenced by operating policy and management efficiency. If the statement of income showed these expenses as a single line item, this would not communicate much information to the users of the statement. Breaking out each of the significant operating expenses allows management and others to readily identify expense areas that may be excessive and that call for further analysis and possible corrective action. A brief explanation of the line items included under operating expenses on the statements of income for Deb's Steakhouse follows.

Salaries and Wages. This line item includes the regular salaries and wages, extra wages, overtime pay, vacation pay, and any commission or bonus payments to employees. Note that the figure shown as salaries and wages for the corporate form of Deb's Steakhouse is greater than the salaries and wages figure shown for the proprietorship form of Deb's Steakhouse. This difference results from the fact that the owner of a proprietorship cannot be paid a salary or wage.

Specifically, the difference can be accounted for in the following salaries and wages analysis:

Corporation	$55,000
Proprietorship	36,000
Attributable to owner	$19,000

Employee Benefits. This line item includes the cost of free employee meals, social security and Medicare taxes (FICA), federal and state unemployment taxes, union and nonunion insurance premiums, state health insurance, union and nonunion pension fund contributions, medical expenses, workers' compensation insurance, and other similar expenses. Expenses related to employee benefits can be significant for restaurant operations. Note that the amount for employee benefits shown for Deb's Steakhouse, Inc., is greater than that shown for Deb's Steakhouse (proprietorship). This difference arises because: (a) an owner of a proprietorship cannot deduct benefits on his or her behalf, and (b) there are no payroll taxes on behalf of the owner, since wages cannot be paid to an owner.

Specifically, the difference can be accounted for in the following employee benefits analysis:

Corporation	$7,900
Proprietorship	6,900
Attributable to owner	$1,000

China, Glassware, and Silverware. These items are generally considered direct service expenses rather than repair and maintenance expenses. Therefore, replacement costs for china, glassware, and silverware appear here as a separate item under Operating Expenses. This line item also includes the depreciation expense for china, glassware, and silverware.

Kitchen Fuel. This line item includes only the cost of fuel used for cooking, such as gas, coal, charcoal briquettes, steam, electricity, or hickory chips.

Laundry and Dry Cleaning. This line item includes the cost of laundering table linens and uniforms; contracting for napkin, towel, and apron service; and cleaning uniforms, wall and window hangings, and floor coverings.

Credit Card Fees. This item includes the amount paid to credit card organizations for central billing and collection of credit card accounts.

Operating Supplies. This item represents supplies that have been used and are not includable as inventory. These include cleaning supplies, paper supplies, guest supplies, and bar supplies. The statements of income for Deb's Steakhouse list Operating Supplies as a single line item. However, large operations may list the categories of operating supplies separately on the statement of income.

Advertising. *Marketing* is the more general term used to describe the varied expenses incurred in promoting a restaurant operation to the public. Items listed under marketing vary with the needs and requirements of individual properties. Deb's Steakhouse is a relatively small operation, so its marketing expenses consistently include only advertising costs such as newspaper ads, circulars, and brochures. Therefore, it is more appropriate and informative for that operation to list Advertising instead of marketing as the operating expense item on the statement of income. Large restaurant operations, on the other hand, may incur significant marketing expenses in such areas as sales, advertising, and public relations. It would be appropriate for these properties to list the term *Marketing* as a direct expense line item on the statement of income.

Utilities. This line item includes the cost of electricity, fuel, water, ice and refrigeration supplies, waste removal, and engineer's supplies. Note, however, that the Utilities item does not include fuel used for cooking purposes. The cost of energy used for cooking purposes appears as a separate line item. If electricity or gas is used as kitchen fuel and for heating and lighting, it is necessary to use meter readings or to estimate usage to isolate kitchen fuel expense.

Repairs and Maintenance. This line item includes the cost of plastering, painting, decorating, repairing dining room furniture and kitchen equipment, plumbing and heating repairs, and other maintenance and repair expenses.

Income Before Fixed Charges and Income Taxes

The figure for income before fixed charges and income taxes is used to measure the success of operations and the effectiveness and efficiency of management. Therefore, this section of the statement of income is extremely important to management. This figure is calculated by subtracting total operating expenses from the gross profit figure.

Note in Exhibit 1 that, for a proprietorship form of business organization, this section of the statement of income reads as "Income Before Fixed Charges." Income taxes are not mentioned because a proprietorship does not pay income taxes—the owner does. A proprietorship's business income is reported on the owner's personal income tax return.

The difference between the proprietorship and corporation income before income taxes (IBIT) is as follows:

Proprietorship IBIT	$37,000
Corporation IBIT	17,000
Difference	$20,000

This difference can be accounted for as follows:

Owner's salary	$19,000
Owner's fringe benefits	1,000
Total	$20,000

Fixed Charges

The **fixed charges** section of the statement of income includes rent, property taxes, property insurance, interest expense, and depreciation. Fixed charges are those expenses that are incurred regardless of whether the business is open or closed, and they remain relatively constant even with changes in sales volume.

Income Before Income Taxes

For a corporation, fixed charges are subtracted from income before fixed charges and income taxes to arrive at the amount of income before income taxes.

Note that the statement of income for a proprietorship (Exhibit 1) does not include this line item. Again, this is because a business organized as a proprietorship does not pay income taxes—the owner does.

Income Taxes

The income taxes section of the statement of income includes federal and other government income taxes. Again, note that this line item does not appear on the statement of income for a proprietorship.

Net Income (or Loss)

The bottom line of the statement of income reveals the net income (or loss) of the operation for a stated period. This figure will indicate the overall success of operations for the period of time covered by the statement of income. The amount of net income shown for the corporate form of Deb's Steakhouse differs from that of the proprietorship form of business organization because:

- The owner of a proprietorship cannot be paid a salary or wage; thus there are also no applicable payroll taxes on that salary or wage.
- The owner of a proprietorship is not entitled to deductible benefits.
- The owner of a proprietorship pays the income taxes of the business on his or her personal income tax return.

The net income difference of $22,000 ($37,000 − $15,000) between the proprietorship and corporation is accounted for as follows:

Salary and fringe benefits attributable to the owner	$20,000
Income taxes of the corporation	2,000
Total	$22,000

Equity Statements

Equity statements reflect changes in equity that occurred during an accounting period. Exhibit 3 illustrates a statement of owner's equity prepared for a proprietorship; Exhibit 4 depicts a statement of retained earnings prepared for a corporation. The following sections explain the line items that appear on these equity statements.

Statement of Owner's Equity

The **statement of owner's equity** is prepared for a proprietorship form of business organization. The owner's capital account reflects the owner's residual claims to the assets of the business. The owner's claims are residual because they follow any claims to assets that creditors may have, as represented by the liabilities section of the balance sheet.

Exhibit 3 shows the statement of owner's equity for Deb's Steakhouse. Deb Barry's equity for the period just ended is calculated by adding net income and subtracting withdrawals from the amount of owner's equity shown on the previous statement of owner's equity prepared for the prior period. (Normally, the owner's investments are also added; however, the proprietor in this example did not make such investments in her business during the current year.) The net income figure is the same figure that appears on the bottom line of the statement of income in Exhibit 1.

Exhibit 3   **Statement of Owner's Equity for a Proprietorship**

Deb's Steakhouse
Statement of Owner's Equity
For the Year Ended December 31, 20X2

Deb Barry, Capital—January 1, 20X2	$ 81,000
Add Owner's Investments during the year	0
Add Net Income for the year ended December 31, 20X2	37,000
Total	118,000
Less Withdrawals during the year	20,000
Deb Barry, Capital—December 31, 20X2	$ 98,000

Notes:

1. The net income figure is from the Statement of Income illustrated in Exhibit 1.

2. The ending capital amount is transferred to the Balance Sheet illustrated in Exhibit 5.

Exhibit 4 **Statement of Retained Earnings for a Corporation**

Deb's Steakhouse, Inc.
Statement of Retained Earnings
For the Year Ended December 31, 20X2

Retained Earnings, January 1, 20X2	$43,000
Add Net Income for the year ended December 31, 20X2	15,000
Total	58,000
Less Dividends Declared during the year	0
Retained Earnings, December 31, 20X2	$58,000

Notes:

1. The net income figure is from the Statement of Income illustrated in Exhibit 2.

2. The ending retained earnings amount is transferred to the Balance Sheet illustrated in Exhibit 6.

Statement of Retained Earnings

The **statement of retained earnings** is prepared for the corporate form of business organization. Its purpose is to compute the amount of earnings retained by the corporation. *Retained Earnings* represents the lifetime profits of the business that have not been declared as dividends to the shareholders.

Exhibit 4 illustrates the statement of retained earnings for Deb's Steakhouse, Inc. Note that the amount of retained earnings for the period just ended is calculated by adding net income and subtracting dividends declared from the amount of retained earnings shown on the previous statement of retained earnings prepared for the prior period. The net income figure is the same as that appearing on the bottom line of the statement of income in Exhibit 2. *Dividends Declared* includes all dividends declared during the current accounting year regardless of whether they are paid or unpaid.

Balance Sheet

The **balance sheet** shows assets, liabilities, and equity, revealing the *financial position* of a business. This information is presented as of the close of business on a certain date. The expression used by accountants is that the balance sheet provides information *on a given date.* The phrase *on a given date* has an entirely different meaning from the phrase *for a stated period of time,* which is used to describe the time period covered by an income statement.

For example, a balance sheet dated March 31 would present the status of financial information as of the close of business on that particular day. If you were counting the cash you presently have, you would state a dollar amount as it exists on the date you performed the count. All amounts shown on the balance sheet represent a status of existence on a certain day.

The balance sheet is composed of three major sections:

- Assets
- Liabilities
- Equity

Assets represent cash, receivables, inventories, equipment, property, and rights acquired by the business either by purchase or stockholder investment. Assets are items that are not used up at present; they have future utility or value.

Liabilities represent the debts of the business. Liabilities represent claims on assets by outsiders.

Equity represents the owner's financial interest in the business. Equity also represents a claim on the assets; however, this claim is by the owners, and it is a residual claim to those of the creditors.

Another way of looking at the balance sheet is that the assets represent the resources of the business, while the liabilities and equity represent the claims on those resources. This pragmatic relationship is represented in the accounting equation:

$$\text{Assets} = \text{Liabilities} + \text{Equity}$$

The following sections discuss the assets, liabilities, and equity sections of the proprietorship and corporate balance sheets for Deb's Steakhouse as illustrated by Exhibits 5 and 6, respectively. A brief explanation of the line items appearing under the basic balance sheet categories is also provided. The only significant difference between balance sheets prepared for proprietorships and those prepared for corporations is in the equity section.

Exhibit 5   Balance Sheet for a Proprietorship

Deb's Steakhouse
Balance Sheet
December 31, 20X2

ASSETS

CURRENT ASSETS

Cash	$34,000	
Accounts Receivable	4,000	
Inventories	5,000	
Prepaid Expenses	2,000	
Total Current Assets		$ 45,000

PROPERTY AND EQUIPMENT

	Cost	Accumulated Depreciation	
Land	$ 30,000		
Building	60,000	$15,000	
Furniture and Equipment	52,000	25,000	
China, Glassware, Silver	8,000		
Total	150,000	40,000	110,000

OTHER ASSETS

Security Deposits	1,500	
Preopening Expenses	2,500	
Total Other Assets		4,000

TOTAL ASSETS		**$159,000**

LIABILITIES

CURRENT LIABILITIES

Accounts Payable	$11,000	
Sales Tax Payable	1,000	
Accrued Expenses	9,000	
Current Portion of Long-Term Debt	6,000	
Total Current Liabilities		$ 27,000

LONG-TERM LIABILITIES

Mortgage Payable	40,000	
Less Current Portion of Long-Term Debt	6,000	
Net Long-Term Liabilities		34,000

TOTAL LIABILITIES		61,000

OWNER'S EQUITY

Capital, Deb Barry—December 31, 20X2		98,000

TOTAL LIABILITIES AND OWNER'S EQUITY		**$159,000**

Exhibit 6   Balance Sheet for a Corporation

Deb's Steakhouse, Inc.
Balance Sheet
December 31, 20X2

ASSETS

CURRENT ASSETS

Cash	$34,000	
Accounts Receivable	4,000	
Inventories	5,000	
Prepaid Expenses	2,000	
Total Current Assets		$ 45,000

PROPERTY AND EQUIPMENT

	Cost	Accumulated Depreciation	
Land	$ 30,000		
Building	60,000	$15,000	
Furniture and Equipment	52,000	25,000	
China, Glassware, Silver	8,000		
Total	150,000	40,000	110,000

OTHER ASSETS

Security Deposits	1,500	
Preopening Expenses	2,500	
Total Other Assets		4,000
TOTAL ASSETS		**$159,000**

LIABILITIES

CURRENT LIABILITIES

Accounts Payable	$11,000	
Sales Tax Payable	1,000	
Accrued Expenses	9,000	
Current Portion of Long-Term Debt	6,000	
Total Current Liabilities		$ 27,000

LONG-TERM LIABILITIES

Mortgage Payable	40,000	
Less Current Portion of Long-Term Debt	6,000	
Net Long-Term Liabilities		34,000
TOTAL LIABILITIES		61,000

STOCKHOLDERS' EQUITY

Common Stock		
Par Value $1		
Authorized 50,000 shares		
Issued 25,000 shares	25,000	
Additional Paid-In Capital	15,000	
Total Paid-In Capital		40,000
Retained Earnings, December 31, 20X2		58,000
TOTAL STOCKHOLDERS' EQUITY		98,000
TOTAL LIABILITIES AND STOCKHOLDERS' EQUITY		**$159,000**

Current Assets

Current assets are defined as those assets that are convertible to cash within 12 months of the balance sheet date. Items appearing as current assets are usually listed in the order of their liquidity (that is, the ease with which they can be converted to cash).

Cash. Cash consists of cash in house banks, cash in checking and savings accounts, and certificates of deposit.

Accounts Receivable. This line item includes all amounts due from customers carried by the restaurant on open accounts.

Inventories. This line item includes merchandise held for resale, such as food provisions and liquor stock. Inventories also include operating supplies such as guest supplies, office supplies, and cleaning supplies.

Prepaid Expenses. This line item shows the value of prepayments whose benefits will expire within 12 months of the balance sheet date. Prepaid expense items may include prepaid interest, rent, taxes, and licenses.

Property and Equipment

The property and equipment portion of the balance sheet lists noncurrent assets. The major noncurrent assets are land, buildings, and equipment. The costs for Building and for Furniture and Equipment that appear on the balance sheets for Deb's Steakhouse are decreased by amounts shown as Accumulated Depreciation.

    Depreciation spreads the cost of an asset over the term of its useful life. **Depreciation expense** is the cost of depreciation for only the current accounting period; it is shown on the statement of income. **Accumulated depreciation** is the sum of all depreciation from prior years to the present and is shown on the balance sheet. It is important to stress that this procedure is not an attempt to establish the market values of assets. The cost of the asset minus the amount of its accumulated depreciation leaves the net asset value, or what is sometimes called the *book value*. This should not be confused with market value (the value that the asset could bring if sold on the open market).

    Accumulated depreciation does not affect the noncurrent asset Land because land does not wear out *in the normal course of business*. Accumulated depreciation also does not affect China, Glassware, and Silver on the balance sheet because amounts for deterioration, breakage, and loss have already been deducted directly from this asset account.

Other Assets

The other assets portion of the balance sheet includes assets that do not apply to line items previously discussed. Security deposits include funds deposited with public utility companies (for instance, telephone, water, electric, and gas companies) and other funds used for similar types of deposits. Preopening expenses include capitalized expenses incurred before the opening of the property.

Current Liabilities

Current liabilities are obligations that will require settlement within 12 months of the balance sheet date. The total current liabilities figure alerts the restaurant operator to the operation's cash requirements and is often compared with the total figure for current assets.

Accounts Payable. This line item shows the total of unpaid invoices due to creditors from whom the restaurant receives merchandise or services in the ordinary course of business.

Sales Tax Payable. This line item includes all sales taxes collected from customers that are payable to federal or local government agencies.

Accrued Expenses. This line item lists the total amount of expenses incurred for the period up to the balance sheet date but that are not payable until after the balance sheet date and have not been shown elsewhere as a current liability.

Current Portion of Long-Term Debt. Since the total figure for current liabilities includes all obligations that will require an outlay of cash within 12 months of the balance sheet date, this line item includes the principal portion of long-term debt that is due within one year of the balance sheet date.

Long-Term Liabilities

A **long-term liability** (also called long-term debt) is any debt *not* due within 12 months of the balance sheet date. Any portion of long-term debt that is due within 12 months of the balance sheet date is subtracted from the total outstanding obligation and is shown in the current liabilities portion of the balance sheet.

Equity Section

Exhibit 5 shows the equity section of the balance sheet prepared for a proprietorship. The Owner's Equity line item shows the interests of the sole owner in the assets of Deb's Steakhouse. The figure for Deb Barry's Capital account in Exhibit 5 is the same figure that appears as the current balance on the statement of owner's equity in Exhibit 3. If the balance sheet were prepared for a partnership, the interests of each partner would be shown as line items under Partners' Equity. Changes in equity accounts of the partners would be shown in a statement of partners' equity whose format would be similar to that of the statement of owner's equity.

Exhibit 6 shows the equity section of the balance sheet prepared for a corporate form of business organization. *Common Stock* shows the par value, the number of shares authorized, and the number of shares issued. *Additional Paid-In Capital* shows the total amount for cash, property, and other capital contributed by stockholders in excess of the par value of the common stock. *Retained Earnings* includes that portion of net income earned by the corporation that is not distributed as dividends, but is retained in the business. The figure for Retained Earnings in Exhibit 6 is the same as that shown at the bottom of the statement of retained earnings in Exhibit 4.

Exhibit 7   Statement of Cash Flows

Deb's Steakhouse, Inc. **Statement of Cash Flows** **December 31, 20X2**		
Cash Flows from Operating Activities:		
Cash provided from operations		$ 27,000
Cash Flows from Investing Activities:		
Cash proceeds from sale of equipment	$ 5,000	
Deposit on vehicles	(20,000)	
Cash used by investing activities		(15,000)
Cash Flows from Financing Activities:		
Issuance of 1,000 shares of common stock	11,000	
Payment of 20X1 dividends declared	(1,000)	
Cash provided from financing activities		10,000
Increase (decrease) in cash for the year		$ 22,000
Cash at the beginning of the year		12,000
Cash at the end of the year		$ 34,000

Statement of Cash Flows

The major purpose of the **statement of cash flows (SCF)** is to provide information about where a company's cash came from and where that cash was spent. Its
focus is on **cash provided** or **cash used** and not on profit or loss. Cash flow is the
net result of cash receipts minus cash payments. If cash receipts exceed cash payments, the cash flow is positive, also called a cash inflow, meaning cash has been
provided by an activity. If the cash payments exceed the cash receipts, the cash flow
is negative, also called a cash outflow, meaning cash has been *used* by an activity.
The SCF is shown in Exhibit 7; note that it has three major sections:

- Operating Activities
- Investing Activities
- Financing Activities

    The ending cash shown on the SCF must reconcile with the cash shown on the
balance sheet. Note that the ending cash of $34,000 on the SCF in Exhibit 7 is equal
to the cash amount on the balance sheet in Exhibit 6.

Operating Activities

The **operating activities** section shows either the cash provided or cash used
from the primary day-to-day operating activity of a business. For a restaurant, the
primary day-to-day operating activity is cash generated from sales of food and
beverages. For a hotel, the primary day-to-day operating activity is cash generated from rooms, dining room, gift shop, and other departments of the hotel. The

generation of cash will be different from income because not all sales result in an immediate cash receipt and not all expenses require an immediate cash payment.

Investing Activities

The **investing activities** section shows the cash provided from the sale of or cash used for the purchase of:

- Short-term and other investments
- Land, buildings, and other property
- Equipment

For example, if a hotel purchased several vehicles with a $20,000 cash deposit and a $75,000 bank loan, the cash *used* is $20,000; this amount would appear in the investing activities section of the statement of cash flows.

Financing Activities

The **financing activities** section shows the cash provided from activities such as issuance of capital stock or bonds and cash borrowings.

The financing activities section also shows cash used from activities such as payment of dividends and payment on the debt portion of cash borrowings.

 **Key Terms** ───

accumulated depreciation—The sum of all depreciation from prior years to the present. It is recorded on the balance sheet.

annual financial statements—Statements issued at the end of a business year.

assets—Cash, receivables, inventories, equipment, property, and other rights of a business.

balance sheet—A financial statement showing a business's financial position on a given date in terms of assets, liabilities, and equity.

cash provided—A positive cash flow resulting when cash receipts exceed cash payments; also called *cash inflow*.

cash used—A negative cash flow resulting when cash payments exceed cash receipts; also called *cash outflow*.

cost of sales—A term that shows the cost of merchandise used in the sales process; also referred to as *cost of goods sold*.

current assets—Cash and other assets that can be converted to cash within 12 months of the balance sheet date.

current liabilities—Debts of the business that must be settled within 12 months of the balance sheet date.

depreciation—The accounting practice of spreading the cost of an asset over the term of its useful life.

depreciated expense—The cost of depreciation for only the current accounting period. It is recorded on the income statement.

equity—The owner's financial interest in the business.

financing activities—A section of the statement of cash flows that shows either the cash provided or cash used in transactions involving capital stock, cash loans, payment of dividends, and the debt portion of cash borrowings.

fiscal year—Business year. Can be any 12 consecutive months.

fixed charges—Expenses incurred regardless of sales volume. Also referred to as *occupancy costs*.

gross profit—The result of net sales minus cost of sales.

interim financial statements—Statements issued during the business year.

investing activities—A section of the statement of cash flows that shows either the cash provided or the cash used in transactions involving investments, property, and equipment.

liabilities—The debts of a business.

long-term liability—Any debt not due within 12 months of the balance sheet date. Also called *long-term debt*.

operating expenses—A section of the statement of income that lists expenses that are most directly influenced by operating policy and management efficiency.

operating activities—A section of the statement of cash flows that shows either the cash provided or the cash used by the primary day-to-day business activity.

revenue—The amounts billed for sales of merchandise and services.

statement of cash flows (SCF)—A financial statement showing where cash came from and how it was spent. Its focus is on cash provided or cash used, not on profit or loss.

statement of income—A financial statement showing revenue and expenses for the purpose of reporting on the results of operations.

statement of owner's equity—A financial statement prepared for a proprietorship that shows the owner's capital interest, which is the sum of his or her investments and income or assets not withdrawn for personal use.

statement of retained earnings—A financial statement prepared for a corporation that shows the business's lifetime earnings that have not been declared as dividends.

 # Review Questions

1. What is the purpose of the statement of income?
2. What are the basic categories that appear on the statement of income?
3. What is the difference between revenue and net income?

4. What is the purpose of the statement of owner's equity and the statement of retained earnings?

5. What is the purpose of the balance sheet?

6. What are the major categories that appear on the balance sheet?

7. What is the definition of current assets? What are some examples?

8. What is the definition of property and equipment? What are some examples?

9. What is the purpose of the statement of cash flows?

10. What are the three activities sections on the statement of cash flows? What is the purpose of each?

Internet Sites

For more information, visit the following Internet sites. Remember that Internet addresses can change without notice. If the site is no longer there, you can use a search engine to look for additional sites.

Balance Sheet
www.investopedia.com/
 articles/04/031004.asp

Beginner's Guide to Financial State-
 ments—The SEC
www.sec.gov/investor/pubs/
 begfinstmtguide.htm

Cash Flow Statement
www.investopedia.com/
 articles/04/033104.asp

Income Statement
www.investopedia.com/
 articles/04/022504.asp

Problems

Problem 1

Compute the cost of sales from the following information.

Food Sales	$80,000
Cost of Food Used	23,000
Employee Meals Served	500

Problem 2

Compute the gross profit from the following information:

Sales	$100,000
Cost of Sales	33,000
Payroll	30,000
Operating Expenses	12,000

Problem 3

Compute the total assets from the following information.

Cash	$ 15,000
Food Inventory	4,000
Food Sales	100,000
Common Stock Issued	26,000
Accounts Receivable	5,000
Land	30,000
Retained Earnings	32,000
Building	80,000
Furniture & Equipment	22,000
Accounts Payable	2,500
Additional Paid-In Capital	8,000

Problem 4

On which financial statements would the following items be presented?

Cash	_____
Accounts Payable	_____
Food Sales	_____
Withdrawals	_____
Common Stock Issued	_____
Dividends Payable	_____
Payroll Expense	_____
Food Inventory	_____
Prepaid Expenses	_____
Cost of Sales	_____
Land	_____
Accounts Receivable	_____
Advertising Expense	_____
Prepaid Advertising	_____
Mortgage Payable	_____

Problem 5

Sales are $50,000; cost of sales is $15,000; and all other expenses total $40,000. Determine the amount of revenue based on this information.

Problem 6

Compute the ending cash balance if the beginning cash balance was $40,000 and the SCF shows the following:

Cash Used by Operating Activities	$10,000
Cash Used by Investing Activities	20,000
Cash Provided by Financing Activities	25,000

Problem 7

Decide whether each of the following statements is true or false.

1. The income statement represents the financial position of a business.

2. Retained earnings represent the lifetime profits of the business that have not been declared as dividends to the shareholders.

3. The proper way to write a date for a balance sheet as of the year ended December 31, 20XX, is as follows: December 31, 20XX.

4. *Fiscal year* is another term for *business year*.

5. *Accumulated depreciation* is another term for *depreciation expense*.

6. *Dividends declared* is another term for *dividends payable*.

7. *Cost of goods sold* is another term for *cost of sales*.

8. *Sales* is another term for *revenue*.

9. Land is not depreciated in hospitality industry accounting.

10. The balance sheet shows revenue and expenses.

Problem 8

Use the following information to prepare an income statement for Wings Diner, Inc., for the year ended March 31, 20XX. Use the proper statement heading and a format similar to that used in the chapter for Deb's Steakhouse, Inc.

Payroll	$ 50,000
Employee Benefits	9,500
Cost of Food Sold	30,000
Cost of Liquor Sold	15,000
Food Sales	100,000
Utilities	5,000
Depreciation	10,000
Income Taxes	300
Property Insurance	6,000
Supplies Expense	3,000
Rent	8,750
Liquor Sales	50,000
Interest	7,000
Advertising	2,250
Property Taxes	2,000

Problem 9

An analysis of a business's financial information shows that the business's debts total $307,000 and that the owner's equity in the business is $182,000. From this information, determine the total assets of this company.

Problem 10

Curfew Inn is a proprietorship owned by Susan Plies. For the year ended December 31, 20X2, the net income of the lodging operation was $38,500. During that year, Susan invested $20,000 and withdrew $27,000. The financial records show that the bookkeeping account called *Capital, Susan Plies* had a balance of $12,750 on December 31, 20X1.

Prepare a statement of owner's equity for the year ended December 31, 20X2.

Problem 11

For the year ended December 31, 20X9, the net income of National Motels, Inc., was $85,900. The Retained Earnings account on January 1, 20X9, showed a balance of $62,000. During the year 20X9 the board of directors declared the following dividends to its stockholders:

May 21:	$8,500
November 28:	$8,500

The dividends declared on November 28 have not been paid as of December 31, 20X9. Prepare a statement of retained earnings for the year ended December 31, 20X9.

Problem 12

Using the following information, prepare a balance sheet on December 31, 20X7, for the Summer Resort, a proprietorship owned by Stan Robins. The statement of owner's equity prepared for the year ended December 31, 20X7, shows a total of $97,000. The asset and liability bookkeeping accounts show the following balances on December 31, 20X7:

Accumulated Depreciation on Equipment	$ 5,000
Accounts Receivable	9,000
Cost of Furniture	40,000
Cost of Equipment	10,000
Accumulated Depreciation on Building	20,000
Accumulated Depreciation on Furniture	20,000
Cost of Building	182,000
Cash	16,500
Land	20,000
Accounts Payable	8,000
Accrued Expenses	9,700
Prepaid Expenses	2,500
Wages Payable	4,100
Inventories	3,800

Mortgage Payable is $120,000, of which $15,000 is due currently.

Problem 13

Prepare the statement of cash flows from the following information:

Cash at Beginning of Year	$45,000
Cash Provided from Operations	30,000
Cash Proceeds from Sale of Equipment	10,000
Deposit on New Equipment	12,000
Issuance of Capital Stock	15,000
Payment of Dividends Declared	7,000

Ethics Case

Dekkon Foods & Lodging, Inc., is managed by executives who understand the value of ethics in the hospitality industry. They want to sharpen their

(continued)

(continued)

own ideological ethical attitudes and foster those of their supervisory employees in order to benefit the company's customers, employees, and other stakeholders.

To accomplish this purpose, management has hired a consultant to conduct several seminars on ethics. The first seminar covered the following three basic principles involved in ethical decision-making:

- The Principle of Utilitarianism. This principle asks, "What decision will provide the greatest amount of good for the greatest amount of people?"

- The Principle of Rights. This principle states that human beings have certain moral rights that must be respected at all times regardless of factors such as race, religion, or economic status.

- The Principle of Justice. This principle states that everyone should be treated fairly in matters that involve administration of rules, assignment of job duties, promotions, and compensation.

1. Which principle(s) is/are involved when management is considering the administration of lie detector tests to employees? Discuss any controversial elements or constraints involved in evaluating this action.

2. Which principle(s) is/are involved when management is writing policies for promotion? Discuss any controversial elements or constraints involved in evaluating this action.

3. Which principle(s) is/are involved when management is estimating the staffing levels required to serve guests? Discuss any controversial elements or constraints involved in evaluating this action.

Chapter 4 Outline

Preparation of the Balance Sheet
Asset Classification
Current Asset Accounts
    Cash
    Short-Term Investments
    Accounts Receivable
    Inventories
    Prepaid Expenses
Noncurrent Asset Accounts
    Investments
    Property and Equipment
    Other Assets
Liability Classification
Current Liability Accounts
    Accounts Payable
    Sales Tax Payable
    Income Taxes Payable
    Accrued Payables
    Advance Deposits
    Current Maturities of Long-Term Debt
Long-Term Liability Accounts
    Reclassification Example
Bonds
    Types of Bonds
    Bond Prices
    Bonds Issued at a Discount
    Bonds Issued at a Premium
    Bond Sinking Fund
Equity Classification
Proprietorship Equity Accounts
    Capital
    Withdrawals
Partnership Equity Accounts
Corporation Equity Accounts
    Common Stock Issued
    Additional Paid-In Capital
    Retained Earnings
    Preferred Stock Issued
    Donated Capital
    Treasury Stock
    Stockholders' Equity on the Balance
        Sheet
Limited Liability Company Equity
  Accounts

Competencies

1. Identify the accounts used to prepare a balance sheet, and identify and describe the asset accounts. (pp. 79–87)

2. Identify and describe the liability accounts. (pp. 87–91)

3. Identify types of bonds, and describe accounting for them. (pp. 91–93)

4. Identify and describe the equity accounts. (pp. 93–100)

4

Exploring the Balance Sheet

THE THREE MAJOR FINANCIAL STATEMENTS are the balance sheet, income statement, and statement of cash flows. Of these three, the balance sheet receives the least attention because of its lackluster content and complexity. The balance sheet reports on the financial position of a company; in other words, the balance sheet reveals the financial health of a company. Instead of looking at where a company has been (income statement), the financial data on the balance sheet reports on the *present status* of a company. This status can give an indication of inherent future difficulties for the company to operate as a going concern.

The balance sheet shows:

- What a company owns (called *assets*)
- What a company owes (called *liabilities*)
- What the owners have invested in the company (called *equity*)

The assets and liabilities give a picture of the financial condition of the company at the end of an accounting period. The assets and liabilities are further categorized by short-term and long-term characteristics.

The balance sheet got its name because the total of the assets will always be equal to—that is, in balance with—the combined total of liabilities and equity.

This chapter gives an in-depth description of the balance sheet accounts and provides answers to such questions as the following:

1. Which accounts are current assets, investments, property and equipment, and other assets?

2. Which accounts are current liabilities and long-term liabilities?

3. What are bonds payable, types of bonds, bond prices, and sinking funds?

4. What are the components of equity for a proprietorship, partnership, and corporation?

Preparation of the Balance Sheet

Not all of the bookkeeping accounts are used to prepare a balance sheet; different classifications of accounts are used to prepare the statement of income and the balance sheet. The selected bookkeeping accounts used to prepare the balance sheet are classified as:

Exhibit 1   Balance Sheet Accounts

ASSET ACCOUNTS

Cash	Land
Short-Term Investments	Building
Accounts Receivable	Furniture & Equipment
Food Inventory	China, Glassware, Silver
Beverage Inventory	Linen
Office Supplies Inventory	Uniforms
Operating Supplies Inventory	Organization Costs
Prepaid Insurance	Security Deposits
Prepaid Rent	

LIABILITY ACCOUNTS

Accounts Payable	Accrued Interest
Sales Tax Payable	Advance Deposits
Income Taxes Payable	Current Maturities of Long-Term Debt
Accrued Payroll	Notes Payable
Accrued Payroll Taxes	Mortgage Payable
Accrued Property Taxes	

EQUITY ACCOUNTS

For Corporations:	**For Proprietorships or Partnerships:**
Common Stock Issued	Capital, (owner's name)
Additional Paid-In Capital	Withdrawals, (owner's name)
Retained Earnings	

- Assets
- Liabilities
- Equity

These three types of bookkeeping accounts are collectively referred to as **balance sheet accounts**.

Exhibit 1 shows a representative listing of the balance sheet accounts used in most hospitality companies. The specific kinds of balance sheet accounts a company uses depend on its size, activities, and industry. All companies will have the asset account called Cash. However, a hospitality company will not have an asset account called Paint Inventory, as would a car manufacturer. Not all hospitality companies will have a liability account called Mortgage Payable, because some restaurants rent instead of own their facilities, or an established company may have paid off its mortgage. Just these few examples indicate the importance of analyzing balance sheet accounts.

The balance sheet may show assets, liabilities, and equity in either of two formats. The *account format* has two columns, listing assets on the left side of the balance sheet, and liabilities and equity on the right. The *report format* shows the three sections sequentially following each other; assets at the top, followed by liabilities, and finally the equity section. Most accountants and readers prefer the report format.

The composition of the balance sheet illustrates the accounting equation:

$$\text{Assets} = \text{Liabilities} + \text{Equity}$$

Asset Classification

Assets are items owned by a business that have a commercial or exchange value and are expected to provide a future use or benefit to the business. Ownership in this case refers to possession of legal title and, thus, applies to assets purchased on credit or financed by borrowings, in addition to those assets purchased with cash.

If the balance sheet simply listed all of these assets under one grouping, it would be difficult for the reader to easily perform analyses regarding the financial position of the company. For this reason, these assets are further divided into the following meaningful groups:

- Current assets: cash, short-term investments, accounts receivable, inventories, prepaid expenses
- Noncurrent assets: investments, property and equipment, other assets

The following sections define each of these categories and discuss individual accounts in some detail.

Current Asset Accounts

Current assets consist of cash or assets that are convertible to cash within 12 months of the balance sheet date. To be considered a current asset, an asset must be available without restriction for use in payment of current liabilities.

Among the major categories of current assets are the following accounts, listed here in order of liquidity:

- Cash
- Short-Term Investments
- Accounts Receivable
- Inventories
- Prepaid Expenses

Cash

Cash refers to currency, personal checks, travelers checks, and possibly credit and debit cards. Credit and debit card transactions are treated as cash if the cash is instantly available upon depositing the credit card vouchers with a local bank or processing through a merchant credit card services provider. Credit and debit cards are subject to credit card fees (also called commissions) that are an expense of doing business. If credit card volume is significant, these fees should be monitored and recorded daily. If they are not, the cash balance will be inflated.

For example, if a merchant (such as a hospitality business) processes $5,000 of credit card sales with a merchant credit card services provider and its fee is one percent, the provider transmits a deposit of $4,950 to the designated bank account of the hospitality business.

The bankcards (MasterCard and Visa) offer merchants a direct deposit service if a manual credit card voucher system is used. Under this direct bank deposit arrangement, the merchant receives funds for credit card deposits faster than if the merchant were on an electronic system with a credit card services provider. The retailer manually deposits the credit card vouchers at the retailer's bank and the deposit is treated like a cash deposit; there is no wait for a third party (the credit card service provider) to transmit the deposit. The disadvantage of using credit card vouchers for manual direct deposit is that the credit card fee is generally higher.

Manual credit card preparation is not common in the hospitality industry. Most hospitality operations use an electronic credit card swipe machine that produces a credit card receipt voucher. These swipe machines are stand-alone units that are integrated with an electronic cash register (ECR) or point-of-sale (POS) system.

Any cash that is restricted for current use must be disclosed as such in the financial statements and a determination made as to whether the cash is to show under current assets or noncurrent assets. Two examples of restricted cash funds are *compensating balances* and *special-purpose funds.*

A compensating balance usually takes the form of a minimum amount that must be maintained in a checking account as a stipulation of a borrowing arrangement with a bank. These compensating balances may be included under current assets if the arrangement is a short-term one. Compensating balances required by long-term borrowing arrangements should be included under noncurrent assets, preferably Investments.

Special-purpose funds may be deposited in a special bank account and set aside by management for a specific purpose, such as acquisition of property or equipment. Cash that is earmarked, either voluntarily or by contract, for a special purpose relating to long-term needs should be included under noncurrent assets, preferably Investments.

Short-Term Investments

Short-term investments, known also as **marketable securities,** are trading securities (stocks, bonds) that are (1) readily marketable, and (2) earmarked by management for conversion into cash should the need arise.

Accounts Receivable

The most common receivable is **accounts receivable**, which represents the amounts owed to a firm by its customers.

A business that does not have banking arrangements for converting credit card vouchers into immediate cash must treat its credit card vouchers as accounts receivable.

A hospitality business may issue its own credit cards (usually referred to as in-house credit cards) to the public. Any transactions on these cards are included in accounts receivable because the firm directly invoices and collects from the guest.

Allowance for Doubtful Accounts. A bookkeeping account called **Allowance for Doubtful Accounts** represents an estimate of potential receivables that may

Exhibit 2   Explanation of a Promissory Note Form

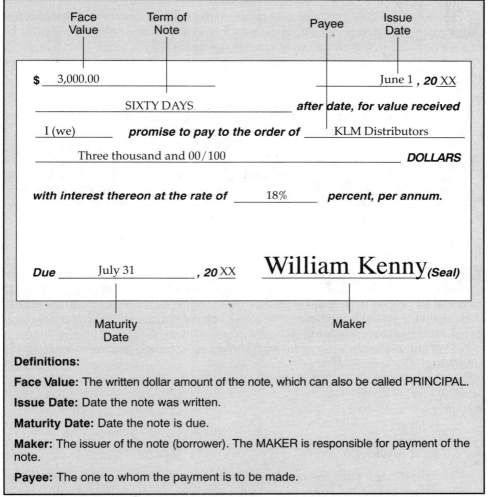

Source: Raymond Cote, *Business Math Concepts* (Providence, R.I.: P.A.R. Inc., 1985), p. 54.

become uncollectible. Historical analysis and aging of the receivables are used to compute the estimated doubtful accounts. The allowance for doubtful accounts is a contra-asset account because it reduces a related asset—in this case, the receivables.

Notes Receivable. A promissory note (see Exhibit 2) is a written promise to pay a definite sum of money at some future date. When a promissory note is made payable to the hospitality company, the company is called the *payee* of the note. Promissory notes have two characteristics not normally associated with accounts receivable. First, they are negotiable instruments because they are legally transferable among parties by endorsement. Second, these notes generally involve the payment of interest in addition to the principal (the amount of the loan).

Notes receivable that are collectible within one year of the balance sheet date can be included under current assets. Long-term notes receivable should be included with the noncurrent assets under Investments.

Inventories

This current asset account includes stocks of food and beverage merchandise held for resale; stocks of operating supplies such as guest supplies, office supplies, cleaning supplies, and engineering supplies; and other supplies held for future use. **Inventories** are recorded in such bookkeeping accounts as Food Inventory, Beverage Inventory (Liquor Inventory), Gift Shop Inventory, Operating Supplies, Cleaning Supplies, Office Supplies, and Restaurant Supplies. Supplies of china, glassware, and silver are not current assets; these items are not intended to be consumed in the short term. They are longer-lived assets and properly belong in the Property and Equipment category.

Prepaid Expenses

Prepaid expenses are expenditures, usually recurring, that produce a measurable benefit that will affect more than one accounting period, but no more than 12 months. Examples of prepaid expenses include prepaid rent (excluding security deposits) and prepaid insurance premiums, both of which are paid in advance and benefit future accounting periods.

Prepaid expenses are commonly shown in separate accounts such as the following:

- Prepaid Rent

- Prepaid Insurance

- Prepaid Interest

- Prepaid Service Contracts

Technically, prepaid expenses are unexpired costs that will benefit future periods but are expected to expire within a relatively short period, usually within 12 months of the current accounting period.

For example, payment of the current month's rent on the first of the month or after is *not* a prepaid expense because it is for the current month of the accounting period. However, if the rent for July is paid in June, the payment of the July rent is recorded as prepaid rent in June.

Noncurrent Asset Accounts

Current assets are those assets that are convertible to cash within 12 months of the balance sheet date. By contrast, noncurrent assets are those assets that are *not* to be converted to cash within 12 months of the balance sheet date. The three major categories of noncurrent assets are:

- Investments
- Property and Equipment
- Other Assets

The following sections discuss these three categories in more detail, providing definitions for some noncurrent asset accounts found in most businesses.

Investments

The Investments category can be bewildering because it has a different meaning in accounting and finance. In accounting, the term **investments** is a balance sheet category that does *not* include short-term investments. Instead, Investments is used to indicate noncurrent assets.

The most likely item to appear under Investments is the purchased corporate stock of affiliated companies or other companies for the purpose of influence or control. Other items that can appear under Investments are those securities that failed the short-term investment test, land held for expansion or future sale, and restricted cash accounts that are not readily available for use.

Property and Equipment

The noncurrent asset category of **Property and Equipment** includes those assets of a relatively permanent nature that are **tangible** (they possess physical substance) and are used in the business operation to generate sales. These **long-lived assets**, which have a life expectancy of more than one year, are also referred to as *plant assets* or **fixed assets**.

Property and Equipment accounts include such noncurrent assets as land, buildings, furniture, fixtures, vehicles, ovens, dishwashing machines, and similar long-lived assets. The following are typical fixed-asset accounts:

- Land
- Buildings
- Furniture and Equipment
- Transportation Equipment
- China, Glassware, Silver, Linen, and Uniforms

The preferred accounting treatment for china, glassware, silver, linens, and uniforms is to capitalize the cost of the initial purchase or complete replacement of the items.

Accumulated Depreciation. Depreciation is a method for allocating the cost of an asset over its useful life. The bookkeeping account **Accumulated Depreciation** contains the sum of these depreciation allocations for all prior years up to the present period. Accumulated Depreciation is a contra-asset account because it reduces a related asset account. The following do not have a related accumulated depreciation account:

- Land
- China, Glassware, Silver

- Linen

- Uniforms

In hospitality, as in most industries, land is not depreciated because it does not wear out or become consumed. (Land *can* be depreciated in such industries as mining and forestry; such depreciation is called *depletion*.) China, glassware, silver, linen, and uniforms are treated with a different method of accounting for their limited life. Instead of being reduced through an accumulated depreciation account, the cost of these assets is directly reduced by a *depreciation factor*. The *Uniform System of Accounts for the Lodging Industry* recommends a life not to exceed three years and expensing any replacements.

Other Assets

The noncurrent asset category **Other Assets** consists of purchased **intangible assets** that are long-lived but have no physical substance; their ownership conveys certain rights and privileges to their owner.

Intangible assets are also depreciated, except that accounting uses the term *amortization* to represent the cost allocation of an intangible asset over its useful life. Another difference is that the amortization calculation is not set up in an accumulated account; instead, the calculation directly reduces the cost of the intangible assets.

The following sections discuss some of the more common intangible assets.

Security Deposits. Security deposits include funds deposited to secure occupancy or utility services (such as telephone, water, electricity, and gas) and any similar types of deposits.

Preopening Expenses. The *Uniform System of Accounts for the Lodging Industry* now recommends that preopening expenses should no longer be capitalized (recorded as an asset), but rather should be expensed in the year incurred. Those companies who previously capitalized preopening expenses may continue to show the remaining unamortized cost as an asset until it reaches zero. For that reason, this chapter will present a discussion of preopening expenses as an asset. Importantly, it is acceptable for companies outside the United States to continue capitalizing and amortizing preopening expenses.

Organization Costs. Organization costs are expenditures incurred while legally forming a corporation and include such items as legal fees, stock certificate costs, accounting fees, promotional fees, incorporator's expenses, and underwriting fees to issue publicly held stock.

Trademarks and Trade Names. The federal government provides legal protection for trademarks and trade names if they are registered with the U.S. Patent Office. Material costs associated with their purchase are recorded as Trademarks and Trade Names, a noncurrent asset account.

Franchise Right. Franchising involves a long-term contract wherein the franchisor agrees to lend its name, goodwill, and back-up support to the franchisee. For these benefits, the franchisee agrees to maintain required quality standards and follow certain operating procedures. In addition, the franchisee pays the franchisor in the form of initial costs and annual fees.

An account called Franchise Right may be used to record the initial franchise cost, if material. Annual payments under a franchise agreement should be *expensed* by recording these expenditures to an expense account such as Franchise Fees Expense or Royalties Expense.

Goodwill. Goodwill has different meanings in the fields of marketing and finance (accounting). A company may enjoy a superior product or reputation that obviously generates goodwill. However, any value for this goodwill would be arbitrary and cannot appear on the balance sheet of such company.

Goodwill *can* be recorded if it is the result of the purchase of a business and the price paid for the assets is in excess of the fair market value (FMV) of those assets. For example, a business purchased for $875,000 as shown below results in goodwill of $75,000:

	FMV
Land	$200,000
Building	500,000
Furniture & Equipment	100,000
Total FMV of assets purchased	$800,000
Price paid for the assets	875,000

Goodwill = Excess over FMV = $75,000

Liability Classification

Liabilities are the debts of the business (that is, what the business owes its creditors). Liabilities represent the claims of creditors on the assets of a business and are sometimes referred to as *creditors' equities.*

Liability is important because it reflects a present and future demand on the cash flow of a company. For this reason, the liabilities section of the balance sheet is divided into current liabilities and long-term liabilities.

Current Liability Accounts

Current liabilities are those liabilities that are due within 12 months of the balance sheet date. The settlement of current liabilities can be achieved by the payment of cash, the exchange of another current asset, replacement by another current liability, or other new financing. The customary current liability accounts are:

- Accounts Payable
- Sales Tax Payable
- Income Taxes Payable
- Accrued Payables
- Advance Deposits
- Current Maturities of Long-Term Debt

Accounts Payable

Accounts payable result from verbal or implied promises to pay at some short-term future date. Such transactions usually arise when food, beverages, supplies, services, or utilities are purchased from vendors (also called suppliers or purveyors) *on credit*. Accounts payable are sometimes referred to as *trade payables*.

Sales Tax Payable

Taxes on retail sales are levied by many states and some cities. Usually the sales tax is imposed on the consumer; however, it is the seller who must collect the tax from the buyer, file the appropriate sales tax return, and remit the sales tax collected. Essentially, the seller acts as a collection agent for the taxing authority. Thus, sales taxes collected are a liability and are excluded from revenue (sales).

Income Taxes Payable

This account generally applies only to corporations. The federal government, most states, and some municipalities impose taxes on the taxable income of a corporation. A corporation might have three accounts as follows:

- Federal Income Tax Payable
- State Income Tax Payable
- Municipal Income Tax Payable

Accrued Payables

Accrued payables represent unrecorded expenses that, at the end of an accounting period, have been incurred but not yet paid. These unpaid expenses often require estimates, which may be computed by reference to historical data or by prescribed analytical procedures. The accrual of expenses is performed to comply with the matching principle—that is, to record expenses to the period in which they are incurred. Typical examples are:

- Accrued Payroll
- Accrued Payroll Taxes
- Accrued Property Taxes
- Accrued Interest Expense

Advance Deposits

Advance deposits are guest payments to the business for goods and services that have not yet been provided. Advance deposits are customary for reservations for banquets and rooms. Advance deposits cannot be treated as revenue because the sale has not been earned; instead, the cash received is treated as a liability.

Current Maturities of Long-Term Debt

This is not a bookkeeping account. Instead, it is an amount transferred from long-term liabilities that is due within 12 months of the balance sheet date. These current

Exhibit 3   Status of Note at Time of Loan: 2/15/X1

Amount Unpaid: $14,000	Number of Payments Remaining	Amount Due Within 12 Months: $12,000			
$1,000 due 3/15/X1	1	$1,000 due 8/15/X1	6	$1,000 due 1/15/X2	11
$1,000 due 4/15/X1	2	$1,000 due 9/15/X1	7	$1,000 due 2/15/X2	12
$1,000 due 5/15/X1	3	$1,000 due 10/15/X1	8	$1,000 due 3/15/X2	13
$1,000 due 6/15/X1	4	$1,000 due 11/15/X1	9	$1,000 due 4/15/X2	14
$1,000 due 7/15/X1	5	$1,000 due 12/15/X1	10		

maturities are also called **current portion of long-term debt**. A thorough explanation of current portion of long-term debt is provided in the following discussion of long-term liabilities.

Long-Term Liability Accounts

Long-term liabilities can consist of the following:

- Notes payable
- Mortgages payable
- Bonds payable

Long-term liabilities are a **hybrid liability** because part of the liability can constitute a current liability and the remainder a long-term liability. A note or mortgage payable usually has monthly payment provisions and special attention is required for proper placement on the balance sheet. Each payment due within 12 months of the balance sheet date is reclassified and the sum is shown under current liabilities; the amount due after this 12-month period is shown under long-term liabilities.

Bonds are a major form of financing and are discussed later in the chapter.

Reclassification Example

This example uses a 14-month note to illustrate how *reclassification* of long-term debt is performed. Assume that on February 15, 20X1, a business executed a 14-month loan for $14,000, with payment terms of $1,000 per month plus interest at a specified rate. Exhibit 3 shows the debt structure of this loan on the day the funds were borrowed.

Exhibit 4   Status of Note after First Payment: 3/16/X1

Amount Unpaid: $13,000		Amount Due Within 12 Months: $12,000			
	Number of Payments Remaining	$1,000 due 8/15/X1	5	$1,000 due 1/15/X2	10
$1,000 due 4/15/X1	1	$1,000 due 9/15/X1	6	$1,000 due 2/15/X2	11
$1,000 due 5/15/X1	2	$1,000 due 10/15/X1	7	$1,000 due 3/15/X2	12
$1,000 due 6/15/X1	3	$1,000 due 11/15/X1	8	$1,000 due 4/15/X2	13
$1,000 due 7/15/X1	4	$1,000 due 12/15/X1	9		

The $14,000 debt requires monthly payments; therefore, the next 12 monthly payments of $1,000 represent a current liability called *current portion of long-term debt*, and the balance is classified as long-term debt. Since no payments have yet been made, the balance sheet at the end of the month will appear as follows:

Balance Sheet
February 28, 20X1

Current Liabilities:		
Current portion of long-term debt		$12,000
Long-Term Liabilities:		
Note Payable	$14,000	
Less current portion due	12,000	
Long-term debt		2,000

On March 15, a payment of $1,000 plus interest is made on the loan. Now the unpaid balance is $13,000. Exhibit 4 shows the debt structure of this loan after the first payment has been made.

The $13,000 unpaid balance requires monthly payments; therefore, the next 12 monthly payments of $1,000 represent a current liability, and the balance is classified as long-term debt. The balance sheet at the end of the month will appear as follows:

Balance Sheet
March 31, 20X1

Current Liabilities:		
Current portion of long-term debt		$12,000
Long-Term Liabilities:		
Note Payable	$13,000	
Less current portion due	12,000	
Long-term debt		1,000

Exhibit 5 Status of Note after Second Payment: 4/16/X1

Amount Unpaid: $12,000			Amount Due Within 12 Months: $12,000			
			$1,000 due 8/15/X1	4	$1,000 due 1/15/X2	9
	Number of Payments Remaining		$1,000 due 9/15/X1	5	$1,000 due 2/15/X2	10
$1,000 due 5/15/X1	1		$1,000 due 10/15/X1	6	$1,000 due 3/15/X2	11
$1,000 due 6/15/X1	2		$1,000 due 11/15/X1	7	$1,000 due 4/15/X2	12
$1,000 due 7/15/X1	3		$1,000 due 12/15/X1	8		

On April 15, another payment of $1,000 plus interest is made on the loan. Now the unpaid balance is $12,000. Exhibit 5 shows the debt structure of this loan after the second payment has been made.

At this phase of the loan, only 12 monthly payments remain. Therefore, the complete unpaid balance of $12,000 represents a current liability. The balance sheet at the end of the month will appear as follows:

Balance Sheet
April 30, 20X1

Current Liabilities:
    Note Payable $12,000

Bonds

Bonds are a long-term liability and another form of notes payable. Companies might find it more attractive to raise large amounts of cash by issuing bonds than by taking out a commercial loan. Well-known companies can issue bonds with a lower interest rate than they would pay on a commercial loan. Bonds are typically sold in units of $1,000 (the **face value** or maturity value). Bonds generally pay interest twice a year to the bondholders. The issuing company is obligated to pay the holder of the bond its face value at a specified future date called the **maturity date.**

A **bond certificate** is evidence of ownership. A supporting legal document called a **bond indenture** explains the rights and privileges of the owner and any special terms and features.

Types of Bonds

Types of bonds are defined by their maturity dates, collateral, registration, and other properties. A bond may have one or more of these features.

Term and Serial Bonds. A bond that matures at a specified maturity date at its full face value is a **term bond**. A **serial bond** spreads the payment of its face value over several maturity dates.

Secured and Unsecured Bonds. Bonds backed with collateral of specific assets are **secured bonds**, also called *mortgage bonds*. **Debenture bonds** are unsecured bonds backed only by the issuer's good faith.

Registered and Bearer Bonds. Bonds issued in the name of the owner are **registered bonds**. Bonds not registered in any name are called **bearer bonds** or *coupon bonds* because the holder must send in coupons to receive interest payments. Most bonds issued are registered bonds.

Convertible and Callable Bonds. Bonds that can be converted into common stock are **convertible bonds**. Bonds that can be called in and paid before the maturity date are **callable bonds**.

Bond Prices

Bonds, like stock, are traded on national markets and are attractive to many investors. A bond might not necessarily sell in these markets at its face value. If a bond bears an interest rate more attractive than current offerings or money market rates, that bond could sell for more than its face value. Conversely, if money market rates are more attractive than a bond's stated rate, it might sell at less than its face value. Bond prices are quoted at a percentage of their maturity value. A bond quoted at 100 means its price is $1,000 (100% × $1,000), and a bond quoted at 95 means its price is $950 (95% × $1,000). A bond may be originally issued at a discount or a premium from its face value. Many factors influence the price of bonds, such as interest rate trends, the issuer's reputation, and market conditions.

Bonds Issued at a Discount

At original issue, a bond might sell at less than its face value because of the issuer's reputation or because the bond's stated interest rate is less than market rates. For example, a company may issue $3,000,000 of face value bonds but sell them at $2,700,000. The $300,000 is called a **discount** and is an expense that will be amortized over the life of the bond, because, at maturity, the issuing company must pay the $3,000,000 face value.

Bonds Issued at a Premium

At original issue, a bond might sell at more than its face value because the bond's stated interest rate is more than market rates. For example, a company may issue $3,000,000 of face value bonds but sell them at $3,200,000. The $200,000 is called a **premium**; it is treated as a reduction of interest expense and the premium will be amortized over the life of the bond because, at maturity, the issuing company need pay only the $3,000,000 face value.

Bond Sinking Fund

To make a bond more attractive, a **sinking fund** provision under the control of a trustee such as a bank or trust company is used. A sinking fund is cash (or other

Exhibit 6 Financial Structure of a Proprietorship

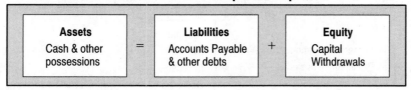

assets) periodically put aside specifically to retire the bond debt. This cash can be invested, and it is expected that the sinking fund payments and any interest or other income will be sufficient to pay the face value at maturity date. The sinking fund is reported in the investment section of the balance sheet.

Equity Classification

The **equity accounts** represent the claims of the owner(s) on the assets of the business. By contrast, the liability accounts represent creditors' claims on the assets. Taken together, these accounts support the fundamental accounting equation:

$$\text{Assets} = \text{Liabilities} + \text{Equity}$$

This equation can be restated as:

$$\text{Assets} = \text{Claims of Creditors} + \text{Claims of Owners}$$

The types of equity accounts depend upon whether the company is a proprietorship, partnership, corporation, or limited liability company.

Proprietorship Equity Accounts

A proprietorship requires only two equity accounts: a *capital account* to represent the owner's financial interest in the business, and a *withdrawals account* to accumulate the cash drawings or other assets withdrawn from the business by the owner. Exhibit 6 shows the financial structure and the components of the equity section of a proprietorship. The two bookkeeping accounts used to record equity transactions are *Capital (Owner's Name)* and *Withdrawals (Owner's Name)*.

The types of equity transactions that may occur for a proprietorship form of business organization include the following:

- The owner investing personal cash or property in the business

- The owner withdrawing cash or property from the business for personal use

- The business recording either an operating profit or loss for the accounting period

Exhibit 7 illustrates how various equity transactions affect the equity section of a proprietorship.

Exhibit 7   Effect of Equity Transactions in a Proprietorship

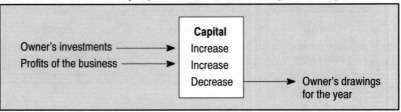

Capital

The **Capital Account** represents the owner's financial interest in the business. It reflects the equity transactions between the business and its owner.

An owner's financial interest in the proprietorship is increased whenever the owner makes personal investments in the business. These personal investments can be in the form of cash, equipment, or property.

The Capital Account is also increased by the profits of the business because the profits belong to the owner of a proprietorship. These profits increase the account regardless of the amount of withdrawals made by the owner.

Withdrawals

The **Withdrawals Account** is a temporary bookkeeping account used to accumulate the owner's drawings from the proprietorship. Some accountants refer to this account as the *drawings account.*

An owner may withdraw cash, inventory, or other assets from the business. The effect of these drawings is to reduce his or her financial interest (equity) in the proprietorship. The sum in the withdrawals account is used to reduce the capital account.

Partnership Equity Accounts

Accounting for a partnership is similar to that of a proprietorship, with the exception that the transactions of two or more owners are involved. Therefore, each owner requires individual capital and withdrawals accounts. The partnership's net income or loss is allocated to each partner in accordance with the division of profits as specified in the partnership agreement. In the absence of an agreement, the income (or loss) of the partnership is divided equally among the partners.

Exhibit 8 shows the financial structure and the components of the equity section of a partnership having two partners. Notice that each partner has his or her own capital and withdrawals account.

Corporation Equity Accounts

The equity section for a corporation may be labeled Stockholders' Equity or Shareholders' Equity; the terms are interchangeable. The equity section of a corporation

Exhibit 8   Financial Structure of a Partnership

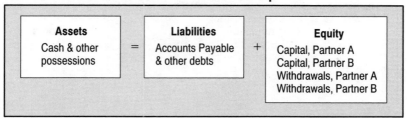

Assets		**Liabilities**		**Equity**
Cash & other possessions	=	Accounts Payable & other debts	+	Capital, Partner A Capital, Partner B Withdrawals, Partner A Withdrawals, Partner B

Exhibit 9   Financial Structure of a Corporation

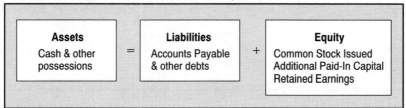

Assets		**Liabilities**		**Equity**
Cash & other possessions	=	Accounts Payable & other debts	+	Common Stock Issued Additional Paid-In Capital Retained Earnings

is more involved than that for a proprietorship or partnership because the corporation is a legal entity separate from its owners.

A simple corporate structure, as shown in Exhibit 9, includes the following equity accounts:

- Common Stock Issued

- Additional Paid-In Capital

- Retained Earnings

A more complex corporate structure might include these equity accounts:

- Preferred Stock Issued

- Donated Capital

- Treasury Stock

A corporation owns its assets, owes its liabilities, and has legal claim to its earnings. Earnings may be distributed to stockholders in the form of dividends. These dividends first must be declared by the corporation's board of directors. The board is the only governing body with the power to declare dividends.

Usually, the owner's original investment to start a business is used to purchase stock of the corporation. This stock provides the owner with voting rights used for, among other things, the election of the board of directors. The purchase of this stock may result in additional paid-in capital, as explained later. The corporation's earnings are kept (retained) by the corporation until they are declared as dividends to the shareholders.

Exhibit 10 shows how the equity section of a corporation is affected by the various equity transactions.

Exhibit 10   Effect of Equity Transactions in a Corporation

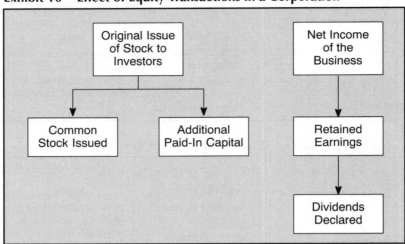

Common Stock Issued

The stock issued as shown on the financial statement of a corporation is the original issue of its stock to its initial investors. After this original issue, the investors may sell their stock to other investors. This after-issue sale of stock does not affect the corporation's financial records because the corporation is not a party to these market transactions.

Common stock issued is shown on the financial statement at **par value**. The par value is selected by the corporation when it files its articles of incorporation; par value does not have any relationship whatsoever to its real value.

Usually, the par value selected is very low, generally ranging from 1¢ to $1 per share. Low par values are selected because certain states levy a tax on the corporation for its par value of stock, and par value represents the legal capital that must be retained by the corporation for protection of its creditors. Thus, most states mandate that a corporation cannot sell its stock below par value.

Because of the confusion between par value and market value, some corporations issue *no-par value stock*. The entire proceeds received from the sale of no-par value stock becomes the legal capital per share, and this amount is the basis for recording to Common Stock Issued. For example, if $50,000 was received from the original sale of no-par value stock, $50,000 would be recorded to the Cash account and the Common Stock Issued account. One disadvantage of no-par value stock is that some states levy a high tax on this type of common stock.

In many states, a company's board of directors is permitted to assign a stated value to no-par value stock, which becomes the legal capital per share. Stated value, like par value, has no relationship to market value. The board of directors may change the stated value at any time.

Exhibit 11   Common Stock Issued and Additional Paid-In Capital

Stock	Amount Recorded as Common Stock Issued	Amount Recorded as Additional Paid-In Capital
Par value	Par value	Excess over par value
No-par with stated value	Stated value	Excess over stated value
No-par without stated value	Entire proceeds	None

Additional Paid-In Capital

Because par value or stated value does not reflect the stock's real value, the proceeds received from the original issue of a corporation's stock are usually greater than the par or stated value. The amount in excess of par value or stated value is called **additional paid-in capital**.

Some accountants prefer to use an account called Paid-In Capital in Excess of Par Value or Paid-In Capital in Excess of Stated Value. Regardless of the account title used, the computations are identical and all are equity accounts.

If no-par value stock without a stated value is issued, the entire proceeds from the original issuance of the corporation's stock are recorded as common stock issued and no entry is made to Additional Paid-In Capital.

Exhibit 11 shows the amounts recorded in the Common Stock Issued and Additional Paid-In Capital accounts when par value stock, no-par with stated value, and no-par without stated value are issued.

To better understand how additional paid-in capital arises, study the following example. Assume the following information for a corporation:

> Authorized stock: 50,000 shares of $1 par value common stock
> Stock to be issued: 10,000 shares
> Selling price per share: $7

The issuance of this stock will produce the following results in the bookkeeping records:

> Cash Received: $70,000 (10,000 shares × $7)
> Common Stock Issued: $10,000 (10,000 shares × $1 par value)
> Additional Paid-In Capital: $60,000 ($70,000 − $10,000)

The $70,000 cash received is the proceeds from the selling price of $7 per share multiplied by the total number of shares sold (10,000 shares in this case). Note that the corporation is not issuing all of its authorized shares. This is not uncommon; a corporation usually applies for more authorized shares than it intends to originally issue. The corporation uses this strategy to avoid having to amend its corporate charter should the company desire to issue more stock in the future due to working capital needs, expansion, or other reasons.

The common stock issued is always recorded at its par value, if any. In this example, 10,000 shares of $1 par value stock were issued for a total of $10,000 par value.

The $60,000 additional paid-in capital is the amount received of $70,000 less the total par value issued of $10,000. An alternate method of determining the amount in excess of par value is to compute it on a per-share basis. For example, the selling price of $7 per share represents a premium of $6 over the par value of $1 per share. This premium of $6 per share multiplied by the number of shares issued (10,000) also results in additional paid-in capital of $60,000.

Retained Earnings

Retained Earnings is an account that represents the lifetime earnings of the corporation not distributed to shareholders in the form of dividends. The net income of the business is an *increase* to Retained Earnings.

Cash dividends declared are recorded as a *decrease* to Retained Earnings. This decrease is recorded at the time the dividends are declared by the board of directors, not when they are paid. The payment of dividends affects cash; the declaration of dividends is an allocation of earnings to the shareholders that is recorded at the time the board declares the dividend and the liability for payment at a future date. The declaration of dividends affects corporate equity accounts by way of a *decrease* in the Retained Earnings account and an *increase* in the Dividends Payable account.

The Dividends Payable account is a liability account and will be decreased when the dividends are paid at a future date.

The following is a history of the Retained Earnings account for a corporation that has been in existence for seven years:

Business Year	Net Income	Dividends Declared	Retained Earnings
1	$ 9,000		$ 9,000
2	15,000		24,000
3	17,000	$7,000	34,000
4	12,000	7,000	39,000
5	(4,000)		35,000
6	(2,000)		33,000
7	10,000		43,000

Preferred Stock Issued

Preferred stock is a special kind of stock corporations use to attract a different kind of investor, thus expanding the corporation's ability to raise funds. The accounting procedures for preferred stock are similar to those for common stock and will not be enumerated here. One obvious difference is the terminology; the issuance of preferred stock is recorded as *preferred stock issued* rather than *common stock issued*. This distinguishes the different kinds of capital stock issued by the corporation.

The dividend on preferred stock is usually stated as a percentage of par value. In this case, par values are *not* set at a nominal amount. For example, a $100 par value preferred stock with a dividend stated at eight percent will receive an $8 dividend per year. If the preferred stock has no par value, the dividend would be stated as a dollar amount per share.

Dividends on preferred stock, like common stock, must be declared by the board of directors. However, preferred stockholders receive priority over common stockholders as to the receipt of dividends. Thus, it is possible for dividends to be declared on preferred stock and not on common stock.

The right to vote is ordinarily not permitted for preferred stockholders, but some states allow corporations to issue voting preferred stock if they desire. Preferred stock offers features common stock does not, such as the following:

- Dividend privileges
- Conversion privilege
- Liquidation preference
- Callability

Dividend Privileges. What if a company's board decides not to declare dividends on any of its outstanding stock for a period of time? To make preferred stock more attractive, the preferred stock could be issued as *cumulative preferred stock*. Past dividends that have not been paid to cumulative preferred stockholders are called *dividends in arrears*, which must be paid to the preferred stockholders before any dividends can be declared on the common stock.

Conversion Privilege. The market value of common stock usually reacts more favorably than preferred stock when a company is growing or has a favorable profit pattern. Owners of *convertible preferred stock* have a right to exchange their preferred stock for common stock as stipulated on the stock certificate. For example, a preferred stock could be exchanged at the rate of one preferred share for four shares of common stock, or some other exchange ratio.

Liquidation Preference. Most preferred stock carries a feature that provides a measure of security for its holders. In the case of corporate dissolution, after all priority claims are paid, the preferred stockholders have first claim over the common stockholders on the remaining assets of the business.

Callability. The special provisions that make preferred stock more attractive may in time become too expensive for a corporation to sustain. Also, the demands of these special features might work against the common stockholders. To guard against these problems, most preferred stock is issued as *callable preferred stock*. This means that a corporation may buy back *(call)* its preferred stock and retire it. The *call price* is usually higher than the preferred stock's par or stated value. When preferred stock is callable, the call price per share usually acts as a price ceiling on the open market.

Donated Capital

Sometimes corporations receive assets (such as land) as gifts from states, cities, or benefactors to increase local employment or encourage business activity in a locality. In such cases, the appropriate asset account would be increased and the **donated capital** equity account would be increased accordingly.

Treasury Stock

A corporation may reacquire shares of its previously issued stock to reduce the number of outstanding and issued shares. This is sometimes done to increase

Exhibit 12   Equity Section of a Corporate Balance Sheet

STOCKHOLDERS' EQUITY	
Paid-In Capital	
Preferred Stock, 9% dividends, $100 par, cumulative, callable, 600 shares authorized and issued	$ 60,000
Common Stock, $1 par, 200,000 shares authorized, 50,000 shares issued, treasury stock 5,000 shares, which are deducted below	50,000
Additional Paid-In Capital	70,000
Total Paid-In Capital	$ 180,000
Donated Capital	30,000
Retained Earnings	65,000
Total	$ 275,000
Deduct: Common Treasury Stock at Cost	17,000
Total Stockholders' Equity	$ 258,000

the figure computed for earnings per share, which some regard as an investment guideline, or it may be done simply to reduce outside ownership.

When stock is reacquired, it is called **treasury stock.** Treasury stock is no longer considered *issued and outstanding;* therefore, it does not pay any dividends and is not associated with voting privileges. However, it may later be sold again.

The cost method is generally used to record the purchase of treasury stock. Under this method, the Common Stock Issued account is not affected; rather, a contra-equity account called Treasury Stock is used.

For example, assume that a corporation reacquires 5,000 shares of its $1 par value common stock for a cost of $17,000. The business transaction is recorded as an *increase* of $17,000 in the treasury stock account and a $17,000 *decrease* in the cash account.

Stockholders' Equity on the Balance Sheet

A corporation may present an extensive equity section on its balance sheet depending upon the types of equity transactions it carries out. For example, the equity section of a balance sheet for a particular corporation may appear as in Exhibit 12. The section titled Stockholders' Equity includes the sale of both common and preferred stock, contributions of additional paid-in capital and donated capital, and the deduction of treasury stock reacquired by the corporation.

Limited Liability Company Equity Accounts ————————

A limited liability company (LLC) is a business form that has advantages similar to both a partnership and a corporation. This allows the owners to take advantage of the profit-sharing attributes of a partnership, yet enjoy the limited liability protection of a corporation. Accounting for an LLC is similar to that for a partnership. Each owner has an individual equity account in which profits and distributions are recorded.

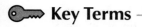 **Key Terms** ————————————————————————————————————

accounts receivable—The amounts owed to a firm by its customers.

accrued payables—Unrecorded liabilities for expenses that have been incurred but not yet paid during the financial reporting period.

accumulated depreciation—An account containing the sum of depreciation allocations for all prior years to the present. It is a contra-asset account because it reduces a related asset.

additional paid-in capital—The amount paid by stockholders in excess of the par or stated value of a stock.

advance deposits—Customer deposits for services not yet rendered or goods not yet delivered.

allowance for doubtful accounts—An account representing an estimate of potential receivables that may become uncollectible. It is a contra-asset account because it reduces accounts receivable.

balance sheet accounts—Accounts known collectively as assets, liabilities, and equity.

bearer bond—A bond with no registered owner's name.

bond certificate—Tangible evidence of ownership of a bond, usually a printed form with information about the bond.

bond indenture—A document that explains the rights and privileges of a bond holder and any special terms and features of the bond.

callable bond—A bond that can be redeemed (called in) and paid by the issuer before the maturity date.

capital account—An equity account showing the financial interest of owners. Used for proprietorships and partnerships.

convertible bond—A bond that can be converted into common stock.

current assets—Cash or assets that are convertible to cash within 12 months of the balance sheet date.

current portion of long-term debt—Portion of long-term liabilities that is due within 12 months of the balance sheet date.

debenture bond—A bond with no collateral behind it.

discount—With regard to bonds, the amount by which the initial selling price is below face value.

donated capital—Assets received by the corporation as a gift.

equity accounts—A section of the balance sheet showing the financial interest of the owners.

face value—The maturity value of a bond.

fixed assets—Noncurrent assets that have a relatively permanent nature, are tangible, and are used to generate sales.

goodwill — An account reflecting the value of intangible assets such as a business's superior products or service. It can be recorded if it is the result of the purchase of a business and the price paid is in excess of the fair market value of the purchased business's assets.

hybrid liability — A long-term liability in which part of the liability is current and part is long-term.

intangible assets — Long-lived assets having no physical substance but conveying certain rights to the owner.

inventories — Items held for sale or consumption.

investments — In accounting, a balance sheet category that does not include short-term investments. The item most likely to appear in this category is the purchased corporate stock of affiliated companies or other companies for the purpose of influence or control. Also included are securities failing the short-term investment test, land held for expansion or sale, and restricted cash accounts.

long-lived assets — Assets with a useful life exceeding 12 months.

long-term liabilities — Liabilities due after 12 months of the balance sheet date.

marketable securities — Trading securities (stocks, bonds) that are readily marketable and earmarked by management for conversion into cash.

maturity date — The date at which the issuer of a bond is obligated to pay the bond's face value to the bondholder.

notes receivable — Promissory notes (promises to pay) made payable to a company. They are negotiable instruments when endorsed and involve the payment of interest.

organization costs — Costs involved with the legal formation of a business; usually associated with the corporate form.

other assets — A noncurrent asset category that includes long-lived intangible assets.

par value — A value for common stock selected by the issuing corporation when it files its articles of incorporation. Par value has no relationship with the stock's real value.

premium — With regard to bonds, the amount by which the initial selling price is greater than the face value of the bonds.

prepaid expenses — A current asset account for items paid in advance. Prepaid items are unexpired expenses that will benefit future periods.

property and equipment — A noncurrent asset category that includes long-lived tangible assets.

registered bond — A bond issued in the name of the owner or buyer of the bond.

retained earnings — The lifetime earnings of a corporation not distributed to shareholders in the form of dividends declared.

secured bonds — Bonds backed with collateral of specific assets. Also called *mortgage bonds*.

serial bond—A bond spreading the payment of its face value over several maturity dates.

short-term investments—Readily marketable securities that management can sell should the need for cash arise.

sinking fund—With regard to bonds, cash or other assets periodically put aside to retire bond debt.

tangible asset—A long-lived asset having physical substance. Examples are land, buildings, and equipment.

term bond—A bond maturing at a specified date at its full face value.

treasury stock—Reacquired stock previously issued by the corporation.

withdrawals account—A temporary account used to accumulate the owner's/ owners' drawings of cash or other assets from a proprietorship or partnership.

 # Review Questions

1. How are the following classifications of bookkeeping accounts defined?
   a. Asset
   b. Liability
   c. Equity

2. How are the following categories defined?
   a. Current Asset
   b. Property and Equipment
   c. Other Assets
   d. Current Liability
   e. Investments

3. What are the definitions of the following current asset accounts?
   a. Cash
   b. Short-Term Investments
   c. Accounts Receivable
   d. Inventories
   e. Prepaid Expenses

4. Why is a 20-year mortgage requiring monthly payments allocated as part current liability and part noncurrent liability on the balance sheet?

5. What are the equity accounts for a proprietorship?

6. What are the equity accounts for a corporation?

7. What is an Allowance for Doubtful Accounts? Where does this account appear on the balance sheet?

8. How are credit card drafts generally treated and recorded?

9. Why are prepaid expenses treated as an asset and not as an expense?

10. When and how is goodwill recorded according to accounting principles?

11. What is the definition of Accumulated Depreciation? Where does this account appear on the balance sheet?

 ## Internet Sites

For more information, visit the following Internet sites. Remember that Internet addresses can change without notice. If the site is no longer there, you can use a search engine to look for additional sites.

Assets
http://en.wikipedia.org/wiki/Asset

Balance Sheet
http://en.wikipedia.org/wiki/
  Balance_sheet

Current and Long-term Liabilities
http://en.wikipedia.org/wiki/Liability

Equity
http://en.wikipedia.org/wiki/
  Equity_(finance)

What Is Inventory?
www.wisegeek.com/what-is-
  inventory.htm

What Are Preferred Stock and Common Stock?
www.investopedia.com/ask/
  answers/182.asp

 ## Problems

Problem 1

Classify each of the following accounts as an asset (A), liability (L), or equity (EQ) account.

_____ Accounts Payable
_____ Short-Term Investments
_____ Land
_____ Mortgage Payable
_____ Capital
_____ Common Stock Issued
_____ Prepaid Rent Expense
_____ Repair Parts Inventory
_____ Accounts Receivable
_____ Investments
_____ Building
_____ Sales Tax Payable
_____ Withdrawals
_____ Retained Earnings
_____ Food Inventory
_____ Paid-In Capital

Problem 2

The Vendome Corporation has purchased 100 shares of stock of the Ford Motor Company, which is listed on the New York Stock Exchange. Would this purchase be recorded as an investment or as short-term investment? State the reason for your conclusion.

Problem 3

The Eller Corporation has purchased 100 percent of the outstanding stock of the Jewel Company. Would this purchase be recorded as an investment or as marketable securities? State the reason for your conclusion.

Problem 4

DORO, Inc., has purchased 1,000 shares of Goldfinders, Inc., from its founder. There is no ready market for this stock. Would this purchase be recorded as an investment or as marketable securities? State the reason for your conclusion.

Problem 5

On March 10, the GGD Company borrowed $36,000 from a bank. The company executed a promissory note for a term of three years, with payments to start on April 10. Monthly payments are required, consisting of $1,000 on the principal plus interest to be computed at the rate specified on the note. On March 31, what amount will appear as a long-term liability on the balance sheet?

Problem 6

For this problem, continue to use the information provided in Problem 5. On April 10, the GGD Company made its first payment on the note; the payment consisted of $1,000 on the principal plus accrued interest on the unpaid balance. On May 10, the company made its second payment on the note, consisting of $1,000 on the principal plus accrued interest on the unpaid balance. What amounts will appear as long-term debt on the balance sheets dated April 30 and May 31?

Problem 7

A corporation issues 100,000 shares of an authorized 500,000 shares of $1 par value common stock. The selling price is $15 per share.

a. How much cash is received?

b. What amount is recorded as common stock issued?

c. What amount, if any, is recorded as additional paid-in capital?

Problem 8

Compute the retained earnings at the end of Year 4 from the following income and dividends records of a corporation:

Income History:

Business Year	Net Income or (Loss)
1	$(7,000)
2	(4,000)
3	25,000
4	35,000

Dividends History:

In Year 4, dividends of $10,000 were declared.
These dividends were paid in Year 5.

Problem 9

Specify whether each of the following statements is true or false.

1. Balance sheet accounts are the revenue and expense accounts.
2. A 20-year mortgage with monthly payment terms is shown on the balance sheet only under long-term debt.
3. Land held for future expansion is shown under Property and Equipment on the balance sheet.
4. MasterCard and Visa card drafts are treated as cash received.
5. An asset can be a future expense.
6. Assets – Liabilities = Equity.
7. China and glassware are long-lived assets appearing in the Property and Equipment section.
8. Treasury stock represents bonds of the United States government.
9. Assets – Equity = Liabilities.
10. Capital stock can consist of common and preferred stock.

Problem 10

A business is recording its sales activity for the day and has the following in its cash register: cash at $3,000; in-house credit card drafts at $1,500; Visa credit card drafts at $4,500; and personal checks from customers at $500. What amount will be recorded as cash in the accounting records?

Problem 11

William Garnett is purchasing the assets of the Delta Company for $310,000. The appraised value of the assets is land at $60,000, building at $200,000, and equipment at $40,000. Show how this transaction would appear in the Assets section of a classified balance sheet.

Problem 12

On March 2, rent of $5,000 is paid, which covers the period of March 1 to March 31. How much of this amount will be recorded as prepaid rent?

Problem 13

Joseph Roland is starting a new business. He has incurred the following expenditures: $1,000 for legal fees for incorporation, $300 for state incorporation fees, $500 to the electric company as security for utility services, and $75,000 to a franchisor for the right to use its name and other support services. Show how this transaction would appear in the Assets section of a balance sheet.

Problem 14

On June 30, 20X7, real estate was purchased with a 15-year mortgage of $270,000. The terms of the mortgage were monthly payments of $1,500 on the principal and 12 percent interest on the unpaid balance, with payments beginning July 30 and due on the 30th of the month thereafter.

   a. Show how the mortgage would be presented on the balance sheet for June 30, 20X7.

   b. Show how the mortgage would be presented on the balance sheet for July 31, 20X7.

   c. Show how the mortgage would be presented on the balance sheet for June 30, 20X8.

Problem 15

A corporation has 750,000 shares of authorized common stock at 10¢ par value. On three separate occasions, it has issued the following shares of common stock:

> 100,000 shares for $700,000
> 200,000 shares for $1,300,000
> 150,000 shares for $900,000

The corporation has since repurchased 50,000 shares for a total of $400,000. It had originally issued this stock for $7 per share.

     The retained earnings for the year ended June 30, 20X8, were $425,000. The corporation's net income for the year ended June 30, 20X9, was $250,000. Dividends declared during the year 20X9 were $75,000. As of June 30, 20X9, $25,000 of the dividends have not been paid. Prepare the Stockholders' Equity section for the balance sheet as of June 30, 20X9.

Problem 16

1. The _____explains the rights and privileges of the bond holder.

2. An unsecured bond is also called a _____.

3. A bond maturing at a specified date is a _____.

4. A bond originally issued at less than face value is a bond issued at a _____.

5. Bonds not registered in any name are _____.

Ethics Case

The class has just been seated for the final exam in Hospitality Accounting I. Marty, one of the students, notices that certain formulas and procedures have been written on the wall next to his desk. They obviously were placed there by a student from the previous class.

     Marty's grades are marginal. He needs to pass the final exam today in order to pass this course. Marty's father has told him that unless Marty passes all his courses, his parents will no longer pay for his education. Also, the college has notified Marty that he is on academic probation and his continued enrollment depends on his overall grade average.

1. Since Marty did not write the material on the wall, why shouldn't he take advantage of the situation? Support your conclusion and comment on any consequences.

2. What should Marty do? Support your decision.

Chapter 5 Outline

Preparation of the Income Statement
Revenue Classification
Sales Accounting
    Sales Taxes
    Servers' Tips
Expense Classification
Cost of Sales Expense
    Food Cost
    Gross Profit
Inventory Systems
    Perpetual Inventory System
    Periodic Inventory System
    Inventories in Service Areas
Other Business Expenses
    Operating Expenses
    Fixed Expenses
    Income Taxes Expense
Depreciation

Competencies

1. Describe the income statement and the accounts used to prepare one, and define the revenue classification. (pp. 109–111)

2. Explain when a sale is recognized, and describe the accounting treatment for sales taxes and servers' tips, employee meals, cost of sales, food used, and gross profit. (pp. 111–114)

3. Explain the accounting procedures for the perpetual inventory system and the periodic inventory system, and describe the differences in accounting for purchases and cost of sales. (pp. 115–123)

4. Describe typical day-to-day operating expenses, fixed expenses, and income taxes expense. (pp. 123–124)

5. Describe depreciation and explain the difference between Depreciation expense and Accumulated Depreciation. (pp. 124–125)

5

Exploring the Income Statement

THE INCOME STATEMENT is the most popular and most analyzed statement of the three major financial statements, mainly because it is a profit-oriented statement and easy to read. The income statement reports on the operating results of a company; that is, the income statement shows whether the company had a profit or loss from its operations. The income statement is historical; it shows what has happened, not what will happen. However, ratio and performance analyses can be used to determine operating weaknesses or inefficiencies, from which corrective action can be planned.

The income statement provides critical information for the company's investors and creditors because its emphasis is on sales and expenses with a conclusion of profitability (or loss). An income statement that shows a loss is usually of concern to investors, because a struggling company cannot grow and increase its stock value. Without recurring profits, it is unlikely that dividends will be paid to investors. A period of sustained losses could lead to bankruptcy; both bond and stock investors would lose some or all of their investment, and creditors would be unpaid.

The income statement affects the company's balance sheet. The profit (or loss) shown on the income statement is recorded to an equity account appearing on the balance sheet. In the case of a corporation, this equity account is called *Retained Earnings*; for proprietorships and partnerships, it is called *Capital*.

The balance sheet presents the financial health or condition of a company; the income statement shows the company's operating results (profit or loss). Without proper financial health, a company cannot operate; without profitable operations, a company cannot sustain its financial health. These facts clearly indicate the relationship of these two financial statements.

This chapter examines the income statement accounts and answers such questions as the following:

1. What accounts are in the revenue classification?

2. When is a sale recognized and recorded in the accounting records?

3. How are sales taxes, credit card transactions, and employee tips treated under sales accounting procedures?

4. What accounts are in the expense classification?

5. What are the perpetual and periodic inventory systems and their effect on cost of sales expense?

6. How are employee meals, direct purchases, and storeroom purchases treated under accounting procedures?

7. What is the relationship between depreciation expense and accumulated depreciation?

Preparation of the Income Statement

Only certain accounts are used to prepare the income statement. The asset, liability, and equity classifications of accounts are used to prepare the balance sheet. The selected bookkeeping accounts to prepare the income statement are classified as:

- Revenue
- Expenses

These two classifications are collectively referred to as **income statement accounts.**

Exhibit 1 shows a representative listing of income statement accounts for a hospitality company. The exact quantity or variety of income statement accounts will vary depending on the type of company, its size, and the industry that it's in. For example, a restaurant will not have a Rooms sales account; a hotel rooms department will not have a Kitchen Fuel expense account.

The income statement can have many names. The old term *Profit and Loss Statement* is still used informally in conversation; however, the term is not used to label the statement itself. The accounting profession now uses various headings on the statement, such as the following:

- Income Statement
- Statement of Income
- Statements of Operations
- Operating Statement

These are just a few examples. The statement's name is not as important as knowing what is on the statement and what its purpose is. The income statement (as this chapter refers to it) starts with sales (revenue accounts), continues with expenses, and arrives at the net income (or net loss) for a period of time (typically a month, quarter, or year).

The relationship of the balance sheet and income statement also extends into the accounting equations. Since the net income (or net loss) is recorded to an equity account on the balance sheet, the short form of the equation does in fact equate to both statements:

$$\text{Assets} = \text{Liabilities} + \text{Equity}$$

Revenue Classification

The largest account in the **revenue** classification is Sales, which represents the amounts billed to guests for the sales of goods and services. A sale is recognized

Exhibit 1   Listing of Income Statement Accounts

Revenue Classification
  Sales Accounts:
    Rooms
    Food
    Beverage
Expense Classification
  Cost of Sales Accounts *(If perpetual inventory system is used):*
    Cost of Food Sales
    Cost of Beverage Sales
  Purchases Accounts *(If periodic inventory system is used):*
    Food Purchases
    Beverage Purchases
  Operating Expenses
    Payroll
    Payroll Taxes
    Employee Benefits
    Employee Meals
    China, Glassware, Silver, Linens, Uniforms
    Supplies
    Advertising
    Telephone
    Kitchen Fuel
    Utilities
    Repairs and Maintenance
  Fixed Expenses
    Rent
    Property Taxes
    Insurance
    Interest
    Depreciation
    Amortization
  Income Taxes Expense

and recorded in the accounting records at the time services are rendered or when the goods are delivered, regardless of whether the guest or customer pays in full or uses an open account privilege. This treatment is in accordance with the *realization principle,* a generally accepted accounting principle.

Some companies may include non-sale items such as interest income and dividends income in the revenue category. Other companies may treat these incidental items in a separate category called *other income.*

Sales Accounting

The recording of a sale is not dependent upon the receipt of cash or the kind of credit card a customer uses; a sale generates a corresponding increase in cash or accounts receivable. When a sale is made, other elements that arise are sales taxes and servers' tips.

Most states apply a sales tax to the retail price of meals and other products or hotel services. Tips are typical in most restaurant establishments, with the exception of quick-service (fast-food) operations. Sales accounting requires special treatment of these items because they are not considered part of the revenue classification.

Sales Taxes

The Sales account does not include amounts charged for sales taxes, since these amounts actually represent a liability rather than revenue. A hospitality business must account for taxes collected from guests and remit these collections to the taxing authority.

For example, assume a guest enjoys dinner at a fine dining establishment and pays $25 for the dinner plus a six percent sales tax (imposed by the state). Suppose the guest pays the tab with cash. This business transaction creates the following events:

1. The Food Sales account (a revenue account) is increased by $25.00.

2. The Sales Tax Payable account (a liability account) is increased by $1.50 ($25.00 × 6%).

3. The Cash account (an asset account) is increased by $26.50.

Servers' Tips

Guests may include service gratuities (tips for servers) on the credit card drafts. However, any tips entered on credit card drafts are excluded from revenue, since these amounts belong to employees, not the hospitality company. To facilitate accounting for these tips, hospitality firms often pay the tips to employees at the end of each shift, and then wait for collection from the credit card company.

Expense Classification

The **expense** classification includes those accounts that represent day-to-day expenses incurred in operating the business, expired costs of assets charged to expense by depreciation, and costs of assets (such as inventory) that are consumed in operating the business.

For purposes of discussion, expenses have been grouped into the following topical categories:

- Cost of sales expense

- Operating expenses

- Income taxes expense

- Depreciation

Cost of Sales Expense

Cost of sales expense represents the cost of inventory products used in the selling process, and, therefore, applies only to revenue-producing centers.

Separate accounting is performed for cost of beverage sales and cost of food sales. Cost of beverage sales is the cost of liquor and mixes used to generate sales. Cost of food sales is the cost of food used in the preparation process for resale to guests. The *net food cost* (that is, cost of food sales) does not include meals provided to employees.

Unlike the food and beverage department, the rooms department does not have a cost of room sales account. Rooms are not consumed, nor do they involve a sale of inventory; it is room occupancy that is sold. Expenses associated with the upkeep of rooms (for instance, guest supplies, cleaning supplies, and housekeeping labor) are recorded in various operating expense accounts, rather than a cost of sales account.

Food Cost

Cost of sales is a truly representative accounting term: it is the cost of the raw materials used to make a sale to guests. In a restaurant, this raw material is food; therefore, *food cost* means the same as *cost of sales*. Another accounting term used as a substitute for cost of sales is *cost of goods sold*.

What is food cost? If a restaurant has $1,000 of food used, is the cost of sales (food cost) $1,000? Probably not! Remember that cost of sales represents the cost of food *served to guests*. Many restaurants also provide meals to their employees at no charge or at a nominal charge. The food cost (cost of sales) appearing on the financial statements must not include the cost of employee meals.

Continuing with our example of $1,000 of food used, assume that the cost of employee meals is $50 (before employee payments, if any). The cost of food sold is computed as follows:

Food used	$1,000
Less cost of employee meals	50
Cost of sales	$ 950

Where does this food come from? Food comes from the storeroom; all food in the storeroom is called *inventory*. When the inventory is pulled out and used, it then becomes *cost of sales* and *employee meals expense*.

Exhibit 2 shows that there is food worth a total of $5,000 in the storeroom, which is called *Food Inventory*. The kitchen then requisitions food worth $1,000 and processes it, which is called *Food Used*. The employees ate food costing $50, which is called *Employee Meals Expense*; this is an operating expense and not a cost of sales expense. The balance of $950 was used to prepare food for guests and is called *Cost of Sales*.

Gross Profit

The amount of $950 used to serve guests resulted in billings of $2,800; this would be recorded to a *revenue* account called Sales. The profit on the raw materials is called *gross profit* and is calculated as follows:

Exhibit 2   Food Cycle: From Inventory, to Expense, to Sales

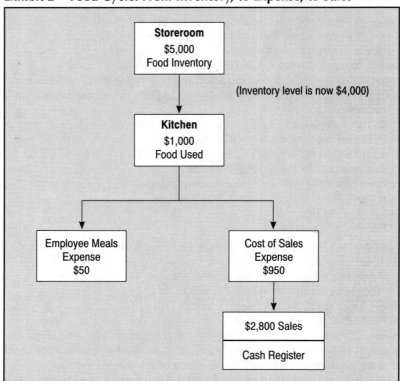

Sales	$2,800
Cost of sales	$ 950
Gross profit	$1,850

After the gross profit would appear the deductions for *employee meals, payroll,* and *other operating expenses.* In our example, the employee meals would be a $50 operating expense.

What if the employees were charged for their meals? Continuing with our example, assume employees were charged $30 for their meals. In this case, the operating expense called Employee Meals Expense would appear on the financial statements as $20, which is the result of the employee meals of $50 reduced by the employee collections of $30.

The preceding material shows that there is an interrelationship among inventory, cost of sales, and sales. It is important to understand this relationship because both the balance sheet and income statement are affected, as shown in Exhibit 3. This exhibit shows the flow of financial transactions for these items. Food not used is an asset on the balance sheet called Food Inventory. As it is used for guest purposes, it is converted to an expense called Cost of Sales.

Exhibit 3   Relationship of Inventory, Cost of Sales, and Sales

Inventory Systems

In addition to providing internal control, inventory systems are designed to supply information about inventory and cost of sales. Inventory represents the *products not used*, and cost of sales represents the *products used* to produce guest sales.

The specific procedures for recording inventories or cost of sales depend on the type of inventory accounting system a hospitality business uses. Any business that sells inventory may use either the *perpetual inventory system* or the *periodic inventory system*, or a combination of both.

Perpetual Inventory System

Under a **perpetual inventory system,** the operations area of a hospitality business constantly updates its records on its inventory of food, beverage items, or other inventory products on hand. This means that every time inventory is acquired for the storeroom, the merchandise inventory record is increased; whenever issues are made to the kitchen from the storeroom, inventory is decreased.

Exhibit 4 shows how this flow of purchases and issues is processed in the storeroom and shows the subsequent flow of documents to the accounting department. To accomplish the constant updating of information about inventory on hand, the storeroom clerk or other responsible individual must record the receipts and issues on a special document. Exhibit 5 features a perpetual inventory form commonly used for this purpose.

One advantage of the perpetual inventory system is that it provides instant inventory status information from the inventory cards. There is no urgent need to count the inventory in the stockroom to determine if a reorder is necessary. In addition, inventory management may be improved if reorder points and reorder quantities are printed on the inventory card.

Another advantage of the perpetual inventory system is internal control. The inventory records specify the quantities of each item that *should* be available in the storeroom. During the month, management can conduct quick spot-checks by physically counting selected items and comparing the quantity counted against the amount shown on the inventory cards. Any overages or shortages can then be analyzed to determine if discrepancies are due to paperwork errors or if losses are due to theft.

Exhibit 4   Operations Flowchart for a Perpetual Inventory System

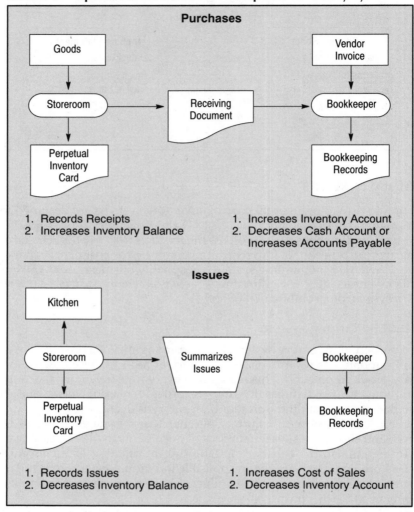

Another benefit of this system is that it allows a hospitality business to completely count its inventory any time during the month instead of only at the end of the month.

Perpetual Bookkeeping Accounts. The storeroom sends the receiving documents and requisitions (issues) to the accounting department, which matches the receiving reports with vendor invoices and processes the invoices for journalizing and subsequent payment.

If the storeroom clerk has not costed and summarized the issues, accounting now performs this procedure. The bookkeeping entry for issues is usually made at the end of the month.

Exhibit 5   Sample Perpetual Inventory Form

| | | | Inventory Ledger Card | | | | | | | | |

		Purchases			Issues			Balance on Hand			
Date	Ref.	Units	Unit Cost	Total	Units	Unit Cost	Total	Units	Unit Cost	Total	

No. _____   Description _____

The general ledger contains the following accounts that will be used to record the activities of the food storeroom and kitchen:

- Inventory
- Cost of Sales
- Employee Meals Expense

Inventory account. Separate Inventory accounts are maintained for food, beverage items, and merchandise in the gift shop. The Inventory account is a current asset account. Its balance at the end of the month should agree with the total of all of the perpetual inventory records in the storeroom. This result provides internal control benefits.

In a perpetual system, the Inventory account is constantly updated for purchases and issues that affect inventory. Exhibit 6 shows which accounts are affected when purchases are recorded. The bookkeeping accounts used to record purchases depend on whether the purchase is a *storeroom purchase* or a *direct purchase.*

A **storeroom purchase** is for goods that will be delivered to the storeroom for later use. Storeroom purchases are recorded as an increase to the Inventory account.

A **direct purchase** is for goods that the supplier will deliver directly to the kitchen for immediate consumption. Direct purchases are recorded to the Cost of Sales bookkeeping account.

Cost of Sales account. Separate Cost of Sales accounts are maintained to identify the cost of goods sold (food, beverage items, and gift shop merchandise). The total issues (at cost) decrease the Inventory account and increase the Cost of Sales account.

Employee Meals Expense account. This account is used to record the cost of employee meals. Each department would have an Employee Meals Expense

Exhibit 6   Recording of Purchases

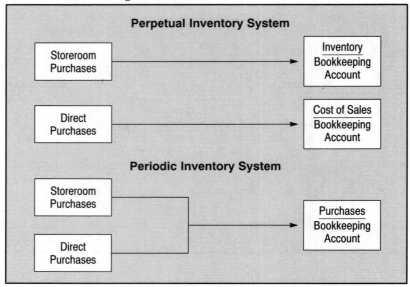

account, such as Rooms Department—Employee Meals, Food and Beverage Department—Employee Meals, and Administrative and General Department—Employee Meals.

Perpetual Inventory Accounting. The accounting department processes various documents that are recorded to the bookkeeping accounts in the general ledger. The storeroom requisitions represent issues from the storeroom and usage for sales. Invoices for storeroom purchases are recorded to an Inventory account, while invoices for direct purchases are recorded to a Cost of Sales account. The Employee Meals Report is used to correct the amount previously recorded to Cost of Sales and to charge each department for its share of the expense for meals provided to employees. These documents affect the bookkeeping accounts as follows:

Transaction	Bookkeeping Account	Effect on Account
Storeroom purchase	Inventory	Increase
Direct purchase	Cost of Sales	Increase
Issues	Inventory	Decrease
	Cost of Sales	Increase
Employee meals	Cost of Sales	Decrease
	Employee Meals Expense	Increase

Exhibit 7 diagrams the perpetual inventory accounting method. The ending inventory on May 31 was $3,800, which becomes the beginning inventory for June. In June, purchases of $12,200 were made. Therefore, the total goods available for June were $16,000 *at cost*. Since the issues were $12,000 *at cost* for June, this means that the storeroom should have $4,000 of inventory *at cost*. This important inventory management data can be computed as follows:

Exhibit 7   Perpetual Inventory Accounting Method

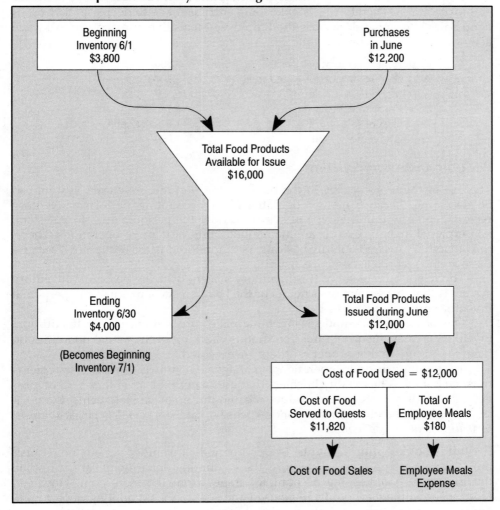

Beginning inventory, 6/1	$ 3,800	
Add: Storeroom purchases in June	12,200	
Cost of goods available	16,000	*(food for use)*
Less: Issues for June	12,000	*(food used)*
Ending inventory, 6/30	$ 4,000	*(food not used)*

The purchases would have been recorded as an increase to the Food Inventory account. The issues would have been recorded as an increase to the Cost of Food Sales account, also referred to as Cost of Food Sold.

However, the $12,000 recorded to the Cost of Food Sales account needs refinement. Remember that *food used* might represent not only food prepared for guest consumption, but also food provided to employees. In this case, $180 went for employee meals. Therefore, a bookkeeping entry is made to decrease the Cost of Food Sales account and increase the Employee Meals Expense account. All these activities can be presented as follows:

Beginning inventory, 6/1	$ 3,800
Add: Storeroom purchases in June	12,200
Cost of goods available	16,000
Less: Employee meals	180
Less: Cost of sales	11,820 (12,000 − 180)
Ending inventory, 6/30	$ 4,000

Periodic Inventory System

The use of the word *system* in the name of the **periodic inventory system** can be deceiving, because neither operations nor accounting performs inventory recordkeeping within this type of system. Under the periodic inventory system, no perpetual inventory cards are maintained in the storeroom operations. Therefore, inventory ins and outs are basically not monitored with checkpoints, because there are no records to compare against.

The major advantage of this inventory system over the perpetual inventory system is that this system does not incur the heavy costs of maintaining perpetual inventory cards.

One obvious disadvantage is that internal control suffers greatly. In addition, inventory management requires continuous checking of the actual quantities on hand and usage so that proper reorders are executed.

To accomplish good operational management, timely financial statements must be issued. A hospitality business that uses a periodic inventory system faces yet another disadvantage: to produce meaningful financial statements, the business must face the inconvenience and expense of taking *a complete physical inventory at the end of each month.*

Periodic Bookkeeping Accounts. Under a periodic inventory system, no requisitions (issues) are prepared. Therefore, the accounting department cannot update the Inventory bookkeeping account for issues from the storeroom. However, receiving documents should still be used and sent to the accounting department, which will match them with the invoices so that proper payment can be made.

Under a periodic inventory system, the general ledger contains the following bookkeeping accounts:

- Inventory
- Purchases
- Employee Meals Expense
- Employee Meals Credit

Notice that the bookkeeping accounts used in this inventory system *do not include a Cost of Sales account.* This is because the issues are not documented by operations and thus cannot be recorded by the accounting department.

Inventory account. As in the perpetual inventory system, the periodic system uses separate Inventory accounts for food, beverage items, and merchandise from the gift shop. Unlike the procedure followed under the perpetual system, no recording of inventory activity is made to Inventory account.

Because no activity is recorded to the Inventory account, the account's balance will always reflect the inventory balance at the beginning of the accounting period.

Purchases. Recall that, in the perpetual inventory system, storeroom purchases increase an Inventory account, while direct purchases are recorded to Cost of Sales. Storeroom and direct purchases are handled very differently in a periodic inventory system. Both storeroom and direct purchases are recorded to a book-keeping account called *Purchases*. Exhibit 6 shows where purchases are recorded under a periodic system.

Employee Meals Expense account. As in the perpetual inventory system, this account is used in the periodic inventory system to record the cost of employee meals. Each department would have an Employee Meals Expense account.

If an employee pays part or all of his or her meal cost, this account is shown at net of the payment. For example, if the cost of employee meals for the rooms department is $100 and the employees have contributed $40, Rooms Department—Employee Meals is shown at a net cost of $60.

Employee Meals Credit. This account represents employee meals for all departments of the hospitality business. It is used to eliminate the cost of employee meals from food used to arrive at food prepared for guests, which is called Cost of Sales.

It is important to fully understand the difference between the Employee Meals Expense account and the Employee Meals Credit account. The expense account is a departmental account that appears on each department's financial statement, charging the department for the cost of meals consumed by its staff. The effect of the Employee Meals Credit account is to remove the cost of food consumed by all employees from the Food Department.

Periodic Inventory Accounting. Under a periodic inventory accounting method, the general ledger accounts provide very little information that readily shows the inventory balance or cost of sales for the period. To understand how to arrive at these figures, recall the month-end status of the bookkeeping accounts:

1. The Inventory account contains only the balance as of the beginning of the period. No purchases or issues are recorded to this account. Therefore, to determine the ending inventory, a physical count and costing of the inventory must be performed.

2. A Cost of Sales account does not exist under a periodic inventory system because issues are not recorded.

3. A Purchases account contains the total purchases for the period.

Exhibit 8 reveals the limited accounting information provided by a periodic inventory accounting method. However, after the physical inventory has been completed, calculating the cost of sales is simple, using the following logic:

• Inventory represents product not used.

• Cost of Sales represents product used for guests.

Exhibit 8   Periodic Inventory Accounting Method

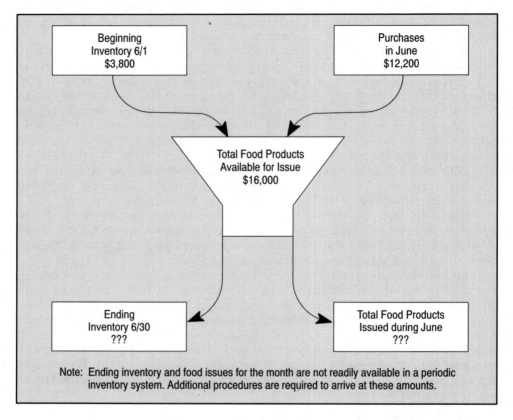

Note: Ending inventory and food issues for the month are not readily available in a periodic inventory system. Additional procedures are required to arrive at these amounts.

The accounting records reveal that:

- Beginning inventory is $3,800.
- Purchases for June were $12,200.

The physical inventory shows the following:

- Ending inventory as of June 30 is $4,000 at cost.

The food and beverage manager turns in a monthly report showing the following information:

- Employee meals are $180 at cost.

Accountants have devised a procedure to compute cost of sales from this limited information. The calculations in this procedure are performed as follows:

Beginning inventory, 6/1	$ 3,800
Add: Purchases for June	12,200
Cost of goods available	16,000 *(food for use)*

Less: Ending inventory, 6/30	4,000	*(food not used)*
Cost of food used	12,000	*(food used — total)*
Less: Employee meals	180	*(food used — employees)*
Cost of sales	$11,820	*(food used — guests)*

Inventories in Service Areas

The net income shown on the financial statements depends on the accuracy of the ending inventory dollar amount. In the hospitality industry, many items are requisitioned from the storeroom and stored temporarily in the bar or the kitchen so that employees can provide quality and prompt guest service.

Measuring inventory of bar stock is required so that records reflect accurate amounts of items not consumed and sold. Full and open bottles of liquor, wine and beer in kegs, and other beverage inventories on hand must be physically counted, since these items are usually of material value.

Larger hotels measure inventory of food items in the kitchen area at the end of each month, a required procedure due to the inventory's materiality to the financial statements. Small restaurant operations may not perform such procedures for various reasons, such as when the effort expended is likely to exceed the intended benefits (cost-benefit rule), or when the results are not expected to have any material effect on the net income.

Other Business Expenses

Cost of sales is only one type of expense incurred in a hospitality business. The other business expenses can be separated into groups such as operating expenses, fixed expenses, and income taxes. This grouping allows the preparation of a classified income statement that will be more meaningful and easier to read.

Operating Expenses

The day-to-day expenses incurred by a business during its operational activities are referred to as *operating expenses*. The following are typical examples:

Payroll	Supplies
Payroll Taxes	Kitchen Fuel
Employee Meals	Utilities
Advertising	Telephone

Fixed Expenses

Certain kinds of expenses are not an active part of operations, but are incurred regardless of the level of business, even when the business is closed for any reason. These expenses are referred to as *fixed expenses*. The following are examples of fixed expenses:

Rent	Interest
Property Taxes	Depreciation
Property Insurance	Amortization

Income Taxes Expense

These taxes are levied by the federal and state governments on the income of a corporation. Some municipalities may also tax business income. It is possible for a corporation to pay income taxes even if it had a loss for the year, because some states require the "income tax" payment to be the largest amount resulting from the following three computations:

- A specified minimum payment
- A tax computed on corporate equity
- A tax computed on taxable income

Depreciation

Depreciation allocates the purchase cost of a tangible long-lived asset such as a building or piece of equipment over its estimated useful life. Accountants also refer to tangible long-lived assets as *fixed assets*. Not all fixed assets are depreciated. For instance, land is not a depreciable fixed asset because its life is infinite in the hospitality industry environment.

When an asset is purchased, its cost is recorded to a balance sheet account. Time and usage will decrease the utility of this asset. Remember that anything *used up* is an expense. However, the use of a long-lived asset is fragmented: some is used this year, some next year, and so on.

How is this fragmented usage measured so that a portion of the cost can be transferred to expense? No scientific methods are available. However, one common method of computing the portion of the cost of a fixed asset that has expired is to allocate the cost over a period of time.

For example, assume that a company purchases a vehicle for $12,000. Based on published industry guidelines or the company's planned usage of the vehicle, the accountant determines that the vehicle's useful life is expected to be three years. This means that the asset should be decreased by $4,000 and an expense be increased by $4,000 each year over a three-year period.

The income statement will show the allocation of the asset's cost for this period in an account called Depreciation. As with all income statement accounts, Depreciation expense is set to zero at the end of the year to start counting the expense for the next year.

The asset cost on the balance sheet never changes. In this example, it will always be $12,000. An account called Accumulated Depreciation is used to record the reduction of the asset's cost basis. This account will contain the sum of all depreciation charges over the life of the asset. Unlike the Depreciation expense account, the Accumulated Depreciation account maintains a cumulative balance; it is not set to zero. Accumulated Depreciation is referred to as a *contra-asset account* because it reduces the basis of another asset.

The **book value** of an asset is not an indication of its market value. Book value is an accounting term that represents the undepreciated cost of an asset. Accountants determine an asset's book value by subtracting the amount of accumulated depreciation from the asset's cost.

The relationship of asset cost, depreciation, and accumulated depreciation is best shown through analysis of the balance sheets and income statements over the three-year period of ownership of the vehicle just described:

	Balance Sheets		
	End of 1st year	End of 2nd year	End of 3rd year
Property and Equipment Section:			
Vehicle, at cost	$12,000	$12,000	$12,000
Less Accumulated Depreciation	4,000	8,000	12,000
Undepreciated Cost	8,000	4,000	0

	Income Statements		
	End of 1st year	End of 2nd year	End of 3rd year
Depreciation	4,000	4,000	4,000

Key Terms

book value—Asset cost minus accumulated depreciation.

direct purchase—Food purchased for immediate use and delivered by the purveyor to the kitchen.

expense—Cost of items used to produce revenue, cost of items consumed, or the expired cost of assets.

income statement accounts—Revenue and expense accounts.

periodic inventory system—A system of inventory accounting in which no perpetual inventory records are maintained and cost of sales must be manually computed.

perpetual inventory system—A system of inventory accounting in which inventory records are continuously maintained, supplying instant inventory information.

revenue—A classification that includes sales and might also include interest income and dividends income.

storeroom purchase—Goods purchased that are delivered to the storeroom for later use.

Review Questions

1. How is the Revenue classification defined?
2. How is the Expense classification defined?
3. At what point is a sale recorded?
4. How does the Sales account differ from the Cost of Sales account?
5. What are the major differences between the perpetual and periodic inventory systems?

6. What are advantages and disadvantages of the two inventory systems discussed in this chapter?

7. How do accounting treatments of storeroom purchases and direct purchases differ under the two types of inventory systems?

8. What is the difference between the expense account Depreciation and the contra-asset account Accumulated Depreciation?

Internet Sites

For more information, visit the following Internet sites. Remember that Internet addresses can change without notice. If the site is no longer there, you can use a search engine to look for additional sites.

Cost of Goods Sold for a Restaurant Operation
www.foodservicewarehouse.com/
education/restaurant-operations/
managing-cogs.aspx
www.restaurantreport.com/features/
ft_inventory.html

Depreciation
http://en.wikipedia.org/wiki/
Depreciation
www.irs.gov/businesses/small/
article/0,,id=137026,00.html

Income Statement
http://en.wikipedia.org/wiki/
Income_statement

Inventory Barcode Technology
www.barcodesinc.com/articles/
inventory-control-system.htm

Perpetual vs. Periodic Inventory Systems
www.ehow.com/about_5527717_
perpetual-vs-periodic-inventory-
system.html
http://blog.accountingcoach.com/
purchases-inventory/

Prime Cost
www.whitehutchinson.com/leisure/
articles/primetime.shtml

Problems

Problem 1

A restaurant started the month with a food inventory of $3,000 in the storeroom. During the month, food purchases totaling $9,000 were delivered to the storeroom and food totaling $8,000 was issued from the storeroom. What was the cost of food available for the month?

Problem 2

The accounting records for a restaurant indicate that food sales were $18,000, food used was $5,800, and employee meals at cost were $50. What is the cost of sales?

Problem 3

The accounting records for a restaurant indicate that food sales were $25,000, food used was $8,100, and employee meals at cost were $75. What is the gross profit?

Problem 4

A restaurant started the month with a food inventory of $2,000. Its purchases for the month were $10,000 and its cost of food used was $9,000. What is its ending inventory?

Problem 5

A restaurant ended the month with a food inventory of $4,000. Its purchases for the month were $12,000 and its cost of food used was $11,000. What was its beginning inventory?

Problem 6

An asset was purchased at a cost of $20,000. It is being depreciated at the rate of $4,000 per year. What is its useful life expressed in years?

Problem 7

Decide whether each of the following statements is true or false.

1. Balance sheet accounts are the revenue and expense accounts.
2. Land is a depreciable fixed asset in the hospitality industry.
3. If a guest tab shows food at $40 and sales tax of $2.40, the amount recorded as a sale will be $42.40.
4. If a guest orders a $2,000 banquet and pays $2,000 on the banquet to be scheduled next month, a sale of $2,000 is recorded.
5. Storeroom purchases under a periodic inventory system are recorded to an Inventory account.
6. Direct purchases under a periodic inventory system are recorded to a Cost of Sales account.
7. Accumulated Depreciation is an expense account.
8. A guest tab shows food at $80 and sales tax of $4.80; the guest pays with an in-house credit card. The $80 amount cannot be treated as a sale.
9. *Food used* is the same as *cost of food sold.*
10. The income statement accounts do not affect the accounting equation: Assets = Liabilities + Equity.

Problem 8

Calculate the cost of food sales under a periodic inventory system for the period ended October 31 given the following information:

Inventory on October 31 is $7,000
Sales for the period were $200,000
Purchases for the period were $69,000
Inventory on September 30 was $8,000

Free employee meals for the period were as follows:

Rooms Department	$500
Food Department	900
Administrative and General Department	375

Problem 9

Calculate the cost of food sales under a perpetual inventory system for the month ended March 31 given the following information:

> Inventory on March 31 was $2,900
> Storeroom purchases for the month were $36,000
> Storeroom issues for the month were $36,500
> Direct purchases for the month were $626
> Free employee meals for the month were $225

Problem 10

A building is purchased on January 1 for $240,000. The cost of this asset is to be allocated on the basis of $8,000 per year. What is its book value at the end of the first year?

Problem 11

Equipment is purchased on June 1 for $7,500 and its cost is to be allocated at $625 per month.

a.   What would be its book value on June 30?

b.   What would be its book value on July 31?

Problem 12

A vehicle is purchased for $10,200 and is estimated to have a useful life of three years. At the end of three years, its estimated book value is zero. What should be the annual charge to depreciation expense?

Problem 13

A hospitality company uses the perpetual inventory system. Its food inventory was $2,700 on August 1 and $3,000 on August 31. Total deliveries to the storeroom in August were $15,000. What were the food issues from the storeroom in August?

Problem 14

A hospitality business uses the perpetual inventory system. For October, storeroom issues (food used) totaled $25,875 and the cost of sales equaled $25,615. What was the amount for free employee meals for October?

Problem 15

A hospitality business uses the periodic inventory system. On November 1, the food inventory was $2,000. During November, food purchases totaled $9,000 and free employee meals were $200. The cost of food sales for the month equaled $4,000. What is the ending inventory on November 30?

Problem 16

Specify whether each of the following is an operating expense, a fixed expense, or a cost of sales item.

	Operating Expense	Fixed Expense	Cost of Sales
Payroll			
Utilities			
Advertising			
Rent			
Insurance			
Property Taxes			
Kitchen Fuel			
Employee Benefits			
China, Glassware			
Repairs			
Cost of Food Sold			
Food Purchases			
Depreciation			
Interest			
Amortization			

Ethics Case

Brady Dumais owns a small proprietorship that operates on a cash-only basis; no credit cards are accepted. Brady has taken a bookkeeping course and a tax preparation course. With the help of his spouse, he is able to perform all the bookkeeping duties and prepare his tax returns.

Brady discovers that federal and state income taxes take away 35 percent of his profits. Because his is a cash business, Brady has started the practice of "skimming" sales. Because these sales will not appear in the business records, they will escape taxation, and Brady will be able to retain 100 percent of these revenue dollars.

1. Identify the stakeholders in this case.

2. Comment on the legal and ethical issues involved in skimming.

Chapter 6 Outline

Origins of Bookkeeping
21ˢᵗ Century Bookkeeping
    Double-Entry Accounting
Bookkeeping Accounts
    Account Balance
    Computer Processing of Accounts
    General Ledger
Learning Debits and Credits
    Methods of Learning Debits and
        Credits
Analyzing Business Transactions
Analyzing 21 Universal Transactions
The Nature of Debits and Credits
    Equality of Debits and Credits
    Computer Audit Trail
    Debit and Credit Rules
Recording 21 Universal Transactions
Contra Accounts
Normal Account Balance

Competencies

1. Define and describe bookkeeping and double-entry accounting, and identify common bookkeeping accounts and tools. (pp. 131–135)

2. Describe learning debits and credits, and use three basic questions to analyze business transactions. (pp. 136–143)

3. Define debits and credits and use them to record business transactions. (pp. 143–152)

4. Define contra accounts, identify common contra accounts, and explain how these accounts are used. (pp. 152–154)

5. Identify the normal account balances for each account classification. (pp. 154–155)

6

The Bookkeeping Process

COMPUTERS HAVE SIMPLIFIED AND EXPEDITED the bookkeeping process. However, a computer cannot analyze a business transaction and determine the proper accounts that are involved. The proper application of debits and credits to the correct accounts is vital to the accuracy of any management information system. To successfully process a business transaction, one must be absolutely familiar with the accounts in the five classifications (assets, liabilities, equity, revenue, and expenses). It is impossible to clearly analyze a business transaction and easily understand the debit and credit rules if one does not first fully learn the accounts in these five classifications.

Properly designed input forms and accounting procedures simplify the determination of debits and credits critical to a reliable financial system. Despite the use of computer and other modern systems, it is imperative that a hospitality businessperson possess a strong understanding of debits and credits.

This chapter presents the essential information every well-grounded businessperson should know. First, the chapter analyzes 21 business transactions representing a majority of day-to-day operations for the transactions' effects on the bookkeeping accounts. Next, the chapter shows how these 21 transactions are recorded, using debits and credits.

This chapter provides answers to such questions as:

1. What is double-entry accounting?
2. What is a bookkeeping account?
3. What is the general ledger?
4. How are business transactions analyzed?
5. What are the debit and credit rules?
6. What are contra accounts?
7. What is a normal balance in a general ledger account?

Origins of Bookkeeping

While the history of accounting may not be important to the learning of accounting, its history presents some interesting facts relative to its importance in the business world. It is impossible to find the birthplace or birth date of bookkeeping. Instead, historians analyze the development of bookkeeping from simple records to the framework that has evolved into today's bookkeeping principles. From the early days of Roman history, there was always some form of recordkeeping, even though it was in the simple form of a cash book. Then the rapid growth of business and the rise of merchants in the 1400s brought a need for refinement in the process of keeping records. In 1458 Benedetto Cotrugli wrote *Della mercatura et del mercante perfectto*, a textbook that presented a ledger, a journal, and memorandum books for merchants.

Then, in 1494, an Italian monk, Luca Pacioli (pronounced "Pot-CHEE-oh-lee") wrote the first treatise on double-entry accounting.[1] The topic of accounting was one of five sections in Pacioli's mathematics book, entitled *Everything about Arithmetic, Geometry, and Proportions.* Historians claim that his contribution to the accounting field was in writing down what was already known, rather than in inventing the system of double-entry bookkeeping. Nonetheless, his dissertation was so complete and accurate that he is called "the Father of Accounting." Luca Pacioli researched and wrote about a method used by merchants in Venice during the Italian Renaissance period. His publication included the accounting cycle, equality of debits and credits, assets, liabilities, capital, income, expense accounts, closing entries, and trial balances. From his works, further development has produced today's sophisticated method of accounting.

21st Century Bookkeeping

Bookkeeping is the first function in the accounting department. Without bookkeeping, there would be no financial information or statements. Business transactions trigger the bookkeeping process. Evidential matter, such as invoices, checks, cash register tapes, bank deposits, and contracts, supports business transactions.

A *business transaction* is an exchange of property, goods, or services for cash or a promise to pay. Purchases and sales transactions make up the largest volume of business transactions. A business may purchase goods, property, or services by the payment of cash or a promise to pay. A business's promise to pay its purveyors (suppliers) is an *accounts payable* transaction. Customers of a business may purchase its goods, property, or services with the payment of cash or a promise to pay. A promise to pay by a customer of a business is an *accounts receivable* transaction.

Modern bookkeeping now is an *input* function, coding the proper accounts and amounts affected by business transactions. After coding, these transactions are processed by a computerized accounting application called general ledger accounting software.

Double-Entry Accounting

Double-entry accounting is a bookkeeping process in which every business transaction affects two or more bookkeeping accounts. This ancient standard has proven itself through time and experience. It has been in use since the first bookkeeping system and likely will always be the basis of any accounting system. Double-entry accounting provides built-in checks and balances to determine the accuracy of recording amounts. It would be impossible to generate the multitude of financial information and statements without double-entry accounting.

Luca Pacioli: The Father of Accounting

Early in his career, Luca Pacioli joined a Franciscan monastery in Sansepulcro and became an apprentice to a local businessman. He later went to Venice to tutor the three sons of a rich merchant. During this time, in the year 1470, at the age of twenty-five, Pacioli wrote his first manuscript, about algebra. Pacioli then quit his apprenticeship to work as a mathematics scholar.

In 1475, Pacioli became a teacher at the University of Perugia, where he stayed for six years. He was the first lecturer to hold a chair in math at the university. In his lectures, Pacioli stressed the importance of putting theory to practical use. His 1494 book *Everything about Arithmetic, Geometry, and Proportions* made him famous, and he was invited to teach mathematics at the Court of Duke Lodovico Maria Sforzo in Milan. One of his pupils was Leonardo da Vinci; they became good friends. In 1510, Pacioli was appointed director of the Franciscan monastery in Sansepulcro. In 1514, Pope Leo III called Pacioli to the papacy in Rome to become a teacher there. Scholars are unsure about what happened to Pacioli afterward, but they believe that he never made it to Rome; he probably died on June 19, 1517, in the monastery in Sansepulcro.

Bookkeeping Accounts

Financial statements or information reports cannot be produced without an orderly and logical arrangement of headings and account titles. A **bookkeeping account** is an individual record for each account a business uses to record its business transactions. Every hospitality business will use a multitude of accounts from each of the five account classifications. In the initial design phase of a management information system, the accountant, in consultation with executives and managers, determines the bookkeeping accounts necessary to produce the desired financial information and statements. These bookkeeping accounts are listed in an accounting document called the **chart of accounts**. This document is functionally a *table of contents* listing the only authorized bookkeeping accounts in an accounting system. Exhibit 1 shows a typical chart of accounts. We will use this chart to process the 21 universal transactions presented later in the chapter. Review these accounts well before proceeding; a thorough understanding of the accounts will greatly simplify the learning of debits and credits.

Account Balance

Each bookkeeping account is headed by its name, followed by entries consisting of a date, a source reference, and an amount. At this stage, we do not concern ourselves with this level of detail or whether the amount is a debit or credit. A bookkeeping account is much like a bin containing numerical results that increase or decrease its balance. The bin concept of an account is shown in Exhibit 2. The account balance is computed by taking the beginning balance and increasing or decreasing that balance to arrive at an ending balance.

Exhibit 1   Sample Chart of Accounts

Asset Accounts

Cash
Marketable Securities
Accounts Receivable
Food Inventory
Beverage Inventory
Supplies Inventory
Prepaid Insurance
Prepaid Rent
Land
Building
Furniture and Equipment
China, Glassware, Silver, Linen, Uniforms
Organization Costs
Security Deposits

Liability Accounts

Accounts Payable
Sales Tax Payable
Income Taxes Payable
Accrued Payroll
Accrued Payroll Taxes
Advance Deposits
Current Maturities of Long-Term Debt
Notes Payable
Mortgage Payable

Equity Accounts

For Corporations:	*For Proprietorships or Partnerships:*
Common Stock Issued	Capital, (owner's name)
Additional Paid-In Capital	Withdrawals, (owner's name)
Retained Earnings	

Revenue Accounts

Room Sales
Food Sales
Beverage Sales

Expense Accounts

Cost of Food Sold (If perpetual inventory system is used)
Cost of Beverage Sold (If perpetual inventory system is used)
Food Purchases (If periodic inventory system is used)
Beverage Purchases (If periodic inventory system is used)
Salaries and Wages
Payroll Taxes
Employee Benefits
Food Department—Employee Meals

Exhibit 1 *(continued)*

Rooms Department—Employee Meals
China, Glassware, Silver, Linen, Uniforms
Supplies
Advertising
Telephone
Utilities
Repairs and Maintenance
Rent
Property Taxes
Property Insurance
Interest
Depreciation
Amortization
Income Taxes

Exhibit 2   Bin Concept of an Account

Account Title: Cash	
Increase	$1,000
Increase	2,000
Decrease	500
Increase	700
Decrease	1,000
Account Balance	$2,200

Computer Processing of Accounts

In a computerized general ledger system, all accounts have a unique identification number that serves as the basis for computer input. This account number is listed in the chart of accounts. A properly designed computerized general ledger program will reject any business transaction that is not recognized by the official chart of accounts.

General Ledger

General ledger is simply a term that refers collectively to all the bookkeeping accounts. It is a part of accounting terminology that all business students and professionals must know. Instead of going to the bookkeeper and asking for "all the bookkeeping accounts," it is more professionally appropriate to ask for "the general ledger." In computer systems, the general ledger is stored on tape, disk, or CD. A printout of the general ledger shows several accounts per page.

Learning Debits and Credits ————————————————

It has long been a student tradition to fear the learning of debits and credits. Therefore, many students take their first accounting course with preconceived negativism that is ill-founded. For many years, the teaching of debits and credits started with pluses and minuses in the accounting equation. This approach was quite confusing and turned off many students; therefore, it is not addressed in this chapter.

The learning of debits and credits does not have to be a nightmare. Debits and credits are simple to learn and are based on logic. The key is to know the different types of bookkeeping accounts before starting any learning of debits and credits. Once a student has learned the bookkeeping accounts classified as *asset, liability, equity, revenue,* and *expense,* the next step is to follow the simple precepts presented in this chapter. By doing so, the student will soon be skilled in the application of debits and credits.

Methods of Learning Debits and Credits

As just stated, this chapter does not address the plus/minus approach using the accounting equation. Instead, the chapter uses the method called the "Increase/Decrease effect of business transactions on the bookkeeping accounts." This method is easy to learn; one need only determine if a business transaction increases or decreases a bookkeeping account's monetary amount. For example, cash received increases the monetary amount of the *Cash* bookkeeping account. The business's writing of a check decreases the monetary amount of the *Cash* bookkeeping account. A sale increases the *Sales* bookkeeping account. The purchase of inventory with credit privileges increases two bookkeeping accounts: *Inventory* and *Accounts Payable.*

Someone using the increase/decrease effect method analyzes a business transaction, determines the bookkeeping accounts affected, and applies the debits and credits based on the increase or decrease effect to the bookkeeping accounts. (This method will be discussed in detail later in the chapter.)

Analyzing Business Transactions ————————————————

Before any business transaction can be processed in the bookkeeping phase, the transaction must be analyzed. This is relatively simple if three basic questions are answered in a specific sequence for every transaction:

1. Which two or more bookkeeping accounts are affected?

2. What are the account classifications (asset, liability, equity, revenue, expense) of these bookkeeping accounts?

3. Is the balance of the bookkeeping account increased or decreased by this business transaction?

The following examples demonstrate the sequence and logic involved in analyzing business transactions.

Example A. Cash food sales for the day total $8,000. (We will disregard sales taxes for this example.)

1. Bookkeeping accounts affected?
   Cash
   Food Sales

2. Classification of accounts?
   Assets (Cash)
   Revenue (Food Sales)

3. Increase/Decrease?
   Cash account is increased. (Receipt of cash always increases the cash account.)
   Food Sales account is increased.

Example B. The owner of a proprietorship, B. Mercedes, invests personal cash of $50,000.

1. Bookkeeping accounts affected?
   Cash
   Capital, B. Mercedes

2. Classification of accounts?
   Assets (Cash)
   Equity (Capital)

3. Increase/Decrease?
   Cash account is increased.
   Capital account of B. Mercedes is increased.

Example C. On June 1, a restaurant purchases advertising for $1,000 on open account. The newspaper ad will run on June 11 and 12.

1. Bookkeeping accounts affected?
   Advertising
   Accounts Payable

2. Classification of accounts?
   Expense (Advertising)
   Liabilities (Accounts Payable)

3. Increase/Decrease?
   Advertising expense account is increased.
   Accounts Payable account is increased.

Example D. The restaurant in Example C now pays the open account of $1,000.

1. Bookkeeping accounts affected?
   Cash
   Accounts Payable (Advertising cannot be used; if it were used, it would create a duplicate entry.)

2. Classification of accounts?
   Assets (Cash)
   Liabilities (Accounts Payable)

3. Increase/Decrease?
   Cash account is decreased. (Payment of cash is always a decrease to cash.)
   Accounts Payable account is decreased.

Analyzing 21 Universal Transactions

You should now be ready to test your skills at analyzing transactions. The following 21 transactions represent the bulk of day-to-day business transactions and some month-end adjustments. Read each transaction carefully. Ask yourself the three basic questions as you analyze the transaction.

Do only one at a time. Resist any impulse to look at the textbook's answer and explanation that follow each example transaction. Determine your own answers. Then read the text's answers, and compare your answers with them.

After we analyze these 21 transactions, we will apply debits and credits.

Example #1. A motel writes a $1,500 check to pay its current monthly rent.

Account	Classification	Effect
Cash	Asset	*Decrease*
Rent Expense	Expense	*Increase*

Reason: An expense (rent) has been incurred, which requires the use of cash. This reduces the balance in the Cash account. The account Rent Expense is incremented (increased) for the period.

Example #2. A lodging operation writes a $1,500 check on April 15, paying its rent for May.

Account	Classification	Effect
Cash	Asset	*Decrease*
Prepaid Rent	Asset	*Increase*

Reason: When rent is paid in advance of the accounting period it affects, it cannot be charged to Rent Expense. Rather, the prepayment of rent creates an asset (an item that benefits more than one accounting period). This increments the asset account called Prepaid Rent. Issuing a check always reduces cash.

Example #3. A lodging business writes a $1,500 check on August 1, paying its rent for August.

Account	Classification	Effect
Cash	Asset	*Decrease*
Rent Expense	Expense	*Increase*

Reason: While this may appear to be paying the rent in advance, this is not actually the case. Since August is the current accounting period, payment of the August rent on August 1 is an expense incurred *within* that period.

Example #4. A guest's invoice was $50.00 for meals, plus $3.00 for sales tax. The guest pays the $53.00 tab with cash.

Account	Classification	Effect
Cash	Asset	*Increase*
Food Sales	Revenue	*Increase*
Sales Tax Payable	Liability	*Increase*

Reason: All three accounts are incremented by this transaction. Note that a restaurant acts as a collection agent for the state; ultimately, the sales taxes collected for a period must be remitted to the state.

Example #5. A guest's invoice was $50.00 for meals, plus $3.00 for sales tax. The guest uses an open account authorized by the restaurant and charges the total tab of $53.00.

Account	Classification	Effect
Accounts Receivable	Asset	*Increase*
Food Sales	Revenue	*Increase*
Sales Tax Payable	Liability	*Increase*

Reason: The only difference between this transaction and that in Example #4 is that the guest did not pay by cash or cash equivalent. Instead, the restaurant gets the guest's promise to pay in the future.

Example #6. One week after the transaction of Example #5, the restaurant receives a personal check for $53.00 from the guest.

Account	Classification	Effect
Cash	Asset	*Increase*
Accounts Receivable	Asset	*Decrease*

Reason: The receipt of cash is an increase. The guest's payment results in a reduction of the Accounts Receivable balance.

Example #7. A hotel buys $65.00 worth of food provisions for its storeroom and pays cash on delivery. It uses the perpetual inventory system.

Account	Classification	Effect
Cash	Asset	*Decrease*
Food Inventory	Asset	*Increase*

Reason: Under the perpetual inventory system, the Food Inventory account is used to record purchases of food provisions. Food Inventory is incremented by this purchase.

Example #8. A hotel buys $1,200 worth of food provisions for its storeroom and uses an open account previously arranged with the supplier. The hotel uses the perpetual inventory system.

Account	Classification	Effect
Food Inventory	Asset	*Increase*
Accounts Payable	Liability	*Increase*

Reason: The hotel has made a promise to pay at some future date; this has increased its liabilities. Purchases on open account are recorded as Accounts Payable.

Example #9. The hotel in Example #8 remits a check for $1,200 to the supplier in payment of inventory purchases that had been made on open account.

Account	Classification	Effect
Cash	Asset	*Decrease*
Accounts Payable	Liability	*Decrease*

Reason: When the purchases were initially made (see Example #8), Accounts Payable was increased to reflect the increase in the hotel's liabilities. The remittance of a check has now reduced this liability.

Example #10. A hotel buys $55.00 worth of food provisions for its storeroom and pays cash on delivery. The hotel uses the periodic inventory system.

Account	Classification	Effect
Cash	Asset	*Decrease*
Food Purchases	Expense	*Increase*

Reason: Under the periodic inventory system, the account called Food Purchases is used to record purchases of food inventory items. In this transaction, the Food Purchases account is incremented by the purchase of additional food provisions.

Example #11. A hotel buys $900 worth of food provisions for its storeroom and uses an open account previously arranged with the purveyor (supplier). The hotel uses the periodic inventory system.

Account	Classification	Effect
Food Purchases	Expense	*Increase*
Accounts Payable	Liability	*Increase*

Reason: The hotel has made a promise to pay at some future date; this promise has increased its liabilities. Purchases on open account are recorded as Accounts Payable.

Example #12. Ken Thomas is starting a new business, a proprietorship called Ken's Restaurant Supply Company. In a single transaction, Ken invests cash of $55,000, plus land and building with a basis, respectively, of $40,000 and $175,000.

Account	Classification	Effect
Cash	Asset	*Increase*
Land	Asset	*Increase*
Building	Asset	*Increase*
Capital, Ken Thomas	Equity	*Increase*

Reason: The assets of the business have been increased by the owner's investment of cash, land, and a building. The Capital account of Ken Thomas is incremented, since he has increased his ownership interest in the business. An alternate view is that Ken Thomas has increased his claim to the assets of the business by investing personal assets.

Example #13. Mae Brentwood is starting a new hospitality establishment called Brentwood, Inc. She invests $50,000 into the business for 4,000 shares of $1 par common stock.

Account	Classification	Effect
Cash	Asset	*Increase*
Common Stock Issued	Equity	*Increase*
Additional Paid-In Capital	Equity	*Increase*

Reason: Brentwood, Inc., has received cash, thus incrementing its Cash account. The corporation has also increased its issued and outstanding common stock. Since the corporation has received $50,000 for stock issued at a total par value of $4,000, the stock has been issued at a premium of $46,000. Therefore, the account Additional Paid-In Capital is incremented.

Example #14. Deb Stephens is starting a new lodging operation called Dotco, Inc. She invests $50,000 into the business for 4,000 shares of no-par common stock.

Account	Classification	Effect
Cash	Asset	*Increase*
Common Stock Issued	Equity	*Increase*

Reason: The corporation has received cash and increased its issued and outstanding common stock. There is no premium to record because the corporation issued no-par stock with no stated value.

Example #15. Ann Cole is starting a new restaurant called Dorco, Inc. She invests $50,000 into the business for 4,000 shares of no-par common stock that has a stated value of $8 per share.

Account	Classification	Effect
Cash	Asset	*Increase*
Common Stock Issued	Equity	*Increase*
Additional Paid-In Capital	Equity	*Increase*

Reason: The corporation has received cash and increased its issued and outstanding common stock. While the stock issued had no par value, the stock did have a stated value. Since the corporation has received $50,000 for stock issued at a total stated value of $32,000, the stock has been issued at a premium of $18,000. Therefore, the account Additional Paid-In Capital is incremented.

Example #16. A restaurant uses a perpetual inventory system. Issues from the storeroom total $15,000 for the month. This amount represents food the kitchen uses to generate sales and prepare employee meals.

Account	Classification	Effect
Cost of Food Sales	Expense	*Increase*
Food Inventory	Asset	*Decrease*

Reason: Under a perpetual inventory system, the inventory records reflect the cost of food issued from the storeroom. Issues are treated as a reduction to the Food Inventory account and an increase to the expense account called Cost of Food Sales. In the next example, this account is adjusted for the cost of free employee meals.

Example #17. Of the $15,000 total for food issued in Example #16, $300 was used for free employee meals ($200 to Rooms Department employees and $100 to Food Department employees).

Account	Classification	Effect
Rooms Department— Employee Meals Expense	Expense	*Increase*
Food Department— Employee Meals Expense	Expense	*Increase*
Cost of Food Sales	Expense	*Decrease*

Reason: The Cost of Food Sales account should reflect only the cost of food used in the selling process. Therefore, an adjustment must be made for free employee meals, whose total reduces the Cost of Food Sales account. The costs of free employee meals increase departmental expense accounts.

Example #18. A restaurant uses a periodic inventory system. Issues from its storeroom total $15,000 for the month. This amount represents food the kitchen uses to generate sales and prepare employee meals.

> *Effect*
>
> No bookkeeping entries are made for issues under a periodic inventory system.

Reason: Under a periodic inventory system, inventory purchases are recorded as Purchases. Issues from the storeroom are not recorded (but they are under a perpetual inventory system).

At the end of each accounting period, the inventory is physically counted and priced at cost, or it is estimated using a procedure such as the gross profit method. After ending inventory has been determined, the following procedure can be used (on either the financial statements or supporting schedules) to compute the cost of food sold:

	Beginning Food Inventory
Plus:	Food Purchases
Result:	Cost of Food Available for Sale
Minus:	Ending Food Inventory
Result:	Cost of Food Used
Minus:	Employee Meals, at cost
Result:	Cost of Food Sold

Example #19. A hospitality operation purchases $875 worth of office supplies from a vendor and charges the purchases to an open account.

To properly analyze this transaction, you must know that there are two methods of accounting for operating supplies and office supplies: the asset method and the expense method. The asset method records the initial purchase to a *Supplies Inventory* account, while the expense method records it to a *Supplies Expense* account. At the end of the accounting period, a physical inventory is taken and the bookkeeping accounts are adjusted to reflect the proper inventory balances and expense (usage); at this time, both methods produce the same amount. This example uses the asset method

Account	Classification	Effect
Supplies Inventory	Asset	*Increase*
Accounts Payable	Liability	*Increase*

Reason: The asset method is used to record the purchase of office supplies. The supplies were purchased on open account.

Example #20. A check is issued for $1,200 on 3/1/X1 in payment of a property insurance policy with a term of 3/1/X1 to 3/1/X2.

Account	Classification	Effect
Cash	Asset	*Decrease*
Prepaid Insurance	Asset	*Increase*

Reason: This payment is for an insurance policy with a term of one year. Prepaid insurance is an asset. Each month, the passage of time will expire a portion of the asset. The only entry required at this time is that of recording the purchase of prepaid insurance, which is a temporary asset benefiting future periods.

Example #21. It is now 3/31/X1 for the company in Example #20. The insurance accountant submits the following adjusting entry for the above policy.

Account	Classification	Effect
Prepaid Insurance	Asset	*Decrease*
Insurance Expense	Expense	*Increase*

Reason: The passage of one month has expired $1/12$ of the prepaid insurance amount.

The Nature of Debits and Credits

Recording business transactions requires a standard system to produce consistent results. The double-entry accounting system requires that each business transaction affect two or more bookkeeping accounts. Using records that indicate *"increase"* and *"decrease"* next to amounts would be difficult to read and process, especially by a computerized system. Instead of stating *"increase"* or *"decrease,"* debits and credits are used in the double-entry system.

Exhibit 3 addresses some common fallacies regarding what debits and credits really mean and what they do. In accounting, **debit** means to record an amount in the left side of an account. The term **credit** means to record an amount in the right side of an account. To illustrate, we use a two-column account format. This two-column format is also called a *T-account* because it resembles the letter *T*.

Exhibit 3   Common Debit/Credit Misconceptions

Misconception	Truth
Debits add and credits subtract.	False. Debits add *and* subtract. Credits also add *and* subtract.
Debits are positive and credits are negative.	False. Positive and negative have no relation to debits and credits.
Debits and credits do not make sense.	False. Their use is based on logic.
Learning debits and credits is complex.	False. Only a basic knowledge of the classification of accounts and the increase/decrease effect of a business transaction is required.
I do not really need to know about debits and credits.	False. You do not need to be an expert, but, as a business student and aspiring professional, you should have a working knowledge because the person you will someday compete with for a promotion has that knowledge.

Name of Account

Debit	Credit
(Dr)	(Cr)

Notice the placement of debits and credits in this T-account. Debits are in the left side and credits are in the right side. The abbreviations **dr** and **cr** indicate debit and credit, respectively. The **account balance** (the difference between the total debits and total credits) can be either a debit balance or a credit balance, depending on which side has the larger amount.

Equality of Debits and Credits

A benefit of the double-entry system is that the accuracy of recording dollar amounts can be verified. For example, if cash is debited for $100, any credit entry or entries must also total $100. This is referred to as the **equality of debits and credits**. Therefore, in the recording of any business transaction, the sum of the debit dollars must equal the sum of the credit dollars. Keep in mind, however, that testing the equality of debits and credits does not verify that the amounts were recorded in the *correct* accounts; for example, the recording of equal debit and credit amounts in two incorrect accounts will result in an equality of debits and credits.

Computer Audit Trail

A batch number for control purposes is manually assigned to an assemblage of entries before they are submitted for computer processing. During computer processing, each entry is given a computer-generated sequence number for identification. Computerized general ledger software applications have a routine in their data entry program that checks the equality of debits and credits. If an out-of-balance condition occurs, the entry with an input error can easily be located and corrected.

A printout listing the computer-processed entries shows the batch number, the processed entries, and dollar totals of debits and credits. Some programs compare these totals and print a message such as "Batch in Balance" or "Batch Out of Balance" (depending on condition) at the bottom of the report.

Debit and Credit Rules

Before attempting to learn the rules of debits and credits, you should be capable of (1) classifying accounts, and (2) analyzing a business transaction.

There are many ways to learn the rules for applying debits and credits to record business transactions. The easiest and fastest way involves learning one central rule and then applying logic to that central rule.

The basic central rule governing the use of debits and credits is:

> **Use a debit to *increase* an asset or expense account.**

With this central *rule of increase*, we can use simple logic to determine how to increase the other three classifications. If we use a debit to increase an asset or expense account, the only remaining option is to use a credit to increase the other three classifications. With logic, we can visualize the debit and credit rules as follows:

Rule of Increase

	Debit	Credit
Asset	X	
Liability		X
Equity		X
Revenue		X
Expense	X	

Readers may ask, "How do you *decrease* an account?" Many of you already have the answer because you continued the process of logic. To *decrease an account*, do the *opposite of the rule of increase*. Therefore, the debit and credit rules can be concluded as follows:

	Increase	Decrease
Asset	Debit	Credit
Liability	Credit	Debit
Equity	Credit	Debit
Revenue	Credit	Debit
Expense	Debit	Credit

Thus far, we have examined how to analyze a business transaction and have learned the debit and credit rules. The next step is to journalize these transactions. Journalizing can be done on a two-column amount journal or an in-house custom-designed input form. To simplify learning debits and credits, we dispense with technical format considerations and, for academic purposes, treat each entry as a separate item to allow for discussion.

Recording 21 Universal Transactions

The following are the 21 transactions we analyzed earlier in the chapter. Two standard procedures in journalizing entries state that the debit part of an entry is written before the credit part, and the credit part of an entry is indented for additional sight verification.

Consult the chart of accounts in Exhibit 1 as you process these 21 business transactions. For each transaction, perform the analysis and apply the debits and credits. Look at the first entry to familiarize yourself with the academic format used to record these business transactions. Thereafter, solve each successive entry, compare your answer with the text result, and resolve any issues before proceeding to the next entry.

Example #1. A motel writes a $1,500 check to pay its current monthly rent.

Date	Description		Debit			Credit		
1.	Rent Expense		1	500	00			
	Cash					1	500	00

Account	Classification	Effect	Debit/Credit
Cash	Asset	*Decrease*	Credit
Rent Expense	Expense	*Increase*	Debit

Example #2. A lodging operation writes a $1,500 check on April 15, paying its rent for May.

2.	Prepaid Rent		1	500	00			
	Cash					1	500	00

Account	Classification	Effect	Debit/Credit
Cash	Asset	*Decrease*	Credit
Prepaid Rent	Asset	*Increase*	Debit

Example #3. A lodging business writes a $1,500 check on August 1, paying its rent for August.

3.	Rent Expense		1	500	00			
	Cash					1	500	00

Account	Classification	Effect	Debit/Credit
Cash	Asset	*Decrease*	Credit
Rent Expense	Expense	*Increase*	Debit

Example #4. A guest's invoice was $50.00 for meals, plus $3.00 for sales tax. The guest pays the $53.00 tab with cash.

4.	Cash			53	00			
	Food Sales						50	00
	Sales Tax Payable						3	00

Account	Classification	Effect	Debit/Credit
Cash	Asset	*Increase*	Debit
Food Sales	Revenue	*Increase*	Credit
Sales Tax Payable	Liability	*Increase*	Credit

Example #5. A guest's invoice was $50.00 for meals, plus $3.00 for sales tax. The guest uses an open account authorized by the restaurant and charges the total tab of $53.00.

5.	Accounts Receivable			53	00			
	Food Sales						50	00
	Sales Tax Payable						3	00

Account	Classification	Effect	Debit/Credit
Accounts Receivable	Asset	*Increase*	Debit
Food Sales	Revenue	*Increase*	Credit
Sales Tax Payable	Liability	*Increase*	Credit

Example #6. One week following the transaction in Example #5, the restaurant receives a personal check for $53.00 from the guest.

6.	Cash			53	00			
	Accounts Receivable						53	00

Account	Classification	Effect	Debit/Credit
Cash	Asset	*Increase*	Debit
Accounts Receivable	Asset	*Decrease*	Credit

Example #7. A hotel buys $65.00 worth of food provisions for its storeroom and pays cash on delivery. The hotel uses the perpetual inventory system.

	7.	Food Inventory			65	00			
		Cash						65	00

Account	Classification	Effect	Debit/Credit
Cash	Asset	*Decrease*	Credit
Food Inventory	Asset	*Increase*	Debit

Example #8. A hotel buys $1,200 worth of food provisions for its storeroom and uses an open account previously arranged with the supplier. The hotel uses the perpetual inventory system.

	8.	Food Inventory		1	200	00			
		Accounts Payable					1	200	00

Account	Classification	Effect	Debit/Credit
Food Inventory	Asset	*Increase*	Debit
Accounts Payable	Liability	*Increase*	Credit

Example #9. The hotel in Example #8 remits a check for $1,200 to the supplier in payment of inventory purchases that had been made on open account.

	9.	Accounts Payable		1	200	00			
		Cash					1	200	00

Account	Classification	Effect	Debit/Credit
Cash	Asset	*Decrease*	Credit
Accounts Payable	Liability	*Decrease*	Debit

Example #10. A hotel buys $55.00 worth of food provisions for its storeroom and pays cash on delivery. The hotel uses the periodic inventory system.

	10.	Food Purchases			55	00			
		Cash						55	00

Account	Classification	Effect	Debit/Credit
Cash	Asset	*Decrease*	Credit
Food Purchases	Expense	*Increase*	Debit

Example #11. A hotel buys $900 worth of food provisions for its storeroom and uses an open account previously arranged with the purveyor (supplier). The hotel uses the periodic inventory system.

11.	Food Purchases			900	00			
	Accounts Payable						900	00

Account	Classification	Effect	Debit/Credit
Food Purchases	Expense	*Increase*	Debit
Accounts Payable	Liability	*Increase*	Credit

Example #12. Ken Thomas is starting a new business, a proprietorship called Ken's Restaurant Supply Company. In a single transaction, Ken invests cash of $55,000, plus land and building with a basis, respectively, of $40,000 and $175,000.

12.	Cash		55	000	00			
	Land		40	000	00			
	Building		175	000	00			
	Capital, Ken Thomas					270	000	00

Account	Classification	Effect	Debit/Credit
Cash	Asset	*Increase*	Debit
Land	Asset	*Increase*	Debit
Building	Asset	*Increase*	Debit
Capital, Ken Thomas	Equity	*Increase*	Credit

Example #13. Mae Brentwood is starting a new hospitality establishment called Brentwood, Inc. She invests $50,000 in the business for 4,000 shares of $1 par common stock.

13.	Cash		50	000	00			
	Common Stock Issued					4	000	00
	Additional Paid-In Capital					46	000	00

Account	Classification	Effect	Debit/Credit
Cash	Asset	*Increase*	Debit
Common Stock Issued	Equity	*Increase*	Credit
Additional Paid-In Capital	Equity	*Increase*	Credit

Example #14. Deb Stephens is starting a new lodging operation called Dotco, Inc. She invests $50,000 in the business for 4,000 shares of no-par common stock.

14.	Cash		50	000	00			
	Common Stock Issued					50	000	00

Account	Classification	Effect	Debit/Credit
Cash	Asset	*Increase*	Debit
Common Stock Issued	Equity	*Increase*	Credit

Example #15. Ann Cole is starting a new restaurant called Dorco, Inc. She invests $50,000 in the business for 4,000 shares of no-par common stock that has a stated value of $8 per share.

15.	Cash		50	000	00			
	Common Stock Issued					32	000	00
	Additional Paid-In Capital					18	000	00

Account	Classification	Effect	Debit/Credit
Cash	Asset	*Increase*	Debit
Common Stock Issued	Equity	*Increase*	Credit
Additional Paid-In Capital	Equity	*Increase*	Credit

Example #16. A restaurant uses a perpetual inventory system. Issues from the storeroom total $15,000 for the month. This amount represents food the kitchen uses to generate sales and prepare employee meals.

16.	Cost of Food Sales		15	000	00			
	Food Inventory					15	000	00

Account	Classification	Effect	Debit/Credit
Cost of Food Sales	Expense	*Increase*	Debit
Food Inventory	Asset	*Decrease*	Credit

Example #17. Of the $15,000 total for food issued in Example #16, $300 was used for free employee meals ($200 to Rooms Department employees and $100 to Food Department employees).

17.	Rooms Dept.—Employee Meals			200	00				
	Food Dept.—Employee Meals			100	00				
	Cost of Food Sales						300	00	

Account	Classification	Effect	Debit/Credit
Rooms Department— Employee Meals	Expense	*Increase*	Debit
Food Department— Employee Meals	Expense	*Increase*	Debit
Cost of Food Sales	Expense	*Decrease*	Credit

Example #18. A restaurant uses a periodic inventory system. Issues from its store-room total $15,000 for the month. This amount represents food used by the kitchen in generating sales and preparing employee meals.

Effect

No bookkeeping entries are made for issues under a periodic inventory system.

Example #19. A hospitality operation purchases $875 worth of office supplies from a vendor and charges the purchase to an open account. The asset method is used to record supplies.

19.	Supplies Inventory			875	00			
	Accounts Payable					875	00	

Account	Classification	Effect	Debit/Credit
Supplies Inventory	Asset	*Increase*	Debit
Accounts Payable	Liability	*Increase*	Credit

Example #20. A check is issued for $1,200 on 3/1/X1 in payment of a property insurance policy with a term of 3/1/X1 to 3/1/X2.

20.	Prepaid Insurance		1	200	00			
	Cash					1	200	00

Account	Classification	Effect	Debit/Credit
Cash	Asset	*Decrease*	Credit
Prepaid Insurance	Asset	*Increase*	Debit

Example #21. It is now 3/31/X1 for the company in Example #20. The insurance accountant submits the following adjusting entry for the above policy.

21.	Insurance Expense		100	00			
	Prepaid Insurance					100	00

Account	Classification	Effect	Debit/Credit
Insurance Expense	Expense	*Increase*	Debit
Prepaid Insurance	Asset	*Decrease*	Credit

Contra Accounts

Contra accounts are bookkeeping accounts that have a *contrary* or *reverse* effect in their account classification. For example, accumulated depreciation is a contra-asset account; its function is a minus in the asset section. Contra accounts generally exist only in the following account classifications:

- Assets
- Equity
- Revenue

Learning the debit and credit rule for contra accounts is actually quite simple if we use *reverse logic* regarding the central rule of increase for assets and state the *rule of increase for contra accounts* as:

> Use a credit to *increase* a contra-asset account.

Continuing with contra-account logic, it follows that a *debit* is used to increase *contra-equity* or *contra-revenue* accounts. The following is a listing of the common contra accounts and how they are increased:

Contra Account	Classification	Rule of Increase
Allowance for Doubtful Accounts	Asset	Credit

Accumulated Depreciation	Asset	Credit
Withdrawals	Equity	Debit
Treasury Stock	Equity	Debit
Sales Allowances	Revenue	Debit

Following are three sample entries involving contra accounts.

Withdrawals. Ken Thomas owns a proprietorship called Ken's Restaurant Supply Company. Because a proprietorship cannot pay salaries or wages to its owner, Ken Thomas must draw funds from the business as necessary. A business check is issued for $1,000, payable to Ken Thomas.

Account	Classification	Effect	Debit/Credit
Cash	Asset	*Decrease*	Credit
Withdrawals, Ken Thomas	Equity (Contra)	*Increase*	Debit

The journal entry to record the $1,000 withdrawal of funds is as follows:

	Withdrawals, Ken Thomas	1	000	00			
	Cash				1	000	00

Allowance for Doubtful Accounts. The contra-asset account called *Allowance for Doubtful Accounts* contains an estimated amount of accounts receivable that might become a bad debt. When the estimate is updated, an expense account called *Bad Debts Expense* (or *Provision for Doubtful Accounts*) is charged.

An aging of accounts receivable indicates that the Allowance for Doubtful Accounts should be increased by $1,000. An analysis of this transaction shows:

Account	Classification	Effect	Debit/Credit
Bad Debts Expense	Expense	*Increase*	Debit
Allowance for Doubtful Accounts	Asset (Contra)	*Increase*	Credit

The journal entry to record this estimate is as follows:

	Bad Debts Expense	1	000	00			
	Allowance for Doubtful Accounts				1	000	00

Accumulated Depreciation. The contra-asset account called *Accumulated Depreciation* contains the depreciation for all prior periods up to the current period. When accumulated depreciation is updated, an expense account called Depreciation Expense is charged.

Exhibit 4   Entries and Account Balance

Cash	
1000	500
2000	1000
700	
Total 3700	1500
Balance 2200	

(Translation: Account has a debit balance of $2200.)

An asset depreciation study shows that depreciation for the current month is $2,000. An analysis of this transaction shows the following:

Account	Classification	Effect	Debit/Credit
Depreciation Expense	Expense	*Increase*	Debit
Accumulated Depreciation	Asset (Contra)	*Increase*	Credit

The entry to record the $2,000 depreciation for the current period is as follows:

Depreciation Expense	2	000	00			
Accumulated Depreciation				2	000	00

Normal Account Balance

The balance of an account is determined by the difference of its debit and credit amounts. The account has a debit balance if the debit total is greater or a credit balance if the credit total is greater. Exhibit 4 shows one way to determine an account balance. The type of account balance (debit or credit) is another important audit tool. If debits are used to increase an asset account, it follows that an asset account should have a debit balance; otherwise the account might need analysis. For example, cash should have a debit balance of not less than zero. A credit balance would indicate either an error in recording an entry or an overdrawn condition. In either case, investigation is necessary.

The **normal account balance** rule is that the account should have a balance in conformity with the rules of increase. Exhibit 5 illustrates the normal balances of accounts. This exhibit is also useful in learning the rules of increase for the account classifications.

Exhibit 5   Summary of Normal Balances by Classification

```
                    ┌─────────────────┐
                    │     ACCOUNT     │
                    └─────────────────┘
                             │
                    ┌─────────────────┐
                    │  Classification │
                    └─────────────────┘
              ┌──────────────┴──────────────┐
   ┌──────────────────┐          ┌──────────────────┐
   │      Asset       │          │    Liability,    │
   │        or        │          │    Equity, or    │
   │     Expense      │          │     Revenue      │
   └──────────────────┘          └──────────────────┘
              │                            │
   ┌──────────────────┐          ┌──────────────────┐
   │  Normal Balance  │          │  Normal Balance  │
   │      is a        │          │      is a        │
   │     DEBIT        │          │     CREDIT       │
   └──────────────────┘          └──────────────────┘
```

Endnote

1. http://acct.tamu.edu/smith/ethics/pacioli.htm

Key Terms

account balance—The difference between the total debits and credits in an account. The larger amount determines whether the balance is debit or credit.

bookkeeping account—An individual record for each account a business uses to record its business transactions.

chart of accounts—A table of contents listing every authorized bookkeeping account in a business's accounting system.

contra accounts—Bookkeeping accounts that have a contrary or reverse effect in their account classifications.

cr—Abbreviation for credit.

credit—A term indicating that amounts are to be recorded in the right side of an account. A credit increases a liability, equity, or revenue account.

debit—A term indicating that amounts are to be recorded in the left side of an account. A debit increases an asset or expense account.

double-entry accounting—A bookkeeping process in which every business transaction affects two or more bookkeeping accounts.

dr—Abbreviation for debit.

equality of debits and credits—A condition in which the sum of the debit dollars equals the sum of the credit dollars. Equality confirms that the correct amounts were recorded; however, it does not verify that they were recorded in the correct accounts.

general ledger—A term that refers collectively to all the bookkeeping accounts.

normal account balance—The type of balance (debit or credit) an account should have, based on its classification. Each asset and expense account should have a debit balance, while each liability, equity, and revenue account should have a credit balance.

Review Questions

1. What is double-entry accounting?

2. What is a bookkeeping account?

3. What is a chart of accounts?

4. What is a general ledger?

5. What are the three basic questions applied in analyzing a business transaction?

6. What is meant by the equality of debits and credits?

7. With the exception of contra accounts, a debit will increase which of the five classifications of accounts?

8. With the exception of contra accounts, a credit will increase which of the five classifications of accounts?

9. What is a contra account?

10. What is a normal account balance?

Internet Sites

For more information, visit the following Internet sites. Remember that Internet addresses can change without notice. If the site is no longer there, you can use a search engine to look for additional sites.

Audit Trail
www.investopedia.com/terms/a/
  audittrail.asp

Business Transaction Source Documents
www.netmba.com/accounting/fin/
  process/source/

*Canada Chart of Accounts Standard for
  Reporting*
www.statcan.gc.ca/subjects-sujets/
  standard-norme/fpp-sfrf/5000044-
  eng.htm

Chart of Accounts
www.netmba.com/accounting/fin/
  accounts/chart/

Contra-Asset Accounts
www.suite101.com/content/
  accounting-101-contra-asset-gl-
  accounts-a185711

Contra-Revenue Accounts
www.wikicfo.com/wiki/Net%20Sales.
  ashx

Debit and Credit Rules Explained
www.moneyinstructor.com/doc/
   debitrule.asp

http://en.wikipedia.org/wiki/
   Debits_and_credits

General Journal Entries
www.netmba.com/accounting/fin/
   process/journal/

General Ledger
www.toolkit.com/small_business_guide/
   sbg.aspx?nid=P06_1450

 # Problems

Problem 1

Classify the following accounts as Asset (A), Liability (L), Equity (EQ), Revenue (R), or Expense (EX).

a. Accrued Payroll

b. Payroll

c. Prepaid Rent

d. Rent

e. Cash

f. Accounts Payable

g. Supplies Inventory

h. Supplies

i. Food Sales

j. Food Inventory

k. Retained Earnings

l. Building

m. Common Stock Issued

n. Owner's Capital

o. Owner's Withdrawals

p. Payroll Taxes

q. Accounts Receivable

r. Additional Paid-In Capital

Problem 2

Indicate whether Cash is increased or decreased by the following business transactions:

1. The owner invests cash in the business.

2. Cash sales for the day are $2,000.

3. The business issues a check.

4. The business receives payment from a customer who had made a previous purchase on open account.

5. The business pays its outstanding balance on an account payable.

Problem 3

Complete the following statements by specifying whether the stated accounts are increased or decreased by the business transaction:

1. A business incurs a repair expense of $200. The account Repairs Expense is _____.

2. A customer buys services on open account. The account called Accounts Receivable is _____.

3. A customer pays his/her open account balance. The account called Accounts Receivable is _____.

4. On March 10, a business writes a check for the April rent. The account Prepaid Rent is _____.

5. In April, the account Prepaid Rent referred to in the previous transaction (Number 4) is _____ and the account Rent Expense is _____.

Problem 4

For the following business transactions, identify the bookkeeping accounts affected; classify the bookkeeping accounts as Asset (A), Liability (L), Equity (EQ), Revenue (R), or Expense (EX); and determine whether the effect is an increase or decrease on the bookkeeping accounts.

1. On July 5, a lodging business issues a check paying the July rent.

2. A hospitality operation uses the asset method of accounting for supplies. Supplies of $600 are purchased on open account.

3. A hospitality facility uses the perpetual inventory system. Storeroom purchases of $1,000 are made on open account.

4. A hospitality business uses the perpetual inventory system. The Storeroom Requisitions Report shows that food provisions of $3,000 were issued for the month.

5. Continue using the information from the previous transaction (Number 4). The food and beverage manager's report shows that total employee meals for the month were $60.

6. A guest tab shows the following information: food at $60, beverage at $20, and sales tax at $4.80. The guest paid with a Visa credit card.

7. A business issues a check paying the currently due mortgage. The principal is $800 and the interest is $900.

Problem 5

Determine whether each of the following statements is true or false.

1. A business transaction is initially recorded in the general ledger.

2. Posting is the process of entering a transaction in a journal.

3. In a periodic inventory system, purchases of storeroom food inventory are recorded in an account called Food Inventory.

4. The account Cost of Food Sales is found in the periodic inventory system.

5. Inventory is an expense account.

6. The equity accounts for a proprietorship are Capital and Withdrawals.

7. Sales is a revenue account.

8. Cost of Sales is an expense account under the perpetual inventory accounting method.

9. Purchases is an expense account under the periodic inventory accounting method.

10. Prepaid Expense is an asset account.

Problem 6

Assume that a hospitality operation uses a perpetual inventory system. Name the accounts affected by the following transactions and specify whether the effect is an increase or a decrease.

a. Liquor sales for the day total $525, $400 of which was paid in cash with the balance charged to guests' open accounts.

b. A storeroom purchase of liquor totaling $725 is charged by the operation to an open account.

c. A direct purchase of liquor totaling $67 is made. Check number 978 is issued upon purchase.

d. Issues from the liquor storeroom for the month total $1,525.

Problem 7

Assume the hospitality operation instead uses a periodic inventory system. Name the accounts affected by the following transactions and specify whether the effect is an increase or a decrease.

a. Liquor sales for the day total $525, $400 of which was paid in cash with the balance charged to guests' open accounts.

b. A storeroom purchase of liquor totaling $725 is charged by the operation to an open account.

c. A direct purchase of liquor totaling $67 is made. Check number 978 is issued upon purchase.

Problem 8

Specify which of the following account classifications are increased by the use of a debit. (Write the word *debit* in the blank next to the appropriate account classifications.)

Account Classification	To Increase
Asset	_____
Liability	_____
Equity	_____
Revenue	_____
Expense	_____

Problem 9

Specify which of the following account classifications are increased by the use of a credit. (Write the word *credit* in the blank next to the appropriate account classifications.)

Account Classification	To Increase
Asset	_____
Liability	_____
Equity	_____
Revenue	_____
Expense	_____

Problem 10

Classify the following contra accounts.

Allowance for Doubtful Accounts	Contra	_____
Accumulated Depreciation	Contra	_____

Withdrawals	Contra	_____
Treasury Stock	Contra	_____
Allowances	Contra	_____

Problem 11

Indicate whether a debit or a credit will increase the balance of the following contra accounts.

Allowance for Doubtful Accounts	_____
Accumulated Depreciation	_____
Withdrawals	_____
Treasury Stock	_____
Allowances	_____

Problem 12

Identify which account will be debited in each of the following circumstances if the transaction shown is a credit to Accounts Payable.

Transaction	Inventory System	Account Debited
a. Purchase of food for storeroom	Perpetual	_____
b. Purchase of food for kitchen	Perpetual	_____
c. Purchase of food for storeroom	Periodic	_____
d. Purchase of food for kitchen	Periodic	_____
e. Purchase of liquor for storeroom	Perpetual	_____
f. Purchase of liquor for storeroom	Periodic	_____
g. Purchase of office supplies	Asset	_____

Problem 13

Assume that a hospitality operation uses a perpetual inventory system. Journalize the following transactions on a two-column journal.

a. Liquor sales for the day total $525, $400 of which was paid in cash with the balance charged to guests' open accounts.

b. A storeroom purchase of liquor totaling $725 is charged by the operation to an open account.

c. A direct purchase of liquor totaling $67 is made. Check number 978 is issued upon purchase.

d. Issues from the liquor storeroom for the month total $1,525.

Problem 14

Assume the hospitality operation instead uses a periodic inventory system. Journalize the following transactions on a two-column journal.

a. Liquor sales for the day total $525, $400 of which was paid in cash with the balance charged to guests' open accounts.

b. A storeroom purchase of liquor totaling $725 is charged by the operation to an open account.

c. A direct purchase of liquor totaling $67 is made. Check number 978 is issued upon purchase.

Problem 15

The Blue Ribbon Steakhouse uses a perpetual inventory system for food and beverages. Supplies inventory and expense accounts are separately maintained for the following types of supplies: Guest, Cleaning, Office, and Kitchen. Purchases of supplies are charged to either an inventory (asset) account or an expense account based on the destination of the supplies (storeroom or direct use).

Journalize the following transactions on a two-column journal for the Blue Ribbon Steakhouse.

20X1

March 1: The sales report for the day presented the following information:

Food	$1,985.75
Beverage	425.00
Sales Tax	144.65
Cash received and bank credit cards	1,550.65
In-house credit cards	1,003.68
Cash shortage	1.07

(Cash shortages or overages are recorded to one account called Cash Short or Over.)

March 1: Issued check number 645 for $1,600 to Baker Realty in payment of the March rent.

March 1: Purchased $900 of food provisions for the storeroom on open account from Daxell Supply.

March 1: Purchased $250 of liquor on open account for the storeroom from Tri-State Distributors.

March 1: Paid for newspaper advertising to run on March 15. Issued check number 646 for $350 to *City News*.

March 2: The sales report for the day presented the following information:

Food	$1,856.50
Beverage	395.00
Sales Tax	135.09
Cash received and bank credit cards	1,495.84
In-house credit cards	891.13
Cash overage	.38

March 2: Issued check number 647 for $1,500 to Capital Insurance for a one-year policy on contents of building. Term of the policy is March 8, 20X1, to March 8, 20X2.

March 2: Paid for newspaper advertising to run on April 8. Issued check number 648 for $850 to *City News*.

March 2: Issued check number 649 for $225 to Eastern Telephone for the period March 1 to March 31.

March 2: Purchased (on open account) the following items from Kimble Supply, intended for the storerooms:

Kitchen utensils, paper, twine, pots, and pans	$980.00
Pens, pencils, cash register rolls, staplers, and pads	200.00
Matchbooks provided free to guests	150.00
Cleaning solvents and polish	175.00

March 2: Recorded the following issues reports from the storerooms:

Issues from the storeroom to the kitchen	$1,225
Issues from the storeroom to the bar	200

March 2: The cost of free employee meals is recorded in a Food Department Employee Meals Expense account and a Beverage Department Employee Meals Expense account for management information purposes. Recorded the food manager's report of free meals provided to employees for March 1 and 2, which provided the following information:

Free meals to bar employees, at cost	$15
Free meals to food department employees, at cost	40

Problem 16

The Sunshine Motel uses a perpetual inventory system for food and beverages. Inventory and expense accounts are separately maintained for the following types of supplies: Rooms, Restaurant, and Administrative Supplies. Purchases of supplies are charged to either an inventory (asset) account or an expense account based on the destination of the supplies (storeroom or direct use).

Journalize the following transactions involving the Sunshine Motel on a two-column journal.

20X8

May 1: The sales report for the day presented the following information:

Room Sales	$5,210.00
Food	1,863.25
Beverage	375.00
Sales Tax	372.41
Cash received and bank credit cards	2,125.83
In-house credit cards	5,695.68
Cash overage	.85

May 2: Purchased $875 of food provisions for the storeroom on open account from Prince Supply.

May 2: Purchased $315 of liquor for the storeroom on open account from Hodges Distributors.

May 2: Paid for newspaper advertising which ran on March 9. Issued check number 864 for $350 to *State Tribune.*

May 2: The sales report for the day presented the following information:

Room Sales	$4,968.50
Food	2,265.95

Beverage	575.00
Sales Tax	390.47
Cash received and bank credit cards	5,365.38
In-house credit cards	2,834.09
Cash shortage	.45

May 2: Issued check number 865 for $4,200 to Zenith Insurance for a one-year workers' compensation policy. Term of the policy is May 1, 20X8, to May 1, 20X9.

May 2: Issued check number 866 for $625 to Central Telephone for the period May 1 to May 31.

May 2: Purchased (on open account) the following items from Kimble Supply, intended for the storerooms:

Amenities for room guests	$750.00
Pens, pencils, and other office supplies	500.00
Kitchen utensils, paper, twine, pots, and pans	600.00

May 3: Recorded the following issues reports from the storerooms:

Issues from the storeroom to the kitchen	$1,500
Issues from the storeroom to the bar	300

May 3: The cost of free employee meals is recorded to separate departmental expense accounts. Recorded the food manager's report of free meals furnished to employees for May 1 and 2, which provided the following information:

Free meals to rooms department employees, at cost	$75
Free meals to food and bar department employees, at cost	50
Free meals to administrative and general department employees, at cost	25

Problem 17

Judy Barnes starts a new proprietorship called the Rialto Bistro on April 5, 20X5. The operation does not serve liquor; it uses a periodic inventory system for food items. Inventory and expense accounts are set up for Operating Supplies and Office Supplies (four separate accounts). Purchases of storeroom supplies are recorded to an inventory account; direct purchases are recorded to an expense account.

Journalize the following transactions on a two-column journal.

20X5

April 5: Judy invested $75,000 in the business. This amount was used to open a business checking account.

April 5: Purchased the following property:

Land	$ 45,000
Building	165,000
	$210,000

Issued check number 101 for $40,000 to State Bank, and financed the balance by a mortgage with State Bank.

April 5:   Issued check number 102 for $5,000 to National Supply and executed a $35,000 promissory note payable to National Supply to purchase the following items:

Operating Supplies	$ 1,200
Office Supplies	800
Furniture	18,000
Equipment	14,000
China, Glassware, Silver	6,000

April 5:   Issued check number 103 for $1,400 to Fidelity Insurance for a one-year fire insurance policy.

April 5:   Issued check number 104 for $200 to City Utilities as a deposit for utility services.

April 5:   Purchased $2,500 of food provisions on open account from Statewide Purveyors.

April 8:   Issued check number 105 for $500 to Judy Barnes for personal use.

Problem 18

Joshua Kim starts a new corporation called Jokim, Inc., on May 12, 20X7. The operation uses a periodic inventory system for food items. The inventory and expense accounts set up for supplies are Operating Supplies and Office Supplies. Purchases of storeroom supplies are recorded to an inventory account, and direct purchases are recorded to a supplies expense account.

Journalize the following transactions on a two-column journal.

20X7

May 12:   Jokim, Inc., issues 200,000 authorized shares of $1 par common stock. Of this total, 10,000 shares are issued to the owner, Joshua Kim, for $80,000. The owner issues a personal check payable to Jokim, Inc., which is used to open a company checking account.

May 12:   Purchased the following property:

Land	$ 35,000
Building	155,000
	$190,000

Issued check number 101 for $50,000 to County Bank, and financed the balance by a mortgage with County Bank.

May 12:   Issued check number 102 for $7,000 to Provident Supply, and executed a $40,000 promissory note with Provident Supply to purchase the following items:

Operating Supplies	$ 900
Office Supplies	600
Furniture	19,500
Equipment	18,000
China, Glassware, Silver	8,000

May 12:   Issued check number 103 for $400 to City Utilities as a deposit for utility services.

May 15:   Issued check number 104 for $2,100 to Fidelity Insurance for a one-year fire insurance policy.

May 16:   Purchased $6,700 of food provisions on open account from Star Purveyors.

Ethics Case

The accounting department of Dandon Corporation is preparing the company's monthly financial statements. After reviewing the data, the company's controller, Sue Roberts, discovers that Dandon's current liabilities exceed its current assets. This latest information brings the company's poor liquidity position to light.

The company has an outstanding bank loan that requires that monthly financial statements be provided to the bank's commercial loan department. The terms of the loan provide protection for the bank should the security of repayment become doubtful: the bank may call for full payment, demand more collateral, or increase the rate of interest.

Dandon Corporation's profits have been satisfactory, and it has made timely payments to the bank during the course of the loan. The corporation foresees no difficulty in the future in continuing to make the loan payments.

However, to avoid any potential problems with the bank, the president of Dandon instructs Sue to treat all of a loan with another bank as a long-term liability. If Sue makes this change, the current portion of this other bank loan would be eliminated from current liabilities and instead show up as long-term debt. This change in accounting would make the company's current assets larger than its current liabilities.

1. Should the controller follow the president's instructions?

2. Comment on the change in accounting treatment.

3. What real harm is caused by temporarily changing the current versus the long-term portion of a loan? Doesn't all debt require payment anyway?

Chapter 7 Outline

Advantages of Computerized Systems
    Potential Disadvantages
Input Forms
    General Journal
    Special Journals
Output Forms
    Three-Column Account Format
    Subsidiary Ledgers
    Guest and City Ledgers
Online Accounting System
    Point-of-Sale Terminals
    Electronic Cash Registers
    Barcodes
Features of Accounting Packages
Standard General Ledger Modules
    Chart of Accounts Module
    Starting Balances Module
    Comparative Data Module
    Journal and Posting Module
    Trial Balance Module
    Financial Statements Module
    General Ledger Printout Module
    Year-End Module
Selecting General Ledger Accounting
    Software

Competencies

1. Describe the advantages and potential disadvantages of using a computerized accounting system. (pp. 167–169)

2. Describe the general journal and the various special journals. (pp. 169–170)

3. Describe the three-column account format and the various ledgers that can be used. (pp. 170–174)

4. Describe an online accounting system and its hardware components. (pp. 174–176)

5. Identify the standard modules in a general ledger software package and describe the function of each module. (pp. 176–183)

6. List factors to consider when selecting a general ledger software package. (pp. 183–184)

7

Computerized Accounting System: An Introduction

UNTIL RELATIVELY RECENTLY, only mainframe computers were available to businesses, and only large companies could afford them. In addition to their high cost, mainframes also needed programmers and other technicians. Now, with the microcomputer or personal computer (PC), even small businesses can computerize their accounting systems and other operations. A variety of ready-to-use business application software is available at modest cost. Numerous inexpensive accounting software packages are available that offer turnkey installations. The features provided by these packages range from fundamental to sophisticated, although all of them can do the following:

- Record transactions
- Post transactions
- Print a trial balance
- Print a general ledger
- Print financial statements

Computers make the accounting and bookkeeping processes easier, faster, and more accurate. Little computer expertise is necessary, and the *initial* bookkeeping procedures are similar whether they are performed manually or on a computer. A meaningful advantage of computerized accounting is that the tedious and repetitive clerical procedures have been eliminated or significantly reduced.

This chapter describes computerized general ledger accounting software. The terms and content apply to most commercially available packages. In addition, the chapter answers such questions as the following:

1. What are the advantages of a computerized accounting system?

2. What are the typical input and output forms in a computerized accounting system?

3. What is an online accounting system?

4. What are the features and modules of a general ledger software application?

5. What are the functions of the various modules in general ledger software?

6. What factors should a business consider while selecting a general ledger software package?

Advantages of Computerized Systems

The computer has become an integral tool in managing a hospitality business because it can process data quickly, accurately, and efficiently. Computerized accounting systems offer the following advantages over manual systems:

- *Speed.* A computer can process a vast amount of data at speeds that human effort cannot approach. Once the data is entered, it can be processed in any sequence and retrieved with minimal clerical effort.

- *Error safeguards.* A computer does not make errors in math or posting in an account. Furthermore, good computer programs scrutinize incoming data and will not allow faulty transactions such as invalid account numbers and out-of-balance journals. Computerized general ledgers may have other features that safeguard the validity of financial data as well.

- *Automatic posting.* In a manual system, the first bookkeeping procedures are journalizing and then transferring the information from a journal to the bookkeeping accounts. In a computerized system, the journals still require manual input, but the posting is automatic. Once the computer receives the journal input, it readily transfers this data to the specified bookkeeping accounts. This feature is a fantastic time-saver and significantly reduces errors. Typically, the manual posting process is slow, tedious, and prone to math errors, and posting is too often performed to the wrong accounts.

- *Automatic account balance calculation.* In a manual system, after the month-end posting process is completed, the bookkeeper has to go through each bookkeeping account and bring the account balances up to date. This procedure also contributes to computational errors and an out-of-balance general ledger that compound problems with a trial balance and worksheet. A computerized accounting system is designed to update the account balances immediately after posting, and these up-to-date records are available at any time for management's analysis.

- *Automatic report generation.* Because the data is stored in a computer file, it can be sorted in any sequence, and a user can quickly provide monitor displays or printouts of the general ledger, financial statements, and management reports.

Potential Disadvantages

The biggest potential disadvantage of any computerized system is power failure or computer breakdown. Unless contingent manual procedures are developed, computerized tasks come to a halt. Emergency alternatives include the use of a battery backup or use of another computer system.

Computerized operations usually require painstaking adherence to procedures. Any departure from procedures might disrupt the entire operation,

Exhibit 1   General Journal

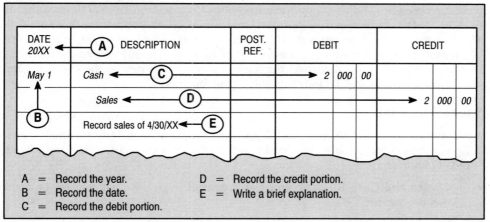

DATE 20XX	DESCRIPTION	POST. REF.	DEBIT	CREDIT
May 1	Cash		2 000 00	
	Sales			2 000 00
	Record sales of 4/30/XX			

A = Record the year.   D = Record the credit portion.
B = Record the date.   E = Write a brief explanation.
C = Record the debit portion.

especially if the operation uses an integrated accounting package (described later). Both the efficiency and quality of guest service may be affected.

In addition, the technical nature and detailed requirements of a computerized application may require personnel with higher skill levels than those the business has. It may be necessary to invest in special training and/or recruiting efforts.

Input Forms

Any computer system must be given the transactions that are to be processed. An **input form** is any document or form that contains information to be entered into the computer system. In addition to business transactions, an accounting system must also process other non-daily transactions, such as end-of-month Prepaid Insurance, Accumulated Depreciation, and any of a number of other accounts needing adjustment.

A skilled accountant can select or design input forms that are easy to use and require minimal training. Properly designed input forms reduce errors and provide internal control. Using a manual entry system, these transactions are written on an input form and entered with a keyboard.

General Journal

Entering transaction data (journal entries) on a form is called **journalizing**. The **general journal** is a two-column form used to enter transaction data (see Exhibit 1). This simple, traditional general journal is used in all accounting systems. Notice that the debit amount is on the left side and the credit amount is on the right side. While the debited account name is to the left and the credited account name is indented to the right, this procedure is optional in a computerized system.

As its name implies, the general journal is a general form. It can be used for many purposes, from recording business transactions to recording adjustment transactions. Its universal use is well known. The general journal format works well for recording adjustments or summaries of business transactions, such as monthly totals. However, it is not designed to record daily business transactions. This is because every account must be identified on a line-by-line basis; for example, if cash is in ten transactions, cash must be identified ten times and the amounts would also have to be recorded the same number of times in the bookkeeping account. The use of special journals solves this problem.

Special Journals

Accountants favor the use of **special journals** for recording daily business transactions. These journals are designed specifically for a particular company. They typically include:

- A **Sales and Cash Receipts Journal** prepared from the cash register tapes or cashier's report.

- An **Accounts Payable Journal** prepared from invoices received from suppliers and service providers.

- A **Cash Payments Journal** prepared from the checks issued to suppliers and service providers; this is sometimes called a *check register.*

- A **Payroll Journal** prepared from the checks issued to employees for salaries and wages.

Examples of these special journals are shown in Exhibit 2. Notice that the column headings feature the account name and code and whether the account is debited or credited. The **sundry column** is for those accounts for which a specific column is not provided. Items that appear in the sundry column are those that do not have frequent and repetitive entries. Special journals do not necessarily follow the *debits on left side and credits on right side* format. One design approach is to place the most active columns nearest the description column; another is to place the accounts to be debited first (left side), followed by all accounts to be credited. The arrangement is immaterial, because, in the end, only the total of each column is posted.

Note that the columns in Exhibit 2 have been totaled. Totaling the amounts in a column (a vertical process) is called **footing.** When you calculate the sum of each column total by adding the debits and subtracting the credits, the result should be zero, indicating equality of debits and credits. Totaling amounts in a row (a horizontal process) is called **crossfooting.**

The special journal can serve as an input form, or the summary totals of each column and the individual sundry entries could be entered on a general journal.

Output Forms

An **output form** is any document, report, or form produced by a computer system. Computerized financial statements and other outputs are similar between a manual system and a computer system. Within an accounting system are various types of ledgers such as the general ledger and subsidiary ledgers.

Exhibit 2 Special Journals

Sales and Cash Receipts Journal

Date	Food Sales cr 401		Sales Tax Payable cr 211		Customer Collections cr 112		Cash to Bank dr 102		Customer Charges dr 112		Cash Short (Over) dr (cr) 754	Account Title	Acct. No.	Amount dr	
Dec. 8	1	350 67		81 04		185 00	1	407 06		200 00		90	Cost of Food Sales	501	8 75
15	1	268 52		76 11		—	1	286 93		48 65		(40)	Operating Supplies	727	9 45
Total	2	619 19		157 15		185 00	2	693 99		248 65		50			18 20

Accounts Payable Journal

Date	Vendor	Accounts Payable cr 201		Food Inventory dr 121		Supplies Inventory dr 131		Utilities dr 712		Account Title	Acct. No.	Amount dr	
Dec. 7	Star Purveyors	300	00	300	00								
14	Pompano Purveyors	500	00	500	00								
	TOTAL	800	00	800	00	—		—				—	

Cash Payments Journal

Date	Paid To:	Check Number	Cash—Checking cr 102		Food Inventory dr 121		Accounts Payable dr 201		Account Title	Acct. No.	Amount dr	
Dec. 2	DSK Realty	348	800	00					Rent Expense	801	800	00
2	Associated Insurance Co.	349	2 400	00					Prepaid Insurance	132	2 400	00
31	Regional Telephone	358	65	16					Telephone	751	65	16
	TOTAL		10 262	92	200	00	4 600	00			5 462	92

Payroll Journal

Paid To:	Check No.	Gross Wages dr 601		FICA cr 215		FIT cr 215		Net Pay cr 103	
Christine Robert	621	32	16	7	85	2	00	22	31
Elizabeth David	622	30	15	7	36	6	00	16	79
TOTAL		868	71	79	36	59	00	730	35

Exhibit 3   Three-Column Account Format

Title: Accounts Receivable								Account No.: 112		
	Explanation	Ref.	Dr			Cr		Balance		
Nov. 30									185	00
Dec. 31		S	248	65		185	00		248	65

Title: Accounts Payable								Account No.: 201		
	Explanation	Ref.	Dr			Cr		Balance		
Nov. 30								(4	600	00)
Dec. 31		CP	4	600	00					
31		AP				800	00	(800		00)

Three-Column Account Format

Business transactions, adjustments, and other entries must be recorded in the bookkeeping accounts. The three-column account format shown in Exhibit 3 is very popular and easy to read and use. The three columns are for debits, credits, and balances. The debit column is on the left of the credit column. Note that the first amount in the balance column is not marked as a debit or credit amount; this shows that the amount is a beginning balance. Some systems use a *bf* (balance forward) notation or another indicator to highlight a beginning balance.

The posting reference column shows a cross-reference of the source for the entry. In Exhibit 3, the debit and credit entries come from:

- Sales Journal (S)
- Cash Payments Journal (CP)
- Accounts Payable Journal (AP)

If a transaction source document is a general journal, a common practice is to use the letter *J* followed by a number; typically the list begins with the number 1 each month and is incremented for each general journal entry prepared during that month. The codes for source documents are determined at installation design.

The balance column requires a means to identify a debit or credit balance. An accountant *signs* a credit balance by enclosing the amount in parentheses, using a negative sign, or writing *cr* after the amount. An unsigned amount represents a debit balance.

A simple way to compute an account balance is to treat debits as positive and credits as negative. The Accounts Receivable account in Exhibit 3 is one example. The beginning debit balance of $185 and the debit entry of $248.65 are added; the credit entry of $185 is subtracted to arrive at the ending *debit balance* of $248.65.

The Accounts Payable account in Exhibit 3 provides an example of an account that starts with a credit balance. One would compute the balance by starting with a negative amount of $4,600, adding the debit entry of $4,600, and subtracting the credit entry of $800. The resulting *credit balance* is $800.

Exhibit 4   Accounts Receivable Subsidiary Ledger

NAME	DEBCO, Inc.						
ADDRESS							

DATE 20X2	ITEM	POST. REF.	DEBIT		CREDIT	BALANCE	
Dec. 8	Tab 1812	S	200	00		200	00

NAME	J.R. Rickles						
ADDRESS							

DATE 20X2	ITEM	POST. REF.	DEBIT		CREDIT		BALANCE	
Nov. 18	Tab 1511	S	185	00			185	00
Dec. 8	Payment	S			185	00	-0-	
15	Tab 1849	S	48	65			48	65

Subsidiary Ledgers

A **subsidiary ledger** is separate from the general ledger. Its purpose is to provide supporting detail for certain accounts in the general ledger. These accounts are sometimes referred to as *controlling accounts*. For example, the Accounts Receivable account in the general ledger shows only a balance due from all customers; it does not indicate who the customers are. The most common subsidiary ledgers are the accounts receivable subsidiary ledger and the accounts payable subsidiary ledger.

The **accounts receivable subsidiary ledger** lists each customer receivable and supporting detail. A separate record is maintained for each customer. A sample accounts receivable ledger is shown in Exhibit 4. Each record shows the dates of activity, the source of the charge, and any payments.

The **accounts payable subsidiary ledger** shows detailed information about amounts owed by the business to its suppliers and the account activity (dates, purchases, payments). It is a separate subsidiary ledger but its format is identical to the accounts receivable ledger format.

Guest and City Ledgers

Guest ledgers and city ledgers are types of accounts receivable subsidiary ledgers used in a lodging operation. The **guest ledger** is used to record transactions involving registered guests. The **city ledger** is used to record transactions for all customers other than registered guests. Once a registered guest checks out, that person is no longer a registered guest. A city ledger could contain the following:

- Sales transactions for rental of conference rooms
- Unregistered guests charging food purchases
- The unpaid balance for previously registered guests who checked out

Online Accounting System

In an online accounting system, business transactions are recorded as they occur. This type of computerized data entry system is sometimes called a *real-time* system or an *integrated* accounting system. Online systems are popular in areas such as the following:

- Reservations
- Food order entry
- Sales
- Inventory control
- Accounting

Point-of-Sale Terminals

A point-of-sale (POS) terminal contains its own input/output units and possibly a small storage memory. A POS terminal must be connected to a remote central processing unit (CPU), an expensive component that can handle multiple POS terminals. POS terminals can have peripherals such as magnetic stripe readers, check readers, scales, and barcode scanners. Sales POS terminals record the sale and post it in the general ledger almost simultaneously.

Electronic Cash Registers

An electronic cash register (ECR) is a cash register with programmable features that can be customized for specific needs of the user. It is a stand-alone hardware computer system. All the required hardware components are in the ECR, and its keyboard (customized for its particular operation) is the input device. The display unit, storage memory, and CPU are contained within the ECR housing. Its flexibility offers management timely revenue and cash information, resulting in better management and internal control.

Barcodes

Most of us are familiar with the barcode systems used in the retail industry. The product is passed over a scanner that reads the barcode. In these systems, the following events occur concurrently:

- The selling price is displayed to the customer.
- The selling price is recorded in a sales journal.
- The sale is recorded in the general ledger.
- Inventory records are updated.

Barcodes can be used to track products from receiving through sale, making possible an automated perpetual inventory system.

Features of Accounting Packages

Sophisticated accounting packages can provide the following automated accounting capabilities:

- Billing
- Accounts receivable
- Accounts payable
- Inventory control
- Depreciation
- Payroll

Basic accounting packages merely perform the bookkeeping function, while the more sophisticated packages automate much of the clerical function. Regardless of its sophistication, each package has the following:

- Modules
- Menus/windows
- Audit trails
- Computer fraud safeguards

Modules. Accounting software packages are designed to perform designated tasks through a series of callable programs usually referred to as *modules*. Pull-down menus or windows are used to select these modules.

Pull-Down Menus. With menu-driven programs, the computer monitor displays a list of menu options. The user can *pull down* (select) a menu by using the computer mouse to position the cursor over the list of options, clicking and holding the mouse button, moving the cursor down (scrolling) through the options, and releasing the mouse button when the desired option is highlighted.

Windows. A window is an area on the computer screen that is used by the program to furnish the same capability as a menu but offers other features, such as the following:

- Menu items are represented by *icons* (pictures) and *buttons*. A user "pushes" a button by positioning the cursor over it and clicking the mouse button. Menu items represented by icons are activated in the same way, except that the user is often required to click the mouse button twice.

- A windows environment often lets the user run several applications at the same time. The *taskbar* (usually located at the bottom of the screen) indicates which applications are running.

- A windows environment also allows the user to access more than one document at a time.

Audit Trails. An **audit trail** allows a user to trace transactions that were processed in the computerized accounting system. Any sophisticated computerized accounting system (1) permits the user to trace entries back to a source document, and (2) furnishes a record of any data entered into the accounting system.

Computer Fraud Safeguards. As with any manual system, the safeguarding of business assets and confidential information is a major challenge in computer systems. Protecting the business against computer fraud requires an effective system of internal control characterized by authoritative management policies and assurance that employees are following the safeguards.

Standard General Ledger Modules

The purpose of a *manual* general ledger system is to update the general ledger, print a trial balance, and, finally, assemble the financial statements. A *computerized* general ledger can also perform these functions, because it likewise has a separate record for each bookkeeping account, showing the account's identification number, title, and changes to its balance.

A typical computerized accounting package consists of the following **modules**:

- Chart of Accounts
- Starting Balances
- Comparative Data
- Journal and Posting
- Trial Balance
- Financial Statements
- General Ledger Printout
- Year-end

Chart of Accounts Module

The Chart of Accounts Module allows the user to set up the bookkeeping accounts and perform routine file maintenance on these accounts. This module permits the user to:

- Set up the bookkeeping account titles and account identification numbers.
- Enter the current account balances.
- Add or change account titles and account identification numbers.

Entering the Bookkeeping Accounts. The requirements for entering the bookkeeping accounts depend on the accounting package; each has its own procedures. A versatile package permits the user to select account titles and account identification numbers. The account identification numbers that can be assigned must be within the range allowed by the general ledger package. Some packages allow only three-digit account numbers, while others allow account numbers with four digits or more. Many accounting packages do not allow the user to select an

Exhibit 5   Computerized Chart of Accounts

```
101   Cash on Hand                        ACC
102   Cash-Regular Checking               ACC
103   Cash-Payroll Checking               ACC
112   Accounts Receivable                 ACR
121   Food Inventory                      ACI
131   Supplies Inventory                  ACI
132   Prepaid Insurance                   ACP
147   Furniture & Equipment               AFF
149   China, Glassware & Silver           AFF
157   Accumulated Depreciation            AFD
201   Accounts Payable                    LCA
211   Sales Tax Payable                   LCE
215   Employee Taxes Withheld             LCE
231   Accrued Payroll                     LCE
232   Accrued Payroll Taxes               LCE
301   Capital, Ann Dancer                 CSC
```

account number composed of all nines, such as 999 or 9999. The reason is that the computer software reserves these numbers for either suspense accounts (described later) or its internal function of determining profit or loss.

A user must exercise caution when setting up the account numbers. The computer will sort or group accounts based on selected parameters within the report program modules. Therefore, the numbering system should have the capacity for new accounts as needed.

Many general ledger modules do not require an Income Summary account in the general ledger, because the determination of income or loss is built into the program.

Classification of Account Numbers. The method for classifying accounts as assets, liabilities, equity, revenue, or expenses varies by general ledger package. All packages contain specific instructions for account number classifications. The accounting package might stipulate that asset accounts be numbered between 1000–1999 and liability accounts between 2000–2999, and that the equity, revenue, and expense accounts also be within specific number ranges.

Level of Account. In addition to the type of account, some packages require that each account be described in terms of its *level*, which refers to how the account will appear on the financial statements. The level describes whether the account is to be printed individually on a single line or combined with other accounts and printed as one caption (line item) on the financial statements. In some packages, the level is defined in the Report Format Module instead of the chart of accounts module.

Exhibit 5 shows one format of a chart of accounts. The level of the account is not required in this particular Chart of Accounts Module. In the exhibit, assets are in the 1000–1999 range, with current assets (CA) in the 1000 series and property and equipment in the 1500 series. Current liabilities (CL) are in the 2000 series, and equity (EQ) in the 3000 series. (Though not shown in the exhibit, sales [REV] would fall in the 4000 series, and expenses [EX] in the 5000 series.)

Starting Balances Module

It is unlikely that a computerized general ledger will be started on the first day of a business year for an existing business. Therefore, programmers have provided ways for existing businesses to enter the starting balances when converting from a manual system to a computerized system.

Some packages let the user set up a chart of accounts with the starting balances. Other packages require that a chart of accounts be set up first, and afterward the current account balances are transferred from a general journal. The general ledger package has built-in safeguards against alterations of the balance without an authorized transaction that provides an audit trail.

Comparative Data Module

More sophisticated general ledger packages have features that allow the entry of last year's balances, budgets, or other comparative data that can be used to produce comparative financial statements or other comparative reports for management. Generally, only the income statement accounts contain budgeted data, because operating budgets are revenue- and expense-oriented.

Many computerized systems allow the retention of data from the previous year *(year-1 past)* and the year prior to the previous year *(year-2 past)*. After a system is computerized and has gone through a year-end closing, there is no need to enter the previous year's balances, because each year at year-end the computer software automatically moves the current closing balances to year-1 past data and the old year-1 balances to year-2 past data.

Journal and Posting Module

This module records the journal entries in the bookkeeping accounts and prints the journals or a journal summary. The recording of journal entries in bookkeeping accounts is called **posting**. Some general ledger packages might call this module a *Journal Module* or a *Posting Module*; regardless of its name, they all perform the same function. Even though a system may be online, certain transactions must be entered using input forms. There are many ways to prepare computer input; cost, hardware, software, and skilled personnel all play a role in determining how input is prepared.

Smaller companies with single-page journals might use the original journals as the input documents. Larger companies (not on an integrated system) have journals consisting of numerous entries and pages; therefore, they may prefer to use a separate input form for the convenience of the keyboard operator and for internal control reasons.

The data on the input document is entered with a keyboard. The Journal and Posting Module then prints a summary journal and posts the data to the

Exhibit 6   Sales and Cash Receipts Journal

										Sundry Items		
		SALES & CASH RECEIPTS JOURNAL (S) December 20X2										
Date	Food Sales cr 401			Sales Tax Payable cr 211		Customer Collections cr 112	Cash to Bank dr 102		Customer Charges dr 112	Cash Short (Over) dr (cr) 754	Account Title	Acct. No.	Amount dr
Dec. 8	1	350	67	81	04	185 00	1	407 06	200 00	90	Cost of Food Sales	501 ✓	8 75
15	1	268	52	76	11	—	1	286 93	48 65	(40)	Operating Supplies	727 ✓	9 45
Total	2	619	19	157	15	185 00	2	693 99	248 65	50			18 20
		✓		✓		✓		✓	✓	✓			

bookkeeping accounts. The journal printout serves as an audit trail to substantiate the changes to the general ledger (bookkeeping accounts). In some packages, the printout shows an *entry sequence number* that serves as an identification number should analysis be necessary due to an input error. Some packages also allow the entry of a *batch control number* to provide more controls and audit trails.

Suspense Account. A **suspense account** is an account in which the computer software posts an amount if the computer cannot find the account number in its chart of accounts. This prevents the general ledger from being out of balance, but the suspense account may contain several transactions that will require analysis. The suspense account should be cleared before any further processing is performed.

Some packages do not have a suspense account, because they will not process input data that is out of balance. Instead, the software either rejects the batch or prints an error message during processing and lets the user instantly make the correction.

Most software packages print an "in balance" statement at the bottom of the journal printout to indicate that the debit and credit totals are in balance. Conversely, an "out of balance" message will print if a balance error occurs.

Exhibit 6 shows a sales and cash receipts journal that was prepared manually. This journal was used as a source document to prepare the computer input form shown in Exhibit 7. The input form is given to a keyboard operator who enters the information into the computer software's Journal and Posting Module. Exhibit 8 shows the computerized audit trail that indicates that the journal was processed (posted) and account balances (the general ledger) were updated.

Trial Balance Module

This module prints a trial balance that is a primary tool the accountant uses to prepare analyses, reconciliations, and adjusting entries. A **trial balance** is a listing of all the general ledger accounts with their balances. The accountant uses a trial

Exhibit 7   Input Form for Keyboard Operator

Journal Input Form
Posting Date: 12/30/X2   Batch No: 1
Journal Code: S

Account	Debit	Credit
401		2 | 619 | 19
211		157 | 15
112		185 | 00
102	2 | 693 | 99	
112	248 | 65	
754	| 50	
501	8 | 75	
727	9 | 45	
Batch Total	2 | 961 | 34	2 | 961 | 34

Exhibit 8   Journal Printed by Computer

Journal: S
Posting Date: 12/31/X2   Batch Number: 1
Run Date: 1/10/X3

Sequence	Account		Debit	Credit
001	102	Cash—Regular Checking	2,693.99	
002	112	Accounts Receivable	248.65	185.00
003	211	Sales Tax Payable		157.15
004	401	Food Sales		2,619.19
005	501	Cost of Food Sales	8.75	
006	727	Operating Supplies	9.45	
007	754	Cash Short or Over	.50	
Batch Total			2,961.34	2,961.34
			IN BALANCE	

balance to examine the accounts, prepare adjustments, and verify the equality of debits and credits. The following is a typical procedure an accountant might use:

1. Analyze the trial balance to determine adjustments.
2. Prepare the adjusting entries and forward them to the keyboard operator.
3. Have the Journal and Posting Module process the adjusting entries.
4. Request a new trial balance.

Exhibit 9 shows one format used for trial balances. Some computerized systems print the balances in only a single column; credit balances are enclosed by parentheses.

Exhibit 9   Trial Balance

		Trial Balance Dr				Cr		
101	Cash on Hand	1	000	00				
102	Cash—Regular Checking	18	223	23				
103	Cash—Payroll Checking		200	00				
112	Accounts Receivable		248	65				
121	Food Inventory	5	875	00				
131	Supplies Inventory	1	100	00				
132	Prepaid Insurance	2	400	00				
147	Furniture & Equipment	45	000	00				
149	China, Glassware & Silver	9	000	00				
157	Acc. Depreciation—F&E					27	000	00
201	Accounts Payable						800	00
211	Sales Tax Payable						157	15
215	Employee Taxes Withheld						138	36
231	Accrued Payroll							
232	Accrued Payroll Taxes							
301	Capital, Ann Dancer					74	324	73
302	Withdrawals, Ann Dancer	38	000	00				
401	Food Sales					165	209	94
501	Cost of Food Sales	57	158	75				
601	Payroll	49	774	87				
602	Payroll Taxes	4	788	75				
605	Employee Benefits	2	164	18				
607	Employee Meals	2	875	00				
712	Utilities	3	345	31				
721	China, Glassware & Silver	1	650	00				
727	Operating Supplies	2	908	11				
751	Telephone		915	44				
752	Office Supplies		923	14				
753	Credit Card Fees	1	868	75				
754	Cash Short or Over		137	66				
761	Repairs & Maintenance	2	489	34				
801	Rent	9	600	00				
821	Insurance	1	859	00				
891	Depreciation	4	125	00				
	TOTAL	267	630	18		267	630	18

Financial Statements Module

All general ledger packages print the income statement, balance sheet, statement of retained earnings, and statement of owner's equity. Not all packages can print the statement of cash flows, and not all packages offer the same flexibility in formatting the financial statements.

Some general ledger packages allow the user to customize the financial statements in any format desired, with customized headings and totals. Other packages do not allow any flexibility; the user must adopt the headings, line totals, and format provided by the software. Most packages offer reasonable capability to format a user's financial statements according to the user's requirements.

Exhibit 10   Computer General Ledger Account Format

102	Cash—Regular Checking		25,792.16
	12/31/X9 CP	(10,262.92)	
	12/31/X9 S	2,693.99	
			18,223.23

Comments:

- The account number is 102. The name of the account follows its number code.
- The beginning balance of 25,792.16 is shown at the rightmost position.
- This general ledger software shows credit amounts in parentheses.
- The posting references are the journals CP and S shown next to the transaction date of 12/31/X9.
- This general ledger software highlights the ending balance with a "star."

General Ledger Printout Module

This module prints the general ledger, usually in a three-column account format. Most packages permit the following options:

- Print the entire general ledger.
- Print a series of accounts.
- Print one account.

At first, reading an account printed by a General Ledger Module might be puzzling. Depending on the software, the account format might be different from what is customary with a manual system. Exhibit 10 shows an account printed by a computerized general ledger. Notice the balance column showing the beginning balance and ending balance. However, there are no separate debit and credit columns. Instead, the debits are shown as positive numbers and the credits are shown as negative numbers (using parentheses). To better grasp the general ledger concept, rework the amounts in the account shown in Exhibit 10 and check your result with the ending balance.

Year-End Module

This module clears the balances in the revenue and expense accounts (and the withdrawals account, if applicable) and updates the retained earnings account or capital account without any need for closing entries. The accountant merely activates the Year-end Module from among the menu options and the year-end closing process is executed. Some packages automatically print a post-closing trial balance, while others require that it be requested via a menu print option.

A **post-closing trial balance** is a listing of the balance sheet accounts. It lists only the balance sheet accounts because, after the year-end closing entries are performed, the income statement accounts contain only zero balances. Exhibit 11 shows a post-closing trial balance. The purpose of the post-closing trial balance is to show the equality of debits and credits after the closing process and to serve as

Exhibit 11   Post-Closing Trial Balance

101	Cash on Hand	1	000	00			
102	Cash—Regular Checking	18	223	23			
103	Cash—Payroll Checking		200	00			
112	Accounts Receivable		248	65			
121	Food Inventory	5	157	00			
131	Supplies Inventory	1	000	00			
132	Prepaid Insurance	2	200	00			
147	Furniture & Equipment	45	000	00			
149	China, Glassware & Silver	8	850	00			
157	Accumulated Depreciation—F&E				27	375	00
201	Accounts Payable					800	00
211	Sales Tax Payable					157	15
215	Employee Taxes Withheld					138	36
231	Accrued Payroll					385	00
232	Accrued Payroll Taxes					366	00
301	Capital, Ann Dancer				52	657	37
	Total	81	878	88	81	878	88

an audit trail when the ending balances are carried over as beginning balances for the next accounting year.

In addition to performing the closing process, this module may automatically move the revenue and expense closing balances to year-1 past data, and the old year-1 past data to year-2 past data.

Selecting General Ledger Accounting Software

Naturally, when a business is considering which software to purchase, it is worthwhile to actually see the software in action, especially when it is operating at a real company instead of a seminar or trade show. Even this visual experience requires investigating certain features, because not all companies have identical staff, resources, and needs. No checklist can be considered complete, but the following are some features to explore when selecting general ledger accounting software.

Basic Considerations

- Audit trails of input
- Flexible chart of accounts for customization of account names and codes
- Inquiry capability to examine balances and transactions

- Audit trails:
    - Unauthorized account numbers
    - Out-of-balance entries or batches
    - Reference to source documents or input identification
    - Accounting period date
    - Processed date
- Special journal formats appropriate for your requirements
- Customization of financial statements
- Physical limitations of software:
    - Number of accounts
    - Maximum entry amount
    - Maximum account balance
    - Maximum characters in account description
    - Maximum number of journal entries
- Rounding of dollar amounts in financial reporting

Advanced Considerations

- Departmentalized accounting
- Consolidation of multiple locations or companies
- Comparative reports (budgets, history)
- Online capability
- Other built-in applications:
    - Accounts receivable
    - Accounts payable
    - Payroll
    - Fixed assets
    - Inventory
    - Order entry
    - Purchase order
- Flash reports
- Graphical reports

Final considerations, of course, are the cost of the software and the level of customer support provided by the supplier after the purchase.

Key Terms

accounts payable journal—A special journal prepared from invoices received from suppliers and service providers.

accounts payable subsidiary ledger—A ledger showing the account activity and detail of amounts owed to suppliers and service providers.

accounts receivable subsidiary ledger—A ledger showing the activity and supporting detail for each customer receivable.

audit trail—Any computerized accounting system reference or document that allows the tracing of transactions back to a source document and that provides a record of any data entered into the system.

cash payments journal—A special journal prepared from checks issued to suppliers and service providers.

city ledger—An accounts receivable subsidiary ledger that lodging operations use to record transactions for all customers other than registered guests.

crossfooting—Totaling the amounts in a row (a horizontal process).

footing—Totaling the amounts in a column (a vertical process).

general journal—A two-column journal form used to enter transaction data.

guest ledger—An accounts receivable subsidiary ledger used in lodging operations to record transactions by registered guests.

input form—Any document or form containing information to be entered into a computer system.

journalizing—The entering of transaction data in the form of journal entries on a journal form.

modules—Computerized accounting programs that perform specific tasks.

output form—Any document, report, or form produced by a computer system.

payroll journal—A special journal prepared from checks issued to employees for salaries and wages.

post-closing trial balance—A trial balance (after closing entries are processed) listing the balance sheet accounts with their balances.

posting—The recording of journal entries in bookkeeping accounts.

sales and cash receipts journal—A special journal prepared from cash register tapes or cashier's reports.

special journal—A journal that is specifically designed for a particular use.

subsidiary ledger—A ledger, separate from the general ledger, in which supporting detail is kept for certain accounts in the general ledger.

sundry column—A column in a special journal for those accounts not having a specific column.

suspense account—An account in which computer software posts an amount if the account number being processed is not authorized by the chart of accounts.

trial balance—A listing of all the general ledger accounts with their balances.

 Review Questions ───────────────────────────────

1. What are the advantages and disadvantages of a computerized accounting system?

2. What is the definition of general journal? special journal? sundry column?

3. From which source are the following special journals prepared?

   a. Sales and Cash Receipts Journal
   b. Accounts Payable Journal
   c. Cash Payments Journal
   d. Payroll Journal

4. What are footing and crossfooting?

5. What is the definition of each of the following terms?

   a. Subsidiary Ledger
   b. Accounts Receivable Subsidiary Ledger
   c. Accounts Payable Subsidiary Ledger
   d. Guest Ledger
   e. City Ledger

6. What are a point-of-sale terminal and an electronic cash register?

7. How are each of the following modules in a general ledger software package used?

   a. Chart of Accounts Module
   b. Starting Balances Module
   c. Comparative Data Module
   d. Journal and Posting Module
   e. Trial Balance Module
   f. Financial Statements Module
   g. General Ledger Printout Module
   h. Year-End Module

8. What is a suspense account?

9. What is an audit trail?

10. What is a three-column account form?

11. How are the following terms defined?

   a. Journalizing
   b. Posting
   c. Trial Balance
   d. Post-closing Trial Balance

Internet Sites

For more information, visit the following Internet sites. Remember that Internet addresses can change without notice. If the site is no longer there, you can use a search engine to look for additional sites.

Accounting Cycle
www.quickmba.com/accounting/fin/
  cycle/

Computers in the Hospitality Industry
www.hotelmule.com/management/
  html/20/n-820.html
http://en.wikipedia.org/wiki/
  Point_of_sale
http://en.wikipedia.org/wiki/
  Application_software

General Ledger and Subsidiary Ledgers
www.businesstown.com/accounting/
  basic-general.asp

History of Computers in Business
http://library.thinkquest.org/3205/
  Comp.html
www.topaccountingdegrees.com/how-
  technology-has-changed-accounting
http://ezinearticles.com/?The-Role-
  of-Computers-in-the-Modern-
  World&id=2585965
www.cs.iupui.edu/~aharris/mmcc/
  mod2/abwww0.html

Source Documents
www.quickmba.com/accounting/fin/
  source-document/

Trial Balance
www.quickmba.com/accounting/fin/
  trial-balance/

Problems

Problem 1

Indicate the journal in which the following transactions will be recorded by making a checkmark under the appropriate heading.

	Sales	Accounts Payable	Payroll	Cash Payments
a. Payroll checks	_____	_____	_____	_____
b. Checks to suppliers	_____	_____	_____	_____
c. Sales for the day	_____	_____	_____	_____
d. Invoice to be paid next week	_____	_____	_____	_____
e. Issued check for rent payment	_____	_____	_____	_____

Problem 2

Specify whether each column in the following special journals is a debit or a credit. Columns not applicable to a particular journal are indicated with an "x."

Journal Column	Sales & Cash Receipts	Accounts Payable	Cash Payments
Cash	_____	x	_____

Sales Tax Payable	___	x	
Customer Collections	___	x	x
Customer Charges	___	x	x
Accounts Payable	x	___	___
Food Sales	___	x	x
Food Inventory	x	___	___
Allowances	___	x	x
Cash Shortage	___	x	x
Sundry Items	___	___	___

Problem 3

Prepare a general journal entry in proper format using the following totals as shown on a payroll journal:

Gross wages	$5,000
FICA withheld	400
FIT withheld	800

Problem 4

Compute the ending balance in the following accounts:

Title: Food Inventory   **Account No.: 121**

	Explanation	Ref.	Dr	Cr	Balance
Nov. 30					4 875 00
Dec. 31		CP	200 00		
31		AP	800 00		5 875 00
31		J6		718 00	

Title: Sales Tax Payable   **Account No.: 211**

	Explanation	Ref.	Dr	Cr	Balance
Nov. 30					(1 216 75)
Dec. 31		S		157 15	
31		CP	1 216 75		

Problem 5

A hotel has the following subsidiary ledgers:

Guest Ledger	$250,000
City Ledger	120,000
Accounts Payable	60,000

What amount will appear as Accounts Receivable on the balance sheet?

Problem 6

The following is an abstract of an accounts payable journal with footings. Analyze and comment.

	Accounts Payable cr	Inventory dr	Utilities dr	Advertising dr
3/4	1,000	1,000		
3/8	125		125	
3/15	69			96
3/31	416	416		
3/31	87		87	
Totals	1,697	1,416	212	96

Problem 7

Determine whether each of the following statements is true or false.

1. Journalizing is the process of transferring an amount to an account.

2. The total of the sundry column in a special journal is posted in the general ledger.

3. Special journals have a special design that is suitable for any company.

4. A post-closing trial balance shows the balance sheet and income statement accounts with their balances.

5. A suspense account contains a reserve amount for casualties such as fire or theft.

6. Computer software packages cannot print financial statements.

7. The most popular account format in a general ledger software package is the T-account.

8. A city ledger is a custom-designed ledger for municipalities.

9. Conversion from a manual system to a computerized system must start at the beginning of a year because account balances during a year cannot be brought forward.

10. A trial balance shows only suspense accounts in the general ledger.

Ethics Case

Al Bender is the controller of the Diabco Company. Sara Labont is the assistant controller. Al is a close friend of the company president, and Sara is a relatively new employee. Sara is a recent college graduate with high honors from a prestigious university.

Prior to Sara's employment, the company's accounting system did not produce the timely, useful information that management required. After

(continued)

(continued)

Sara was hired, Al assigned her the task of designing a new accounting system. He also told Sara to devote all of her effort to this assignment. After several months of Sara's hard work and long hours, the new system was completed, installed, and highly successful.

The company's executive managers have been greatly impressed with the new system's results and the significant improvement in accuracy and turnaround time. Recently, Diabco's president asked Al who designed the system. Al, seeking an opportunity to promote his image, told the president that the system was his original idea and design. Further, he told the president that, while the development of the system required a tremendous amount of his personal time, the company's needs have priority.

Later, Al tells Sara about his conversation with the president. Al suggests to Sara that her silence would be her best course of action in this matter.

1. What are the relevant facts in this case?

2. What are the ethical issues?

3. What are Sara's possible alternatives for her next course of action?

Chapter 8 Outline

Accounting Cycle
    Cash Basis Accounting
    Accrual Basis Accounting
    Manual vs. Computerized Accounting
        Cycle
Tower Restaurant: A Computerized
    Demonstration
    Tower's Input Procedures
    Tower's Computer Software
Conversion from Manual to Computer
    System
    Setting Up the Computer Chart of
        Accounts
    Computer Input of Account Balances
Journalizing the Monthly Business
    Transactions
Computerized Posting of the Special
    Journals
End-of-Month Accounting
    Working Trial Balance
    Adjusting Entries
    Computer Input of Adjusting Entries
Computation of Net Income or Loss
    Proprietorship Net Income
    Corporation Net Income
Computerized Financial Statements
Computerized General Ledger
Reversing Entries
Computerized Year-End Processing
    Automatic Closing Entries
    Post-Closing Trial Balance

Competencies

1. Describe the accounting cycle and the difference between accrual and cash basis accounting. (pp. 193–195)

2. Explain the steps necessary to convert from a manual accounting system to a computerized accounting system. (pp. 195–198)

3. Describe how special journals can be used as source documents for input to the computerized accounting system. (pp. 199–202)

4. Describe a working trial balance and identify adjusting entries. (pp. 202–209)

5. Explain how net income or loss is manually calculated to verify the accuracy of the computerized financial statements. (pp. 209–211)

6. Describe computerized year-end accounting activities, including printing the general ledger and preparing reversing entries, closing entries, and the post-closing trial balance. (pp. 211–216)

8

Computerized Accounting Cycle: A Demonstration

THE EXACT METHOD OF PROCESSING TRANSACTIONS in a computerized accounting system depends on the type of computer (mainframe or personal) and general ledger software used. Nevertheless, all computerized systems require similar input and produce similar output.

Despite all its advantages, the computer has not eliminated the need for human professional judgment. An accountant still must analyze data for correctness and up-to-date status. Errors can occur during the journalizing process because, even though a computer system may reject unauthorized account numbers, it cannot determine if a valid account might actually be an incorrect account for a particular transaction. Most companies need monthly financial statements for successful management. Reliable financial statements require the expertise of an accountant to analyze such items as expired insurance, depreciation, doubtful accounts, and other entries that must be updated with adjusting entries.

The accounting cycle begins with business transactions, continues with month-end adjusting entries and printing of financial statements, and terminates with the year-end process. This chapter covers a computerized accounting cycle from start to finish, using Tower Restaurant as a demonstration case. To make the chapter more pragmatic, Tower Restaurant, currently on a manual accounting system, will convert to a computerized accounting system. The chapter provides comprehensive coverage of the operation of a computerized accounting system and answers such questions as the following:

1. How is a manual system converted to a computerized accounting system?

2. How are business transactions processed in a computerized accounting system?

3. What are adjusting entries? How are they determined and processed?

4. How can net income (or loss) be manually verified?

5. Which financial statements are produced in a computerized accounting system?

6. What is the computerized year-end process?

Accounting Cycle

The **accounting cycle** is the sequence of accounting procedures performed during an accounting period; it is a continuing process of recording and reporting

Exhibit 1   Accounting Cycle

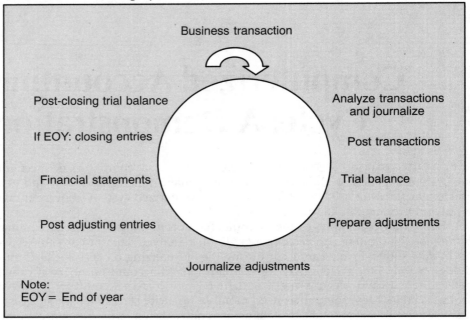

financial information. An *accounting system* is a database of financial information about a company. No two companies have exactly the same database because each company has different information requirements that vary with size, industry, and customer market. However, the accounting cycle illustrated in Exhibit 1 is the one attribute of an accounting system that *is a constant*. The following list summarizes the functions of the accounting cycle:

- Analyze and journalize transactions.
- Post transactions to the general ledger.
- Print a trial balance.
- Analyze the trial balance; prepare, journalize, and post adjusting entries.
- Issue the financial statements.
- At end of year, close income statement accounts; print post-closing trial balance.

Cash Basis Accounting

Under **cash basis accounting**, revenue is recorded only when cash is received, and an expense is recorded only when cash is paid. This basis of accounting produces misleading information because it fails to record revenue when earned (realization principle) and does not enter expenses incurred in the production of this revenue (matching principle). Therefore, cash basis accounting *is not in compliance with generally accepted accounting principles (GAAP).*

A small business is justified in keeping its books on the cash basis of accounting; however, an accountant will prepare a worksheet and convert these records to accrual basis accounting if financial statements are to be issued to external users.

Accrual Basis Accounting

Under **accrual basis accounting**, all revenue and expense transactions are recorded in the period in which they occur. The accrual basis of accounting is in compliance with GAAP and must be used by accountants in the preparation of financial statements. To comply with the matching principle, the accrual basis of accounting also requires adjustments prior to preparation of financial statements for particulars such as invoices not yet received, expired assets (prepaid items, depreciation), potential bad debts, and other items.

Manual vs. Computerized Accounting Cycle

The elements of the accounting cycle are identical for manual and computerized accounting systems. Each phase of the cycle is required. The only difference is the method of processing, manual vs. computer. This chapter covers the computer process; for those interested in the manual elements of accounting, such as the formidable worksheet and reversing entries, an example is provided in Appendix A at the end of the chapter.

Tower Restaurant: A Computerized Demonstration ———

Tower Restaurant is a family-operated small business formed as a proprietorship and owned by Ann Dancer, who is a full-time hospitality teacher. It is a relatively new business and its market is local residents in a rural town. Tower's accounting year is the calendar year. The restaurant has used a manual accounting system and is planning to convert to a computerized accounting system. The management of Tower has elected to end its manual system as of the November 30 accounting period, which is the end of its busy season. The restaurant will be closed for most of December except for two small banquets, one on December 8 and the other on December 15. Therefore, this cutoff of the manual system is an ideal time for a conversion to an automated system.

Tower's Input Procedures

Because Tower is a small business, its management has decided not to invest in an online system or enter daily transactions in the computer system. After consultation with the restaurant's accountant, Tower management decided on the following procedure for processing the restaurant's business transactions:

- Continue to use the existing special journals:
  - Sales and Cash Receipts Journal
  - Cash Payments Journal

- Accounts Payable Journal
- Payroll Journal

- Enter the data manually on these journals.
- At the end of the month, use the journal footings and individual sundry items as input to the computer system.

Tower's Computer Software

Tower purchased a low-cost computer and an inexpensive, commercially available general ledger software package. The software's specific features include capabilities that:

- Show credit amounts in parentheses and debit amounts unsigned.
- Display equality of debits and credits as "Net DR/CR $0.00."
- Customize a chart of accounts.
- Customize financial statements.

Since December is the last month of Tower's business year, its management has decided not to enter any comparative or historical data in the Comparative Data Module. Tower has decided to use the following modules of this computer package:

- Chart of Accounts
- Starting Balances
- Posting
- Trial Balance
- Financial Statements
- General Ledger
- Year-end

For the conversion to a computerized accounting system, Tower's accountant has the following assignment:

- Set up a computerized chart of accounts.
- Enter the starting balances in the computer system.
- Manually enter the December transactions on special journals.
- Post the special journals in the computer system.
- Print a trial balance.
- Analyze the trial balance.
- Determine adjustments.
- Journalize and post the adjusting entries in the computer system.
- Print financial statements.

- Print the general ledger.
- Perform the year-end process (December 31 is the end of the accounting year):
  - Closing entries
  - Post-closing trial balance

Conversion from Manual to Computerized System

All software packages allow the user to set up account balances so that a conversion from a manual system to a computerized system can take place at any time of the year. Some software packages allow the use of existing account numbers or provide flexibility in designing an account number coding system. Setting up a chart of accounts for a computerized system requires that each bookkeeping account be assigned an account number and an account type.

An account number is required in computer systems to simplify the input process and avoid writing the account name in journal entries to the computer, which can lead to rejections or errors.

Setting Up the Computer Chart of Accounts

The general ledger package permits Tower Restaurant to use its existing chart of accounts. Fortunately, the manual account coding system was logically designed by Tower's accountant and can be used by the software. Tower uses a three-digit numbering code as follows:

1xx	Assets
2xx	Liabilities
3xx	Equity
4xx	Revenue
5xx	Cost of sales expense
6xx	Payroll and related expenses
7xx	Operating expenses
8xx	Fixed expenses

The second digit of the number code also has a special meaning. For example, assets were further subdivided as follows:

10x	Cash items
11x	Receivables
12x	Food and other merchandise inventories
13x	Supplies inventory
14x	Fixed assets
15x	Accumulated depreciation

For the other classifications of accounts, a similar indexing approach was used for the second digit of the account number. The third digit of the number code is a sequential number, leaving open numbers for expansion. 9xx numbers were not used so as to avoid conflict with any built-in suspense account or automatic functions of the package.

The *type* of account must be specified because these letter codes are used to customize the printing of financial statements. This particular computer package uses a three-letter code to specify the type of account. Easy-to-follow instructions to code the accounts are provided. A sample of the type of account coding follows:

```
A = Asset
   C = Current
         C  =  Cash
         R  =  Receivable
         I  =  Inventory
         P  =  Prepaid
   F = Fixed asset
         F  =  Furniture and equipment
         D  =  Depreciation
L = Liability
   C = Current
         A  =  Accounts payable
```

The software package allows the accountant to set up the chart of accounts and enter the beginning balances during the same computer processing operation. Therefore, the accountant decides to use this feature and enter the account balances before submitting any input to the computer.

Computer Input of Account Balances

After the codes are determined, the next step is to enter the beginning balances of each account. The ending balances as of November 30 are entered because they also represent the beginning balances for December 1. The codes and balances have been manually entered on a form, which could be either a two-column journal or some other useful format. This form is input to the computer software's Chart of Accounts Module, and the data is entered via a keyboard. The computer processing result is shown in Exhibit 2, which indicates that the chart of accounts is now computerized, the balances are entered, and there was equality of debits and credits.

Journalizing the Monthly Business Transactions ——————

The business transactions during December have been manually recorded in the special journals. The entries in these journals are shown in Exhibits 3 through 6.

Notice that these journals are footed. The accountant has proven the equality of debits and credits by crossfooting the columnar totals. These journals will be input documents for the computer system.

The columnar headings on each journal indicate the account number and identify the column as either a debit or credit entry. In parentheses immediately following the journal name is the posting reference; in this case, the posting references are S, CP, AP, and PR, as assigned to the specific journal.

Exhibit 2   Chart of Accounts with Starting Balances

CHART OF ACCOUNTS
Tower Restaurant

Account	Description	Type	11/30/X8
101	Cash on Hand	ACC	1,000.00
102	Cash-Regular Checking	ACC	25,792.16
103	Cash-Payroll Checking	ACC	200.00
112	Accounts Receivable	ACR	185.00
121	Food Inventory	ACI	4,875.00
131	Supplies Inventory	ACI	1,100.00
132	Prepaid Insurance	ACP	0.00
147	Furniture & Equipment	AFF	45,000.00
149	China, Glassware & Silver	AFF	9,000.00
157	Accumulated Depreciation	AFD	(27,000.00)
201	Accounts Payable	LCA	(4,600.00)
211	Sales Tax Payable	LCE	(1,216.75)
215	Employee Taxes Withheld	LCE	0.00
231	Accrued Payroll	LCE	0.00
232	Accrued Payroll Taxes	LCE	0.00
301	Capital, Ann Dancer	CSC	(74,324.73)
302	Withdrawals, Ann Dancer	CST	38,000.00
401	Food Sales	ISS	(162,590.75)
501	Cost of Food Sales	ECP	57,150.00
601	Payroll	EOA	48,906.16
602	Payroll Taxes	EOA	4,788.75
605	Employee Benefits	EOA	2,164.18
607	Employee Meals	EOA	2,875.00
712	Utilities	EOO	3,094.65
721	China, Glassware & Silver	EOO	1,650.00
727	Operating Supplies	EOO	2,898.66
751	Telephone	EOO	850.28
752	Office Supplies	EOO	923.14
753	Credit Card Fees	EOO	1,868.75
754	Cash Short or Over	EOO	137.16
761	Repairs & Maintenance	EOO	2,489.34
801	Rent	EOF	8,800.00
821	Insurance	EOF	1,859.00
891	Depreciation	EOF	4,125.00
	NET DR/CR		0.00

Computerized Posting of the Special Journals

Special journals become input to the computer software's Posting Module; the data is entered via a keyboard. The footing of each column for a specific account is entered, but each item in the sundry column must be individually entered, because the total of a sundry column is not representative of any one particular account. The computer processing result is shown in Exhibits 7 through 10. Notice that the computer report is in two sections for each journal. The top section shows the following:

- A posting reference called Journal Number, in this case S, CP, AP, and PR
- A replication of the sequence of the items as they were on the source document (special journal)
- The account number
- The debit or credit amount posted to the account number
- Equality of debits and credits

Exhibit 3 Manual Sales & Cash Receipts Journal

Tower Restaurant
SALES & CASH RECEIPTS JOURNAL (S)
December 20X8

Date	Food Sales cr 401			Sales Tax Payable cr 211		Customer Collections cr 112		Cash to Bank dr 102			Customer Charges dr 112		Cash Short (Over) dr (cr) 754		Sundry Items			
															Account Title	Acct. No.	Amount dr	
Dec. 8	1	350	67	81	04	185	00	1	407	06	200	00		90	Cost of Food Sales	501	8	75
15	1	268	52	76	11	—		1	286	93	48	65		(40)	Operating Supplies	727	9	45
Total	2	619	19	157	15	185	00	2	693	99	248	65		50			18	20

Exhibit 4 Manual Cash Payments Journal

Tower Restaurant
CASH PAYMENTS JOURNAL (CP)
December 20X8

Date	Paid To:	Check Number	Cash— Checking cr 102			Food Inventory dr 121		Accounts Payable dr 201			Sundry Items			
											Account Title	Acct. No.	Amount dr	
Dec. 2	DSK Realty	348		800	00						Rent Expense	801	800	00
2	Associated Insurance Co.	349	2	400	00						Prepaid Insurance	132	2 400	00
6	Star Purveyors	350	2	150	00			2	150	00				
6	VOID	351		—										
7	Tom's Seafood	352		75	00	75	00							
7	State Dept. of Taxation	353	1	216	75						Sales Tax Payable	211	1 216	75
9	Pompano Purveyors	354	2	450	00			2	450	00				
14	Tom's Seafood	355		125	00	125	00							
16	Tower Payroll Account	356		730	35						Cash—Payroll Checking	103	730	35
31	City Utilities	357		250	66						Utilities	712	250	66
31	Regional Telephone	358		65	16						Telephone	751	65	16
	TOTAL		10	262	92	200	00	4	600	00			5 462	92

Exhibit 5   Manual Accounts Payable Journal

				Tower Restaurant **ACCOUNTS PAYABLE JOURNAL (AP)** *December 20X8*				

Date	Vendor	Accounts Payable cr 201	Food Inventory dr 121	Supplies Inventory dr 131	Utilities dr 712	Sundry Items		
						Account Title	Acct. No.	Amount dr
Dec. 7	Star Purveyors	300 00	300 00					
14	Pompano Purveyors	500 00	500 00					
	TOTAL	800 00	800 00	—	—			—

Exhibit 6   Manual Payroll Journal

				Tower Restaurant **PAYROLL REGISTER (PR)** *December 16, 20X8*					

		1	2	3	4	5
	Paid To:	Check No.	Gross Wages dr 601	FICA cr 215	FIT cr 215	Net Pay cr 103
	Christine Robert	621	32 16	7 85	2 00	22 31
	Elizabeth David	622	30 15	7 36	6 00	16 79
	Ann Tasha	623	42 00	9 94	10 00	22 06
	Mary Alcrep	624	24 40	2 41	—	21 99
	Tom Paul	625	140 00	9 80	6 00	124 20
	Steve Towe	626	600 00	42 00	35 00	523 00
	TOTAL		868 71	79 36	59 00	730 35

Exhibit 7   Computerized Sales & Cash Receipts Journal

```
                              Tower Restaurant
                         Sales & Cash Receipts Journal        PAGE   1
                            Current P/E Date: 12/31/X8
        Journal Number: S


         Date    Ref #   Description                    Account        Amount

        12/31            Food Sales                       401        (2,619.19)
        12/31            Sales Tax Payable                211          (157.15)
        12/31            Customer Collections             112          (185.00)
        12/31            Cash to Bank                     102         2,693.99
        12/31            Customer Charges                 112           248.65
        12/31            Cash Short                       754             0.50
        12/31            Cost of Food Sales               501             8.75
        12/31            Operating Supplies               727             9.45
                                                                    ---------------

                                                 Net DR/CR              $0.00



                                        Journal Summary
                    Account Description                             Net Posting

               102  Cash-Regular Checking                            2,693.99
               112  Accounts Receivable                                 63.65
               211  Sales Tax Payable                                 (157.15)
               401  Food Sales                                      (2,619.19)
               501  Cost of Food Sales                                   8.75
               727  Operating Supplies                                   9.45
               754  Cash Short or Over                                   0.50
                                                                    ---------------

                                                 Net DR/CR              $0.00
```

The bottom section of the report is a Journal Summary, which shows the same information, but by account number sequence.

End-of-Month Accounting

The business transactions that have been posted were for the month of December. If financial statements were printed at this time, they would be incomplete because adjustments must be determined and posted. This is probably the most complex phase of the accounting process and usually requires the experience of an accountant.

In a manual system, a multi-section worksheet is required, its sections consisting of Trial Balance, Adjustments, Adjusted Trial Balance, Income Statement, and Balance Sheet. Each section is separated into a debit and credit column. First, the accounts and their balances are entered in the trial balance section. Then the accountant computes and enters the adjustments in the adjustment column. The remainder of the worksheet can then be completed. This is a tedious, time-consuming process subject to mathematical errors that require even more time to correct. The complete worksheet procedure and associated exhibits appear in Appendix A at the end of the chapter.

Exhibit 8   Computerized Cash Payments Journal

```
                           Tower Restaurant
                         Cash Payments Journal
                       Current P/E Date: 12/31/X8          PAGE    1

      Journal Number: CP


       Date    Ref #   Description                  Account        Amount


      12/31            Cash-Checking                  102        (10,262.92)
      12/31            Food Inventory                 121            200.00
      12/31            Accounts Payable               201          4,600.00
      12/31            Rent Expense                   801            800.00
      12/31            Prepaid Insurance              132          2,400.00
      12/31            Sales Tax Payable              211          1,216.75
      12/31            Cash-Payroll Checking          103            730.35
      12/31            Utilities                      712            250.66
      12/31            Telephone                      751             65.16
                                                                -------------

                                              Net DR/CR            $0.00


                                          Journal Summary
                 Account Description                          Net Posting


            102  Cash-Regular Checking                        (10,262.92)
            103  Cash-Payroll Checking                            730.35
            121  Food Inventory                                   200.00
            132  Prepaid Insurance                              2,400.00
            201  Accounts Payable                               4,600.00
            211  Sales Tax Payable                              1,216.75
            712  Utilities                                        250.66
            751  Telephone                                         65.16
            801  Rent                                             800.00
                                                            -------------

                                              Net DR/CR            $0.00
```

Exhibit 9   Computerized Accounts Payable Journal

```
                           Tower Restaurant
                       Accounts Payable Journal
                       Current P/E Date: 12/31/X8
                                                           PAGE    1

      Journal Number: AP


       Date    Ref #   Description                  Account        Amount


      12/31            Accounts Payable               201          (800.00)
      12/31            Food Inventory                 121           800.00
                                                                -------------

                                              Net DR/CR            $0.00


                                          Journal Summary
                 Account Description                          Net Posting


            121  Food Inventory                                   800.00
            201  Accounts Payable                                (800.00)
                                                            -------------

                                              Net DR/CR            $0.00
```

Exhibit 10   Computerized Payroll Journal

```
┌────────────────────────────────────────────────────────────────────┐
│                         Tower Restaurant                             │
│                          Payroll Journal                             │
│                     Current P/E Date: 12/31/X8                       │
│                                                      PAGE   1         │
│                                                                      │
│  Journal Number: PR                                                  │
│ ──────────────────────────────────────────────────────────────────  │
│                                                                      │
│   Date     Ref #   Description              Account        Amount    │
│                                                                      │
│   12/31            Gross Wages                601         868.71     │
│   12/31            FICA                       215         (79.36)    │
│   12/31            FIT                        215         (59.00)    │
│   12/31            Net Pay                    103        (730.35)    │
│                                                        ───────────    │
│                                                                      │
│                                          Net DR/CR        $0.00      │
│                                                                      │
│                                                                      │
│                                 Journal Summary                      │
│              Account Description                      Net Posting     │
│ ──────────────────────────────────────────────────────────────────  │
│                                                                      │
│        103   Cash-Payroll Checking                     (730.35)     │
│        215   Employee Taxes Withheld                   (138.36)     │
│        601   Payroll                                    868.71      │
│                                                        ───────────    │
│                                                                      │
│                                          Net DR/CR        $0.00      │
└────────────────────────────────────────────────────────────────────┘
```

Working Trial Balance

Since Tower is using a computerized system, a worksheet is not necessary. Nevertheless, an accountant must manually determine the adjustments. The first step is to use the Trial Balance Module and print a preliminary trial balance called a **working trial balance** (also called an *unadjusted trial balance*). The working trial balance is shown in Exhibit 11, indicating a net income before adjustments of $18,626.64.

The next step is the most difficult. Adjustments must be determined and computed, requiring the skill and knowledge of an experienced accountant. The adjustments for Tower are not highly complex because it is a small business. Typically, a hospitality business will adjust for the following items at month end:

- Cost of food used in the revenue process
- Cost of employee meals
- Supplies consumed during the month
- Prepaid insurance expired by the passage of one month
- Depreciation increase by the passage of one month
- Depreciation of china, glassware, and silver
- Unpaid payroll days at the end of the month
- Unpaid payroll taxes at the end of the month

Exhibit 11 Computerized Working Trial Balance

Tower Restaurant
Working Trial Balance
Current P/E Date: 12/31/X8

Account	Unadjusted Balance		Adjustments	
	Debit	Credit	Debit	Credit
101 Cash on Hand	1,000.00			
102 Cash—Regular Checking	18,223.23			
103 Cash—Payroll Checking	200.00			
112 Accounts Receivable	248.65			
121 Food Inventory	5,875.00			
131 Supplies Inventory	1,100.00			
132 Prepaid Insurance	2,400.00			
147 Furniture & Equipment	45,000.00			
149 China, Glassware & Silver	9,000.00			
157 Accumulated Depreciation		27,000.00		
201 Accounts Payable		800.00		
211 Sales Tax Payable		157.15		
215 Employee Taxes Withheld		138.36		
231 Accrued Payroll		0.00		
232 Accrued Payroll Taxes		0.00		
301 Capital, Ann Dancer		74,324.73		
302 Withdrawals	38,000.00			
401 Food Sales		165,209.94		
501 Cost of Food Sales	57,158.75			
601 Payroll	49,774.87			
602 Payroll Taxes	4,788.75			
605 Employee Benefits	2,164.18			
607 Employee Meals	2,875.00			
712 Utilities	3,345.31			
721 China, Glassware & Silver	1,650.00			
727 Operating Supplies	2,908.11			
751 Telephone	915.44			
752 Office Supplies	923.14			
753 Credit Card Fees	1,868.75			
754 Cash Short or Over	137.66			
764 Repairs & Maintenance	2,489.34			
801 Rent	9,600.00			
821 Insurance	1,859.00			
891 Depreciation	4,125.00			
Total	267,630.18	267,630.18		

Net income before adjustments 18,626.64

Adjusting Entries

The purpose of **adjusting entries** is to bring the general ledger up to date to comply with the revenue recognition principle and the matching principle. The day-to-day transactions do not take into account items such as consumption of inventories, estimates of depreciation, or unpaid payrolls. As the accountant determines the adjustments, each adjusting entry is entered in a general journal. Exhibit 12 shows the adjusting entries manually entered on this journal. Note that the journal is numbered J1 (first general journal in December) and each entry is separated by a letter code in this fashion: (a), (b), (c), etc. This letter code is not required, but it provides additional reference for audit trail purposes.

Correcting Entries. The term *adjusting entries* is not used for any entries whose purpose is to fix errors in the general ledger; error-fixing entries are called **correcting entries**.

Cost of Sales. Tower uses the perpetual inventory system. The issues from the storeroom total $718. See entry (a) in Exhibit 12, which *increases* cost of food sales expense and *reduces* the food inventory.

Employee Meals. The storeroom issues in entry (a) include food served to both guests and employees, which is a problem because the cost of food sales account must show only the cost of food served to guests. Therefore, an adjustment is necessary to remove that portion applicable to food served to employees. The food manager's listing showing a $35 cost for employee meals is used to prepare this adjustment. See entry (b) in Exhibit 12, which *increases* the employee meals expense and *reduces* the cost of food sales expense.

Supplies Used. Tower uses the asset method to record purchases of supplies. The asset method records all purchases to supplies inventory. A listing of supplies drawn from the inventory is used to process this transaction; the supplies used this month total $100. See entry (c) in Exhibit 12, which *increases* the supplies expense and *reduces* the supplies inventory.

Prepaid Insurance. On December 2, Tower Restaurant purchased a $2,400 property and liability insurance policy and set up an asset called Prepaid Insurance (see Cash Payments Journal). The $2,400 premium was for 12 months, starting December 2 of this year and ending on December 2 of next year. Therefore, $200 of the policy's cost basis expires each month ($1/12$ of $2,400). See entry (d) in Exhibit 12, which *increases* the insurance expense and *reduces* the prepaid insurance.

Depreciation. The purchase of all long-lived assets is recorded to a type of property and equipment asset account. Depreciation is a method in which the cost of a long-lived tangible asset is allocated over its useful life. Depreciation has been calculated at $375 for December. See entry (e) in Exhibit 12, which *increases* depreciation expense and *increases* the Accumulated Depreciation contra-asset account.

China, Glassware, Silver. Replacements of china, glassware, and silver are charged to expense; however, the initial purchase had been charged to an asset account. This group of assets is depreciated over its useful life, but the entry is

Exhibit 12   Manual Adjusting Entries

	JOURNAL					Page *J1*	
Date 20X8	Description	Post. Ref.	Debit			Credit	
	(a)						
Dec. 31	Cost of Food Sales	501	718	00			
	Food Inventory	121				718	00
	Record storeroom issues to kitchen						
	(b)						
31	Employee Meals	607	35	00			
	Cost of Food Sales	501				35	00
	Record food used for free employee meals						
	(c)						
31	Operating Supplies	727	100	00			
	Supplies Inventory	131				100	00
	Adjust inventory account to physical						
	(d)						
31	Insurance	821	200	00			
	Prepaid Insurance	132				200	00
	Charge expired premium to expense						
	(e)						
31	Depreciation	891	375	00			
	Accumulated Depreciation—F & E	157				375	00
	Record $1/12$ annual depreciation						
	(f)						
31	China, Glassware & Silver (Expense)	721	150	00			
	China, Glassware & Silver (Asset)	149				150	00
	Record $1/12$ annual depreciation						
	(g)						
31	Payroll	601	385	00			
	Accrued Payroll	231				385	00
	Record unpaid wages as of 12/31						
	(h)						
31	Payroll Taxes	602	366	00			
	Accrued Payroll Taxes	232				366	00
	Record unpaid employer's taxes as of 12/31						

slightly different from that for buildings, furniture, and equipment. An accumu- lated depreciation account is not used; instead, the depreciation computation is used to reduce the cost basis of the asset. Depreciation has been calculated at $150 for December. See entry (f) in Exhibit 12, which *increases* the china, glassware, and silver expense and *reduces* the cost basis of these assets.

Payroll. A business will always have unpaid payroll at the end of any week or month. The reason is that the workweek and payday are different. For example, a workweek of Sunday to Saturday might be paid on Wednesday (payday) of the following week. This is shown in the following partial calendar:

End of March/Beginning of April

S	M	T	W	T	F	S
27	28	29	30	31	1	2
3	4	5	6	7	8	9

The workweek ended April 2 was paid on April 6. The result is that the workdays from March 27 to March 31 are unpaid as of March 31, and a payroll adjusting entry is required to properly reflect the payroll expense for March.

In Tower's case, the unpaid workdays total $385. See entry (g) in Exhibit 12, which *increases* the payroll expense and *increases* the Accrued Payroll liability account.

Payroll Taxes. Federal and state governments levy payroll taxes on the employer, with payment due the following month or at some later date. The unpaid payroll taxes for Tower amount to $366. See entry (h) in Exhibit 12, which *increases* the payroll taxes expense and *increases* the Accrued Payroll Taxes liability account.

Computer Input of Adjusting Entries

The adjusting entries that have been manually entered on a general journal are input to the computer system. The Posting Module is again used to input the jour- nal entries. Exhibit 13 shows the computer printout after the computer has posted the journal entries. Notice that the change to net income is a reduction of $2,294.

At this point, the accountant could have the financial statements printed. However, it is more prudent to review another trial balance to ensure that all accounts requiring adjustment have indeed been adjusted. This additional trial balance also ensures that there are no problems involving posting to incorrect accounts during the adjustment phase and that all account balances are normal. Therefore, the accountant again uses the Trial Balance Module. This trial balance can also be called an *adjusted trial balance,* because the account balances shown are those reflecting the posting of adjusting entries. Exhibit 14 shows the resulting computerized adjusted trial balance and a net income of $16,332.64. Using audit trails, we can verify the mathematical accuracy of this amount as follows:

- The unadjusted trial balance (Exhibit 11) shows net income of $18,626.64.

Exhibit 13   Computerized Adjusting Entries

**Tower Restaurant
Adjusting Entries
Current P/E Date: 12/31/X8**

Journal Number: J1

		Debit	Credit
501	Cost of Food Sales	718.00	
121	Food Inventory		718.00
607	Employee Meals	35.00	
501	Cost of Food Sales		35.00
727	Operating Supplies	100.00	
131	Supplies Inventory		100.00
821	Insurance	200.00	
132	Prepaid Insurance		200.00
891	Depreciation	375.00	
157	Accumulated Depreciation		375.00
721	China, Glassware & Silver	150.00	
149	China, Glassware & Silver		150.00
601	Payroll	385.00	
231	Accrued Payroll		385.00
602	Payroll Taxes	366.00	
232	Accrued Payroll Taxes		366.00
	TOTALS	2,329.00	2,329.00

Effect on Net Income   (2,294.00)

- The adjustments entered in the computer system (Exhibit 13) show a net reduction to income of $2,294.

- Net income of $18,626.64 minus a net reduction to income of $2,294.00 does in fact equal $16,332.64, as shown on the adjusted trial balance (Exhibit 14).

Computation of Net Income or Loss

Though the computer is capable of computing net income or net loss without human intervention, all accomplished business students or professionals should be familiar with this easy procedure. Only the revenue and expense accounts are used to compute net income or loss. One procedure is as follows:

- Add sales and other credit accounts in the revenue classification.
- Add up the expenses.
- Subtract expenses from revenue.
- If the revenue is larger, the difference is income.

Exhibit 14   Computerized Adjusted Trial Balance

Tower Restaurant
Adjusted Trial Balance
Current P/E Date: 12/31/X8

Account

		Debit	Credit
101	Cash on Hand	1,000.00	
102	Cash—Regular Checking	18,223.23	
103	Cash—Payroll Checking	200.00	
112	Accounts Receivable	248.65	
121	Food Inventory	5,157.00	
131	Supplies Inventory	1,000.00	
132	Prepaid Insurance	2,200.00	
147	Furniture & Equipment	45,000.00	
149	China, Glassware & Silver	8,850.00	
157	Accumulated Depreciation		27,375.00
201	Accounts Payable		800.00
211	Sales Tax Payable		157.15
215	Employee Taxes Withheld		138.36
231	Accrued Payroll	385.00	
232	Accrued Payroll Taxes		366.00
301	Capital, Ann Dancer		74,324.73
302	Withdrawals	38,000.00	
401	Food Sales		165,209.94
501	Cost of Food Sales	57,841.75	
601	Payroll	50,159.87	
602	Payroll Taxes	5,154.75	
605	Employee Benefits	2,164.18	
607	Employee Meals	2,910.00	
712	Utilities	3,345.31	
721	China, Glassware & Silver	1,800.00	
727	Operating Supplies	3,008.11	
751	Telephone	915.44	
752	Office Supplies	923.14	
753	Credit Card Fees	1,868.75	
754	Cash Short or Over	137.66	
764	Repairs & Maintenance	2,489.34	
801	Rent	9,600.00	
821	Insurance	2,059.00	
891	Depreciation	4,500.00	
	Total	268,756.18	268,756.18

Net income   16,332.64

To apply this procedure to Exhibit 14, total the revenue accounts (account 401) and then calculate the total of the expense accounts (accounts 501–891). The results are as follows:

Revenue total	$165,209.94
Expenses total	148,877.30
Net income	$ 16,332.64

Here is another method. The normal balance of sales is a credit, and expenses have a normal debit balance. The *excess of credits indicates net income*. In Exhibit 14, use accounts 401–891, subtract credits and add debits, and arrive at a credit of $16,332.64, indicating net income.

Proprietorship Net Income

The equity accounts of a proprietorship are Capital and Withdrawals. The net income from operations of the business increases owner's capital; a net loss decreases owner's capital. The owner's withdrawals are not necessarily related to net income. Generally, withdrawals—a reduction of owner's capital—are limited to cash or other assets on hand.

Corporation Net Income

The net income of a corporation belongs to the corporation and cannot be with-drawn unless the board of directors declares a dividend. The equity accounts of a corporation are related to stock issued, paid-in capital, and retained earnings. A Dividends Declared account is not necessary because the declaration of dividends can be treated as a direct reduction of Retained Earnings. The net income from operations is an increase to Retained Earnings.

Computerized Financial Statements

After reviewing the adjusted trial balance, the accountant concludes that all adjustments have been entered and the general ledger contains reliable and up-to-date financial information. Without further clerical effort, the Financial Statements Module is used to print the financial statements. Tower has elected to show only rounded dollar amounts in the financial statements. The three major financial statements are shown in Exhibits 15 through 17.

The statement of owner's equity is not required because the changes to equity are shown in the equity section of the balance sheet.

Computerized General Ledger

Printing the general ledger is time-consuming because of its volume. In a computerized system, the general ledger does not have to be printed until after the financial statements are completed, owing to the inquiry capabilities of the software. If an account requires analysis, the General Ledger Module can be used to display one account or a series of accounts on the computer screen or as printer output.

All computer software packages demand some compromise. In this case, the popular three-column account format is not available. Instead, the beginning and

Exhibit 15 Computerized Income Statement

Tower Restaurant
Income Statement
For the Period Ended December 31, 20X8

REVENUE	
Sales	$ 165,210
COST OF SALES	
Cost of Food Sales	57,842
GROSS PROFIT (LOSS)	107,368
OPERATING EXPENSES	
Payroll & Related	
Payroll	50,160
Payroll Taxes	5,155
Employee Benefits	2,164
Employee Meals	2,910
Total Payroll & Related	60,389
Other Operating Expenses	
Utilities	3,345
China, Glassware & Silver	1,800
Operating Supplies	3,008
Telephone	915
Office Supplies	923
Credit Card Fees	1,869
Cash Short or Over	138
Repairs & Maintenance	2,489
Total Operating Expenses	14,487
Fixed Expenses	
Rent	9,600
Insurance	2,059
Depreciation	4,500
Total Fixed Expenses	16,159
Total Expenses	91,035
Net Income (Loss)	$ 16,333

ending balances are shown in the right-most column; to the left of this column are the posting entries. Credits are shown in parentheses and debits are unsigned. The General Ledger Module is used to print the entire general ledger. Exhibit 18 shows a sampling of general ledger accounts; the complete general ledger for Tower Restaurant is not illustrated due to space limitations. Note that an ending account balance is indicated by a star (*). Each general ledger account ending balance is identical to the balance shown in the adjusted trial balance and in the financial statements.

Exhibit 16 Computerized Balance Sheet

Tower Restaurant
Balance Sheet
December 31, 20X8

ASSETS

CURRENT ASSETS	
Cash	$ 19,423
Accounts Receivable	249
Food Inventory	5,157
Supplies Inventory	1,000
Prepaid Insurance	2,200
TOTAL CURRENT ASSETS	28,029
PROPERTY and EQUIPMENT	
Furniture and Fixtures	45,000
Accumulated Depreciation	(27,375)
China, Glassware & Silver	8,850
TOTAL PROPERTY and EQUIPMENT	26,475
TOTAL ASSETS	$ 54,504

LIABILITIES & OWNER'S EQUITY

CURRENT LIABILITIES	
Accounts Payable	$ 800
Sales Tax Payable	157
Employee Taxes Withheld	138
Accrued Payroll	385
Accrued Payroll Taxes	366
TOTAL CURRENT LIABILITIES	1,846
TOTAL LIABILITIES	1,846
OWNER'S EQUITY	
Capital, Ann Dancer	74,325
Withdrawals, Ann Dancer	(38,000)
Net Income	16,333
TOTAL OWNER'S EQUITY	52,658
TOTAL LIABILITIES & OWNER'S EQUITY	$ 54,504

Reversing Entries

After the financial statements and general ledger have been printed, it is often helpful to prepare reversing entries (an optional bookkeeping procedure) before the start of the next accounting period. A reversing entry is the exact opposite of an adjusting entry. The accountant must determine which adjusting entries posted in the period just ended should be reversed. Reversing entries are usually dated as of

Exhibit 17   Computerized Statement of Cash Flows

Tower Restaurant	
Statement of Cash Flows	
For the Period Ended December 31, 20X8	
Cash Flows from Operating Activities:	
Cash provided from operations	$ 22,933
Cash Flows from Investing Activities:	
Cash purchase of equipment	(10,000)
Cash used by investing activities	(10,000)
Cash Flows from Financing Activities	0
Increase (decrease) in cash for the year	12,933
Cash at the beginning of the year	6,490
Cash at the end of the year	$ 19,423

the first day of the next accounting period. Appendix B of this chapter presents an in-depth description and demonstration of reversing entries.

Computerized Year-End Processing

In older manual systems, the year-just-ended accounting activities generally required considerable time and effort. **Closing entries** were manually prepared and posted, a post-closing trial balance was manually prepared, and the ending balances for all balance sheet accounts had to be transferred to the new general ledger for the next business year. These manual procedures also were prone to errors. While these errors were detected, even more clerical effort was required to correct them and review the data again.

Automatic Closing Entries

At the end of a business year, all the income statement accounts and withdrawals (and dividends declared, if any) must be set to zero with closing entries, to avoid bringing these balances forward to the next year. The balance sheet account balances are brought forward because they represent beginning balances for the new business year. The technicalities of closing entries are no longer a task in a computerized system. The Year-End Module automatically performs these tasks without a need for manual closing entries.

In addition to performing the closing process tasks, the Year-End Module automatically moves the account balances to year-1 past data, making it possible for comparative reports in the following year. At the option of the user, the previous year-1 past data can be shifted to year-2 past data.

Post-Closing Trial Balance

A post-closing trial balance shows only the balance sheet accounts, since the income statement accounts have been set to zero. The Trial Balance Module is

Exhibit 18 Computerized General Ledger

Tower Restaurant
General Ledger
December 31, 20X8

101	Cash on Hand			1,000.00 *
102	Cash – Regular Checking			25,792.16
	12/31/X8	CP	(10,262.92)	
	12/31/X8	S	2,693.99	
				18,223.23 *
103	Cash – Payroll Checking			200.00
	12/31/X8	CP	730.35	
	12/31/X8	PR	(730.35)	
				200.00 *
112	Accounts Receivable			185.00
	12/31/X8	S	(185.00)	
	12/31/X8	S	248.65	
				248.65 *
121	Food Inventory			4,875.00
	12/31/X8	CP	800.00	
	12/31/X8	AP	200.00	
	12/31/X8	J1	(718.00)	5,157.00 *
131	Supplies Inventory			1,100.00
	12/31/X8	J1	(100.00)	
				1,000.00 *
201	Accounts Payable			(4,600.00)
	12/31/X8	CP	4,600.00	
	12/31/X8	AP	800.00	(800.00)*
401	Food Sales			(162,590.75)
	12/31/X8	S	(2,619.19)	
				(165,209.94)*

used to print a post-closing trial balance. The post-closing trial balance is an audit trail verifying that the year-end process was properly performed.

Exhibit 19 shows a computerized post-closing trial balance. Notice that the capital account has been updated for the withdrawals and net income of the business and is now $52,657.37. This amount reconciles with the equity total of $52,658 shown on the balance sheet (except for a $1 variance due to rounding in the financial statements).

The post-closing trial balance signifies the end of the accounting cycle for the business year just ended; the transfer of balance sheet amounts to the new ledger initiates the accounting cycle for the new business year.

Exhibit 19   Computerized Post-Closing Trial Balance

Tower Restaurant Post-Closing Trial Balance December 31, 20X8		
Account	**Debit**	**Credit**
101 Cash on Hand	1,000.00	
102 Cash – Regular Checking	18,223.23	
103 Cash – Payroll Checking	200.00	
112 Accounts Receivable	248.65	
121 Food Inventory	5,157.00	
131 Supplies Inventory	1,000.00	
132 Prepaid Insurance	2,200.00	
147 Furniture & Equipment	45,000.00	
149 China, Glassware & Silver	8,850.00	
157 Accumulated Depreciation		27,375.00
201 Accounts Payable		800.00
211 Sales Tax Payable		157.15
215 Employee Taxes Withheld		138.36
231 Accrued Payroll		385.00
232 Accrued Payroll Taxes		366.00
301 Capital, Ann Dancer		52,657.37
302 Withdrawals		0.00
Total	81,878.88	81,878.88

Key Terms

accounting cycle—The sequence of accounting procedures during an accounting period. It is a continuing process of recording and reporting financial information.

accrual basis accounting—An accounting method in which all revenue and expenses are recorded in the period in which they occur. This requires adjustments be made before financial statements are prepared (to comply with matching principle).

adjusting entries—Entries that bring the general ledger up to date to comply with the revenue recognition and matching principles.

cash basis accounting—An accounting method in which revenue is recorded only when cash is received and expenses are recorded only when paid. It is not in compliance with GAAP.

closing entries—Entries that set the revenue, expense, withdrawals, and dividends declared accounts to zero at the end of the business year.

correcting entries—Entries that fix errors in the general ledger. They are not adjusting entries.

working trial balance—A preliminary trial balance listing the accounts with their unadjusted balances. The accountant uses this trial balance to determine and compute adjustments. Also called an *unadjusted trial balance*.

Review Questions

1. What is an accounting cycle?

2. What are cash basis accounting and accrual basis accounting?

3. What is the posting procedure for special journals?

4. What is a working trial balance? What is its purpose?

5. What is the purpose of adjusting entries and correcting entries?

6. What are some typical adjustment areas any hospitality business might have at month end?

7. Why does a business using the perpetual inventory system need to adjust the Cost of Food Sales account after storeroom issues are recorded?

8. Why does any business have an unpaid payroll on the same day that payroll checks are given to its employees?

9. What does the computerized year-end process accomplish?

10. What does the post-closing trial balance signify?

Internet Sites

For more information, visit the following Internet sites. Remember that Internet addresses can change without notice. If the site is no longer there, you can use a search engine to look for additional sites.

Accounting Cycle
www.netmba.com/accounting/fin/
    process/

Accrual Basis Accounting
www.wisegeek.com/what-is-accrual-
    basis-accounting.htm

Adjusting Entries
www.netmba.com/accounting/fin/
    process/adjusting/

Closing Entries and Post-Closing Trial Balance
www.quickmba.com/accounting/fin/
    closing-entries/

Closing Entries
www.toolkit.com/small_business_
    guide/sbg.aspx?nid=P06_1580
www.netmba.com/accounting/fin/
    process/closing/

Reversing Entries
www.netmba.com/accounting/fin/
    process/reversing/

Royal Canada Accounting—Accounting Cycle
www2.mtroyal.ab.ca/~wirvine/
    webcoursesept6/accountingcycle.html

Problems

Problem 1

1. A small hotel is designing its chart of accounts for conversion to a computerized software package. The package allows the use of a three-digit identification system as follows:

Assets   1xx
      Current   11x
      Property & Equipment   15x
Liabilities 2xx
      Current   22x
      Long-term   25x
Equity   3xx
      Capital   31x
      Withdrawals   39x
Revenue   4xx
      Room Sales   41x
Expense   5xx
      Payroll   51x
      Payroll Taxes   51x
      Advertising   52x
      Commissions   53x
      Telephone   54x

Specify the first two digits of the three-digit account number for the following:

_____	Cash	_____	Wages Expense
_____	Owner's Capital	_____	Building
_____	Accounts Receivable	_____	Accumulated Depreciation
_____	Accounts Payable	_____	Room Sales
_____	Land	_____	Mortgage Payable
_____	Sales Tax Payable	_____	Supplies Inventory

Problem 2

Rearrange the steps below into the proper sequence for converting from a manual accounting system to a computerized accounting system.

    a. Print financial statements.
    b. Post the current month's activity.
    c. Set up a chart of accounts.
    d. Enter starting balances.
    e. Request a trial balance.

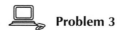
Problem 3

Computer Assignment: The following problem for Roman II Restaurant can be performed on any computerized general ledger.

Requirements:

1. Convert the manual general ledger to a computerized general ledger.
2. Process the current month's journals.
3. Print a trial balance.
4. Process the adjusting entries.
5. Print a trial balance.
6. Print the financial statements.
7. Print the general ledger.

Chart of Accounts and Balances as of August 31, 20X7:

No.	Dr	Cr
101 Cash on Hand	1,500.00	
102 Cash—Regular Checking	20,201.16	
103 Cash—Payroll Checking	400.00	
112 Accounts Receivable	250.00	
121 Food Inventory	5,100.00	
131 Supplies Inventory	1,200.00	
132 Prepaid Insurance	1,000.00	
147 Furniture & Equipment	39,000.00	
149 China, Glassware, & Silver	7,500.00	
157 Accumulated Depreciation		22,000.00
201 Accounts Payable		5,100.00
211 Sales Tax Payable		1,418.29
215 Employee Taxes Withheld		419.20
231 Accrued Payroll		1,200.00
232 Accrued Payroll Taxes		700.00
301 Capital, Ann Dancer		56,134.27
302 Withdrawals	20,000.00	
401 Food Sales		108,393.84
501 Cost of Food Sales	38,296.50	
601 Payroll	32,767.43	
602 Payroll Taxes	3,208.63	
605 Employee Benefits	1,450.00	
607 Employee Meals	1,926.00	
712 Utilities	2,073.65	
721 China, Glassware, & Silver	1,105.00	
727 Operating Supplies	1,942.33	
751 Telephone	570.17	
752 Office Supplies	618.41	
753 Credit Card Fees	1,252.56	
754 Cash Short or Over	91.79	
764 Repairs & Maintenance	1,666.97	
801 Rent	8,000.00	
821 Insurance	1,245.00	
891 Depreciation	3,000.00	
Total	195,365.60	195,365.60

The journals for the month of September 20X7 are as follows:

Roman II Restaurant
SALES & CASH RECEIPTS JOURNAL (S)
September 20X7

Date	Food Sales cr 401	Sales Tax Payable cr 211	Customer Collections cr 112	Cash to Bank dr 102	Customer Charges dr 112	Cash Short (Over) dr (cr) 754	Account Title	Acct. No.	Amount dr
TOTAL	14 780 00	886 80	500 00	15 228 82	700 00	2 98			235 00
							Recap of Sundry Items:		
							Cost of Food Sales	501	120 00
							Repairs & Maintenance	761	75 00
							Operating Supplies	727	40 00
							Total Sundry Items		235 00

Roman II Restaurant
CASH PAYMENTS JOURNAL (CP)
September 20X7

Date	Paid To	Check Number	Cash— Checking cr 102	Food Inventory dr 121	Accounts Payable dr 201	Account Title	Acct. No.	Amount dr
	TOTAL		11 057 62	75 00	4 850 25			6 132 37
						Recap of Sundry Items:		
						Cash-Payroll Checking	103	3 630 33
						Sales Tax Payable	211	1 418 29
						Telephone	751	83 75
						Rent	801	1 000 00
						Total Sundry Items		6 132 37

Roman II Restaurant
ACCOUNTS PAYABLE JOURNAL (AP)
September 20X7

Date	Vendor	Accounts Payable cr 201	Food Inventory dr 121	Supplies Inventory dr 131	Utilities dr 712	Account Title	Acct. No.	Amount dr
	TOTAL	5 687 10	4 950 86	415 12	321 12			-

		1	2	3	4	5
			Roman II Restaurant			
			PAYROLL REGISTER (PR)			
			September 20X7			
Paid To		Check No.	Gross Wages dr 601	FICA cr 215	FIT cr 215	Net Pay cr 103
TOTAL			4 446 01	395 68	420 00	3 630 33

The adjusting journal entries for September 30, 20X7, are:

Cost of Food Sold	4,200.00	
Food Inventory		4,200.00
Employee Meals	200.00	
Cost of Food Sold		200.00
Operating Supplies	230.00	
Supplies Inventory		230.00
Insurance	250.00	
Prepaid Insurance		250.00
Depreciation	400.00	
Accumulated Depreciation		400.00
China, Glassware, & Silver (expense)	120.00	
China, Glassware, & Silver		120.00

Problem 4

A company's financial statements show the following sales:

Month of January	$100,000
Two months ended February	180,000
Three months ended March	320,000

What is the sales amount for the month of February?

Problem 5

On July 1, a one-year fire insurance policy was purchased at a cost of $6,000. What is the insurance expense for the month of July?

Problem 6

On July 31, the bookkeeping account Supplies Inventory shows a debit balance of $1,000. A physical inventory taken on that date indicates that $800 of supplies are on hand. What amount of supplies was used in July?

Problem 7

The income statement section of a worksheet shows the following results:

Total debits:	$ 65,000
Total credits:	$ 72,000

Specify whether the company has a net income or loss for the period, and determine the amount.

Problem 8

The income statement section of a worksheet shows the following results:

Total debits:	$ 84,000
Total credits:	$ 78,000

Specify whether the company has a net income or loss for the period, and determine the amount.

Problem 9

A proprietorship shows the following results on its worksheet:

Capital, beginning of year	$50,000
Withdrawals for the year	30,000
Net income for the year	20,000

What will be the new balance in the Capital account after the closing entries have been posted?

Problem 10

Supplement to Manual Worksheet in Chapter Appendix A.

Prepare a complete worksheet from the following information:

	General Ledger		Adjustments	
	Dr	Cr	Dr	Cr
Cash	10,000			
Accounts Receivable	2,000			
Supplies Inventory	1,500			(a) 600
Prepaid Insurance	3,200			(b) 1,500
Equipment	4,000			
Accumulated Depreciation		1,600		(c) 800
Accounts Payable		3,200		
Capital		11,500		
Withdrawals	40,000			
Sales		63,000		
Rent	12,000			
Telephone	2,200			
Advertising	4,400			
Supplies			(a) 600	
Insurance			(b) 1,500	
Depreciation			(c) 800	
Total	79,300	79,300	2,900	2,900

Ethics Case

Jessica Taylor is the director of computer services for the Wallace Corporation. The Wallace Corporation needs to purchase a new computer, so Jessica has been researching the prices and capabilities of various computer models.

After Jessica finishes comparing the different models and prices, her research shows that her final choice is between two different computers; one is offered for sale by the Sterling Computer Company and the other by the Ultra Computer Company. The capabilities of these computers are identical.

The Sterling Company's computer is more expensive than the Ultra Company's computer. However, the Ultra computer is not as mechanically reliable as the Sterling model.

After considering both models, Jessica orders the Sterling computer. The management of the Wallace Corporation is not aware that the salesperson for the Sterling Computer Company is Jessica's brother-in-law.

1. Is Jessica's decision or behavior unethical?

2. What should Jessica do under these circumstances?

Chapter Appendix A: Preparing the Manual Worksheet

A *worksheet* is a multi-column form used as an accounting tool to centralize the trial balance, adjustments, and other data necessary to produce financial statements. Exhibit A-1 illustrates the following five sections of the worksheet:

- Trial Balance
- Adjustments
- Adjusted Trial Balance
- Income Statement
- Balance Sheet

Exhibit A-1   Worksheet Sections and Sources of Data

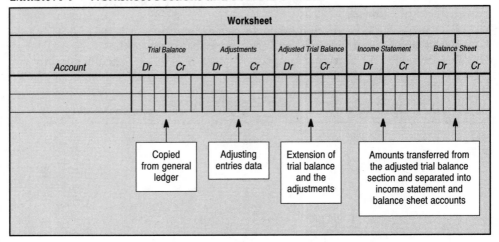

Each section is divided into debit and credit columns. The progression of a worksheet from start to completion for the Tower Restaurant is used as a demonstration. The following are the steps in completing this worksheet:

- The *Trial Balance* section is merely a copy function, copying the accounts and balances from the general ledger. This copy job is shown in Exhibit A-2. Notice the equality of debits and credits of the footings for this section.

- The *Adjustments* section requires a study of the accounts; the entries are those determined by the accountant. These are provided for you and shown in Exhibit A-3. Notice the equality of debits and credits of the footings for this section.

- The *Adjusted Trial Balance* section is the result of a simple math function—adding the debits and subtracting the credits from the Trial Balance section and the Adjustments section. The result is shown in Exhibit A-4. Notice the equality of debits and credits of the footings for this section.

- The *Income Statement* section is the result of examining the Adjusted Trial Balance section and plainly transferring the amounts from the revenue and expense accounts. The result is shown in Exhibit A-5.

  Note that there is no equality of debits and credits in the usual footings. The reason is that only the revenue and expense accounts have been transferred. It is in this section that the net income (or loss) is computed. Notice also that the difference between the footings is a credit of $16,332.64 (indicating net income). A debit is entered in the Income Statement section and a credit is entered in the Balance Sheet section. This is because net income increases the capital account, and a credit is necessary to perform an increase to capital. After the computation of net income, notice that there now is equality of debits and credits of the footings for this section.

- The *Balance Sheet* section is the result of examining the Adjusted Trial Balance section and plainly transferring the amounts from the assets, liabilities, and equity accounts. The result is shown in Exhibit A-5.

  Notice that the preliminary footings do not have equality; however, the entry of net income brings equality to this section.

  The financial statements can now be prepared from the data in the Income Statement section and Balance Sheet section. Trace the amounts from the Income Statement section and Balance Sheet section, respectively, to Exhibit A-6 (Income Statement), Exhibit A-7 (Statement of Owner's Equity), and Exhibit A-8 (Balance Sheet) to complete this demonstration.

Exhibit A-2   Tower Restaurant—Trial Balance on a Worksheet

Tower Restaurant
Worksheet
December 31, 20X8

		1 Trial Balance Dr	2 Trial Balance Cr	3 Adjustments Dr	4 Adjustments Cr	5 Adjusted Trial Balance Dr	6 Adjusted Trial Balance Cr	7 Income Statement Dr	8 Income Statement Cr	9 Balance Sheet Dr	10 Balance Sheet Cr
101	Cash on Hand	1 000 00									
102	Cash—Regular Checking	18 223 23									
103	Cash—Payroll Checking	200 00									
112	Accounts Receivable	248 65									
121	Food Inventory	5 875 00									
131	Supplies Inventory	1 100 00									
132	Prepaid Insurance	2 400 00									
147	Furniture & Equipment	45 000 00									
149	China, Glassware & Silver	9 000 00									
157	Acc. Depreciation—F&E		27 000 00								
201	Accounts Payable		800 00								
211	Sales Tax Payable		157 15								
215	Employee Taxes Withheld		138 36								
231	Accrued Payroll										
232	Accrued Payroll Taxes										
301	Capital, Ann Dancer		74 324 73								
302	Withdrawals, Ann Dancer	38 000 00									
401	Food Sales		165 209 94								
501	Cost of Food Sales	57 158 75									
601	Payroll	49 774 87									
602	Payroll Taxes	4 788 75									
605	Employee Benefits	2 164 18									
607	Employee Meals	2 875 00									
712	Utilities	3 345 31									
721	China, Glassware & Silver	1 650 00									
727	Operating Supplies	2 908 11									
751	Telephone	915 44									
752	Office Supplies	923 14									
753	Credit Card Fees	1 868 75									
754	Cash Short or Over	137 66									
761	Repairs & Maintenance	2 489 34									
801	Rent	9 600 00									
821	Insurance	1 859 00									
891	Depreciation	4 125 00									
	TOTAL	267 630 18	267 630 18								

Exhibit A-3 Tower Restaurant—Worksheet with Adjustments

Tower Restaurant
Worksheet
December 31, 20X8

	Account	1 Trial Balance Dr	2 Trial Balance Cr	3 Adjustments Dr	4 Adjustments Cr	5 Adj. Trial Balance Dr	6 Adj. Trial Balance Cr	7 Income Statement Dr	8 Income Statement Cr	9 Balance Sheet Dr	10 Balance Sheet Cr
101	Cash on Hand	1 000 00									
102	Cash—Regular Checking	18 223 23									
103	Cash—Payroll Checking	200 00									
112	Accounts Receivable	248 65									
121	Food Inventory	5 875 00			(a) 718 00						
131	Supplies Inventory	1 100 00			(c) 100 00						
132	Prepaid Insurance	2 400 00			(d) 200 00						
147	Furniture & Equipment	45 000 00									
149	China, Glassware & Silver	9 000 00			(f) 150 00						
157	Acc. Depreciation—F&E		27 000 00		(e) 375 00						
201	Accounts Payable		800 00								
211	Sales Tax Payable		157 15								
215	Employee Taxes Withheld		138 36								
231	Accrued Payroll				(g) 385 00						
232	Accrued Payroll Taxes				(h) 366 00						
301	Capital, Ann Dancer		74 324 73								
302	Withdrawals, Ann Dancer	38 000 00									
401	Food Sales		165 209 94								
501	Cost of Food Sales	57 158 75		(a) 718 00	(b) 35 00						
601	Payroll	49 774 87		(g) 385 00							
602	Payroll Taxes	4 788 75		(h) 366 00							
605	Employee Benefits	2 164 18									
607	Employee Meals	2 875 00		(b) 35 00							
712	Utilities	3 345 31									
721	China, Glassware & Silver	1 650 00		(f) 150 00							
727	Operating Supplies	2 908 11		(c) 100 00							
751	Telephone	915 44									
752	Office Supplies	923 14									
753	Credit Card Fees	1 868 75									
754	Cash Short or Over	137 66									
761	Repairs & Maintenance	2 489 34									
801	Rent	9 600 00									
821	Insurance	1 859 00		(d) 200 00							
891	Depreciation	4 125 00		(e) 375 00							
	TOTAL	267 630 18	267 630 18	2 329 00	2 329 00						

Exhibit A-4 Tower Restaurant—Worksheet to the Adjusted Trial Balance Sheet

Tower Restaurant
Worksheet
December 31, 20X8

	Account	1 Trial Balance Dr	2 Trial Balance Cr	3 Adjustments Dr	4 Adjustments Cr	5 Adjusted Trial Balance Dr	6 Adjusted Trial Balance Cr	7 Income Statement Dr	8 Income Statement Cr	9 Balance Sheet Dr	10 Balance Sheet Cr
101	Cash on Hand	1 000 00				1 000 00					
102	Cash—Regular Checking	18 223 23				18 223 23					
103	Cash—Payroll Checking	200 00				200 00					
112	Accounts Receivable	248 65				248 65					
121	Food Inventory	5 875 00			(a) 718 00	5 157 00					
131	Supplies Inventory	1 100 00			(c) 100 00	1 000 00					
132	Prepaid Insurance	2 400 00			(d) 200 00	2 200 00					
147	Furniture & Equipment	45 000 00				45 000 00					
149	China, Glassware & Silver	9 000 00			(f) 150 00	8 850 00					
157	Acc. Depreciation—F&E		27 000 00		(e) 375 00		27 375 00				
201	Accounts Payable		800 00				800 00				
211	Sales Tax Payable		157 15				157 15				
215	Employee Taxes Withheld		138 36				138 36				
231	Accrued Payroll				(g) 385 00		385 00				
232	Accrued Payroll Taxes				(h) 366 00		366 00				
301	Capital, Ann Dancer		74 324 73				74 324 73				
302	Withdrawals, Ann Dancer	38 000 00				38 000 00					
401	Food Sales		165 209 94				165 209 94				
501	Cost of Food Sales	57 158 75		(a) 718 00	(b) 35 00	57 841 75					
601	Payroll	49 774 87		(g) 385 00		50 159 87					
602	Payroll Taxes	4 788 75		(h) 366 00		5 154 75					
605	Employee Benefits	2 164 18				2 164 18					
607	Employee Meals	2 875 00		(b) 35 00		2 910 00					
712	Utilities	3 345 31				3 345 31					
721	China, Glassware & Silver	1 650 00		(f) 150 00		1 800 00					
727	Operating Supplies	2 908 11		(c) 100 00		3 008 11					
751	Telephone	915 44				915 44					
752	Office Supplies	923 14				923 14					
753	Credit Card Fees	1 868 75				1 868 75					
754	Cash Short or Over	137 66				137 66					
761	Repairs & Maintenance	2 489 34				2 489 34					
801	Rent	9 600 00				9 600 00					
821	Insurance	1 859 00		(d) 200 00		2 059 00					
891	Depreciation	4 125 00		(e) 375 00		4 500 00					
	TOTAL	267 630 18	267 630 18	2 329 00	2 329 00	268 756 18	268 756 18				

Exhibit A-5 Tower Restaurant—Completed Worksheet

Tower Restaurant
Worksheet
December 31, 20X8

	Account	1 Trial Balance Dr	2 Cr	3 Adjustments Dr	4 Cr	5 Adjusted Trial Balance Dr	6 Cr	7 Income Statement Dr	8 Cr	9 Balance Sheet Dr	10 Cr
101	Cash on Hand	1 000 00				1 000 00				1 000 00	
102	Cash—Regular Checking	18 223 23				18 223 23				18 223 23	
103	Cash—Payroll Checking	200 00				200 00				200 00	
112	Accounts Receivable	248 65				248 65				248 65	
121	Food Inventory	5 875 00			(a) 718 00	5 157 00				5 157 00	
131	Supplies Inventory	1 100 00			(c) 100 00	1 000 00				1 000 00	
132	Prepaid Insurance	2 400 00			(d) 200 00	2 200 00				2 200 00	
147	Furniture & Equipment	45 000 00				45 000 00				45 000 00	
149	China, Glassware & Silver	9 000 00			(f) 150 00	8 850 00				8 850 00	
157	Acc. Depreciation—F&E		27 000 00		(e) 375 00		27 375 00				27 375 00
201	Accounts Payable		800 00				800 00				800 00
211	Sales Tax Payable		157 15				157 15				157 15
215	Employee Taxes Withheld		138 36				138 36				138 36
231	Accrued Payroll				(g) 385 00		385 00				385 00
232	Accrued Payroll Taxes				(h) 366 00		366 00				366 00
301	Capital, Ann Dancer		74 324 73				74 324 73				74 324 73
302	Withdrawals, Ann Dancer	38 000 00				38 000 00				38 000 00	
401	Food Sales		165 209 94				165 209 94		165 209 94		
501	Cost of Food Sales	57 158 75		(a) 718 00	(b) 35 00	57 841 75		57 841 75			
601	Payroll	49 774 87		(g) 385 00		50 159 87		50 159 87			
602	Payroll Taxes	4 788 75		(h) 366 00		5 154 75		5 154 75			
605	Employee Benefits	2 164 18				2 164 18		2 164 18			
607	Employee Meals	2 875 00		(b) 35 00		2 910 00		2 910 00			
712	Utilities	3 345 31				3 345 31		3 345 31			
721	China, Glassware & Silver	1 650 00		(f) 150 00		1 800 00		1 800 00			
727	Operating Supplies	2 908 11		(c) 100 00		3 008 11		3 008 11			
751	Telephone	915 44				915 44		915 44			
752	Office Supplies	923 14				923 14		923 14			
753	Credit Card Fees	1 868 75				1 868 75		1 868 75			
754	Cash Short or Over	137 66				137 66		137 66			
761	Repairs & Maintenance	2 489 34				2 489 34		2 489 34			
801	Rent	9 600 00				9 600 00		9 600 00			
821	Insurance	1 859 00		(d) 200 00		2 059 00		2 059 00			
891	Depreciation	4 125 00		(e) 375 00		4 500 00		4 500 00			
	TOTAL	267 630 18	267 630 18	2 329 00	2 329 00	268 756 18	268 756 18	148 877 30	165 209 94	119 878 88	103 546 24
	Net Income							16 332 64			16 332 64
	TOTAL							165 209 94	165 209 94	119 878 88	119 878 88

Exhibit A-6 Tower Restaurant—Income Statement

Tower Restaurant
Income Statement
For the Year Ended December 31, 20X8

Food Sales	$165,209.94
Cost of Food Sales	57,841.75
Gross Profit	107,368.19
OPERATING EXPENSES:	
Payroll	50,159.87
Payroll Taxes	5,154.75
Employee Meals and Other Benefits	5,074.18
Utilities	3,345.31
China, Glassware & Silver	1,800.00
Operating Supplies	3,008.11
Telephone	915.44
Office Supplies	923.14
Credit Card Fees	1,868.75
Cash Short or Over	137.66
Repairs & Maintenance	2,489.34
Total Operating Expenses	74,876.55
INCOME BEFORE FIXED CHARGES	32,491.64
FIXED CHARGES:	
Rent	9,600.00
Insurance	2,059.00
Depreciation	4,500.00
Total Fixed Charges	16,159.00
NET INCOME	$ 16,332.64

Exhibit A-7   Tower Restaurant—Statement of Owner's Equity

Tower Restaurant
Statement of Owner's Equity
For the Year Ended December 31, 20X8

Ann Dancer, Capital, January 1, 20X8	$74,324.73
Net income for the year	16,332.64
Total	$90,657.37
Less: Withdrawals during the year	38,000.00
Ann Dancer, Capital, December 31, 20X8	$52,657.37

Exhibit A-8   Tower Restaurant—Balance Sheet

Tower Restaurant
Balance Sheet
December 31, 20X8

ASSETS

CURRENT ASSETS

Cash	$19,423.23	
Accounts Receivable	248.65	
Food Inventory	5,157.00	
Supplies Inventory	1,000.00	
Prepaid Insurance	2,200.00	
Total Current Assets		$ 28,028.88

PROPERTY & EQUIPMENT

	Cost	Accumulated Depreciation	
Furniture & Equipment	45,000.00	27,375.00	
China, Glassware, Silver	8,850.00		
Total	53,850.00	27,375.00	26,475.00

TOTAL ASSETS $ 54,503.88

LIABILITIES AND OWNER'S EQUITY

CURRENT LIABILITIES

Accounts Payable	$ 800.00	
Sales Tax Payable	157.15	
Employee Taxes Withheld	138.36	
Accrued Expenses	751.00	
Total Current Liabilities		$ 1,846.51

OWNER'S EQUITY

Capital, Ann Dancer	52,657.37

TOTAL LIABILITIES AND OWNER'S EQUITY $ 54,503.88

Chapter Appendix B: Reversing Entries

The use of reversing entries is an optional bookkeeping procedure. The purpose of reversing entries is to simplify the recording of routine transactions such as cash receipts and cash payments in the next period. Without reversing entries, it would be necessary to refer to prior adjusting entries to properly record routine transactions in the next accounting period.

A good case supporting the use of reversing entries is the need to make an adjusting entry to accrue unpaid salaries and wages. For example, earlier in this chapter an adjusting entry was made for a particular business for unpaid payroll as of August 31. Recall that the calendar for August was as follows:

S	M	T	W	T	F	S
	1	2	3	4	5	6
7	8	9	10	11	12	13
14	15	16	17	18	19	20
21	22	23	24	25	26	27
28	29	30	31			

On August 31, employees were paid for the workweek of August 21 to 27. The payroll days of August 28 to 31 will be included in the paycheck for the first Wednesday in September. Therefore, on August 31, there are four days of payroll expenses not recorded in the accounting month of August.

The adjusting entry on August 31 provided for $4/7$ of an average $7,000 payroll week, debiting Payroll Expense for $4,000 and crediting Accrued Payroll for $4,000.

After the journal entry was posted, the general ledger accounts appeared as follows:

Payroll Expense			Accrued Payroll		
8/31 AJE	4,000	(Wages 8/2–8/31)		8/31 AJE	4,000

Scenario When Not Using a Reversing Entry. The wages for the workweek of August 28 to September 3 will be paid on September 7.

	S	M	T	W	T	F	S
August	28	29	30	31			
September				1	2	3
	4	5	6	7			

Payday for previous week
of Sunday to Saturday
(8/28–9/3)

Assume the payroll for the workweek of 8/28 to 9/3 is $7,000. On September 7, this routine transaction is entered in the payroll journal; the gross wages (payroll expense) will be recorded as $7,000 for the first week of September, and the ledger will appear as follows:

Payroll Expense			Accrued Payroll	
8/31 AJE	4,000	(Wages 8/28–8/31)	8/31 AJE	4,000
9/7 PR	7,000	(Wages 8/28–9/3)		

Not all of the $7,000 payroll expense applies to September; this payroll contains $4,000 applicable to August. A reversing entry provides a convenient method to avoid these accounting complications.

Scenario When Using a Reversing Entry. In review, the ledger accounts initially appeared on August 31 as follows:

Payroll Expense			Accrued Payroll	
8/31 AJE	4,000	(Wages 8/28–8/31)	8/31 AJE	4,000

Reversing entries are prepared at the beginning of the new accounting month. As the name implies, a reversing entry is the exact reverse of an adjusting entry. It contains the same account titles and amounts as the adjusting entry, except that the debits and credits are the reverse of those in the adjusting entry.

The reversing entry on September 1 is as follows:

Sep. 1	*Accrued Payroll*		*4*	*000*	*00*			
	Payroll Expense					*4*	*000*	*00*

After posting the reversing entry on September 1, the ledger accounts are as follows:

Payroll Expense				Accrued Payroll			
8/31 AJE	4,000	9/1 RJE	4,000	9/1 RJE	4,000	8/31 AJE	4,000
						Balance	0

After the payroll journal is posted on September 7, the general ledger account Payroll Expense will appear as follows:

Payroll Expense			
8/31 AJE	4,000	9/1 RJE	4,000
9/7 PR	7,000		

The postings of 9/1 and 9/7 now accurately reflect the $3,000 wages expense for September.

Which Adjusting Entries May Require Reversing Entries? Not all adjusting entries require reversing entries. Generally, any adjusting entry that will affect future cash receipts or cash payments should have a reversing entry in the next period. Adjusting entries that affect inventories, supplies on hand, and other items that require adjustment at each month's end may not require a reversing entry, because the next month's adjusting entry will rectify the account balance.

The use of reversing entries depends on the accounting system and conventions of a particular business. Because of the unique nature of reversing entries and the fact that accounting policies vary from business to business, a universal rule is difficult to state. Generally, this set of guidelines may be followed:

1. Search the prior month's adjusting entries and locate any entries that credit a liability account or debit an asset account. These are the entries that increased either a liability or an asset account.

2. When such entries are located, it may be possible to determine whether a reversing entry is required.

Reversing Entries for the Tower Restaurant

The Tower Restaurant uses a simple method to determine those adjusting entries that will require reversing entries. Its policy is to use an "accrued" account to flag those adjustments that are to be reversed on the first day of the next accounting month.

Refer to Exhibit B-1 and search for each adjusting entry that used some type of "accrued" account in its entry. The two entries that meet this parameter are the Accrued Payroll and Accrued Payroll Taxes entries. Note that these adjusting entries also increased liability accounts. The reversing entries are dated January 1, 2009, and are as follows:

Jan. 1	Accrued Payroll			385	00		
	Payroll Expense					385	00
Jan. 1	Accrued Payroll Taxes			366	00		
	Payroll Taxes Expense					366	00

Exhibit B-1   Tower Restaurant—Journalized Adjusting Entries

Date 20X8	Description	Post. Ref.	Debit		Credit	
	JOURNAL				**Page J6**	
	(a)					
Dec. 31	Cost of Food Sales	501	718	00		
	Food Inventory	121			718	00
	Record storeroom issues to kitchen					
	(b)					
31	Employee Meals	607	35	00		
	Cost of Food Sales	501			35	00
	Record food used for free employee meals					
	(c)					
31	Operating Supplies	727	100	00		
	Supplies Inventory	131			100	00
	Adjust inventory account to physical					
	(d)					
31	Insurance	821	200	00		
	Prepaid Insurance	132			200	00
	Charge expired premium to expense					
	(e)					
31	Depreciation	891	375	00		
	Accumulated Depreciation—F & E	157			375	00
	Record $1/12$ annual depreciation					
	(f)					
31	China, Glassware & Silver (Expense)	721	150	00		
	China, Glassware & Silver (Asset)	149			150	00
	Record $1/12$ annual depreciation					
	(g)					
31	Payroll	601	385	00		
	Accrued Payroll	231			385	00
	Record unpaid wages as of 12/31/X8					
	(h)					
31	Payroll Taxes	602	366	00		
	Accrued Payroll Taxes	232			366	00
	Record unpaid employer's taxes as of 12/31/X8					

Chapter 9 Outline

Restaurant Income Statement
Significance of Restaurant Accounting
Food Sales Accounting
    Coupons
    Service Charges
Beverage Sales Accounting
    Cashiering Single Price, Sales Tax
        Included
Cost of Sales
    Fast-Food Restaurants
    Employee Meals and Officers' Checks
    Perpetual Inventory System
    Periodic Inventory System
Operating Expenses
    Salaries and Wages
    Employee Benefits
    Direct Operating Expenses
    Music and Entertainment
    Marketing Expenses
    Utility Services
    Repairs and Maintenance
    Occupancy Expenses
    Depreciation
    Administrative and General
    Other Income
Restaurant Balance Sheet
Chart of Accounts for Restaurants
Food and Beverage Ratio Analysis
    Food Cost Percentage
    Beverage Cost Percentage
Food Sales Statistics and Analysis
    Food Sales Analysis by Meal Period
    Food Sales Analysis by Dining Facility
    Average Food Check
    Average Food Sale per Seat
    Seat Turnover
Beverage Sales Statistics
    Beverage Sales by Meal Period
    Beverage/Food Sales Ratio
    Beverage Sales by Type
    Beverage Sales by Facility

Competencies

1. Describe the income statements and the accounting procedures for full-service and fast-food restaurants in accordance with the *Uniform System of Accounts for Restaurants.* (pp. 237–238)

2. Summarize the significance of restaurant accounting, and describe basic elements for food and beverage sales accounting. (pp. 238–242)

3. Describe the measurement of food and beverage costs and the various operating expenses. (pp. 242–250)

4. List sources of other income and describe accounting procedures for recording other income. (pp. 251–252)

5. Describe how a restaurant's balance sheet and chart of accounts may differ from those of other industries. (pp. 252–253)

6. Identify and explain the various food sales and beverage sales analysis statistics. (pp. 253–259)

Restaurant Accounting and Financial Analysis

RESTAURANT ACCOUNTING IS A BROAD TERM that encompasses a multitude of different restaurant operations: stand-alone restaurants, chain operations, in-plant operations, department store restaurants, and restaurants in hotels, clubs, hospitals, and other institutions.

Stand-alone commercial restaurants must absorb all expenses, including occupancy costs, depreciation, and interest. Restaurants in department stores, hotels, clubs, and hospitals have the benefit of other income-producing departments contributing to the support of their overhead and fixed expenses. Hospitals and other institutions often have accounting systems to comply with governmental regulations, while in-plant operations are often under contract and in many instances subsidized by their contractor.

These different facilities make it impossible to generalize about restaurant accounting. Therefore, this chapter concentrates on the commercial restaurant, which is an operation unto itself and not an ancillary department such as a restaurant in a hotel, hospital, or subsidized operation.

The accounting procedures and statements appearing in this chapter are those endorsed in the *Uniform System of Accounts for Restaurants (USAR)*,[1] the accounting standard adopted and recommended by the National Restaurant Association. This chapter addresses such questions as:

1. Which financial statement formats for full-service restaurants and fast-food restaurants are recommended by the *USAR*?

2. What sales and expense accounting procedures for full-service restaurants and fast-food restaurants are recommended by the *USAR*?

3. How are service charges and other income treated?

4. What are occupancy expenses?

5. What ratios and statistical analyses are useful in measuring the efficiency of food and beverage operations?

Restaurant Income Statement

The *USAR* provides financial statement formats for various restaurant operations. The major components of an income statement common to any restaurant are:

$$
\begin{aligned}
&\quad\ \text{Sales} \\
-&\quad\ \underline{\text{Cost of Sales}} \\
=&\quad\ \text{Gross Profit} \\
-&\quad\ \underline{\text{Operating Expenses}} \\
=&\quad\ \text{Operating Income} \\
-&\quad\ \underline{\text{Interest}} \\
=&\quad\ \text{Income Before Income Taxes} \\
-&\quad\ \underline{\text{Income Taxes}} \\
=&\quad\ \text{Net Income}
\end{aligned}
$$

An income statement is usually accompanied by numerous supporting schedules that itemize the various components of a single line item on the statement. For example, the line item *food sales* will have supporting schedules such as food sales by facility (outlet) and food sales by meal period. Similar supporting schedules are prepared for beverage sales. Other supporting schedules detail salaries and wages, employee benefits, and each expense appearing as a line item on the income statement. Several of these schedules are explained in the following paragraphs.

The distinction between full-service and limited-service restaurants is sometimes vague, because today's limited-service restaurants can have extensive menus. Instead, we will distinguish between full-service and fast-food operations.

Full-service restaurants sell food and beverages in an elegant or casual setting characterized by distinctive customer attention and table service that distinguishes them from fast-food operations. The income statement in Exhibit 1 depicts an income statement from the *USAR* for a full-service restaurant with food and beverage sales. Such statements can be adapted for a small restaurant, large restaurant, or chain operation.

Fast-food restaurants offer convenience, predictable quality, and expeditious food delivery. Fast food has become a part of the American lifestyle. A fast-food operation serves food quickly but with little or no customer service. Typically, the menu is on a display board and customers order from a cashier, pay for the order, progress in line, and receive their meals. The customer may order the meal to take out or elect to sit at a table. Exhibit 2 shows an income statement from the *USAR* for a fast-food restaurant serving food only. Notice the addition of the paper goods part of cost of sales for a fast-food restaurant. Paper goods are described in detail in the cost of sales section later in this chapter.

Significance of Restaurant Accounting

Building a successful restaurant business is more than just designing menus, preparing food, knowing wines, and using computer systems. What is the one most important element for success? The answer is: There is no one most important element; a business needs personnel, operating procedures, and accounting systems that produce results. All of these elements are interrelated, and all must work for the restaurant to be a success. The restaurant owner need not be an expert in all facets of the business, but he or she must possess enough knowledge to be a professional manager. Since this chapter is about accounting, it will concentrate on that

Exhibit 1   Income Statement: Full-Service Restaurant with Food and Beverage Sales

Sales:
Food $
Beverage
 Total Sales

Cost of Sales:
Food
Beverage
 Total Cost of Sales

Gross Profit

Operating Expenses:
Salaries and Wages
Employee Benefits
Direct Operating Expenses
Music and Entertainment
Marketing
Utility Services
Repairs and Maintenance
Occupancy
Depreciation
Administrative and General Expenses
Other Income
 Total Operating Expenses

Operating Income:
Interest Expense
Income Before Income Taxes
Income Taxes

Net Income $_____

issue. Good recordkeeping of sales and expenses is necessary for the profitable management of a restaurant. Inaccurate records make it impossible to measure the degree of a restaurant's profitability or take timely corrective action when needed.

Restaurant accounting is a specialized field; it is not the same as shoe store accounting or manufacturing accounting. Yes, the rules for debits and credits are the same. However, debits and credits do not make a management information system; they are merely a means of recording data. Before the data is recorded, a logical and meaningful chart of accounts is necessary. After the data is recorded in the bookkeeping accounts, financial statements can be produced. Analysis of the financial statements results in statistical evaluations that may point to areas

Exhibit 2   Income Statement: Fast-Food Restaurant Selling Food Only

Sales:
Food $

Cost of Sales:
Food
Paper Goods
   Total Cost of Sales

Gross Profit

Operating Expenses:
Salaries and Wages
Employee Benefits
Direct Operating Expenses
Marketing
Utility Services
Repairs and Maintenance
Occupancy
Depreciation
Administrative and General Expenses
Other Income
   Total Operating Expenses

Operating Income
Interest Expense
Income Before Income Taxes
Income Taxes

Net Income $ _____

needing further study and action. Ratios such as food cost percentage, labor cost percentage, average food check, and seat turnover are only a few of the statistical tools that are critical to proper restaurant management.

Some may say that a restaurant owner doesn't have to know anything about accounting; he or she can just hire an accountant. However, the accountant does not have a financial stake in the business and will not dedicate his or her full-time attention to the financial-management needs of the business. In any case, an owner *must* understand the basics of accounting and their application to successful management to maximize customer satisfaction and the restaurant's profitability. In the end, it's the owner's personal credit and money on the line, not the accountant's.

The balance sheet and the income statement are two very important financial statements for the restaurant owner or manager. The balance sheet shows the restaurant's financial condition, and the income statement summarizes the profitability of the restaurant's operations. These statements can be supplemented by many financial analyses.

Food Sales Accounting

Food sales include the sales of food, coffee, tea, milk, and fruit juices. Sales of soft drinks are included in food sales if there is no service of liquor, beer, and wine. Sales taxes are not part of food sales because the collection of these taxes is a liability until they are paid to the government.

If pastry or baked goods are sold at a counter, it might be advantageous to account for these sales separately. The same might be true of take-out sales of prepared foods which, if sufficiently large, may require a separate departmental statement. The separation of sales among food, beverage, and other noteworthy categories is important for the calculation of meaningful operating ratios and cost measurement.

Coupons

Coupons and other discount programs are used as promotions to increase business. The treatment of coupon sales must comply with any sales tax regulations in effect. One method is to register the sale at normal retail and enter the coupon amount as a reduction. This procedure keeps track of coupon usage and its promotional effectiveness. Coupon usage can be recorded to a contra-sales account such as Sales Discounts—Coupons.

Service Charges

Some hospitality operations are adopting a policy of adding a **service charge** to customers' checks in lieu of tips. Advantages of this policy include a standard gratuity for employees and elimination of the governmental requirement of tip recordkeeping. However, public acceptance of this policy is mixed. Management must consider the possibility that some waitstaff feel there no longer is a need to earn a tip, resulting in an impairment of customer service.

Service charges are not recorded to food sales; they are recorded as Other Income. Some operations distribute the entire amount of service charges collected to their employees, while others retain a small portion to cover such items as administrative costs or payment of bonuses. Regardless of the method of distributing service charges to employees, 100 percent of the amount collected is recorded to Other Income. When the service charge is distributed, Other Income is reduced.

Beverage Sales Accounting

Beverage sales include all alcoholic beverages and soft drinks. (Coffee, tea, milk, and fruit juices are food items.) Sales taxes are not part of beverage sales. Food sales and beverage sales must be recorded in separate bookkeeping accounts to provide management with meaningful sales and cost analyses. Some of the reasons for this separation are the following:

- The markup on liquor is considerably different from that on food.
- Inventory life is longer for liquor than for food.
- Selling liquor is not as labor-intensive as selling food.

Cashiering Single Price, Sales Tax Included

Some restaurants quote a single price for alcoholic beverages with the tax included. For example, a price of $5.30 includes the sales tax, and the amount is cashiered as $5.30. This practice requires special attention because the sale amount includes the sales tax. A simple method to restate the cashiered beverage amounts into sales and sales tax is:

$$\frac{\text{Amount Cashiered}}{100\% + \text{Sales Tax}\%} = \text{Amount of Sale Excluding Sales Tax}$$

For example, assume the $5.30 includes a six percent sales tax:

$$\frac{\text{Amount Cashiered}}{100\% + \text{Sales Tax}\%} = \frac{\$5.30}{106\%} \quad \$5.00 \text{ Amount of Sale}$$

Applying the six percent sales tax to the $5.00 sale yields a $.30 sales tax. The sale of $5.00 plus the sales tax of $.30 reconciles to the original $5.30 cashiered amount. This calculation is performed daily or at the end of the month.

Liquor laws vary by state and can be troublesome to interpret. While a state might allow cashiering drinks at a single price that includes the sales tax, a rate of higher than the stated tax rate (in this case six percent) might be imposed on the facility unless its drink prices are posted and show the selling price and sales tax amount separately.

Cost of Sales ───────────────────────────────────

The costs of sales for food and beverages are accounted for independently and represent the cost of food or beverage used to generate a customer sale. *Cost of food sales* can also be called *cost of food sold* or **net food cost**. *Cost of beverage sales* is also called *cost of beverage sold* or **net beverage cost**.

The cost of employee meals and officers' checks should not be included in the cost of sales amount. The computation of cost of sales depends on the type of inventory system used in the storeroom. Some restaurants use the periodic system for food and the perpetual system for beverages, especially when expensive wines are involved.

Fast-Food Restaurants

The procedure for computing food cost is identical for a full-service restaurant, limited-service restaurant, or fast-food restaurant. However, the food cost of sales for a fast-food restaurant has an additional cost. Unlike table service restaurants, fast-food restaurants package the meal and supply disposable meal utensils. These packaging materials are called paper goods (see Exhibit 2) and include items such as the following:

- Paper wrappers and napkins
- Paper and foam cups
- Take-out containers
- Plastic utensils and straws

Employee Meals and Officers' Checks

Various methods are used to calculate cost of employee meals. The most convenient is to use an estimated or standard cost based on the type of meal—breakfast, lunch, or dinner. Multiplying this standard cost by the number of meals served to employees results in the total cost of employee meals.

Certain employees, such as executives and department heads, may have dining room privileges, with their meals recorded *at menu prices* on **officers' checks.** These checks are not cashiered as a customer sale. An easy way to arrive at the cost of officers' meals is to use a standard food cost percentage. For example, if officers' checks total $2,000 at menu price for a month and the usual food cost is 30 percent, the cost of officers' meals is $600 ($2,000 × 30%).

Perpetual Inventory System

A perpetual inventory system has many advantages, such as inventory control and daily balances. In addition, its recordkeeping function automatically provides the cost of sales information. However, the recordkeeping can be expensive, even if a computerized system is used, because every receipt and issue requires clerical effort in the manual recordkeeping or the computer input process. Smaller operations may find the perpetual system too expensive, time-consuming, and inefficient for its production process.

The following example shows how cost of food sales is computed under a perpetual system:

Storeroom issues	$350,000
Add transfers from bar	400
Less transfers to bar	(100)
Cost of food used	$350,300
Less officers' checks	
($2,000 menu prices × 30% food cost)	(600)
Less employee meals	(200)
Cost of food sold to customers	$349,500

The procedure to compute cost of beverage sold is similar.

Periodic Inventory System

Storeroom inventory records are not maintained in a periodic inventory system; therefore, inventory control is inadequate. Its only advantage is simplicity and low cost. Because no inventory records are kept, it is necessary to take a month-end physical inventory to arrive at an accurate cost of sales. The month-end inventory for the current month becomes the beginning inventory for the next month. Information from the accounting department, such as purchases, is required to compute cost of sales.

The following is an example of how to compute cost of food sales under a periodic system:

Beginning inventory	$ 55,000
Add purchases	375,000

Add transfers from bar	400
Less transfers to bar	(100)
Less ending inventory	(80,000)
Cost of food used	$350,300
Less officers' checks	
($2,000 menu prices × 30% food cost)	(600)
Less employee meals	(200)
Cost of food sold to customers	$349,500

The procedure to compute cost of beverage sold is similar.

Operating Expenses

Operating expenses represent expenses directly related to the day-to-day opera-tions of the business and reflect operating policies and management efficiency. Operating expenses do not include cost of sales, interest expense, and income taxes. Other income is included in the operating expenses section as a contra item; it is subtracted to arrive at total operating expenses.

According to the *USAR*, operating expenses are the following:

- Salaries and wages
- Employee benefits
- Direct operating expenses
- Music and entertainment
- Marketing expenses
- Utility services
- Repairs and maintenance
- Occupancy expenses
- Depreciation
- Administrative and general expenses
- Other income

Salaries and Wages

The largest controllable expense is salaries and wages for management and staff. A proprietorship would not have a payroll expense for its owner because the Internal Revenue Service does not allow such a deduction. However, if the restaurant is a one-owner corporation, a payroll expense is allowed for its owner. The payroll line item on the income statement is supported by a supplementary schedule. Exhibit 3 shows an example of a salaries and wages schedule for a full-service restaurant; Exhibit 4 shows this schedule for a fast-food restaurant.

Employee Benefits

Employee benefits are payroll-related and represent another significant expense. Many employees are not aware that the employer pays significant payroll taxes

Exhibit 3   Salaries and Wages Schedule: Full-Service Restaurant

	Number of Employees	Regular Wages	Other Wages*
SERVICE			
Captains, hostesses		$	$
Waitstaff			
Buspersons			
Cashiers and checkers			
Total Service			
BEVERAGES			
Bartenders			
Bar cashiers			
Wine steward and wine room attendants			
Total Beverage			
PREPARATION			
Chef, head dietitian, kitchen manager			
Cooks and short order cooks			
Pantry, salads, vegetable cleaners			
Potwashers			
Steward and assistants			
Total Preparation			
SANITATION			
Dishwashers			
Cleaners			
Total Sanitation			
PURCHASING AND STORING			
Purchasing steward			
Receiving clerk			
Storeroom personnel			
Food controller			
Total Purchasing and Storing			
ADMINISTRATIVE			
Officers			
Manager			
Manager's staff			
Sales			
Accounting			
Personnel			
Data processing			
Security			
Total Administrative			
OTHER			
Engineers			
Maintenance			
Door attendants			
Parking lot attendants			
Total Other			
TOTAL SALARIES AND WAGES			

* Other wages include overtime, vacation, commissions, and bonuses.

Exhibit 4   Salaries and Wages Schedule: Fast-Food Restaurant

	Number of Employees	Regular Wages	Other Wages*
Service		$	$
Preparation			
Administrative and general			
Other			
Total Salaries and Wages			

* Other wages include overtime, vacation, commissions, and bonuses.

that will provide future benefits for them. The taxes withheld by the employer from the employees are not included in expense; the withholding of payroll taxes is treated as a liability and the funds are forwarded to the taxing agency. The payroll taxes imposed on the employer that provide future employee benefits are the following:

- Social Security taxes that will someday provide a retirement benefit and Medicare

- State and federal unemployment taxes that provide state benefits in the event of involuntary loss of employment

- State disability taxes that provide benefits for work absences due to sickness

The employer also pays workers' compensation insurance, which provides benefits due to job-related injuries. The Employee Benefits line item on the income statement is supported by a supplementary schedule. Exhibit 5 shows an example of an employee benefits schedule. The expense for employee meals could be included in the employee benefits schedule or shown as a single line item on the income statement, depending on its materiality.

Direct Operating Expenses

A **direct operating expense** is an expense directly involved in serving customers (other than payroll and payroll-related). The Direct Operating Expense line item on the income statement is supported by a supplementary schedule. The extent of the detail of this schedule is determined by management's need for such information. Exhibit 6 shows an example of a direct operating expenses schedule for a full-service restaurant; Exhibit 7 is an example of this schedule for a fast-food restaurant.

Many of the items listed under direct operating expenses are self-explanatory. However, a few need commentary. Part of the expense for *China, glassware, and silver* is the cost of their replacement and part is from depreciating the original asset purchase. *Paper supplies* for a full- or limited-service restaurant include items such as liners, napkins, plates, wrapping paper, soufflé cups, pastry bags, other kitchen papers, and twine. Paper supplies for a fast-food restaurant include

Exhibit 5   Employee Benefits Schedule

FEDERAL AND STATE PAYROLL TAXES
Social Security $ _____
Medicare
Federal unemployment
State unemployment
    Total Federal and State Payroll Taxes

SOCIAL INSURANCE
Workers' compensation
Pensions
Health and hospitalization
Group life
    Total Social Insurance

OTHER EMPLOYEE BENEFITS
Tuition reimbursement
Parties
Sports
Credit union
Awards and prizes
    Total Other

TOTAL EMPLOYEE BENEFITS $ _____

Exhibit 6   Direct Operating Expenses Schedule: Full-Service Restaurant

Uniforms $ _____
Laundry
Linen rental
Replacement of china, glassware, silver
Kitchen utensils
Paper supplies
Guest supplies
Bar supplies
Cleaning supplies
Menus
Dry cleaning
Contract cleaning
Flowers and decorations
Employee transportation
Parking lot rental
Licenses and permits
Other
Total Direct Operating Expenses $ _____

Exhibit 7   Direct Operating Expenses Schedule: Fast-Food Restaurant

Uniforms	$ _____
Utensils	
Supplies	
Contract cleaning	
Licenses and permits	
Miscellaneous	
Total Direct Operating Expenses	$ _____

similar items, except for those materials used to package the meal. As previously explained, these packaging items are a cost of food sold expense. *Guest supplies* are items furnished free to guests, such as matches, toothpicks, and other favors. *Contract cleaning* is for services such as janitorial services, window washing, and pest extermination.

Music and Entertainment

Music and entertainment expenses are costs associated with guest entertainment and include items such as the following:

- Fees for booking agents
- Fees for musicians and entertainers
- Meals served to musicians and entertainers
- Mechanical music
- Contracted wire service
- Records, sheet music, programs, and films

Marketing Expenses

Marketing's prime objective is to promote the restaurant's name, location, service, and ambiance through such activities as public relations, advertising, promotional programs, product research, and market research. Because a franchised name is readily noticeable by the public, franchise fees or royalties are charged to marketing. Exhibit 8 shows an example of a marketing expenses schedule for a full-service restaurant; Exhibit 9 is an example of this schedule for a fast-food restaurant.

Utility Services

Expenses associated with utility services—fuel, water, and removal of waste—are included in this line item. *USAR* recommends that electric bulbs and ice for consumption also be charged to utility services. However, some restaurant operators do not agree with this treatment of ice and prefer to treat ice expense as a direct operating expense.

Kitchen fuel is the fuel (gas, electric, charcoal, and other) used for cooking. Unless there is a separate meter in the kitchen, accounting for kitchen fuel might

Exhibit 8   Marketing Expenses Schedule: Full-Service Restaurant

SELLING AND PROMOTION $
    Solicitation travel
    Direct mail
    Promotional entertainment
    Postage
ADVERTISING
    Newspapers
    Magazines and trade journals
    Radio and TV
    Circulars and brochures
    Directories and guides
    Outdoor signs
PUBLIC RELATIONS AND PUBLICITY
    Civic and community projects
    Donations
    Sports team sponsorship
FEES AND COMMISSIONS
    Franchise fees/royalties
    Advertising agency fees
RESEARCH
    Research travel
    Research agency
    Product testing
Total Marketing Expense $ _____

Exhibit 9   Marketing Expenses Schedule: Fast-Food Restaurant

SELLING AND PROMOTION $
    Advertising
    Public relations and publicity
    Franchise fees/royalties
    Research
Total Marketing Expense $ _____

be impractical; furthermore, management might not wish to estimate this expense. Under these conditions, kitchen fuel is included in the Utility Services expense line item on the income statement.

Repairs and Maintenance

The repairs and maintenance expenses include any cost of material, service, or contracts associated with normal maintenance of equipment, buildings, and grounds. These expenses include items such as the following:

- Painting and decorating
- Repairs to furniture, equipment, buildings, and grounds
- Gardening
- Maintenance contracts

Occupancy Expenses

USAR includes the following as occupancy expenses:

- Rent
- Property insurance
- Property taxes

These expenses have fixed characteristics. Regardless of volume, or whether the restaurant is open or closed, these expenses are incurred and cannot be directly managed.

Rent is any payment for rentals of building, grounds, and equipment. Property insurance is property damage insurance on buildings and contents (liability insurance is an administrative and general expense). Property taxes include items such as real estate taxes, personal property taxes, sewer tax, and corporation renewal fees.

Depreciation

Depreciation and amortization are often lumped together and simply called depreciation because both involve allocating the cost of long-lived assets over their useful lives. *Depreciation* is the allocation of the cost of tangible long-lived assets over their useful lives; *amortization* is a similar expense except that it deals with intangible long-lived assets. Unlike other expenses, depreciation and amortization are expenses that never require a cash payment.

Administrative and General

The *Administrative and General* (often referred to as A&G) expenses represent office and management expenses, an overhead expense category not affiliated with directly serving the customer. A&G is charged for some items one would perhaps not expect to find under this heading, such as *bad debts, cash shortages,* and *credit card fees.* The reasons for charging A&G for these operational costs are as follows:

- A&G is accountable for the timely collection of accounts receivable and the prevention of bad debts.

- A&G is responsible for providing internal control and equipment and procedures to eliminate cash shortages.

- Credit card fees are an administrative policy and cannot be considered advertising or marketing.

The A&G line item on the income statement is supported by a supplementary schedule. Exhibit 10 shows an A&G expenses schedule for a full-service restaurant. Exhibit 11 shows this schedule for a fast-food restaurant.

Exhibit 10   Administrative and General Expenses: Full-Service Restaurant

Office stationery $

Postage (except chargeable to advertising department)

Dues and subscriptions

Travel (except chargeable to advertising department)

Insurance—general

Credit card fees

Bad debts expense

Cash shortages

Legal and professional fees

Telephone (except chargeable to advertising department)

Data processing costs

Management fees from central office

Outside management fees

Total Administrative and General Expenses $ _____

Exhibit 11   Administrative and General Expenses: Fast-Food Restaurant

Insurance—general $

Cash shortages

Legal and professional fees

Help wanted ads

Telephone (except chargeable to advertising department)

Data processing costs

Miscellaneous

Total Administrative and General Expenses $ _____

Other Income

The type of activities falling under *Other Income* (also called *Other Revenue*) depends on the nature of ancillary sales in a restaurant operation. Today's restaurants are increasingly creative in their efforts to expand their operations to supplement revenue from food and beverage operations. All items of Other Income should be separately listed in a supplementary schedule attached to the financial statements. The total of this schedule appears as a single line item on the income statement. Other Income includes such items as the following:

- Service charges (net of paid-outs to waitstaff)
- Cover and minimum charges
- Banquet room rentals
- Rental of display cases

- Concession rentals (coat room, parking)
- Vending machine commissions
- Telephone commissions
- Salvage and waste sales
- Menu advertising
- Cash discounts

Cash discounts may be treated as a reduction of the cost of an item and not as other income. This net cost method is more practical for the small restaurant because only one entry is made: the net amount invoiced for the item.

In large operations, grease sales could be credited to cost of food sales instead of salvage and waste sales; however, the removal of what was once salable waste has now changed to an expense in many communities.

Restaurant Balance Sheet

An income statement varies by type of industry because of the differences in sales (products and services) and the kinds of expenses incurred. However, the balance sheet is fairly standard across the industries. Every business has assets, liabilities, and equity. The accounts in these three classifications are also common to any industry. A balance sheet for a restaurant differs from other industries in the following areas:

- China, glassware, silver, linen, and uniforms
- Preopening expenses
- Cost of bar license
- Franchise contract

China, Glassware, Silver, Linen, and Uniforms. The initial cost of purchasing sets of china, glassware, silver, linen, and uniforms is charged to an asset and depreciated. The net asset portion appears in the property and equipment section of the balance sheet. Replacements are charged directly to expense.

Preopening Expenses. Costs incurred before opening a restaurant, such as employee training and grand opening advertising, can be charged directly to expense or set up as a temporary asset and amortized over a 12-month period. A preopening expense asset appears in the Other Assets section of the balance sheet.

Cost of Bar License. In some states, the quantity or type of liquor licenses is restricted and they are available only by purchase on the open market, usually at considerable cost. A purchased liquor license is an asset appearing in the Other Assets section of the balance sheet.

Franchise Contract. This line item represents a deposit on a franchise contract or purchase of a franchise right. The major franchise contract or right appears in the Other Assets section of the balance sheet.

Chart of Accounts for Restaurants

USAR provides a numbering system for the income and expense classifications. It specifies that the codes presented are not the only way to classify the accounts. However, it is an acceptable standard used by many restaurants. The manual further states that its coding system is flexible and accounts can be added or deleted to suit an individual restaurant. The appendix at the end of the chapter is a reproduction of a chart of accounts from *USAR*.

Food and Beverage Ratio Analysis

Ratio analysis involves examining the mathematical relationship between two amounts, with the relationship expressed in percentage or decimal format. This mathematical format is compared to a budget, standard, historical data, or industry average. If it is compared to industry averages, it is important that *USAR* be adopted or that the user be aware of any deviations.

Ratios are only indicators. Decisions should not be based solely on a mathematical result. A ratio that differs significantly from its base of comparison indicates the need for further investigation to determine the cause of variance.

Ratios are used to analyze balance sheet items and income statement items. The ratios used most often by a food and beverage manager are the food cost percentage and the beverage cost percentage.

Food Cost Percentage

The *food cost percentage* measures cost efficiency in generating customer sales. The formula is:

$$\frac{\text{Cost of Food Sold}}{\text{Food Sales}} = \text{Food Cost Percentage}$$

This ratio expresses the food cost as a percentage of (net) food sales. For example, if actual food sales are $100,000 and the actual food cost is $33,000, the food cost percentage is 33 percent, calculated as follows:

$$\frac{\text{Cost of Food Sold}}{\text{Food Sales}} = \frac{\$33,000}{\$100,000} = 33\%$$

If the budgeted food cost was 30 percent, this means that food costs are running three percent higher than expected. This could be due to standard recipes not being followed, increased costs from suppliers, or lower menu prices. The sales mix can have an effect on the departmental food cost percentage because not all meals have the same food cost percentage. Generally, chicken has a lower food cost percentage than steak. If the sales mix shows a trend toward more steak sales than planned, the food cost percentage will increase.

Beverage Cost Percentage

The utility of this ratio is similar to that of the food cost percentage. The formula is:

$$\frac{\text{Cost of Beverage Sold}}{\text{Beverage Sales}} = \text{Beverage Cost Percentage}$$

The beverage cost percentage is more useful if it is maintained by type of drink. The sales mix also has an effect on a restaurant's overall beverage cost percentage because of the differences in costs and pricing for beer, wine, and liquor.

Food Sales Statistics and Analysis

Food sales statistics provide management with a basis for analyzing selling prices, sales mix, efficiency, and profitability. For example, statistics can be used to determine if:

- Menu prices are reasonable.

- Customer volume is satisfactory.

- Average check is adequate.

- Seat turnover is sufficient.

The amount of sales reporting depends on management's desire for detailed information and the operation's sales mix. **Sales mix** is the relationship of an element of sales to the total. The formula for computing sales mix is:

$$\frac{\text{Item Sales \$}}{\text{Total Sales \$}} = \text{Sales Mix \%}$$

For example, if food sales are $80,000 and beverage sales are $20,000, the sales mix is 80 percent food and 20 percent beverage, computed as follows:

Food	Beverage
$\dfrac{\text{Item Sales \$}}{\text{Total Sales \$}} = \dfrac{\$80,000}{\$100,000} = 80\%$	$\dfrac{\$20,000}{\$100,000} = 20\%$

The sales mix can also be used to analyze the relationship of specific food sales such as steak, chicken, and pasta to total food sales.

Food sales statistics are calculated on a daily basis and summarized for the month. Useful statistics are as follows:

- Food sales analysis by meal period

- Food sales analysis by dining facility

- Average food check

- Average food sales per seat

- Customer turnover

Food Sales Analysis by Meal Period

This analysis is helpful in determining whether a particular meal period warrants being open for business or if sales are sufficient for satisfactory profitability. The following is a daily report analyzing sales by meal period:

Schedule of Food Sales by Meal Period

For Tuesday, June 26, 20X8

	Meals Served	Sales	Percentage
Breakfast	120	$ 480	14.6%
Lunch	150	1,200	36.6%
Dinner	80	1,600	48.8%
Total	350	$3,280	100.0%

The percentages are computed by dividing each individual sale amount by the total. For example, the breakfast sales percentage is calculated as follows:

$$\frac{\text{Item Sales } \$}{\text{Total Sales } \$} = \frac{\$480}{\$3,280} = 14.6\%$$

Food Sales Analysis by Dining Facility

Another useful report is one showing the same data arranged by dining facility instead of by meal period. This analysis is helpful in determining whether a given food service facility (outlet) is generating enough business to justify keeping it open. A large food operation may have outlets such as a main dining room, coffee shop, lunch counter, cafeteria, patio, drive-in, and banquet facilities all in one physical location.

The following is a daily report analyzing sales by dining facility:

Schedule of Food Sales by Dining Facility

For Tuesday, June 26, 20X8

	Meals Served	Sales	Percentage
Counter	30	$ 400	12.2%
Dining Room	320	2,880	87.8%
Total	350	$3,280	100.0%

The percentages are computed by dividing each individual sale amount by the total. For example, the counter sales percentage is calculated as follows:

$$\frac{\text{Item Sales } \$}{\text{Total Sales } \$} = \frac{\$400}{\$3,280} = 12.2\%$$

Average Food Check

The average food check statistic reveals how much, on average, a guest is spending. If the average check is lower than projected, the profit target might not be realized, especially if any increase in volume is not sufficient to offset the deficiency. If the average check is higher but guest volume is declining, it is possible that the menu prices are having an adverse effect and will reduce sales in the long run.

The formula for calculating average food check is:

$$\frac{\text{Meal Period Sales } \$}{\text{Number of Customers}} = \text{Average Food Check}$$

The average food check must be computed for each type of meal for the information to be useful. The term **covers** refers to the number of guests served. The following is an average check computation:

Average Food Check

For Tuesday, June 26, 20X8

	Sales	Guests	Average Check
Breakfast	$ 480	120	$ 4.00
Lunch	1,200	150	8.00
Dinner	1,600	80	20.00
Total	$3,280	350	

The sales amount for each meal period is divided by the number of guests for that meal period. For example, the breakfast average check is computed as follows:

$$\frac{\text{Meal Period Sales \$}}{\text{Number of Guests Served}} = \frac{\$480}{120} = \$4$$

Generally, the average check differs by meal period, with breakfast the lowest and dinner the highest.

Average Food Sale per Seat

The average food sale per seat is computed using the total number of available seats in the facility, regardless of whether they were occupied during the meal period. If the average check is satisfactory, but the average sale per seat is too low, an analysis should be made to determine if the size of the facility is much larger than necessary to satisfy customer demand.

The formula is as follows:

$$\frac{\text{Food Sales \$}}{\text{Available Seats}} = \text{Average Food Sale per Seat}$$

The average food sale per seat is more meaningful if it is computed by meal period. The following is a food sale per seat analysis:

Average Food Sale per Seat

For Tuesday, June 26, 20X8

	Sales	Seats	Average per Seat
Breakfast	$480	25	$19.20
Lunch	1,200	80	15.00
Dinner	1,600	70	22.86
Total	$3,280		

The average food sale per seat is an average of all seats available during a meal period. As shown above, this restaurant has different numbers of available seats per meal period based on seating arrangements; the counter seats are available only for breakfast and lunch.

Seat Turnover

Seat turnover is the number of times that a seat is occupied during a meal period. The more times a seat can be occupied by a different guest, the greater the sales generation during a meal period. The meal period, type of menu items, guest market, and staff efficiency affect the seat turnover statistic.

The formula for calculating seat turnover is:

$$\frac{\text{Guests Served}}{\text{Available Seats}} = \text{Seat Turnover}$$

Generally, the turnover is lowest during the dinner period because of the type of meal and dining experience expected by the guest. The following is a seat turnover analysis:

Average Seat Turnover
For Tuesday, June 26, 20X8

	Guests	Seats	Seat Turnover
Breakfast	120	25	4.8
Lunch	150	80	1.9
Dinner	80	70	1.1

The number of guests for each period is divided by the number of seats for that meal period to arrive at seat turnover.

Beverage Sales Statistics

The percentage of cost and gross profit varies considerably among the different kinds of beverage sales (liquor, wine, beer, and soft drinks). Therefore, any point-of-sale system should record the type of beverage sale in addition to the price.

Gathering statistics on the number of guests served and sales per guest can be difficult, if not impossible, because the consumption of beverages is not coincidental with the consumption of food. For example, at a table of five guests, maybe only one purchases a drink. On the other hand, a table of five guests may generate orders for ten drinks.

Some useful beverage sales statistics are the following:

- Sales by meal period
- Food/beverage sales ratio
- Sales by type of drink
- Sales by facility

Beverage Sales by Meal Period

Each state has regulations governing the hours for the legal sale of alcoholic beverages. Additionally, management might decide to limit the sale of beverages to the lunch and dinner periods. The following is a daily report analyzing sales by meal period:

Schedule of Beverage Sales by Meal Period
For Tuesday, June 26, 20X8

	Sales	Percentage
Breakfast	$ 0	n/a
Lunch	240	27.3%
Dinner	640	72.7%
Total	$880	100.0%

Beverage/Food Sales Ratio

While the sales by meal period is important information, supplementing this data with the relationship of beverage sales to food sales improves the usefulness in analyzing beverage sales. This relationship is computed as follows:

$$\frac{\text{Beverage Sales \$}}{\text{Food Sales \$}} = \text{Beverage/Food Ratio}$$

The following is an analysis of the beverage and food sales relationship:

Analysis of Beverage Sales to Food Sales Ratio
For Tuesday, June 26, 20X8

	Food Sales	Beverage Sales	Beverage/Food Ratio
Breakfast	$ 480	$ 0	n/a
Lunch	1,200	240	20%
Dinner	1,600	640	40%
Total	$3,280	880	

The amount of beverage sales for each meal period is divided by the amount of food sales for that meal period. For example, the beverage/food ratio for the lunch period is calculated as follows:

$$\frac{\text{Beverage Sales \$}}{\text{Food Sales \$}} = \frac{\$240}{\$1,200} = 20\%$$

This analysis shows that during the lunch period, beverage sales equal 20 percent of food sales, and, during the dinner period, beverage sales equal 40 percent of food sales. As expected, the beverage/food ratio is higher during the dinner period. These ratios are more meaningful if prior periods, forecasts, or industry statistics are compared against the actual results. Disappointing ratios might indicate the need for training the staff to improve the marketing effort at the customer-service level, table promotions, or other marketing efforts.

Beverage Sales by Type

An analysis of beverage sales by type of drink is helpful for inventory forecasting and profit management. Different drinks produce different profit margins, and the higher-margin drinks might enjoy a sales increase through menu redesign, table promotions, and waitstaff training. The following is an analysis by type of drink:

Schedule of Beverage Sales by Type of Drink
For Tuesday, June 26, 20X8

Mixed drinks and cocktails	$450	51.2% *
Beer and ale	120	13.6%
Wines	200	22.7%
Soft drinks	$110	12.5%
	$880	100.0%

* The actual computation for mixed drinks and cocktails is 51.1 percent. However, when working with percentages, sometimes the sum of the items does not equal 100 percent due to rounding differences. An arbitrary procedure is to adjust the largest number to arrive at a sum of 100 percent.

Beverage Sales by Facility

The following is an analysis format for beverage sales by facility that might be used by an operation with multi-outlet beverage sales:

Schedule of Beverage Sales by Facility
For Tuesday, June 26, 20X8

	Amount	Percentage
Main bar	$	%
Service bar		
Dining room		
Grill		
Banquets and parties	____	____
Total	$	%

An analysis by facility is not necessary if a restaurant sells beverages in only one outlet.

Endnote

1. For a comprehensive description of recognized accounting procedures and statements for the food and beverage industry, refer to the *Uniform System of Accounts for Restaurants*, 7th revised ed. (Washington, D.C.: National Restaurant Association, 1996), prepared by Deloitte & Touche LLP.

Key Terms

covers—The number of guests served.

direct operating expense—An expense directly involved in serving customers (other than payroll and related).

net beverage cost—Another term for *cost of beverage sold* or *cost of beverage sales*.

net food cost—Another term for *cost of food sold* or *cost of food sales*.

officers' checks—Tabs showing meals and beverages provided to executives and department heads at menu prices but not treated as customer sales.

sales mix—The relationship of an element of sales to total sales.

seat turnover—The number of times a seat is occupied during a meal period.

service charge—A separate charge on a customer's tab in lieu of tips.

 Review Questions ————————————————————————

1. What items are included in food sales?
2. What is the definition of sales mix?
3. What is the formula for each of the following?
   a. Sales mix
   b. Average food check
   c. Average food sales per seat
   d. Seat turnover
   e. Beverage/food sales ratio
4. What items are included in beverage sales?
5. What are the major differences between the perpetual and periodic inventory systems for a storeroom?
6. What is the procedure for calculating cost of food sold if a perpetual inventory system is used in the storeroom for a full-service restaurant?
7. What is the procedure for calculating cost of food sold if a periodic inventory system is used in the storeroom for a full-service restaurant?
8. What is a service charge? What should management consider before instituting this policy?
9. What items are considered other income?
10. What are the components of occupancy expense?
11. What is the major difference in accounting for cost of food sold between a full-service restaurant and fast-food restaurant?

 Internet Sites ————————————————————————

For more information, visit the following Internet sites. Remember that Internet addresses can change without notice. If the site is no longer there, you can use a search engine to look for additional sites.

Beginners' Guide to Financial Statements—The SEC
www.sec.gov/investor/pubs/
   begfinstmtguide.htm

How to Read a Balance Sheet
www.inc.com/articles/2000/05/
   18941.html
http://ezinearticles.com/?How-to-
   Read-a-Small-Business-Balance-
   Sheet&id=1280704
www.investopedia.com/articles/
   04/031004.asp#axzz1Pr0OPjfS

Ratio Analysis: Fundamental Analysis
www.investopedia.com/university/
   fundamentalanalysis/
www.investopedia.com/university/
   ratios/ratios.asp#axzz1Pr0OPjfS

The Perpetual and Periodic Inventory
   Systems
http://accountinginfo.com/study/
   inventory/inventory-110.htm
http://accountingaide.com/examples/
   inventory-systems-perpetual-
   periodic.htm

Problems

Problem 1

Food sales are $300,000, cost of food sales $120,000, direct operating expenses $60,000, and occupancy costs $80,000. What is the gross profit?

Problem 2

Meals served are $10,000, coffee $300, milk $200, soft drinks $400, beer $1,000, wine $1,500, mixed drinks $800. What is the amount of food sales?

Problem 3

Complete the following schedule of food sales by meal period. If necessary, show the percentages with one decimal position, properly rounded.

	Meals Served	Sales	Percent
Breakfast	100	$ 375	_____ %
Lunch	200	1,000	_____ %
Dinner	150	$1,200	_____ %
Total	_____	_____	_____ %

Problem 4

Use the data supplied in Problem 3 to compute the average check for each meal period.

Problem 5

The available seats are 35 for breakfast, 75 for lunch, and 75 for dinner. Use the data supplied in Problem 3 to calculate average seat turnover. If necessary, show the percentages with one decimal position, properly rounded.

Problem 6

Beverage sales are $60 breakfast, $268 lunch, and $475 dinner. Use the data supplied in Problem 3 to calculate the beverage/food ratio. If necessary, show the percentages with one decimal position, properly rounded.

Problem 7

The restaurant's cost of sales percentage averages 32 percent for any month. Following are transactions for the month of April:

Transfers from bar	$ 220	
Transfers to bar	75	
Officers' checks	500	at menu price
Employee meals	130	at standard cost
Storeroom issues	$40,000	

Compute the cost of food sold for the month of April if the perpetual inventory system is used in the storeroom.

Problem 8

A restaurant has a food cost average of 30 percent. The inventory on June 30 is $10,000 and the inventory on July 31 is $10,888. The following are transactions for the month of July:

Purchases	$30,000	
Officers' checks	800	at menu price
Employee meals	150	at standard cost
Transfer to bar	70	
Transfer from bar	90	

Compute the cost of food sold for the month of July if the periodic inventory system is used in the storeroom.

Problem 9

The accounting results for a month show food sales of $500,000 and cost of food sold at $175,000. Compute the food cost percentage for the month.

Problem 10

Beverage sales are cashiered with the sales tax included. Compute the separate amounts for beverage sales and sales tax if the total cashiered sales of $114,490 included a seven percent sales tax.

Ethics Case

Hubert Gundan is the senior accountant for Funtime Amusement Parks Company. The company's sales are $30 million, and the company plans to open more amusement parks in the United States.

Funtime's board of directors has scheduled a meeting with bankers to discuss financing the expansion. The company's current financial statements will be an important part of the discussions. Hubert has a deadline for preparing the statements, which must be met without fail. A courier will pick up the financial statements and deliver them to the board's chairperson at 8 A.M. on the day of the meeting.

The day before the deadline, Hubert discovers that the trial balance does not balance. The credits exceed the debits by $1,202.16. Hubert realizes that even if there is no error, he and his staff will be working until at least midnight to prepare the financial statements and supporting schedules. Hubert is forced to make a decision. Because the discrepancy is small, he decides to enter the $1,202.16 as a debit to the Repairs Expense account. He supports this decision with the following reasoning:

- The Repairs Expense account is very active and significant. Entering the small amount of $1,202.16 will not affect anyone's decision-making.

- No one can accuse the company of trying to inflate its profits because the difference has been charged to an expense account.

- High-level executives are waiting for the financial information. It would be embarrassing for the company to cancel its meeting.

1. Who are the stakeholders in this case?
2. What are the ethical issues involved?
3. What alternative courses of action, if any, are available to Hubert?

Chapter Appendix:

Sample Chart of Accounts Based on *Uniform System of Accounts for Restaurants*

The chart of accounts is a numbering system for the income and expense classifications conforming to the *Uniform System of Accounts for Restaurants.* The codes used here are not the only method for classifying the accounts; however, this is an acceptable standard grouping used by many restaurants. The illustrated code-numbering system is designed to be flexible and to be added to or reduced to fit the requirements of the individual restaurant owner. Some type of account code-numbering system must be used.

The listing that follows is intended to be quite comprehensive. Most restaurants will not require all of the account categories listed. If an account is used very rarely (or never), it should not be included in the chart of accounts. Use of fewer accounts definitely results in less complication.

Source: *Uniform System of Accounts for Restaurants,* 7th Revised Edition (Washington, D.C.: National Restaurant Association, 1996), pp. 141–147. Reprinted by permission.

CHART OF ACCOUNTS

ASSETS (1000)

Account Number	Account Name
1100	Cash
1110	Change funds
1120	Cash on deposit
1200	Accounts receivable
1210	Customers
1220	Allowances and complimentaries
1230	Other
1240	Employees' loans and advances
1250	Provision for doubtful accounts
1300	Inventories
1310	Food
1320	Beverages
1330	Supplies
1340	Other
1400	Prepaid expenses
1410	Insurance
1420	Deposits
1430	Taxes
1440	Licenses
1500	Fixed assets
1510	Land
1520	Building
1530	Accumulated depreciation–building
1540	Leasehold improvements
1550	Accumulated amortization of improvements
1560	Furniture, fixtures and equipment (including POS equipment)
1570	Accumulated depreciation–furniture and equipment
1580	Automobiles/trucks
1590	Accumulated depreciation–automobiles/trucks
1600	Deferred charges
1610	Marketing program prepaid
1620	Pre-opening expenses

LIABILITIES (2000)

2100	Payables
2110	Notes payable
2120	Accounts payable
2200	Taxes withheld and accrued
2210	Income Tax
2220	FICA

2230	Federal unemployment tax
2240	State unemployment tax
2250	Sales tax
2260	Employer's share of payroll taxes
2270	City taxes
2300	Accrued expenses
2310	Rent
2320	Payroll
2330	Interest
2340	Water
2350	Gas
2360	Electricity
2370	Personal property taxes
2380	Vacation
2390	Other
2400	Long-term debt
2410	Mortgage debt
2420	Capital leases
2430	Other debt

SHAREHOLDERS' EQUITY (3000)

3100	Common stock
3200	Capital in excess of par
3300	Retained earnings

SALES (4000)

4100	Food
4200	Beverages

COST OF SALES (5000)
(Detailed sub-accounts, if desired, will vary by type of restaurant)

5100	Cost of sales–food
5200	Cost of sales–beverages

OTHER INCOME (6000)

6100	Cover charges and minimums
6200	Commissions
6210	Gift shop operation–net
6220	Telephone commissions
6230	Concessions
6240	Vending machine/game revenue
6300	Salvage and waste sales
6400	Cash discounts
6500	Meeting/banquet room rental
6900	Miscellaneous

OPERATING EXPENSES (7000)

7100	Salaries and wages
7105	Service
7110	Preparation
7115	Sanitation
7120	Beverages
7125	Administrative
7130	Purchasing and storing
7135	Other
7200	Employee benefits
7205	FICA
7210	Federal unemployment tax
7215	State unemployment tax
7220	Workmen's compensation
7225	Group insurance
7230	State health insurance tax
7235	Welfare plan payments
7240	Pension plan payments
7245	Accident and health insurance premiums
7250	Hospitalization, Blue Cross, Blue Shield
7255	Employee meals
7260	Employee instruction and education expenses
7265	Employee Christmas and other parties
7270	Employee sports activities
7275	Medical expenses
7280	Credit union
7285	Awards and prizes
7290	Transportation and housing
7300	Occupancy costs
7305	Rent—minimum or fixed
7310	Percentage rent
7315	Ground rental
7320	Equipment rental
7325	Real estate taxes
7330	Personal property taxes
7335	Other municipal taxes
7340	Franchise tax
7345	Capital stock tax
7350	Partnership or corporation license fees
7360	Insurance on building and contents
7370	Depreciation
7371	Buildings
7372	Amortization of leasehold
7373	Amortization of leasehold improvements
7374	Furniture, fixtures and equipment
7400	Direct operating expenses
7402	Uniforms
7404	Laundry and dry cleaning
7406	Linen rental
7408	Linen
7410	China and glassware

7412	Silverware
7414	Kitchen utensils
7416	Auto and truck expense
7418	Cleaning supplies
7420	Paper supplies
7422	Guest supplies
7424	Bar supplies
7426	Menus and wine lists
7428	Contract cleaning
7430	Exterminating
7432	Flowers and decorations
7436	Parking lot expenses
7438	Licenses and permits
7440	Banquet expenses
7498	Other operating expenses
7500	Music and entertainment
7505	Musicians
7510	Professional entertainers
7520	Mechanical music
7525	Contracted wire services
7530	Piano rental and tuning
7535	Films, records, tapes and sheet music
7540	Programs
7550	Royalties to ASCAP, BMI
7555	Booking agents fees
7560	Meals served to musicians
7600	Marketing
7601	Selling and promotion
7602	Sales representative service
7603	Travel expense on solicitation
7604	Direct mail
7605	Telephone used for advertising and promotion
7606	Complimentary food and beverage (including gratis meals to customers)
7607	Postage
7610	Advertising
7611	Newspaper
7612	Magazines and trade journals
7613	Circulars, brochures, postal cards and other mailing pieces
7614	Outdoor signs
7615	Radio and television
7616	Programs, directories and guides
7617	Preparation of copy, photographs, etc.
7620	Public relations and publicity
7621	Civic and community projects
7622	Donations
7623	Souvenirs, favors, treasure chest items
7630	Fees and commissions
7631	Advertising or promotional agency fees
7640	Research
7641	Travel in connection with research
7642	Outside research agency

7643	Product testing
7700	Utilities
7705	Electric current
7710	Electric bulbs
7715	Water
7720	Removal of waste
7725	Other fuel
7800	Administrative and general expenses
7805	Office stationery, printing and supplies
7810	Data processing costs
7815	Postage
7820	Telegrams and telephone
7825	Dues and subscriptions
7830	Traveling expenses
7835	Insurance—general
7840	Commissions on credit card charges
7845	Provision for doubtful accounts
7850	Cash over or (short)
7855	Professional fees
7860	Protective and bank pick-up services
7865	Bank charges
7870	Miscellaneous
7900	Repairs and maintenance
7902	Furniture and fixtures
7904	Kitchen equipment
7906	Office equipment
7908	Refrigeration
7910	Air conditioning
7912	Plumbing and heating
7914	Electrical and mechanical
7916	Floors and carpets
7918	Buildings
7920	Parking lot
7922	Gardening and grounds maintenance
7924	Building alterations
7928	Painting, plastering and decorating
7990	Maintenance contracts
7996	Autos and trucks
7998	Other equipment and supplies

INTEREST AND CORPORATE OVERHEAD (8000)

8100	Interest
8105	Notes payable
8110	Long-term debt
8115	Other
8200	Corporate or Executive Office overhead
8205	Officers' salaries
8210	Directors' salaries
8215	Corporate office payroll
8220	Corporate office employee benefits
8225	Corporate office rent

8230	Corporate travel and entertainment
8235	Corporate office automobile expense
8240	Corporate office insurance
8245	Corporate office utilities
8250	Corporate office data processing
8255	Legal and accounting expense
8260	Corporate miscellaneous expense

INCOME TAX (9000)

9000	Income Taxes
9010	Federal
9020	State

Chapter 10 Outline

Income Statement for Stockholders and
    Other External Users
    Revenue Section of the Income
        Statement
    Expense Section of the Income
        Statement
    Income Before Income Taxes, Income
        Taxes, and Net Income
Income Statement for Internal Users
    Revenue Section of the Summary
        Operating Statement
    Departmental Expenses
    Total Departmental Income
    Undistributed Operating Expenses
    Gross Operating Profit, Management
        Fees, Income Before Fixed Charges
    Fixed Charges
    Net Operating Income
    Less: Replacement Reserves
    Adjusted Net Operating Income
The Income Statement Package for Internal
    Users
Operating Ratios
    Average Room Rate
    Occupancy Percentage
    Average Food Check
    Food Cost Percentage
    Beverage Cost Percentage
    Labor Cost Percentage
Hotels with Casino Departments
    Statement of Gaming Operations
    Revenue Accounting
    Expense Accounting

Competencies

1. Describe the hotel income statement intended for external users, its three major sections, and what is reported in each. (pp. 273–278)

2. Describe the income statement for internal users, its purpose, and its various line items, as well as the income statement package prepared for internal users. (pp. 278–281)

3. Identify and describe the operating ratios useful to lodging property management. (pp. 281–289)

4. Identify and explain special accounting considerations for hotels with casino departments. (pp. 289–291)

10

Hotel Accounting and Financial Analysis

THE HOTEL INDUSTRY COMPRISES many different types of lodging operations: small and large hotels, casino hotels, resort hotels, motels, bed & breakfasts, boutique hotels, and more. Financial reporting needs and requirements vary across the spectrum of types of hotel operations, from small, privately owned individual inns to large corporate chains. If a hotel's corporate stock is listed on a major stock exchange, the hotel must meet external reporting requirements set forth by the Securities and Exchange Commission (SEC). **External reports** are financial statements issued to stockholders, creditors, banks, and other interested parties.

Internal reports are financial statements prepared particularly for executives and managers of the hotel company. These reports present more detail and confidential information in a format that allows management to make internal operating decisions. Unlike external reports, internal reports do not require preparation by a certified public accounting firm. However, generally accepted accounting principles (GAAP) and the *Uniform System of Accounts for the Lodging Industry* form the basis for their preparation.

The lodging industry benefits from the efforts and cooperation of the American Hotel & Lodging Association (AH&LA), the Hospitality Financial and Technological Professionals (HFTP), and the Hotel Association of New York City (HANYC). These organizations have contributed to drafting the *Uniform System of Accounts for the Lodging Industry (USALI),* now in its 10th edition.

This chapter answers such questions as the following:

1. What is an acceptable income statement format for stockholders?

2. What is an acceptable income statement format for internal users?

3. What other information is provided in the income statement package for internal users?

4. What are operating ratios? What do they measure?

5. What is a statement of gaming operations?

Income Statement for Stockholders and Other External Users

The SEC mandates the information that must be provided to shareholders; however, most leading companies provide their shareholders with much more data about operational and financial results. The content of the statements varies from company to company, because of factors such as a hotel's size, type of operation, level of guest accommodations, and CPA firm's preferred style. The accounting firm must follow GAAP and draft income statements in good form that accommodate the hotel's specific operating characteristics and that serve the best interests of the reader. Readers might be stockholders, banks, creditors, or other independent interested parties.

The external income statement is called the *income statement* (also sometimes called the *statement of operations* or *profit and loss statement*). Its presentation to outside readers is typically brief but must be accompanied by disclosures in the form of notes to the financial statements (also called *footnotes*). Charts, graphs, a narrative of the past year, and other commentary usually accompany the income statement and other statements. (Readers are encouraged to visit the websites of any companies listed on the stock exchange to examine their financial reports to stockholders.)

Exhibit 1 shows an external income statement in the form recommended by *USALI*. The statement is condensed but conveys the necessary information regarding the results of operations for the current year and a comparison of those results to the previous year. The statement is divided into three major sections:

- Revenue
- Expenses
- Income Before Income Taxes, Income Taxes, and Net Income

Revenue Section of the Income Statement

Revenue centers are those departments that generate sales for the hotel. A revenue center owned and operated by the hotel is also called an **operated department**. Small hotels might have only one operated department: the rooms department. If small hotels have a second operated department, it might be food and beverage. Large hotels have many **outlets** that produce revenue. Departments that produce no revenue but provide services to the operated departments (revenue centers) are sometimes called **support centers**.

Revenue represents the amounts billed to guests/customers for the sale of goods and/or services, excluding sales taxes and tips. The sales revenue amount is listed for each major revenue center on the income statement. Sales taxes collected from guests are not part of revenue; they are a liability of the hotel until they are remitted to the governmental agency.

The rooms and the food and beverage (F&B) departments are the hotel's major sources of revenue and are therefore shown as the first and second line items on the income statement. (Refer to Exhibit 1 as you read this discussion of the external income statement and the line items that appear on it.) Rooms is listed first because it generates the largest amount of revenue and it is the hotel's primary business objective. Rooms revenue may include revenue from no-shows and from linen billings if such charges are separately stated on the guest's bill. In addition to food and beverage sales, F&B departments may generate revenue from meeting room rentals, cover charges, and service charges.

Exhibit 1   External Statement of Income per *USALI*

	Period	
	Current Year	Prior Year
REVENUE		
Rooms	$	$
Food and Beverage		
Other Operated Departments		
Rentals and Other Income		
Total Revenue		
EXPENSES		
Rooms		
Food and Beverage		
Other Operated Departments		
Administrative and General		
Sales and Marketing		
Property Operation and Maintenance		
Utilities		
Management Fees		
Rent, Property Taxes, and Insurance		
Interest Expense		
Depreciation and Amortization		
Loss or (Gain) on the Disposition of Assets		
Total Expenses		
INCOME BEFORE INCOME TAXES		
INCOME TAXES		
Current		
Deferred		
Total Income Taxes		
NET INCOME	$	$

The third line item, Other Operated Departments, comprises revenue for operations such as telecommunications, garage/parking fees, laundry, golf fees, and other recreational and service fees.

The fourth line item, Rentals and Other Income, is for income that is not applicable to the major operating centers. This line item might include the following:

- Interest income and dividend income
- Rentals from office space, stores, offices, and clubs
- Concessions income
- Commissions income
- Vending machine net profits (if owned)
- Cash discounts earned (purchase discounts)
- Salvage income

Package Plans. To increase the marketing effort, some hotels sell **package plans,** which offer guest accommodations and other services or products at a single price. This single price might include the room, food, beverages, and a recreational provision. Since the price includes revenue affecting several departments, it is necessary to allocate revenue to the proper departments.

When a package of services is sold, a procedure using market value ratios should allocate each sales item to the appropriate department. The following is an allocation example for a package that sold for $800:

Package	Market Value	Ratio	Sales Allocation
Rooms	$ 500	50%	$400
Food	300	30%	240
Golf	200	20%	160
Total	$1,000	100%	$800

The marketing department provides the market value. The ratio is calculated by dividing each market value by the total market value. For instance, $500 divided by $1,000 equals 50 percent. The sales allocation is computed by multiplying each ratio by the $800 actual selling price. For example, 50 percent times $800 equals $400.

Expense Section of the Income Statement

Hotel accounting is based on the concept of *responsibility accounting:* only expenses that can be directly controlled by the department manager will be charged to that department. The expenses include cost of sales and other operating costs. The expense section reports numerous costs, some of them unique to specific departments. Any expense identifiable and associated with a specific department is called a **direct expense.** Depending on the specific department, expenses might include the following:

- Cost of food and beverage
- Salaries and wages
- Payroll taxes
- Workers' compensation insurance
- Group benefit plans
- Department supplies
- Guest supplies
- Cleaning supplies
- Office supplies
- Advertising
- Music and entertainment

Expenses for the rooms department (shown as the first line item in the Expenses section) include salaries, wages, payroll taxes, and fringe benefits for the supervisors, front office, housekeeping, concierge, and security. The rooms department's additional expenses include cable television, commissions, linens, supplies, uniforms, and guest transportation.

F&B expenses, the second line item in the section, include salaries and wages, payroll taxes, and fringe benefits for the supervisors, kitchen staff, dining room staff, and cashiers, as well as such expenses as cost of the food and beverage, china, glassware, silver, music and entertainment, licenses, and uniforms.

Expenses shown for the third line item, Other Operated Departments, may include salaries and wages, payroll taxes, and fringe benefits for its staff, as well as other direct expenses.

Expenses for four departments—administrative and general (A&G), sales and marketing, property operation and maintenance (POM), and utilities—are classified as **undistributed operating expenses** because they cannot be identified with any one specific revenue center. Undistributed operating expenses are associated with franchise fees and support centers. The A&G, sales and marketing, POM, and utilities departments are charged for their specifically incurred costs as well as a share of undistributed operating expenses due to the concept of responsibility accounting mentioned earlier.

The fourth line item in the section, A&G, shows its expenses for the period, and include salaries and wages for personnel such as the general manager, the general manager's staff, the accounting and payroll departments, and administrative staff in the credit department, computer operations (information systems), and human resources. A&G expenses also include payroll taxes, fringe benefits, and the cost of supplies.

The fifth line item, Sales and Marketing expenses, reports salaries and wages of the sales/marketing director and staff, public relations, and media advertising. Other department expenses include payroll taxes, fringe benefits, and the cost of supplies.

POM expenses, the next line item, include salaries and wages, payroll taxes, and fringe benefits for its staff. Unique in hotel accounting is that this department also is charged for repairs to all furniture and equipment in the rooms, F&B, A&G, marketing, and other departments. The maintenance expense for the building, grounds, landscaping, and elevators is also charged to POM.

Utilities expenses (the seventh line item) includes the hotel's electric, fuel, steam, and water costs for all departments, except for any power used for cooking, which is charged to the food department.

Following these department expenses on the external income statement are charges for costs applicable to the hotel as a whole or costs not controllable by a department manager. **Management fees** may be paid for outside management costs or may be an allocation from the home office.

Notice that expenses for *rent, property taxes, insurance, interest,* and *depreciation and amortization* for building, furniture, and equipment are not charged to any specific revenue or service center.

The loss or gain on the sale of small assets may be included in the expense section.

Income Before Income Taxes, Income Taxes, and Net Income

Revenue less expenses produces a result called Income Before Income Taxes. The Income Taxes lines include federal, state, and any local income taxes currently due or due at some future time. When the income tax provisions are deducted, Net Income is the resulting last line item.

Income Statement for Internal Users

Internal users include upper management, department managers, and other employees that must be informed of the results of operations so that they can properly perform their responsibilities. *USALI* calls the income statement for internal users the *summary operating statement*. This statement and supporting schedules are prepared exclusively for internal use (for management's analytical purposes) and are not necessarily prepared in accordance with GAAP. An example of the format for the summary operating statement, as recommended by *USALI*, is shown in Exhibit 2. (Refer to Exhibit 2 as you read through the following discussion of the summary operating statement.)

The summary operating statement is different from the external income statement in this very important way: it does not report interest, depreciation, amortization, and income taxes. In addition, the summary operating statement features a deductible line item called Replacement Reserves (explained later in the chapter).

The primary reasons for the design and content of the summary operating statement are as follows:

- To provide management with the results of operations

- To facilitate comparison to other hotels' results of operations

- To have comparative standards

Revenue Section of the Summary Operating Statement

There is no change in this part of the statement from that of the external income statement. The total revenue line represents 100 percent. Each line item's dollar amount is divided by the total revenue dollars to arrive at a percentage of sales for that particular item. Adding the percentages for each individual sales line item (Rooms, F&B, and Other Operated Departments) should result in a total of 100 percent.

Departmental Expenses

This section reports only the expenses for the revenue departments, that is, rooms, F&B, and other operated departments. The percentage of the departmental expense is calculated by dividing the expense amount by its corresponding revenue amount. For example, the percentage for the rooms department expense is calculated by dividing the department dollar expense by the department revenue dollar amount.

Exhibit 2   Summary Operating Statement per *USALI*

| | CURRENT PERIOD | | | | | | YEAR-TO-DATE | | | | | |
| | ACTUAL | | FORECAST | | PRIOR YEAR | | ACTUAL | | FORECAST | | PRIOR YEAR | |
	$	%	$	%	$	%	$	%	$	%	$	%
REVENUE												
Rooms												
Food and Beverage												
Other Operated Departments												
Rentals and Other Income												
Total Revenue												
DEPARTMENTAL EXPENSES												
Rooms												
Food and Beverage												
Other Operated Departments												
Total Departmental Expenses												
TOTAL DEPARTMENTAL INCOME												
UNDISTRIBUTED OPERATING EXPENSES												
Administrative and General												
Sales and Marketing												
Property Operation & Maint.												
Utilities												
Total Undistributed Expenses												
GROSS OPERATING PROFIT												
MANAGEMENT FEES												
INCOME BEFORE FIXED CHARGES												
FIXED CHARGES												
Rent												
Property and Other Taxes												
Insurance												
Total Fixed Charges												
NET OPERATING INCOME												
LESS: REPLACEMENT RESERVES												
ADJUSTED NET OPERATING INCOME												

Total Departmental Income

The amount shown in the Total Departmental Income line item is calculated as follows:

Total Revenue − Total Departmental Expenses

The departmental income percentage is calculated by dividing the total departmental income dollar amount by the revenue dollar amount. The accuracy of the result can be verified by subtracting the total departmental expense percentage from the total revenue percentage of 100 percent.

Undistributed Operating Expenses

The undistributed operating expenses section reports the expenses of the service centers, namely A&G, sales and marketing, POM, and utilities, to arrive at a total shown in the line item Total Undistributed Operating Expenses. Each service center line item dollar amount is divided by the total revenue dollar amount to arrive at its respective expense percentage.

Gross Operating Profit, Management Fees, Income Before Fixed Charges

The line item Gross Operating Profit is computed as follows:

Total Departmental Income − Total Undistributed Expenses

The Management Fees line item was explained earlier. This expense may not occur for each hotel property.

The amount for line item Income Before Fixed Charges is computed as follows:

Gross Operating Profit − Management Fees

The percentage for each of these line items is computed by dividing the individual line amount by total revenue.

Fixed Charges

In the summary operating statement, *fixed charges*, also called *fixed costs*, specifically include only the line items Rent, Property and Other Taxes, and Insurance. It is important to recognize that this section of the summary operating statement *does not* include other fixed costs such as interest, depreciation, and amortization. Fixed charges are incurred regardless of volume, even when the hotel is closed. Fixed costs are sometimes called **occupation costs**. The percentage for each of these items is computed by dividing the individual line amount by total revenue.

Net Operating Income

The line item Net Operating Income is computed as follows:

Income Before Fixed Charges − Total Fixed Charges

The line item percentage is computed by dividing net operating income by total revenue.

Less Replacement Reserves

Less Replacement Reserves appears only in the internal income statement. Some management contracts or loan agreements specify an amount for future replacement of assets or capital improvements. The amount shown is a planning estimate, and the company may or may not have the cash funds actually available for those future expenditures. The percentage is computed by dividing the replacement reserve amount by total revenue.

Adjusted Net Operating Income

Adjusted Net Operating Income is the last line in the Summary Operating Statement. Observe that the expense for income taxes is omitted to maintain another objective of the Statement: to facilitate comparison of results between operating properties. Adjusted Net Operating Income is computed as follows:

$$\text{Net Operating Income} - \text{Replacement Reserves}$$

The line item percentage is computed by dividing adjusted net operating income by total revenue.

The Income Statement Package for Internal Users

Many supporting schedules accompany the summary operating statement, providing considerable information for proper planning and management. These include departmental income statements for the operating departments: rooms, food and beverage, and other operated departments. Also included are expense statements for the support departments: A&G, sales and marketing, POM, and utilities. Finally, other schedules serve to explain many other items in the summary income statement.

It is beyond the scope of this chapter to discuss all the schedules included in the typical monthly reporting package to executives and supervisors of even the smallest hotel.[1] However, Exhibits 3–8 feature selected statement formats, as recommended in *USALI:*

- Exhibit 3: Rooms Department Statement
- Exhibit 4: Food and Beverage Department Combined Statement
- Exhibit 5: Rentals and Other Income Statement
- Exhibit 6: Administrative and General Statement
- Exhibit 7: Sales and Marketing Statement
- Exhibit 8: Property Operation and Maintenance Statement

Operating Ratios

Management needs more than just financial statements with dollar amounts to analyze sales statistics and the efficiency of operations. The use of ratio analysis compared to budgeted ratios or goals helps management determine if there is

Exhibit 3   Rooms Department Statement per *USALI*

	CURRENT MONTH			YEAR-TO-DATE		
	ACTUAL	FORECAST	PRIOR YEAR	ACTUAL	FORECAST	PRIOR YEAR
	$ %	$ %	$ %	$ %	$ %	$ %
REVENUE						
Transient Rooms Revenue						
Group Rooms Revenue						
Contract Rooms Revenue						
Other Rooms Revenue						
Less: Allowances						
Total Rooms Revenue						
EXPENSES						
Payroll and Related Expenses						
Salaries, Wages, and Bonuses						
Salaries and Wages						
Bonuses and Incentives						
Total Salaries, Wages, and Bonuses						
Payroll-Related Expenses						
Payroll Taxes						
Supplemental Pay						
Employee Benefits						
Total Payroll-Related Expenses						
Total Payroll and Related Expenses						
Other Expenses						
Cable/Satellite Television						
Cleaning Supplies						
Commissions						
Commissions and Rebates—Group						
Complimentary Services and Gifts						
Contract Services						
Corporate Office Reimbursables						
Decorations						
Dues and Subscriptions						
Equipment Rental						
Guest Relocation						
Guest Supplies						
Guest Transportation						
Laundry and Dry Cleaning						
Licenses and Permits						
Linen						
Miscellaneous						
Operating Supplies						
Printing and Stationery						
Reservations						
Royalty Fees						
Telecommunications						
Training						
Travel—Meals and Entertainment						
Travel—Other						
Uniform Laundry						
Uniforms						
Total Other Expenses						
TOTAL EXPENSES						
DEPARTMENTAL INCOME (LOSS)						

Exhibit 4   Food and Beverage Department Combined Statement per *USALI*

	CURRENT MONTH			YEAR-TO-DATE		
	ACTUAL	FORECAST	PRIOR YEAR	ACTUAL	FORECAST	PRIOR YEAR
	$ %	$ %	$ %	$ %	$ %	$ %
REVENUE						
Outlet Food Revenue						
Outlet Beverage Revenue						
In-Room Dining Food Revenue						
In-Room Dining Beverage Revenue						
Banquet/Catering Food Revenue						
Banquet/Catering Beverage Revenue						
Mini Bar Food Revenue						
Mini Bar Beverage Revenue						
Other Food Revenue						
Other Beverage Revenue						
Less: Allowances						
Total Food and Beverage Revenue						
OTHER REVENUE						
Audiovisual						
Public Room Rentals						
Cover Charges						
Service Charges						
Miscellaneous Other Revenue						
Less: Allowances						
Total Other Revenue						
TOTAL REVENUE						
COST OF FOOD AND BEVERAGE SALES						
Cost of Food Sales						
Cost of Beverage Sales						
Total Cost of Food and Beverage Sales						
COST OF OTHER REVENUE						
Audiovisual Cost						
Miscellaneous Cost						
Total Cost of Other Revenue						
TOTAL COST OF SALES AND OTHER REVENUE						
GROSS PROFIT (LOSS)						
EXPENSES						
Payroll and Related Expenses						
Salaries, Wages, and Bonuses						
Salaries and Wages						
Bonuses and Incentives						
Total Salaries, Wages, and Bonuses						
Payroll-Related Expenses						
Payroll Taxes						
Supplemental Pay						
Employee Benefits						
Total Payroll-Related Expenses						
Total Payroll and Related Expenses						

(continued)

Exhibit 4   *(continued)*

	CURRENT MONTH			YEAR-TO-DATE		
	ACTUAL	FORECAST	PRIOR YEAR	ACTUAL	FORECAST	PRIOR YEAR
	$ | %	$ | %	$ | %	$ | %	$ | %	$ | %
Other Expenses						
Banquet Expense						
China						
Cleaning Supplies						
Complimentary Services and Gifts						
Contract Services						
Corporate Office Reimbursables						
Decorations						
Dishwashing Supplies						
Dues and Subscriptions						
Equipment Rental						
Flatware						
Glassware						
Ice						
Kitchen Fuel						
Laundry and Dry Cleaning						
Licenses and Permits						
Linen						
Management Fees						
Menus and Beverage Lists						
Miscellaneous						
Music and Entertainment						
Operating Supplies						
Paper and Plastics						
Printing and Stationery						
Royalty Fees						
Telecommunications						
Training						
Travel—Meals and Entertainment						
Travel—Other						
Uniform Laundry						
Uniforms						
Utensils						
Total Other Expenses						
TOTAL EXPENSES						
DEPARTMENTAL INCOME (LOSS)						

need for more analysis or corrective action. Some of the more common ratios used by hotel management are:

- Average room rate
- Occupancy percentage
- Average food check
- Food cost percentage
- Beverage cost percentage
- Labor cost percentage

Exhibit 5   Rentals and Other Income Statement per *USALI*

	CURRENT MONTH			YEAR-TO-DATE		
	ACTUAL	FORECAST	PRIOR YEAR	ACTUAL	FORECAST	PRIOR YEAR
	$ | %	$ | %	$ | %	$ | %	$ | %	$ | %
Space Rental and Concessions						
Commissions						
Cash Discounts Earned						
Cancellation Penalties						
Attrition Penalties						
Foreign Currency Transaction Gains (Losses)						
Guest Laundry and Dry Cleaning						
Interest Income						
Proceeds from Business Interruption Insurance						
Other						
TOTAL RENTALS AND OTHER INCOME						

Average Room Rate

Even though room rates vary by room type or class, the calculation of an average room rate provides helpful information. The *average room rate* (*ARR;* also called the *average daily rate* or *ADR*) is actually an average selling price of all the paid rooms occupied. The formula is:

$$\text{Average Room Rate} = \frac{\text{Rooms Revenue}}{\text{Paid Rooms Occupied}}$$

Occupancy Percentage

The occupancy percentage is important because it measures actual sales revenue in relationship to the hotel's sales potential. The formula is:

$$\text{Occupancy Percentage} = \frac{\text{Paid Rooms Occupied}}{\text{Rooms Available}} \times 100$$

This ratio can be computed only if a hotel maintains statistics on rooms available for sale, complimentary rooms, and actual rooms sold (paid rooms occupied).

Average Food Check

The average food check reveals how much, on average, any restaurant (or other food outlet) guest is spending. It is a measure of food sales related to the number of customers (covers). If the average check is lower than projected, the profit goal may not be reached. The formula is:

$$\text{Average Food Check} = \frac{\text{Food Revenue}}{\text{Number of Covers}}$$

For average food check to be useful as management information, it should be computed for each type of meal (breakfast, lunch, and dinner) and each dining facility (coffee shop, fine dining room, and so on).

Exhibit 6   Administrative and General Statement per *USALI*

	CURRENT MONTH						YEAR-TO-DATE					
	ACTUAL		FORECAST		PRIOR YEAR		ACTUAL		FORECAST		PRIOR YEAR	
	$	%	$	%	$	%	$	%	$	%	$	%
EXPENSES												
Payroll and Related Expenses												
Salaries, Wages, and Bonuses												
Salaries and Wages												
Bonuses and Incentives												
Total Salaries, Wages, and Bonuses												
Payroll-Related Expenses												
Payroll Taxes												
Supplemental Pay												
Employee Benefits												
Total Payroll-Related Expenses												
Total Payroll and Related Expenses												
Other Expenses												
Audit Charges												
Bank Charges												
Cash Overages and Shortages												
Centralized Accounting Charges												
Complimentary Services and Gifts												
Contract Services												
Corporate Office Reimbursables												
Credit and Collection												
Credit Card Commissions												
Decorations												
Donations												
Dues and Subscriptions												
Equipment Rental												
Human Resources												
Information Systems												
Laundry and Dry Cleaning												
Legal Services												
Licenses and Permits												
Loss and Damage												
Miscellaneous												
Operating Supplies												
Payroll Processing												
Postage and Overnight Delivery Charges												
Printing and Stationery												
Professional Fees												
Provision for Doubtful Accounts												
Security												
Settlement Costs												
Telecommunications												
Training												
Transportation												
Travel—Meals and Entertainment												
Travel—Other												
Uniform Laundry												
Uniforms												
Total Other Expenses												
TOTAL EXPENSES												

Exhibit 7   Sales and Marketing Statement per *USALI*

	CURRENT MONTH			YEAR-TO-DATE		
	ACTUAL	FORECAST	PRIOR YEAR	ACTUAL	FORECAST	PRIOR YEAR
	$ %	$ %	$ %	$ %	$ %	$ %
EXPENSES						
Payroll and Related Expenses						
Salaries, Wages, and Bonuses						
Salaries and Wages						
Bonuses and Incentives						
Total Salaries, Wages, and Bonuses						
Payroll-Related Expenses						
Payroll Taxes						
Supplemental Pay						
Employee Benefits						
Total Payroll-Related Expenses						
Total Payroll and Related Expenses						
Other Expenses						
Sales Expenses						
Complimentary Services and Gifts						
Contract Services						
Corporate Office Reimbursables						
Decorations						
Dues and Subscriptions						
Equipment Rental						
Fam (Familiarization) Trips						
Laundry and Dry Cleaning						
Miscellaneous						
Operating Supplies						
Outside Sales Representation						
Postage and Overnight Delivery Charges						
Printing and Stationery						
Promotion						
Telecommunications						
Trade Shows						
Training						
Travel—Meals and Entertainment						
Travel—Other						
Total Sales Expenses						
Marketing Expenses						
Agency Fees						
Collateral Material						
Contract Services						
Direct Mail						
E-Commerce						
Franchise and Affiliation Advertising						
Franchise Fees						
In-House Graphics						
Loyalty Programs and Affiliation Fees						
Media						
Miscellaneous						
Outdoor						
Outside Services						
Photography						
Total Marketing Expenses						
Total Other Expenses						
TOTAL EXPENSES						

Exhibit 8 Property Operation and Maintenance Statement per *USALI*

	CURRENT MONTH			YEAR-TO-DATE		
	ACTUAL	FORECAST	PRIOR YEAR	ACTUAL	FORECAST	PRIOR YEAR
	$ | %	$ | %	$ | %	$ | %	$ | %	$ | %
EXPENSES						
Payroll and Related Expenses						
Salaries, Wages, and Bonuses						
Salaries and Wages						
Bonuses and Incentives						
Total Salaries, Wages, and Bonuses						
Payroll-Related Expenses						
Payroll Taxes						
Supplemental Pay						
Employee Benefits						
Total Payroll-Related Expenses						
Total Payroll and Related Expenses						
Other Expenses						
Building						
Complimentary Services and Gifts						
Contract Services						
Corporate Office Reimbursables						
Decorations						
Dues and Subscriptions						
Electrical and Mechanical Equipment						
Elevators and Escalators						
Engineering Supplies						
Equipment Rental						
Floor Covering						
Furniture and Equipment						
Grounds Maintenance and Landscaping						
Heating, Ventilation, and Air Conditioning Equipment						
Kitchen Equipment						
Laundry and Dry Cleaning						
Laundry Equipment						
Licenses and Permits						
Life/Safety						
Light Bulbs						
Miscellaneous						
Operating Supplies						
Painting and Decorating						
Plumbing						
Printing and Stationery						
Swimming Pool						
Telecommunications						
Training						
Travel—Meals and Entertainment						
Travel—Other						
Uniform Laundry						
Uniforms						
Waste Removal						
Total Other Expenses						
TOTAL EXPENSES						

Food Cost Percentage

The food cost percentage shows the relationship of food cost to food sales. This is a popular ratio used to measure the profitability and efficiency of a food outlet. The ratio shows the cost of food per one dollar of sales. The formula is:

$$\text{Food Cost Percentage} = \frac{\text{Cost of Food Sales}}{\text{Food Revenue}} \times 100$$

This ratio is more meaningful if it is computed for each dining facility.

Beverage Cost Percentage

The beverage cost percentage ratio is computed similarly to the food cost percentage, except that beverage statistics are used in the numerator and denominator. The formula is:

$$\text{Beverage Cost Percentage} = \frac{\text{Cost of Beverage Sales}}{\text{Beverage Revenue}} \times 100$$

Brand variation and type of drink affect the beverage cost percentage. This ratio is more meaningful when computed separately for beer, wine, and liquor.

Labor Cost Percentage

Labor can be the largest operating expense for a lodging property. Labor includes payroll and payroll-related expenses. The formula is:

$$\text{Labor Cost Percentage} = \frac{\text{Payroll \& Related}}{\text{Revenue}} \times 100$$

This ratio can be computed for each revenue center or for the hotel as a whole.

Hotels with Casino Departments

Gaming is becoming increasingly popular in the global hospitality environment. A segment of the public enjoys it as a form of recreation, hospitality operations enjoy its income potential, and governments view it as another source of tax revenue.

A hotel-owned-and-operated casino department is a separate revenue center with its own departmental statement that appears on the hotel's Summary Statement of Income.

Statement of Gaming Operations

The statement of gaming operations is prepared for the casino department, as shown in Exhibit 9. Because the format and line items on the statement are general in nature, they may not apply to all lodging properties with a gaming operation as an ancillary revenue source. Individual properties should modify the statement accordingly to fit their particular requirements.

Revenue Accounting

Gaming revenue is the difference between gaming wins and losses; it is not the total amount wagered. The two methods of accounting for gaming revenue are to treat casino revenue as:

Exhibit 9   Statement of Gaming Operations

	Current Period
REVENUE	$
LESS COMPLIMENTARY ALLOWANCES (used only if above revenue includes complimentaries)	_____
NET REVENUE	
PAYROLL AND RELATED EXPENSES	
Salaries and Wages	
Employee Benefits	_____
Total Payroll and Related Expenses	_____
OTHER EXPENSES	
Complimentaries:	
Rooms	
Food	
Beverage	
Travel	
Special Events	
Other Amenities	
Contract Services	
Credit and Collection	
Gaming Taxes, License Fees, and Regulatory Costs	
Operating Supplies	
Postage	
Provision for Doubtful Accounts	
Telecommunications	
Training	
Uniforms	
Other	_____
Total Other Expenses	_____
TOTAL EXPENSES	_____
DEPARTMENTAL INCOME (LOSS)	$ _____

Source: *Uniform System of Accounts for the Lodging Industry,* 9th rev. ed. (Lansing, Mich.: American Hotel & Lodging Educational Institute, 1996), p. 145.

1.   Gaming revenue only.

2.   Gaming revenue *and* the retail value of complimentary items (free amenities to guests).

Complimentary Allowances. The Complimentary Allowances account is used only if total casino revenue is composed of both gaming revenue *and* complimentary items (at retail).

Expense Accounting

Giving free goods and services to guests as complimentary items is a prevalent gaming industry practice. These allowances might include rooms, food, beverage, travel, and other amenities free of charge as an incentive to gamble at the casino. The approximate retail value is used to account for these items.

Payroll, employee benefits, and other expenses for the Casino department are accounted for in similar manner to that of other operating departments. Of special interest are the following:

- Credit and collection expense

- Gaming taxes, licenses, and fees expense

- Postage expense

- **Complimentaries** expense

The credit and collection expenses associated with casino charge account customers are assessed to the casino, unlike other operating departments, where credit and collection expenses are charged to the A&G department.

The specialized casino licensing fees are charged to the casino department, which is similar in logic to charging the beverage department for its special beverage license fee.

Postage expense related to casino promotions or direct mail programs is charged directly to the casino instead of A&G or the marketing department.

The free guest amenities given to casino customers appear as separate line items under Other Expenses listed by type of complimentary. This procedure is used *regardless* of the revenue method of accounting used for the casino department.

Endnote

1. Readers interested in the complete detailed financial statement package are referred to the *Uniform System of Accounts for the Lodging Industry*, 10th rev. ed. (Lansing, Mich.: American Hotel & Lodging Educational Institute, 2006).

Key Terms

complimentaries—In casino hotels, free goods and services given to casino customers.

direct expense—An expense identifiable and associated with one specific department.

gaming revenue—The difference between gaming wins and losses, *not* the total amount wagered.

management fees—Expenses that represent the costs of having an independent management company operate the property; these fees also might be expense allocations from the home office.

occupation costs—Expenses for such items as rent, interest, property taxes, depreciation, and amortization. Also called *fixed charges* and *fixed costs*.

operated department—A revenue center owned and operated by a hotel.

outlets—Revenue centers.

package plans—Hotel promotional packages that may include accommodations, food, recreation, and other incentives for a single price.

support centers—Departments that produce no revenue but provide services to the operated departments (revenue centers).

undistributed operating expenses—Expenses not easily identified with any specific operated department.

 Review Questions ———————————————————————

1. What are the components of labor cost in the hotel industry?

2. What is the name of the external statement showing revenue and expenses and given to shareholders?

3. What are possible revenue sources for the Other Operated Departments line item?

4. What revenue sources might be included in the line item Rentals and Other Income?

5. What types of personnel might be in the A&G department?

6. What is a direct expense?

7. What types of personnel might be in the sales and marketing department?

8. Which department will get charged for repairs to furniture in the Rooms department?

9. What is the name of the internal income statement given to managers?

10. What four specific expenses are purposely excluded from the internal income statement?

11. Which departments are listed as Undistributed Operating Expenses on the internal income statement?

12. What is the line item called Replacement Reserves on the internal income statement?

13. What ratio measures actual room sales against a hotel's potential room sales?

14. What is the definition of *gaming revenue* in a casino operation?

15. When is the Complimentary Allowances account used in a casino operation?

Internet Sites

For more information, visit the following Internet sites. Remember that Internet addresses can change without notice. If the site is no longer there, you can use a search engine to look for additional sites.

American Gaming Association
www.americangaming.org/

Beginners' Guide to Financial Statements — The SEC
www.sec.gov/investor/pubs/
  begfinstmtguide.htm

Hotel Revenue Center Defined
www.businessdictionary.com/
  definition/revenue-center.html

Ratio Analysis: Fundamental Analysis
www.investopedia.com/university/
  fundamentalanalysis/
www.investopedia.com/university/
ratios/ratios.asp

Understanding the Income Statement
www.investopedia.com/
  articles/04/022504.asp

Problems

Problem 1

A hotel's daily cashiers report shows the following:

Room sales	$100,000
Sales tax on rooms	5,000
Food sales	20,000
Sales tax on food	1,000
Beverage sales	4,000
Sales tax on beverages	200

What are the room sales, food sales, and beverage sales?

Problem 2

The rooms department has the following expenses:

Salaries	$7,000
Wages	10,000
Employee meals	200
Health insurance premiums	2,000
Workers' compensation insurance	800
Payroll taxes—federal	1,600
Payroll taxes—state	1,000

Prepare the payroll and related expenses section for the rooms department schedule.

Problem 3

A hotel offers a couples weekend package plan for $300. This plan includes accommodations for two nights, two breakfasts, two dinners, a welcome bottle of champagne, and a cocktail with each dinner. The market value of these items is $350 rooms, $100 food, and $50 beverages. Allocate the revenue to the proper departments for each plan sold.

Problem 4

Identify the following as a revenue center or a support center:

> Administrative and general
> Marketing department
> Rooms department
> Food department
> Telecommunications department
> Property operation and maintenance

Problem 5

A motel has the following annual information. (Net indicates revenue after allowances.)

Rooms revenue (net)	$897,500
Food revenue (net)	358,300
Beverage revenue (net)	159,870
Cost of food sales	135,200
Paid rooms occupied	17,950
Rooms available (75 daily)	27,375 (75 × 365)
Food covers	37,716

Compute the following ratios:

> Average room rate
> Occupancy percentage
> Average food check
> Food cost percentage

Pr.oblem 6

Prepare a Summary Operating Statement according to the format shown in the chapter. Following is the general ledger information for a small hotel. Not all information may be necessary to prepare the statement.

Room Sales	$1,053,890
Food & Beverage Sales	524,570
Rentals and Other Income	19,033
Payroll & Other Expenses: Rooms	334,356
Cost of Food Sales	178,310
Payroll & Other Expenses: F&B	258,883
Administrative and General	164,181
Marketing	67,868
Property Operation & Maintenance	61,554
Utilities	47,312
Management Fees	20,000
Rent	28,500
Property Taxes	45,324
Insurance (Property & Liability)	6,914
Interest	192,153
Depreciation	140,000
Amortization	6,000
Income Taxes Expense	12,000

Note:
The company has estimated its replacement reserve for the period to be $15,000.

Problem 7

Use the information from Problem 6 to prepare an income statement that would be sent to stockholders.

Chapter 11 Outline

Depreciation
    Straight-Line Depreciation Method
    Declining Balance Depreciation
      Method
    MACRS Depreciation Method
    FASB vs. IRS Depreciation Methods
Amortization
    IRS vs. FASB Regarding Intangible
      Assets

Competencies

1. Describe capital assets and the accounting treatment they require, and define fixed, tangible, and intangible assets. (p. 297)

2. Describe depreciation, bookkeeping accounts used for depreciation, and terms used in the depreciation of assets. (pp. 298–299)

3. Explain the various methods of depreciation discussed in the chapter. (pp. 299–302)

4. Explain amortization, accounting procedures for amortization, and the IRS vs. FASB approaches to intangible assets. (pp. 302–304)

11

Depreciation and Amortization Methods

A RESTAURANT OR HOTEL BUSINESS occasionally purchases assets that provide lengthy service of one or more years. These assets are called capital assets and require special accounting treatment. Capital assets cannot be charged directly to expense upon purchase. Accounting principles and the Internal Revenue Code (IRC) specify in considerable detail the assets that must first be coded to an asset account (capitalized) and then expensed through depreciation or amortization. The basic requirements regarding these assets are as follows:

- The asset must be owned (assets purchased with loans are considered owned).

- The asset must be used in business or income-producing activity.

- The asset must have a useful life of more than one year (that is, it must be long-lived).

Depreciation and amortization are terms that are often incorrectly used. While both refer to long-term assets, depreciation is related to assets having a physical form (such as buildings and machinery), while amortization applies to assets having no physical form (such as patents and copyrights). Simply stated, depreciation or amortization spread the cost of a qualified asset over its useful life. Land is not a qualified asset for depreciation or amortization because land has perpetual usefulness, unlike vehicles or equipment. Some readers may have heard the term *depletion*, which is used in the mining of oil, gas, and other natural resources. It is improbable that the hospitality industry student requires any further study regarding the reduction of a natural resource.

Depreciation is sometimes defined as *an annual allowance for wear and tear, deterioration, or obsolescence of the property*. This definition explains why depreciation is allowed, but the definition can be misleading since depreciation and amortization have no relationship to a decline in an asset's market value or its actual wear and tear. In fact, depreciation and amortization generally allocate an item's cost more quickly than any decline in its true market value or usefulness to a company.

The term *fixed assets* has long been a part of business terminology and is still frequently used to refer to long-lived assets (those that last one year or more). Fixed assets may be tangible or intangible. *Tangible assets* have a physical form (for example, buildings, furniture, and vehicles), while *intangible assets* have no physical form or substance (such as patents and copyrights).

This chapter answers such questions as the following:

1. What is the difference between depreciation and amortization? What types of assets are associated with each?

2. What are the straight-line depreciation and the declining balance methods of depreciation?

3. What is the MACRS method of depreciation?

4. What is amortization? What assets does it apply to?

5. How do the IRS and FASB differ in regard to amortized intangible assets?

Depreciation

Depreciation is a method that is associated with tangible long-lived (more than one year) assets (except land), such as the following:

- Buildings
- Machinery
- Vehicles
- Furniture
- Office equipment
- Computers

Accounting principles and the IRC do not allow deducting the purchase cost of these long-lived assets as an immediate business expense.[1] Allowable depreciation methods provide a deduction called Depreciation Expense, which is shown on the income statement as an expense and reduces net income (and taxable income).

Depreciation methods allow the recovery of the cost of a tangible asset over a period of time, called the asset's useful life. For instance, if a qualified asset is purchased for $12,000 with an estimated useful life of five years, one particular depreciation method might result in an annual depreciation expense of $2,400 per year ($12,000 ÷ 5 years). Depreciation and other adjusting entries are usually recorded at the end of each month. Therefore, each month's portion of the annual depreciation of $2,400 would be recorded with the following month-end journal entry:

Depreciation Expense	200	
Accumulated Depreciation		200
To record $^{1}/_{12}$ of $2,400 annual depreciation		

If $2,400 is expensed each year for five years, the $12,000 purchase cost of the asset is fully recovered as a business expense.

Accounting for depreciation requires the use of the following bookkeeping accounts:

- *Asset account*. This account includes the cost of the asset, which is the sum of its purchase price, freight, installation, and other expenses involved in getting it ready for use.

- *Depreciation Expense account.* This is an income statement expense account showing the depreciation calculation for only the current reporting period.

- *Accumulated Depreciation account.* This is a balance sheet account showing the cumulative depreciation amount for all periods. It is subtracted from the asset's cost to show book value of the asset (book value has no relationship to market value).

Other terms used in the depreciation of assets are:

- *Book value* is the result of the cost of the asset minus its accumulated depreciation.

- *Useful life* is the service life of an asset for its particular purpose as determined by the company that owns it. The useful life may or may not coincide with the asset's economic life or physical life.

- *Salvage value* is the estimated scrap or trade-in value of an asset at the end of its useful life.

The two most common financial methods of depreciating qualifying assets over their useful lives are the following:

- Straight-line method
- Declining balance method

The *declining balance method of depreciation* is often referred to as *accelerated depreciation* because the computed depreciation charges are larger in the early years than they are in the *straight-line method.* Nevertheless, the declining balance method and the straight-line method result in the same total depreciation at the end of an asset's useful life. This is because the declining balance method uses lower depreciation computations in the asset's later years than does the straight-line method. The examples in this chapter will illustrate the annual and total depreciation expense for a similar asset using both depreciation methods.

Only the straight-line and declining balance methods of computing depreciation are allowed under the Modified Accelerated Cost Recovery System (MACRS) method prescribed by the Internal Revenue Service (IRS).

Special rules apply for prorating depreciation calculations for the first year of business since a company's first business year is generally shorter than 12 months. To encourage investment in assets, the IRS often provides special tax deductions for qualifying property in the year it is purchased.

Straight-Line Depreciation Method

The straight-line depreciation method calculation produces the same depreciation expense amount each year. At the end of the asset's useful life, salvage value, if any, is used to reduce the asset's depreciable basis.

The formula for computing depreciation under the straight-line method is:

$$\frac{\text{Cost} - \text{Salvage}}{\text{Useful Life}} = \text{Annual Depreciation Expense}$$

For example, an asset's cost is $10,000; its future salvage value is estimated at $2,000; and its useful life is estimated at four years. Its annual depreciation expense over this four-year period is calculated as follows:

$$\frac{\text{Cost} - \text{Salvage}}{\text{Useful Life}} = \frac{\$10,000 - \$2,000}{4} = \frac{\$8,000}{4} = \$2,000 \text{ Annual Depreciation Expense}$$

A *depreciation schedule* shows the depreciation history of an asset. Returning to the previous example, the asset's depreciation schedule is as follows:

Year	Beginning Book Value	Depreciation Expense	Accumulated Depreciation	Book Value
1	$10,000(a)	$2,000	$2,000	$8,000 [$10,000 − $2,000]
2	8,000	2,000	4,000	6,000 [10,000 − 4,000]
3	6,000	2,000	6,000	4,000 [10,000 − 6,000]
4	4,000	2,000	8,000	2,000 [10,000 − 8,000]
Total		$8,000(b)		(c)

Notes:

(a)   At the beginning of an asset's life, the cost is recorded.

(b)   The depreciation expense total for the four years ($8,000) equals the last accumulated depreciation amount shown at the end of the fourth year ($8,000).

(c)   The book value at the end of the asset's useful life equals the salvage value of $2,000.

Optional Depreciation Computation Method. An alternative way to compute the annual depreciation is to use a percentage rate that is applied to the asset's purchase cost minus its estimated salvage value at the end of its useful life. For instance, the percentage rate of depreciation in the example above is 25 percent (100 percent ÷ 4 years = 25 percent per year). The initial book value of $8,000 (purchase cost $10,000 − salvage value of $2,000) multiplied by 25 percent produces a depreciation expense of $2,000 for each year of the asset's four-year estimated life; the results are identical to those in the previous example.

Declining Balance Depreciation Method

The declining balance depreciation method provides the highest depreciation amount in the early years of an asset's life. The most common depreciation rate is twice the straight-line rate; the method using this doubled rate is called the *double declining balance (DDB) method.*

The principles of the DDB method are as follows:

1.   The straight-line percentage rate is doubled.

2.   The doubled percentage rate (called the *DDB rate*) is applied to the full cost excluding salvage value.

3.   The DDB rate is applied on each year's beginning book value to compute the depreciation expense for that particular year.

4. Book value can never go below salvage value. If the book value goes below salvage value in any computation, the depreciation expense must be *squeezed* out through the subtraction of the ending book value from the salvage value.

For illustrative and comparative purposes, we again turn to the previous example. An asset's cost is $10,000; its future salvage value is estimated at $2,000; and its useful life is estimated at four years. Its annual depreciation expense over this four-year period is calculated as follows:

The DDB rate is 50 percent (100 percent ÷ 4 years × 2).

Year	Beginning Book Value	Depreciation Expense	Accumulated Depreciation	Book Value
1	10,000 (a)	5,000 (b)	5,000	5,000
2	5,000	2,500 (c)	7,500	2,500
3	2,500	500 (d)	8,000	2,000
4	2,000	0 (e)	8,000	2,000
Total		8,000		

Notes:

(a) Cost of asset

(b) $10,000 beginning book value (BBV) × DDB rate of 50 percent

(c) $5,000 BBV × DDB rate of 50 percent

(d) The 50 percent rate cannot be applied, because doing so would bring the ending book value below the salvage value (SV) of $2,000:

	BBV	Depreciation	Ending BV
Applying 50%	2,500	1,250	1,250 (Below $2,000 SV)
Allowed	2,500	500	2,000 (Equals $2,000 SV)

"SQUEEZED"
($2,500 − $2,000)

(e) There is no depreciation expense for year 4 because the ending book value ($2,000) was equal to the salvage value at the end of year 3.

MACRS Depreciation Method

Recall that MACRS is an acronym for Modified Accelerated Cost Recovery System. The IRS developed MACRS as a system for depreciating long-lived tangible assets. Its objective is similar to that of the straight-line and declining balance depreciation methods. The IRS provides many MACRS tables for various property classes and recovery periods. (A *recovery period* is a mandated useful life for a particular type [class] of asset.) The date of purchase further dictates whether a half-year, mid-quarter, or mid-month table should be selected. (More information is available in IRS Publication 946.)

Use of these tables requires knowledge of the purchase or disposition date of a particular asset. Salvage values are ignored, meaning that an asset can be depreciated to zero book value.

Once again we'll use the data from the original example: an asset's cost is $10,000, and its future salvage value is estimated at $2,000. This type of asset is mandated by IRS/MACRS to have a three-year recovery period. Its annual depreciation expense is calculated as follows:

First, the applicable MACRS table is consulted as mandated. In this case, the depreciation table for a three-year recovery period with a half-year convention table was mandated and provided the following annual depreciation rates:

Year	Rate
1	33.33%
2	44.45%
3	14.81%
4	7.41%

Remember that salvage value is ignored. The depreciation calculations over the life of this asset are as follows:

Year	Rate	Computation	Depreciation
1	33.33%	$10,000 × 33.33%	$3,333
2	44.45%	$10,000 × 44.45%	4,445
3	14.81%	$10,000 × 14.81%	1,481
4	7.41%	$10,000 × 7.41%	741
Total			$10,000

FASB vs. IRS Depreciation Methods

The Financial Accounting Standards Board (FASB) and its accounting principles formulate depreciation methods based on the matching principle of accounting. In some situations, the IRS allows expensing the entire cost of assets up to a specific ceiling amount. Therefore, it is not unusual for a company to show depreciation expense on its financial statements that is different from that it reports on its federal income tax return.

The differences resulting from these FASB and IRS regulations are called *timing differences*; while the depreciation expense in each year is different between the two, in the end, the total of the depreciation expense will equal the cost of the asset.

Amortization

In accounting terminology, **amortization** is the process that allocates the cost of an intangible long-lived asset over its useful life. An intangible asset is a capital asset that has no physical structure but will last for more than one year. The IRS and the FASB have different accounting policies regarding amortization of intangible assets. According to FASB, examples of long-lived intangible assets include the following:

- Franchise right purchased in a business transaction

- Trademarks or trade names (development, registration, or purchase)

- Patents (development, registration, or purchase)

- Copyrights (development, registration, or purchase)

- Covenant not to compete agreement (payment to seller upon purchase of a business)

Amortization expenses the cost of an intangible asset over its useful life. The useful lives of intangible assets depend on many factors, such as utility to the owner and legal protection provided by the seller or government.

The amortization procedure of expensing the cost of a qualified intangible asset over its useful life is slightly different from that used in a depreciation procedure. For intangible assets, there is no allowance for amortization account; instead, the cost of the intangible asset is directly reduced to reflect its unamortized cost basis.

For example, the journal entry to amortize a copyright asset is as follows:

Amortization Expense	xxx	
Copyright		xxx

The intangible asset account Copyright would appear on the balance sheet at its reduced cost basis. For instance, suppose a business purchased a Franchise Right that initially cost $100,000 and came with a 20-year contractual right. The annual entry to amortize this intangible asset is $5,000 ($100,000 ÷ 20-year life) is as follows:

Amortization Expense	5,000	
Franchise Right		5,000

In the first year, the $5,000 Amortization Expense would appear on the income statement, and the asset Franchise Right remaining to be amortized ($100,000 cost less $5,000) would appear on the balance sheet as a single line item as follows:

Franchise Right	$95,000

In the second year, the annual journal entry would be repeated as follows:

Amortization Expense	5,000	
Franchise Right		5,000

The $5,000 Amortization Expense would appear on the income statement, and the asset Franchise Right remaining to be amortized ($100,000 cost less $10,000) would appear on the balance sheet as a single line item as follows:

Franchise Right	$90,000

Each year the journal process is repeated. The annual amortization expense will appear on the income statement and the asset balance remaining to be amortized will appear on the balance sheet. The franchise right will not appear on the balance sheet when its balance is zero or it is sold or worthless before the end of its useful life.

IRS vs. FASB Regarding Intangible Assets

It is not unusual for IRS accounting principles to differ from generally accepted accounting principles promulgated by the FASB. The subject of amortized intangible assets is complicated due to differences between the IRS and FASB regarding classification and useful lives of assets.

Goodwill, simply stated, is the payment for a business's name or reputation in excess of the purchase value of the business. The IRS allows an income tax deduction for goodwill amortized over five years. However, FASB no longer allows that practice; goodwill from a business acquisition made after June 30, 2001, can no longer be amortized. The amortization of purchased goodwill might appear on some financial statements for any acquisition made before June 30, 2001.

Organization costs include legal, incorporation, and accounting fees incurred in the formation of a corporation. The IRS requires that these fees be amortized over a five-year period. FASB requires that these fees be expensed in the first year of operation.

Endnote

1. For more information about qualifying assets, useful life, and depreciation methods, see the IRC at www.irs.gov/taxpros/article/0,,id=98137,00.html#irc.

Key Terms

Accumulated Depreciation—A balance sheet account showing the depreciation amount for all periods.

amortization—A method of expensing the cost of an intangible asset over its useful or legal life.

book value—Asset cost minus accumulated depreciation.

depreciation—A method of allocating the cost of a tangible long-lived asset over its estimated useful life.

intangible asset—A long-lived asset that has no physical structure.

salvage value—The estimated scrap or trade-in value of an asset at the end of its useful life.

Review Questions

1. The chapter listed basic requirements that certain assets must meet before they are capitalized and then expensed. What are they?

2. What six major asset groups listed in this chapter can be depreciated?

3. What is the definition of the following terms?

   a. Asset cost
   b. Depreciation
   c. Depreciation expense
   d. Accumulated depreciation
   e. Book value
   f. Useful life

    g. Salvage value
    h. Intangible asset
    i. Amortization

 **Problems** —————————————————————————

Problem 1

Complete a Depreciation Schedule for the straight-line method as it is shown in the chapter (without footnote references) for the following asset:

> Asset cost: $28,000
> Salvage: $4,000
> Useful life: 6 years

Problem 2

Use the information in Problem 1 to complete a Depreciation Schedule using the double declining balance (DDB) method. Round the calculated DDB rate to a whole percentage. Round the depreciation expense calculations to the nearest dollar amount.

Problem 3

Write the journal entry recording the $1,000 depreciation for a tangible fixed asset.

Problem 4

Write the journal entry to record the $1,000 amortization for an intangible fixed asset.

Ethics Case

The Dionysus Company is reviewing its Annual Report to Shareholders before it is formally issued. The operating results show a loss, and management is apprehensive about stockholders' discontent. The company president directs the treasurer to change the company's depreciation expense by increasing the useful lives and salvage values of all depreciable assets.

1. What effect will this have on operating income?

2. What ethical issues are involved?

3. What accounting issues are involved?

Chapter 12 Outline

Financial Statement Package
    Notes to the Financial Statements
    Accountant's Letter
The Money Illusion
    Revenue, Expenses, and Net Income
    Assets, Liabilities, and Equity
Overview of Analytical Methods
The Income Statement
    Reading the Income Statement
    Common-Size Analysis
    Comparative Analysis
    Ratio Analysis
The Balance Sheet
    Reading the Balance Sheet
    Common-Size Analysis
    Comparative Analysis
    Ratio Analysis
Statement of Cash Flows
    Reading the SCF
    Cash Flows from Operating Activities
    Cash Flows from Investing Activities
    Cash Flows from Financing Activities

Competencies

1. Explain the composition of a financial statement package. (pp. 307–309)

2. Explain why the monetary amounts on financial statements can give a false illusion, and describe the effect of accrual accounting on revenue, expenses, net income, assets, liabilities, and equity. (pp. 309–310)

3. Describe how to read and analyze the income statement, balance sheet, and statement of cash flows using common analytical methods. (pp. 310–324)

12

How to Analyze Hospitality
Financial Statements

FINANCIAL STATEMENTS SERVE as a means of communication between the issuing company and the statements' readers. These readers may be internal, such as executives and managers, or external, such as stockholders and creditors. The internal and external forms of financial statements differ in their amount of detail. Internal statements are management tools and thus are quite detailed and include departmental statements. External statements are condensed for reader convenience and exclude departmental statements. The term *financial statement package* is often used to describe the complete set of either external or internal financial statements.

While these statements are tools of communication, the reader must know how to read them and how to interpret them. Many readers do not properly interpret important financial statement information because of certain misconceptions.

This chapter is a "capstone" chapter. It is a review of accounting principles and financial statements designed to take the reader to a new level of competence in understanding, interpreting, and analyzing monetary information in the form of financial statements. Each component of the income statement, balance sheet, and statement of cash flows is examined in detail.

This chapter answers such questions as:

1. What is the content of a financial statement package?

2. What different levels of financial statement services are available from a certified public accountant?

3. What are some common money illusions and other misconceptions about financial statements?

4. What are some common analytical methods used to interpret financial statements? How are they applied?

Financial Statement Package

The three basic financial statements in a financial statement package are the income statement, the balance sheet, and the statement of cash flows.

As stated above, the level of detail of a financial statement package depends on whether it is prepared for internal readers, such as executives and managers, or external readers, such as stockholders and creditors. Beyond this difference, a financial statement package intended for external readers consists of more than just financial statements; also included are notes to the financial statements and an accountant's letter.

Notes to the Financial Statements

The notes to the financial statements, also called **footnotes**, supplement the dollar amounts shown on the statements. These notes provide information that explains important non-monetary items or events. The notes serve as disclosures revealing facts or news that the reader should know to be properly informed about the company. These include such items as the following:

- Accounting policies
- Depreciation methods
- Inventory accounting methods
- Leases (terms and conditions)
- Pending lawsuit (contingent liability)
- Procedures for computing income taxes

Accountant's Letter

An accountant (CPA or non-CPA) employed by a hospitality company may prepare statements for internal readers, but since he or she is an employee (therefore not independent), the employee-accountant cannot prepare financial statements intended for stockholders. Independence means freedom of influence from the party for whom the statements are prepared. It is also possible that creditors such as banks or suppliers might demand that the company seeking a loan or credit privileges engage the services of an independent public accountant.

The public accountant will provide an **accountant's letter** to accompany the statements that explains the level of service performed by the accountant. A public accountant may perform an audit, a review, or a compilation.

An **audit** of financial statements is the highest level of service a public accountant can perform. Because it is highly detailed, it is also extremely expensive. An audit is a comprehensive examination of a company's accounting records. It includes observation of physical inventories and confirmation of accounts receivable and accounts payable. The physical inventories include verifying the existence of food, liquor, supplies, investments, autos, equipment, and other assets recorded in the accounting records. The purpose of an audit is to ensure that the information in the financial statements is presented fairly and in conformity with generally accepted accounting principles. The term *present fairly* covers many issues; perhaps the most important is that the information does not deceive the reader. An audit is not intended to detect fraud, comment on the competence of management, or evaluate the company as a quality investment for stockholders or investors.

Because audits are extremely expensive, the Securities and Exchange Commission allows businesses to report their financial positions to stockholders via quarterly reviewed financial statements. Banks and creditors also may agree to accept statements prepared under a review scope of service. A **review** of the financial statements is substantially smaller in scope than an audit. The observation of physical inventories is not part of a review service and the confirmation of accounts receivable and accounts payable is not required. A review service provides limited assurance that no material changes are necessary to the financial statements for conformity with generally accepted accounting principles.

Though a review service is less expensive than an audit, the review services performed by a CPA are still costly. Therefore, banks and creditors may accept statements prepared under a compilation service. Compiled financial statements, also called **compilations**, are the lowest level of service performed by a public accountant. The statements are a representation of management, and the accountant provides assurance only to the extent that the statements were prepared in accordance with standards for unaudited financial statements.

The Money Illusion

Because the financial statements are stated in absolute values (dollars), it is easy to assume that the amounts represent money transactions. However, this is not a valid assumption, in part because the balance sheet and income statement are prepared using the accrual system of accounting. The accrual system ignores whether cash is present in a business transaction; accrual accounting instead looks for the exchange of goods or services for a promise to pay. A customer's promise to pay is called an account receivable; a business's promise to pay is called an account payable. Strict cash-basis accounting is not used to prepare balance sheets or income statements because it ignores accounts receivable and accounts payable transactions. The only statement based on cash transactions is the statement of cash flows.

This *money illusion*—the notion that financial statement figures stated in dollars are somehow equivalent to money or cash—is a misconception that can play out in different ways in different financial statements. Sometimes the accrual accounting system is behind the illusion (as is the case with revenue, expenses, and net income). Sometimes the dollar amounts are not really money or cash amounts for other reasons (as is the case with some balance sheet accounts). Let's look at some specific examples.

Revenue, Expenses, and Net Income

The accrual basis of accounting is used to report revenue and expenses on the income statement. The principle of any accrual system is that revenue is recorded when earned, and expenses are recorded when incurred. The largest revenue item for any hospitality business is sales. Sales can be made instantly, for cash, or billed to a customer, creating an account receivable. Significant credit card volume can also affect cash if the deposit *float* is more than two or three days. A $310,000 sales amount shown on an income statement represents total *billings*, regardless of whether they have been paid by the customer or are still in accounts receivable. The income statement does not reveal the cash sales.

Operating expenses such as payroll, inventories, advertising, utility services, and other items are recorded under the accrual basis of accounting, even though many of these expenses that appear on an income statement have yet to be paid. Part or all of the prior week's payroll for the month ended is recorded in the current month, but paid in the following month. A business has open credit with its suppliers to purchase inventories and services, but payment is usually due in the following month upon receipt of a statement.

Depreciation and amortization are peculiar expenses because they do not and never will require a cash payment. Both of these expenses are the allocation of a long-lived asset's cost over an estimated useful life. Depreciation relates to tangible assets and amortization relates to intangible assets. Because of their similarity, sometimes only the term *depreciation* appears on the financial statements to represent both depreciation and amortization.

Net income does not represent money income because:

- Sales are a combination of cash sales and billings not yet collected (accounts receivable).

- Many expenses are a combination of payments and invoices or charges not yet paid (accounts payable).

- Depreciation and amortization are never a cash expense.

Assets, Liabilities, and Equity

The money illusion may affect balance sheet accounts as well. The accounts receivable shown on a balance sheet may not be 100 percent collectible. The allowance for doubtful accounts (potential bad debts) is an estimate. Also, the amount shown for land, buildings, and other assets may not represent the true cash value of these items.

Even the *Cash* account may not represent the potential cash position. Cash might be inflated because the payment of accounts payable and other liabilities has been deferred. Cash might be understated because short-term investments can always be sold to bolster the cash position. Another consideration is that the cash position of a company does not reflect its borrowing power.

The equity section of a balance sheet is composed of cumulative net income of the present and the past, which does not relate to cash. The stock issued amounts relate to the original issue date and amount; those funds have long been spent.

Overview of Analytical Methods

The income statement, balance sheet, and statement of cash flows are mathematically related. Despite the differences in format, the tools for analyzing these statements are quite similar. The most common of these analytical tools or methods are the following:

- Common-size analysis
- Comparative analysis
- Ratio analysis

Common-size analysis, also called **vertical analysis**, provides a means of evaluating relative values as opposed to absolute values. **Relative values** are stated in percentages. In the case of a common-size analysis, each line item on the financial statement is divided by a common divisor. The common divisor represents 100 percent and each line item represents a part of that 100 percent. The results of a common-size analysis are often used to construct pie charts or other graphic representations.

Comparative analysis, also called **horizontal analysis,** provides a means of evaluating the changes in **absolute** (dollar) **values.** A comparative analysis compares the dollar amount of the current period with that of another period, or a standard, or a budget. Each line item is independently compared and the dollar change becomes the basis of examination.

Ratios are a means of expressing the relationship between two numbers, arrived at by dividing one by the other. The two numbers may come from different financial statements, and, unlike common-size analysis, with **ratio analysis** there is no common divisor. These ratios serve as a benchmark for comparison against industry standards, budgets, or historical data. Ratios are useful in pointing to possible problem areas that might require investigation or study. A number of ratios are used to analyze the many items on the financial statements.

The Income Statement

The income statement, also called the *profit and loss statement,* reports revenue, expenses, and the resulting net income. The reporting period usually shows the current month and the year-to-date results, generally not exceeding one year for the current reporting period. The date of an income statement is specified as:

For the (period) ended (date)

Exhibit 1 shows that the income statement period for Southern Fast Food is one year ending on December 31, 20X2. This means that the monetary amounts are from January 1, 20X2, through December 31, 20X2.

Reading the Income Statement

Income statement formats will vary from industry to industry and company to company, though all follow this general format:

	Sales
−	Allowances, Discounts, Rebates
=	Net Sales
−	Cost of Sales
=	Gross Profit
−	Operating Expenses
=	Operating Income
+	Gains on Sale of Assets
−	Losses on Sale of Assets
=	IBIT (Income Before Income Taxes)

Exhibit 1   Southern Fast Food—Income Statement

Southern Fast Food, Inc.
Income Statement
For the period ended 12/31/X2

Sales	$ 310,000	100.0%
Cost of food and paper goods	122,450	39.5%
Gross profit	187,550	60.5%
OPERATING EXPENSES		
Salaries and wages	64,480	20.8%
Employee benefits	9,300	3.0%
Direct operating expenses	5,580	1.8%
Marketing	28,520	9.2%
Utility services	8,680	2.8%
Occupancy costs	22,630	7.3%
Depreciation	18,000	5.8%
Amortization	500	.2%
General and administrative	6,830	2.2%
Other expenses	8,830	2.8%
Total operating expenses	173,350	55.9%
Operating income	14,200	4.6%
Gain on sale of equipment	1,000	.3%
Loss on sale of marketable securities	(1,200)	(.4%)
Income before income taxes (IBIT)	14,000	4.5%
Income taxes	5,000	1.6%
Net income	$ 9,000	2.9%

−	Income Taxes
=	Net Income

The amount for *Net Sales* is the result of total billings less allowances, discounts, and rebates. Some income statements show the total billings, the deductions, then net sales as follows:

Sales	$311,000
Allowances and rebates	1,000
Net Sales	$310,000

Other income statements may simply start with net sales because the allowances, discounts, and rebates are not material to reading the statement. Most income statements that start with only the net sales amount label that line item simply as *Sales* for purposes of brevity; it is implied that the amount is really net sales. Using Exhibit 1 as an example, the line item labeled *Sales* is actually net sales of $310,000.

The income statement is a series of steps and subtotals. It is relatively easy to read. Again Exhibit 1 provides an example:

- Net sales less cost of sales produces a subtotal called *gross profit;* it represents the profit after deducting the cost of materials used in producing sales to customers.

- Deducting the operating expenses produces another subtotal called *operating income;* it represents the profit made by the business in its day-to-day operations.

- Non-operating gains are added and non-operating losses are subtracted to produce another subtotal called *income before income taxes (IBIT).*

- *Net income* (the final total) is the result of IBIT less income taxes.

Common-Size Analysis

Common-size percentages are computed by dividing every amount on the income statement by *net sales* and may be illustrated by the following formula:

$$\frac{\text{Dollar amount of line item on income statement}}{\text{(Net) Sales}}$$

Using Exhibit 1, the common-size percentage for *depreciation* is computed as follows:

$$\frac{\$18,000}{\$310,000} = 5.8\%$$

The common-size percentage of 5.8 percent means that depreciation amounted to 5.8 percent of net sales, or almost six cents of the sales dollar.

Reading a common-size analysis of an income statement is relatively simple due to the following:

- Each percentage represents a relationship to net sales.

- Each percentage can be restated as a unit of the sales dollar. For example, the line item *Marketing* shows that the marketing expense takes up about nine cents of the sales dollar ($28,520 ÷ $310,000).

- The common-size percentages are mathematically related because a common divisor (net sales) is used. Using Exhibit 1, for example:

  - Sales of 100 percent less cost of sales of 39.5 percent = 60.5 percent gross profit.

  - Adding all the operating expenses = 55.9 percent.

  - Gross profit of 60.5 percent less operating expenses of 55.9 percent = 4.6 percent operating income.

  - Operating income of 4.6 percent plus gains of 0.3 percent less losses of 0.4 percent = 4.5 percent IBIT.

  - 4.5 percent IBIT less income taxes of 1.6 percent = 2.9 percent.

Comparative Analysis

The data for prior periods and budgets can be used to perform a comparative analysis on the income statement. Because budgets are extensively used with income statements and managers often receive bonuses for favorable performance, a budget example is provided. Using Exhibit 1, if the budget for the line item *Sales* is $315,000 and the budget for the line item *Salaries and wages* is $66,480, a budgetary comparative analysis would look like the following:

	Budget	Actual	Over (Under) Budget
Sales	$315,000	$310,000	$ (5,000)
Salaries and wages	66,480	64,480	(2,000)

The sales variance result of $5,000 under budget is *not favorable*. The salaries and wages variance of $2,000 under budget is *favorable*. In simplistic terms, budgetary variances are favorable when actual sales exceed the budget or when actual expenses are under budget.

Computing the variance as a percentage of the budget can expand a comparative analysis. Using this same example, a full comparative analysis would look like this:

	Budget	Actual	Over (Under) Budget	% Variance
Sales	$315,000	$310,000	$ (5,000)	(1.6%)
Salaries and wages	66,480	64,480	(2,000)	(3.0%)

The sales variance percentage of 1.6 percent is computed by dividing its variance of $5,000 by the sales budget of $315,000; the salaries and wages variance is computed by dividing its variance of $2,000 by the salaries and wages budget of $66,480. Notice that the mathematical *sign* of the variance is the same as that of the dollar variance. In this case, sales were under budget by 1.6 percent and other expenses were under budget by 3.0 percent.

Unlike a common-size analysis, the percentages of one line item are not related to the percentages of any other line item, because a common divisor is not used to compute these percentages.

Ratio Analysis

Accountants use a multitude of ratios to analyze the income statement. Ratio analysis of the income statement is used to measure the following:

- Profitability: comparing profit margins and income to sales or equity
- Asset management: measuring income generated by use of assets
- Operating: measuring effectiveness and efficiency of operations
- Occupancy: measuring the success of rooms management at hotels

This chapter focuses on the following most popular of the operating and profitability ratios:

- Food cost percentage
- Beverage cost percentage
- Labor cost percentage
- Prime cost percentage
- Profit margin ratio

Food Cost Percentage. This ratio expresses the food cost as a percentage of (net) food sales. Using Exhibit 1, actual food sales are $310,000 and the actual food cost is $122,450; the food cost percentage is 39.5 percent, calculated as follows:

$$\frac{\text{Cost of Food Sold}}{\text{Food Sales}} = \frac{\$122,450}{\$310,000} = 39.5\%$$

If the budgeted food cost had been 36.5 percent, food costs would be running three percent higher than planned. Such results could be due to not following standard recipes, increased costs from suppliers, or management's decision to lower menu prices. The sales mix can have an effect on the departmental food cost percentage, because not all meals share the same food cost percentage.

Southern Fast Food's cost of food consists of food items plus paper goods, which is standard accounting procedure for fast-food operations. *Paper goods* are items that accompany the meal, such as the following:

- Paper wrappers and napkins
- Paper and foam cups
- Takeout containers
- Plastic utensils and straws

In Southern Fast Food's case, the cost of food sold takes up almost 40 cents of the sales dollar, an amount that would be considered high for a full-service restaurant but is normal for a fast-food operation. Lower labor costs in a fast-food operation offset higher food costs.

Beverage Cost Percentage. Southern Fast Food does not serve liquor. The utility of the beverage cost percentage ratio is similar to that of the food cost percentage ratio. The formula is:

$$\frac{\text{Cost of Beverage Sold}}{\text{Beverage Sales}} = \text{Beverage Cost Percentage}$$

Labor Cost Percentage. Labor cost includes not just salaries and wages, but employee benefits as well (because of their direct relationship to salaries and wages). Employee benefits include such items as payroll taxes, health and life insurance, employee meals, vacations and holidays, and workers' compensation insurance.

The labor cost ratio expresses the total labor cost (payroll and related) as a percentage of (net) food sales. Using Exhibit 1, the labor cost percentage is 23.8 percent, calculated as follows:

$$\frac{\text{Salaries and Wages} + \text{Employee Benefits}}{\text{Food Sales}} = \frac{\$64,480 + \$9,300}{\$310,000} = 23.8\%$$

This ratio tells us that total payroll costs are taking up almost 24 cents of the sales dollar at Southern Fast Food.

Prime Cost Percentage. Prime cost includes cost of sales plus total labor cost (salaries, wages, and employee benefits). It can be computed by adding the dollar amounts for these items and dividing by net sales. Another method is to take the previously computed ratios or common-size percentages and add them as follows:

Cost of food sold	39.5%
Total labor cost ratio	23.8%
Prime Cost Ratio	63.3%

In the case of Southern Fast Food, the prime cost is 63.3 cents of the sales dollar, leaving 36.7 cents of the sales dollar to cover expenses such as direct operating, marketing, occupancy, and other costs. It also leaves something for the profit.

Profit Margin Ratio. The profit margin ratio measures the amount of net income (income after income taxes) produced by each sales dollar.

Actual food sales in Exhibit 1 are $310,000, net income is $9,000, and the profit margin ratio is 2.9 percent, calculated as follows:

$$\frac{\text{Net Income}}{\text{Food Sales}} = \frac{\$9,000}{\$310,000} = 2.9\%$$

For each sales dollar (100 cents), Southern Fast Food realized a net income of almost three cents. Depending on the economy, competition, and geographic location, this profit margin might be acceptable. Southern Fast Food is a corporation and the owner's salary is included in labor; thus, the owner benefits from the salary and benefits paid by the business, as well as its net income. Another benefit is that the customers are indirectly paying for the assets of the business, ultimately producing owner's wealth when the business is sold.

The $9,000 net income might seem small, but remember that looking only at a money amount can be an illusion. Depreciation and amortization are always non-cash expenses. In the case of Southern Fast Food, these expenses total $18,500 and have been deducted to arrive at the $9,000 net income. The statement of cash flows will reveal the true *cash* net income from operations.

The Balance Sheet

The balance sheet reports assets, liabilities, and equity. The reporting period of a balance sheet is a discrete point in time, not a cumulative period of time. The amounts are those as of the close of a business day, typically the last day of the month. The date for a balance sheet is expressed as:

Month, Day, Year

The date on the balance sheet in Exhibit 2 indicates that the monetary columns are for two dates; the left column for the close of business on December 31, 20X2, and the right column for the close of business on December 31, 20X1.

Exhibit 2   Southern Fast Food—Balance Sheet

	20X2	20X1	Increase (Decrease)
Balance Sheet			
Southern Fast Food, Inc.			
12/31/X2 and 12/31/X1			
Cash	$ 39,000	$ 45,000	$ (6,000)
Short-term investments	0	5,000	(5,000)
Accounts receivable (net)	28,000	18,500	9,500
Inventories	10,000	12,000	(2,000)
Prepaid expenses	3,000	2,000	1,000
Total current assets	$ 80,000	$ 82,500	$ (2,500)
Property and equipment (net)	190,000	130,000	60,000
Other assets (net)	5,000	5,500	(500)
Total assets	$ 275,000	$ 218,000	$ 57,000
Accounts payable	$ 88,000	$ 89,500	$ (1,500)
Sales tax payable	2,000	1,200	800
Accrued expenses	6,000	7,300	(1,300)
Dividends payable	3,000	0	3,000
Current portion of mortgage	5,000	0	5,000
Total current liabilities	$ 104,000	$ 98,000	$ 6,000
Mortgage payable (net)	27,000	0	27,000
Note payable due 2/1/X4	30,000	0	30,000
Capital stock issued (no-par)	117,000	108,000	9,000
Treasury stock	(20,000)	0	(20,000)
Retained earnings	17,000	12,000	5,000
Total liabilities and equity	$ 275,000	$ 218,000	$ 57,000

A balance sheet is not useful for day-to-day operations; therefore, department managers seldom receive it. The financial health of a company is the responsibility of executives; they make the decisions to purchase expensive assets or borrow funds. Other readers of the balance sheet are investors, creditors, and others with a vested interest in a company's financial position.

Reading the Balance Sheet

The monetary amounts on the balance sheet do not reflect current market value of land, buildings, and other long-lived assets. A company's well-known *goodwill* does not appear on its balance sheet. The only time goodwill shows on a balance sheet is when a company is purchased at a value higher than the fair market value (FMV) of its assets (the excess over FMV is goodwill).

All balance sheets are divided into three major sections: assets, liabilities, and equity. Each section presents information that is valuable in evaluating the financial health of a company. This evaluation also uses ratio analysis and comparative analysis. To assist in this evaluation, the major sections are further subdivided. The asset section is subdivided into current assets, property and equipment, and other assets. The liabilities section is subdivided into current liabilities and long-term liabilities.

Common-Size Analysis

Common-size percentages are computed by dividing each amount on the balance sheet by total assets. It can be illustrated by the following formula:

$$\frac{\text{Dollar amount of line item on balance sheet}}{\text{Total Assets}}$$

Using Exhibit 2, the common-size percentage for the 20X2 line item *Cash* is computed as follows:

$$\frac{\$39,000}{\$275,000} = 14.2\%$$

This common-size result tells us that cash makes up 14.2 percent of the total assets. Continuing these calculations for the remaining assets will show what part each asset is of total assets. Since the total assets amount and the total liabilities and equity amount are identical, any line item in the liabilities and equity sections can also use the same divisor, except that the result is interpreted as showing what part each liability or equity is to the total liabilities and equity.

Comparative Analysis

Conducting a comparative analysis on a balance sheet is very popular and informative, especially when comparing the end of the current year with the end of the previous year, because this analysis reveals which items increased or decreased from the previous reporting date.

In Exhibit 2, the line item *Cash* decreased by $6,000 from the previous date. The increase or decrease effect is computed as follows:

Amount for current date	$39,000
Less: Amount for prior date	45,000
Difference	$ 6,000

A positive difference is an increase and a negative difference is a decrease. The increases or decreases may also be stated as a percentage of the prior date's amount; this percentage is computed by dividing the increase or decrease amount by the prior date's amount. Using Exhibit 2, the line item *Cash* is analyzed as follows:

	20X2	20X1	Increase (Decrease)	Percentage
Cash	$39,000	$45,000	$(6,000)	(13.3%)

Cash has decreased 13.3 percent, computed by dividing the $6,000 decrease by the prior date's amount of $45,000. These increases and decreases are sometimes related. That is, an increase in an asset may bring a decrease in another asset, or an increase in an asset may bring an increase in liabilities or equity, as in the following examples:

- Cash is down and accounts receivable are up. The change could be due to increased sales or a change in credit policy.

- Cash is up, marketable securities are down. The change could be the result of selling stocks or bonds to increase the cash position.

- Inventories are up, accounts payable are up. The liability has increased to increase an asset.

- Property and equipment is up, and mortgages payable or notes payable are up. This is another case in which liabilities have increased to increase assets.

- Capital stock increases, and cash or another significant asset increases. The corporation may have sold stock to increase its cash position or to purchase property or equipment.

- Treasury stock increases and cash decreases. Cash was used to repurchase the company's own stock.

- Treasury stock decreases. The corporation may have sold its treasury stock to increase its cash position or to purchase property or equipment.

In the case of Southern Fast Food, the obvious major changes and possible reasons for some balance sheet increases and decreases in Exhibit 2 are the following:

- Cash is down, accounts receivable are up. Cash was used to buy back company stock (see treasury stock below).

- Marketable securities have been completely sold. Proceeds might have been used to supplement the purchase of treasury stock.

- Property and equipment is significantly up. There are new liabilities in the form of a mortgage and notes payable.

- New capital stock was issued (sold). Proceeds may have been used to finance day-to-day operations, to make a down payment to purchase significant assets, or to finance the increase in accounts receivable.

- Treasury stock increased. This action may have caused the decrease in cash or short-term investments (marketable securities).

Some of these will become more obvious when the statement of cash flows is analyzed.

Ratio Analysis

Balance sheet ratios are useful in evaluating the following:

- Liquidity: a company's ability to pay its short-term (current) debt

- Solvency: a company's ability to pay all its debt (current and long-term)

- Asset management: a company's efficient and profitable use of its assets

A full discussion of all the ratios used to analyze a balance sheet would require a chapter unto itself. Here we focus on the *current ratio* and the *acid-test ratio*, the two most popular and universal ratios used by executives, investors, creditors, and investment analysts to measure a company's liquidity position.

Current Ratio. The current ratio shows the relationship of current assets to current liabilities. The formula is:

$$\frac{\text{Current Assets}}{\text{Current Liabilities}}$$

Using Exhibit 2, the current ratio at the end of 20X2 is calculated as follows:

$$\frac{\text{Current Assets}}{\text{Current Liabilities}} = \frac{\$80,000}{\$104,000} = 0.77$$

Southern Fast Food has a current ratio that is 0.77 to 1.00, meaning that it has 77 cents of current assets for every dollar of current liabilities. Current ratios should be compared against prior periods or industry standards to make meaningful judgments. However, there is a definite weak liquidity position when a current ratio falls below 1.00. The management of Southern Fast Food must conduct further study to determine corrective action. For example, selling its treasury stock and omitting future dividends would improve Southern Fast Food's liquidity ratio.

Acid-Test Ratio. The acid-test ratio, also called the *quick ratio,* is a more refined version of the current ratio, resulting in a more strict measurement of liquidity. This ratio excludes the less-liquid assets of inventories and prepaid expenses. The formula is:

$$\frac{\text{Cash} + \text{Short-Term Investments} + \text{Receivables (net)}}{\text{Current Liabilities}}$$

Using Exhibit 2, the acid-test ratio at the end of 20X2 is calculated as follows:

$$\frac{\$39,000 + \$0 + \$28,000}{\$104,000} = .64$$

Southern Fast Food's acid-test ratio is 0.64 to 1.00, meaning that it has 64 cents in the most highly liquid current assets for every dollar of current liabilities. Acid-test ratios should be compared against prior periods or industry standards to make an informed judgment.

Note the close results of the current ratio (0.77) and the acid-test ratio (0.64). In the hospitality industry, it is not unusual for the results of these ratios to be relatively close because inventories are a small part of current assets.

Statement of Cash Flows

The statement of cash flows (SCF) is the only statement that is prepared using only cash transactions. Its preparation is tedious and complex. Its purpose is to report on cash receipts and cash paid out (disbursements). The period of time covered is identical to that of the income statement.

Department managers seldom receive the statement of cash flows. Managing cash is the responsibility of executives who make the decisions to purchase costly assets or to borrow funds. Other readers of the SCF are investors, creditors, and others with a vested interest in a company's sources and uses of cash.

Reading the SCF

The statement of cash flows is divided into three major sections of activities:

- Operating
- Investing
- Financing

Cash flow is the net result of cash receipts and cash payments. If the cash receipts exceed the cash payments, the result is labeled as *net cash provided by (name of activities section).* If the cash payments exceed the cash receipts, the result is labeled as *net cash used by (name of activities section).*

The SCF in Exhibit 3 starts with the three activities sections. The totals of each section are as follows:

Operating Activities	$ 17,200
Investing Activities	(41,200)
Financing Activities	18,000

The total of these three sections results in a decrease to cash of $6,000 for the current year for Southern Fast Food ($17,200 − $41,200 + $18,000).

With this background information, the SCF in Exhibit 3 can be easily read as follows:

- The beginning cash balance of $45,000 comes from the end of last year, as shown on the balance sheet (Exhibit 2).
- The $6,000 cash decrease resulting from the three activities sections is subtracted from the beginning cash balance of $45,000 to arrive at $39,000, representing the ending cash balance at the end of the current year.
- The ending cash balance of $39,000 is verifiable because it must equal the cash balance at the end of this year, as shown on the balance sheet (Exhibit 2).

The SCF must have footnotes that address the following certain topics:

- Cash used to pay for interest and income taxes
- Cash used as down payments to purchase assets financed by a mortgage or note payable
- Disclosure of accounting policy

Cash Flows from Operating Activities

The purpose of the operating activities section is to report the net income on the *cash* basis. Either of two methods can be used to prepare this section: the direct method or the indirect method. The indirect method is the more popular procedure

Exhibit 3   Southern Fast Food—Statement of Cash Flows

Statement of Cash Flows
Southern Fast Food, Inc.
For the year ended 12/31/X2

Cash Flows from Operating Activities:

Net income		$ 9,000
Adjustments to reconcile net income to net cash flows from operating activities:		
Depreciation expense	$ 18,000	
Amortization expense	500	
Gain on sale of equipment	(1,000)	
Loss on sale of short-term investments	1,200	
Increase in accounts receivable	(9,500)	
Decrease in inventories	2,000	
Increase in prepaid expenses	(1,000)	
Decrease in accounts payable	(1,500)	
Increase in sales tax payable	800	
Decrease in accrued expenses	(1,300)	8,200
Net cash provided by operating activities		17,200

Cash Flows from Investing Activities:

Proceeds from sale of equipment	6,000	
Proceeds from sale of short-term investments	3,800	
Purchase of equipment	(43,000)	
Down payment on purchase of land	(8,000)	
Net cash used in investing activities		(41,200)

Cash Flows from Financing Activities:

Cash proceeds from note payable due 2/1/X4	30,000	
Proceeds from issuance of no-par capital stock	9,000	
Dividends declared and paid this year	(1,000)	
Purchase of treasury stock	(20,000)	
Net cash provided by financing activities		18,000
Increase (decrease) in cash for the year		(6,000)
Cash at the beginning of the year		45,000
Cash at the end of the year		$ 39,000

Supplemental Disclosures of Cash Flow Information

Cash paid during the year for:

Interest	$ 1,000
Income taxes	$ 2,000

Supplemental Schedule of Noncash Investing and Financing Activities

A parcel of land was purchased in December 20X2 as follows:

Acquisition cost of land	$ 40,000
Cash down-payment	8,000
Balance financed by mortgage	$ 32,000

Disclosure of Accounting Policy

For purposes of the statement of cash flows, the Company considers all highly liquid debt instruments purchased with a maturity of three months or less to be cash equivalents.

in the hospitality industry and is used in this chapter. Refer to the operating activities section in Exhibit 3 and examine the following for Southern Fast Food:

- The operating activities section starts with the net income from Exhibit 1 of $9,000. This net income was computed on the accrual basis, not on the cash basis.

- All the line items in this section also serve as an accounting procedure used in the indirect method to adjust the $9,000 accrual basis net income to its true cash basis of $17,200.

- Unless you have an overwhelming interest in accounting procedures, you can focus on only the $17,200 total of the operating activities section; this will not dilute your reading of the SCF.

Cash Flows from Investing Activities

The purpose of the investing activities section is to report on cash used to purchase investments or long-lived assets, as well as cash received from the sale of investments or long-lived assets. This section does not involve gains or losses on the sale of assets or the purchase cost of assets.

Investments bought or sold for cash may be short-term (marketable securities) or long-term. Long-lived assets generally involve cash transactions regarding property and equipment.

If an asset costing $100,000 is purchased with a $25,000 cash down payment and the balance of $75,000 is financed, only the $25,000 would appear as cash paid out in this section. (Remember, the SCF reports only on *cash* in and *cash* out.)

If an asset is sold for $80,000 cash resulting in a $15,000 loss, only the $80,000 would appear as cash received in this section.

Refer to the investing activities section in Exhibit 3 and examine the following for Southern Fast Food:

- Cash increased because equipment was sold for $6,000 *cash* and investments were sold for $3,800 *cash*. Any gain or loss is ignored in this section.

- Cash decreased because equipment was purchased for $43,000 cash and land was purchased with a down payment of $8,000 cash. (The financing of the land purchase is explained in the footnotes.)

- The cash flows from investing activities for Southern Fast Food results in a net cash decrease of $41,200.

Cash Flows from Financing Activities

The purpose of the financing activities section is to report on cash received or paid out relating to any equity or debt transactions, such as the following:

- Issuance of capital stock or bonds
- Purchase or sale of treasury stock
- Payment of dividends

- Cash borrowings
- Payment of principal portion of debt financing

Refer to the financing activities section in Exhibit 3 and examine the following for Southern Fast Food:

- Cash increased by $30,000 from a cash loan.
- Cash increased by $9,000 from the issuance of capital stock.
- Cash decreased by $1,000 for the payment of dividends.
- Cash decreased by $20,000 for the purchase of treasury stock this year.
- The cash flows from financing activities for Southern Fast Food results in a net cash increase of $18,000.

 **Key Terms** ───────────────────────────────

absolute values—In the context of financial statements, amounts stated in a monetary format.

accountant's letter—A letter accompanying the financial statements explaining the level of service performed by a public accountant.

audit—The highest level of service performed by a public accountant. It is a comprehensive examination of the accounting records, including observation of physical inventories and confirmation of receivables and payables.

common-size analysis—A method that uses a common divisor to evaluate relative values. Also called *vertical analysis*.

comparative analysis—The comparison of absolute values of the current period against a prior period, a standard, or a budget. Also called *horizontal analysis*.

compilation—The lowest level of service performed by a public accountant in the preparation of compiled financial statements. The accountant provides assurance only to the extent that the statements were prepared in accordance with standards for unaudited financial statements.

footnotes—Notes to the financial statements that provide disclosures that supplement the contents of the financial statements and explain important non-monetary items or events, such as pending lawsuits and leases.

horizontal analysis—See comparative analysis.

prime cost—The sum of cost of sales plus payroll and related costs.

ratio analysis—A means of expressing the relationship between two numbers by dividing one by the other. Ratios serve as benchmarks and are useful in pointing to possible problem areas requiring investigation.

relative values—Amounts stated in percentages in common-size analysis.

review—A level of service that is lower than that of an audit. It provides limited assurance that no material changes are necessary to the financial statements.

vertical analysis—See common-size analysis.

Review Questions

1. What specific items might be included in the notes to the financial statements?

2. What are the differences between an audit, a review, and a compilation service in the preparation of financial statements?

3. Why is the net income amount on the income statement not representative of cash income?

4. What are the differences between common-size analysis, comparative analysis, and ratio analysis?

5. What are the purposes of the income statement, balance sheet, and the statement of cash flows?

6. What are the names and representations of the three subtotals of income and final total of income on the income statement?

7. What does the term *liquidity* mean? Which ratios are used to measure liquidity?

8. What are the purposes of the operating activities section, investing activities section, and financing activities section of the statement of cash flows?

Internet Sites

For more information, visit the following Internet sites. Remember that Internet addresses can change without notice. If the site is no longer there, you can use a search engine to look for additional sites.

Balance Sheets
www.businesstown.com/accounting/
  basic-sheets.asp

*Beginners' Guide to Financial
  Statements*
www.sec.gov/investor/pubs/
  begfinstmtguide.htm

Cash Flow Statement
www.jpec.org/handouts/jpec71.pdf

Income Statements
www.businesstown.com/accounting/
  basic-statements.asp

*Using Ratios for Financial Statement
  Analysis*
www.creditguru.com/ratios/
  ratiopg1.htm

Problems

Problem 1

Compute *net sales, gross profit, operating income, income before income taxes,* and *net income* from the following information:

Income taxes	$ 4,000
Cost of sales	70,000
Non-operating losses	7,000

Sales	255,000
Payroll and related	82,000
Allowances and rebates	5,000
Depreciation and amortization	15,000
Other operating expenses	48,000

Problem 2

Compute the common-size percentages from the following partial income statement:

Sales	$425,000
Cost of sales	131,750
Payroll	106,250
Employee benefits	21,250

Problem 3

Compute the over/(under) budgetary variances using a comparative analysis from the following partial income statement:

	Budget	Actual
Sales	$420,000	$425,000
Cost of sales	134,750	131,750
Payroll	107,250	106,250
Employee benefits	20,250	21,250

Problem 4

Compute the food cost percentage, labor cost percentage, prime cost percentage, and profit margin ratio from the following condensed income statement:

Food sales	$425,000
Cost of food sales	131,750
Gross profit	293,250
Payroll	106,250
Employee benefits	21,250
Other operating expenses	130,750
Total operating expenses	258,250
Income before income taxes	35,000
Income taxes	4,000
Net income	$ 31,000

Problem 5

Compute the current assets, property and equipment, other assets, total assets, current liabilities, long-term liabilities, equity, and total liabilities and equity from the following information:

Accounts payable	$11,000
Accounts receivable	4,000
Land	30,000

Taxes and other payables	7,000
Buildings and equipment, net of depreciation	80,000
Supplies inventory	1,000
Cash	34,000
Liquor license (net purchase cost)	4,000
Common stock issued	43,000
Food inventory	6,000
Retained earnings	58,000

Mortgage payable is $40,000, of which $6,000 is due within 12 months of this balance sheet date.

Problem 6

Prepare a comparative analysis from the following partial balance sheet:

	Last Year End	This Year End	Change	% Change
Total Current Assets	$ 29,396	$ 46,550		
Total Assets	151,889	162,350		
Accounts Payable	15,300	25,400		

Problem 7

Compute the common-size percentages from the following partial balance sheet:

Cash	$ 36,500
Total Current Assets	46,550
Total Assets	162,350
Accounts Payable	25,400

Problem 8

Compute the current ratio and acid-test ratio from the following partial balance sheet:

Cash	$ 36,500
Short-term Investments	2,000
Accounts Receivable	1,450
Inventories	4,000
Prepaid Expenses	2,600
Total Current Assets	46,550
Total Assets	162,350
Accounts Payable	25,400
Total Current Liabilities	39,350
Long-term Liabilities	40,000
Total Liabilities	79,350
Total Equity	$162,350

Problem 9

Calculate the cash flow (increase or decrease in cash) for the period, using the following information:

Cash used in operating activities	$(30,000)
Cash provided by investing activities	90,000
Cash used by financing activities	(20,000)
Cash balance at beginning of year	15,000

Problem 10

Compute the cash provided or used for the operating activities section, investing activities section, and the financing activities section from the following information:

Sold equipment for $15,000 cash
Net income on the accrual basis is $65,000
Net income converted to a cash basis is $40,000
Issued common stock for $100,000 cash
Paid dividends in cash $8,000
Purchased land costing $200,000 with a $50,000 down payment and a mortgage of $150,000

Ethics Case

A privately held lodging company, Katymoe Properties, is a member of AH&LA. The association has asked Katymoe to submit data to be used in developing industry statistics. However, the company has experienced a terrible business year and does not want to disclose that fact to anyone.

The company has cooperated in providing its operating results to AH&LA for the last 20 years and does not want to refuse this time. Therefore, Martin Beebee, president of Katymoe, instructs the company's treasurer to calculate an average of the last five years and submit this average as the operating results for its terrible business year.

Because these numbers will be consolidated with data from hundreds of other lodging properties, the final statistics should not be affected.

1. Identify the stakeholders in this case.

2. Analyze and comment on any issues pertinent to this matter.

Chapter 13 Outline

Competencies

1. Summarize the federal government's authority regarding reporting by public companies, and discuss the SEC, the Sarbanes-Oxley Act, and the 10-K report. (pp. 331–334)

2. List and describe the major components of the annual report to shareholders. (pp. 334–337)

13

Annual Report to Shareholders

A WELL-DONE ANNUAL REPORT to shareholders is a masterpiece of financial and other company information. A company's stockholders should read it, as should anyone considering investing in the company. A company's annual report can answer many common stockholder and investor questions. It is more than just a bunch of financial statements; it is a comprehensive presentation full of financial and other information about the company's past, present, and future, and it often requires a sophisticated reader to glean all of the informational gold nuggets that are not apparent to the casual observer.

Stockholders of publicly held companies typically receive annual reports. Those who are not stockholders may request a copy of a company's annual report from the company's investor relations department, or view it on the company's website.

This chapter presents material that will help you answer the following questions:

1. How does governmental legislation affect annual reports?
2. What is the SEC?
3. What is the Sarbanes-Oxley Act of 2002?
4. What is a 10-K report?
5. What is the standard content of an annual report?

Governmental Authority on Reporting by Public Companies

A publicly listed company must abide by considerable governmental filing requirements. The **Securities and Exchange Commission (SEC)** has requirements that under penalty of law must be followed. Numerous reports must be filed with the SEC and other governmental agencies. The SEC plays the major role in the governmental regulation of the securities markets and the reporting that is required of publicly held companies.

The Sarbanes-Oxley Act of 2002 places additional requirements on a company's managers and auditing firm. This Act is very important legislation affecting corporate governance, financial disclosure, and the practice of public accounting.

The SEC requires that a company create two types of annual reports: the 10-K report (also referred to as the Form 10-K report), which is filed with the SEC, and the company's annual report to shareholders. Understanding the annual report to shareholders requires readers to have a basic understanding of the following:

- The SEC
- The Sarbanes-Oxley Act of 2002
- The 10-K report

The following sections will explore these topics.

The SEC

Prior to the Great Stock Market Crash of 1929, most government regulators and financial investors perceived no need for federal regulation of the securities market. Rare recommendations that the federal government (1) require companies to provide financial disclosure, and (2) enact laws to prevent the fraudulent sale of company stock, were never seriously considered.

The SEC was created because of an economic catastrophe that has maintained its notoriety to this day. When the stock market crashed in October 1929, many investors lost fortunes. Banks also were great losers in the Crash, because they had invested heavily in the stock markets. During the Crash, people feared that banks might not be able to pay back the money in their accounts. A run on the banking system caused many bank failures. In response to the crisis, Congress passed the Securities Act of 1933 and the Securities Exchange Act of 1934. These laws were designed to restore investor confidence, regulate the securities market, and regulate shareholder-reporting requirements.

The SEC is a government agency concerned with the securities industry. Its effectiveness is due in large part to its enforcement authority. Its primary mission is to protect investors and maintain the integrity of the securities markets. One reason this agency is so necessary is that stocks, bonds, and other securities can lose their value. This makes government oversight more important. Contrast this with the banking world, where deposits are guaranteed by the federal government.

The laws and rules that govern the securities industry in the United States are derived from this concept: "All investors, whether large institutions or private individuals, should have access to certain basic facts about an investment prior to buying it." To achieve this goal, the SEC requires public companies to disclose meaningful financial and other information to the public.

In addition to monitoring publicly held companies, the SEC oversees stock exchanges, broker-dealers, investment advisors, mutual funds, and public utility holding companies.

The Sarbanes-Oxley Act of 2002

Despite the creation of the SEC, corporate scandals, deceptions, and bankruptcies continued. Especially conspicuous was the period from 2000 to 2002, in which the following happened:

- In 2000: 176 public companies with assets of $95 billion filed for bankruptcy.

- In 2001: 257 public companies with assets of $259 billion filed for bankruptcy.

- In 2002: 189 public companies with assets of $382 billion filed for bankruptcy.

Two of the most infamous corporate bankruptcies and scandals during the period occurred at Enron Corporation and WorldCom, Inc. Tyco International, Ltd., was also involved in a scandal, but bankruptcy was not imminent. Although there were several other notable bankruptcies and scandals during these years, a discussion of these three companies will provide an overview of the types of problems that led to the passage of the Sarbanes-Oxley Act of 2002.

Enron Corporation had 21,000 employees and was one of the world's leading electricity, natural gas, and communications companies. In 2001, Enron filed for bankruptcy—the second largest in U.S. history. This corporate collapse caused big financial losses for creditors, and thousands of employees lost their life savings, because their 401(k) plans were tied to Enron's stock. In 2002, WorldCom (at that time, the nation's No. 2 long-distance phone company, with 60,000 employees) filed for Chapter 11 bankruptcy after it revealed that it had improperly booked $3.8 billion in expenses. WorldCom's bankruptcy is the largest in United States history, dwarfing that of Enron Corp. Again, shareholders and creditors were saddled with huge financial losses. In 2002, Tyco's former managers were charged with improper and illegal activities, including giving nearly $100 million in unauthorized payments to themselves or associates.

The fall of these three mega-companies, as well as other corporate catastrophes, caused public confidence in corporate reporting and the reliability of the public accounting profession to sink to critically low levels. The stock market downturn during 2000–2002 was extensive. The technology stocks bubble that burst in March 2000 also contributed to the volatility of the stock market.

Congress passed the **Sarbanes-Oxley Act of 2002** to protect investors from fraudulent accounting activities perpetrated by publicly held corporations. This legislation improves the accuracy and reliability of corporate disclosures under securities laws. It includes criminal provisions applicable to a company's management and its public auditing firm. These provisions strengthen criminal sanctions for violators by creating new federal criminal offenses and increasing penalties for existing federal criminal offenses.

The Sarbanes-Oxley Act is arranged into 11 titles, or sections, each consisting of several subsections. The more important sections regarding compliance within these titles are sections 302, 401, 404, 409, and 802. The topics covered in these sections are as follows:

- Section 302: Corporate Responsibility for Financial Reports

- Section 401: Disclosures in Periodic Reports

- Section 404: Assessment of Internal Controls

- Section 409: Disclosures

- Section 802: Criminal Penalties

The 10-K Report

The **10-K report** is the official annual business and financial report filed by public companies with the SEC. Companies with at least 500 shareholders of one class of stock and at least $5 million in assets are required to file with the SEC. The 10-K report presents comprehensive information about the company, including financial statements and other financial information; a business summary; and a list of properties, subsidiaries, legal proceedings, and other facts not usually found in the annual report to shareholders.

Annual Report to Shareholders: An Overview ─────

Annual reports give a detailed picture of a company's financial condition and the results of its operations. Annual reports include management's discussion of the current year, an analysis of important company events, the company's stock price history, and financial data presented quantitatively on three financial statements: the income statement, the balance sheet, and the statement of cash flows. Statistics and graphs often accompany these statements.

Under Section 409 of the Sarbanes-Oxley Act, issuers of financial statements are required to disclose information on material changes in their financial condition or operations. These disclosures should be supported by graphic presentations as appropriate.

The SEC requires that audited financial reports be sent to the company's shareholders at the end of a company's fiscal year, as well as a description of the company's operations and future outlook. Many companies go to considerable expense when creating the annual report, using high-quality, glossy paper and color pictures to make their annual report a showcase for the company.

The content of the annual report varies somewhat from one company to another. Some companies include their 10-K report in the annual report, since the 10-K report includes all of the financial statements and other shareholder information required for the annual report. Regardless of the differences in the quality of production and style of reporting, all annual reports to shareholders should feature the following:

- Letter to the shareholders
- Financial statements
- Notes to the financial statements
- Management assessment of internal controls
- Report of independent public accountants
- Certification of the annual report by company executives

These elements are addressed in the following sections.

Letter to the Shareholders

The shareholders' letter highlights the company's activities during the past year, especially its acquisitions and the opening of new outlets. Typically the letter discusses the company's growth activities and accomplishments. Financial high-lights and graphs often are an integral part of the letter. The letter usually ends with upbeat plans for the future. The company's chief executive officer (CEO) signs the letter.

Financial Statements

Financial statements are written reports describing the financial health of a company and its operating results in quantitative terms. They include a balance sheet, income statement, and statement of cash flows. The statements are prepared and certified by a certified public accounting firm (the auditor).

Sometimes a corporation will have control over other corporations through stock ownership of those companies. Based on its control, that corporation may have to include the results of its controlled companies and affiliates in its financial statements. These combined financial statements are called **consolidated financial statements** and report the financial results of all the companies as if they were a single business entity. The combined assets and liabilities are reported on one balance sheet, the combined revenues and expenses are reported on one income statement, and the combined cash flows are reported on one statement of cash flows.

Notes to the Financial Statements

The notes to the financial statements, often simply called *notes* or *footnotes*, are an integral part of the annual report. They are often placed in a separate section of the report following the financial statements, and present clarifying and important information about the facts behind the numbers. The notes to the financial statements are an essential research tool; they are as important as the numbers on the statements. The notes serve as another disclosure vehicle and not only clarify the financial statements but also reveal information not on the statements. This information includes, at minimum, the following:

- The company's accounting policies, depreciation methods, and inventory accounting methods
- Leases—terms and conditions
- Stock-based compensation
- Related-party activity
- Stock options and other benefit plans
- List of directors and officers
- Stock price history
- Pending lawsuits
- Procedure for computing income taxes

Management Assessment of Internal Controls

Under Section 404 of the Sarbanes-Oxley Act, publicly held companies are required to publish information in their annual reports concerning the following:

- The scope and adequacy of the company's internal control structure

- The company's procedures for financial reporting

- A statement assessing the effectiveness of the company's internal controls and procedures

Report of Independent Public Accountants

The report of independent public accountants is often called the *accountant's letter* or *auditor's report*. The auditor or auditing firm certifies that the financial statements meet the requirements of generally accepted accounting principles (GAAP), and that the auditor's examination complied with mandatory auditing standards. In some cases, the auditor may give a certification with restrictions or give no certification at all. Each of these certifications is referred to as an *opinion*, a term which, in regard to financial statements, has legal significance and can be used only by certified public accountants. The opinion can take the form of any of the following:

- Unqualified opinion

- Qualified opinion

- Adverse opinion

- No opinion

An **unqualified opinion** is given when the financial statements present fairly, in all material respects, a company's financial position, results of operations, and cash flows in conformity with GAAP. An unqualified opinion is also called a *clean opinion* and, from the company's viewpoint, is the most desirable form of opinion. A **qualified opinion** is given when, except for a certain specific issue (as described by the auditor or auditing firm), the financial statements fairly present the company's financial position, results of operations, and cash flows in conformity with GAAP. An **adverse opinion** is given when a company's financial statements are not fairly presented, or the company's system of internal controls has deficiencies. In extreme cases, the auditor may express **no opinion** on the financial statements, especially if the scope of the audit was insufficient or impeded by the company's management or staff.

In addition to the auditor's opinion of the financial statements, Section 404 of the Sarbanes-Oxley Act requires that the public accounting firm, in its auditor's report, assess and report on the effectiveness of the company's internal control system and procedures for financial reporting. Under Section 802 of the Sarbanes-Oxley Act, the accountant or accounting team that knowingly and willfully violates the requirement that *all audit or review papers must be maintained for a period of five years* will face fines and/or imprisonment of up to ten years.

CEO and CFO Certification of the Annual Report

Two certifications of the annual report are required. One relates to the 10-K report and is usually signed by the CEO. The other certification relates to the annual report and is usually signed by the CEO and chief financial officer (CFO).

Under Section 302 of the Sarbanes-Oxley Act, executives must certify their company's financial statements. This certification signifies that:

- The signing officers have reviewed the report.

- The report does not contain any misleading or materially untrue statements or material omissions.

- The financial statements and related information fairly present the company's financial condition and results of operations.

- The signing officers are responsible for internal controls and have evaluated these internal controls within the previous 90 days.

- The officers have provided a list of all deficiencies in the internal controls and information on any fraud that involves employees who play an important role in internal controls.

- The officers have disclosed significant changes in internal controls or related factors that could have a negative impact on the internal control system.

Pursuant to Section 401 of the Sarbanes-Oxley Act, financial statements are required to be accurate, containing no incorrect statements.

Under Section 802 of the Sarbanes-Oxley Act, penalties of fines and/or up to 20 years imprisonment are imposed for altering, destroying, mutilating, concealing, or falsifying records with the intent to obstruct, impede, or influence a legal investigation.

 Key Terms

adverse opinion—A statement in an auditor's report given when a company's financial statements are not fairly presented, or the company's system of internal controls has deficiencies.

annual reports—Audited financial reports sent to the company's shareholders as required by the SEC.

consolidated financial statements—Financial statements that present the combined financial data of a corporation and its controlled subsidiaries as if they were a single business entity; that is, the combined assets and liabilities of the companies are reported on one balance sheet, their combined revenues and expenses are reported on one income statement, and their combined cash flows are reported on one statement of cash flows.

no opinion—In extreme cases, a statement in an auditor's report given when the scope of the audit was insufficient or impeded by the company's management or staff.

qualified opinion—A statement in an auditor's report given when, except for a certain specific issue as described therein, a company's financial statements are fairly presented.

Sarbanes-Oxley Act of 2002—An act passed by the U.S. Congress to protect investors from fraudulent accounting activities perpetrated by publicly held companies. It improves the accuracy and reliability of corporate disclosures under securities laws.

Securities and Exchange Commission (SEC)—A government agency regulating the securities industry.

10-K report—The official annual business and financial report filed by public companies with the Securities and Exchange Commission; also called a *Form 10-K report*.

unqualified opinion—A statement in an auditor's report given when a company's financial statements are fairly presented. Also called a *clean opinion*, and, from the company's viewpoint, is the most desirable form of opinion.

 Review Questions

1. What two types of annual reports does the SEC require?

2. What kind of agency is the SEC? What is its primary mission?

3. What is the significance of October 1929?

4. Why was the SEC created?

5. What is the importance of the Sarbanes-Oxley Act of 2002? What do sections 302, 401, 404, 409, and 802 of the Act cover?

6. What is a 10-K report?

7. What types of opinions can a certified public accounting firm give in its auditor's report?

8. What are consolidated financial statements?

9. What are notes to the financial statements? At a minimum, what do the notes include?

10. What is the standard content of an annual report to shareholders?

 Internet Sites

For more information, visit the following Internet sites. Remember that Internet addresses can change without notice. If the site is no longer there, you can use a search engine to look for additional sites.

Annual Report for a Specific Company
Visit the Internet site of any company whose stock is publicly traded. The site should provide a link to access the company's annual statements and other corporate information.

Sarbanes-Oxley Act
www.soxlaw.com/
http://en.wikipedia.org/wiki/
  Sarbanes%E2%80%93Oxley_Act

Securities and Exchange Commission (SEC)
www.sec.gov/

Case Study:
Preparation of an Annual Report to Shareholders

ETOC Hotels, Inc., is a corporation listed on a major stock exchange; its market capitalization is over $900 million and its common stockholders number in excess of 700,000. The company's fiscal year ends on December 31. In April, after the close of the fiscal year, the company's chief executive officer (CEO) and chief financial officer (CFO) are preparing a 10-K report to file with the SEC. The CEO and CFO are also preparing for a meeting with their certified public accounting firm next week.

The CEO and CFO have decided the following issues:

1. The annual report to shareholders will not include color pictures, because they are costly to print.

2. They will insert a copy of the 10-K report in the annual report, in lieu of a separate set of financial statements.

3. The annual report will not feature any graphs, because they are costly to prepare.

A review of the company's financial reports and system of internal controls reveals:

- The financial statements are in compliance with generally accepted accounting principles, and all material representations are included.

- The company did install an internal system of controls and procedures; however, the system is insufficient to determine if any irregularities occurred. However, the CEO and CFO are confident that fraud or irregularities did *not* occur during the year.

ETOC Hotels, Inc., during the fiscal year just ended, made its first acquisition, of YAR, Inc. (a hotel amenities sales company), by purchasing 90 percent of YAR's common stock. The CEO prefers not to include the financial data of this company in ETOC Hotels, Inc.'s, annual report, because YAR's stock has been held just for several months, not for a full year. But, in any case, the CEO will concur with the CFO's decision on this matter.

(continued)

(continued)

Requirements

Based on this information, compose a critique of the annual report of ETOC Hotels, Inc., with references to sections of the Sarbanes-Oxley Act and/or the SEC, as applicable. Specifically:

1. Analyze and comment on the three decisions made by the CEO and CFO.

2. Decide what the auditor's opinion should be of the annual report — that is, whether the auditor should give the company an unqualified opinion, a qualified opinion, an adverse opinion, or a no opinion — regarding the company's financial statements and system of internal controls. Outline why the other types of opinions might not be proper in this instance.

3. Decide whether the CFO should include the financial data of YAR, Inc., in the annual report of ETOC Hotels, Inc. Explain why or why not.

4. Analyze and comment on any other item that requires further consideration.

Chapter 14 Outline

Competencies

1. Summarize the advantages hospitality businesses enjoy if they accept credit cards, and describe merchant accounts. (pp. 343–346)

2. Describe point-of-sale systems. (pp. 346–348)

3. Explain real-time credit card processing, and discuss steps businesses take to combat credit card fraud. (pp. 349–351)

4. List and describe typical merchant account fees. (pp. 351–353)

14

Credit and Debit Cards

ANY SUCCESSFUL HOSPITALITY BUSINESS recognizes that today's consumer is both credit-oriented and convenience-oriented. Cash-only businesses are scarce, and excel only if they can offer consumers special pricing or products and a convenient location. Even with those outstanding qualities, today's cash-only businesses are at a significant disadvantage. Most hospitality customers expect to be able to take advantage of the convenience of credit cards and debit cards wherever they decide to stay or shop. Any retail establishment puts itself at risk if it ignores this expectation. If your business doesn't provide customer convenience, your competitors are ready and eager to do so.

The Internet has provided additional business opportunities for the opportunistic businessperson. In addition to traditional bricks-and-mortar retail establishments, many retailers have Internet stores that sell food items, services, and hard goods. Selling via the Internet is known as **e-commerce.** A retailer's online store can be on the retailer's own website or on a large trading community website such as Amazon, Yahoo, or eBay, where millions of people buy and sell millions of items every day. These trading community websites are worldwide online marketplaces for the sale of goods and services by a diverse community of individuals and businesses. Practically anyone can trade practically anything on them.

The prevailing method of payment online and in most hospitality businesses is the credit card. This chapter will discuss important credit card issues such as the following:

1. Should every hospitality business accept credit cards?

2. What is a merchant account?

3. How does a business get a merchant account?

4. What is a point-of-sale system? What equipment is required?

5. What is real-time credit card processing?

6. What is a payment gateway?

7. How can people protect themselves against credit card fraud?

8. What are the different fees and charges assessed in a merchant account?

Evaluating Credit Card Acceptance

Not every hospitality business needs to accept credit cards; some companies operate successfully without them. Before managers decide whether to accept credit cards, they must thoroughly analyze the facts pertaining to credit-card acceptance and how it will affect the business.

Accepting credit cards offers many advantages to a hospitality business. In most lodging and restaurant establishments, credit cards are the most widely used form of payment, cash being second. Accepting credit cards offers businesses another way to provide customer service, because most consumers like to use credit cards, finding them a faster, more convenient alternative to paying with cash. The use of credit cards gives a business the image of a modern company with a major focus on pleasing the customer.

If a business decides not to accept credit cards, it may alienate some consumers forever. While the cost to the business of accepting and processing credit cards is a consideration, so too is the lost-business cost of not accepting credit cards. When managers weigh costs, they should consider the following:

- The potential loss of customers if credit cards are not accepted

- The inconvenience to customers if the business doesn't accept credit cards

- The business threat posed by competitors who accept credit cards

If a hospitality business decides that it will accept credit card payments from customers (and the vast majority of hospitality businesses do), a merchant account must be established to provide the business with the capability to accept credit cards.

Processing Credit Card Transactions: The Merchant Account

Before a hospitality business can accept credit cards, it must have a **merchant account,** which is a special account set up for a business through a bank or some other financial institution to accept and process credit card orders. The bank (or other financial institution) is a member of a credit card network. After processing a customer's credit card electronically, the transaction goes through a series of complex stages and ultimately transfers the money through the merchant account and makes a deposit into the business's checking account.

Most merchant accounts provide support for all the major credit card brands, such as Visa, MasterCard, and American Express, and many also provide support for other, less-popular or less-known cards, such as Discover and JCB. In most cases, a single merchant account provides the flexibility to accept most credit cards.

A merchant account is not a bank account; it is a special account set up to accept credit cards. It processes credit card payments from customers and then deposits the proceeds into the business's checking account. Fees associated with the merchant account, such as transaction and service fees, are deducted from the business's account. Regardless of how a credit card is accepted—in person, via telephone, fax, e-mail, or website—a merchant account is required. Since most merchant accounts allow the processing of many types of credit cards, only one merchant account should be necessary for a hospitality business. Visa and MasterCard are the most popular and widely used credit cards, and most merchant accounts process these cards.

Selling on the Internet

It's possible for a business to sell on the Internet without accepting credit card payments; it would simply have to ask its customers to send in their orders by snail mail and pay for them with checks or money orders. But there would be repercussions: orders would be delayed as they made their way through the postal system, and another delay would follow once the order and payment arrived, as the business waited for the check to clear the bank. Of course, customers would be affected by these delays as well, as they waited for their products to be shipped. This is an inconvenient way for customers to shop, and many will refuse to do so. Most customers expect to be able to pay by credit or debit card; a company may lose a substantial amount of business if it doesn't provide that convenience for its customers.

Even if a company has a merchant account for its bricks-and-mortar business, that account may not allow the acceptance of credit card payments over the Internet. Companies should check with their merchant account provider; policies vary from provider to provider. A business might need two merchant accounts: one for in-store sales and a separate one for Internet sales.

A business's merchant account is not the only player in the infrastructure that makes possible online credit card transactions. For example, even if the merchant account for a bricks-and-mortar business can also be used for Internet credit card sales, the account may not be compatible with the online storefront software requirements, or the online storefront service may require a separate merchant account regardless of the existing merchant account's capabilities.

Getting a Merchant Account

A **merchant service provider (MSP)** is any business that offers credit card processing services. The two types of MSPs are:

1. Merchant account providers

2. Independent sales organizations

The services offered and the charges for these services vary greatly, depending mostly on the type of service provider the business selects and the business's sales volume. When managers are deciding on which MSP to contract with, they should examine the following costs:

- Setup charges
- Transaction fees
- Equipment rental and expenses
- Monthly fees
- Other fees and charges

The following sections will take a look at the two types of MSPs.

Merchant Account Providers. The term **merchant account provider (MAP)** is often misused. Strictly speaking, MAPs are banks that provide merchant accounts;

such banks are usually called *acquiring banks*. MAPs are secure and reliable, but they are very selective; opening a merchant account with a MAP usually requires a past personal or business relationship with the bank's management. MAPs are typically very demanding during the application process, requiring businesses to submit a large amount of documentation and detailed financial statements. The stiff entry requirements of MAPs have brought about the rise of independent sales organizations as an alternative merchant service provider.

Independent Sales Organizations. An **independent sales organization (ISO)** is a company that acts as a go-between for a business and a MAP (bank). The ISO applies for the account on behalf of merchants. ISOs are not as heavily regulated as banks, and therefore are not subject to the rigid laws under which all banks operate. ISOs can offer merchant accounts to businesses that banks would otherwise reject. For this risk, ISOs charge higher fees and service charges.

Point-of-Sale Systems

A **point-of-sale (POS) system** captures data at the time and place that a sale is made through the use of personal computers or specialized terminals that are combined with cash registers, barcode readers, optical scanners, and magnetic stripe readers to accurately and instantly capture the sales transaction. Today's POS systems save retailers time and money in many ways, including the following:

- POS systems can interact with check-guarantee services and can process credit cards, smart cards, debit cards, electronic checks, and electronic benefit transfer cards offered by state and federal agencies.

- Card-swipe technology eliminates manual key-in processing. Keying in each card number is slow and prone to error or fraud.

- Processing fees are significantly lower with swipe technology because it is much more secure.

- Online retail POS processing options include secure payment gateways and online check-acceptance capabilities.

POS systems can help a business process its sales quickly, safely, and profitably. There are many POS systems to choose from, and they can be equipped with many options, so managers should seek expert assistance before making a final buying decision. To name just one variable, credit card terminals differ in their sophistication and capabilities (Exhibit 1 shows a basic card-swiping terminal). Order-entry, billing, and collection can be simplified with the use of touch-screen terminal equipment (see Exhibit 2 for a sample touch-screen order-entry keyboard). Touch-screen terminals can be used in quick-service (fast-food), carry-out, and table-service operations.

Components of a Point-of-Sale System

For a hospitality business, a POS system might consist of these components:

- *POS software*, computer programs that facilitate the sales process

MAPs and E-Commerce

MAPs (banks) are often reluctant to give merchant accounts to e-commerce businesses, because of the high failure rate of these businesses. Moreover, e-commerce often incurs a high rate of credit card adjustments, which adds to the MAPs' reluctance. For example, an online customer may dispute a purchase or claim that his or her credit card was fraudulently used. Laws regarding credit card fraud are weighted heavily in the customer's favor. When a customer prevails, the customer's credit card company first credits the contested charge to the customer's account, and then passes on the charge to the MAP. If the merchant cannot afford to pay back the MAP or the merchant is out of business, the MAP has to absorb the charge.

Exhibit 1   Credit Card Swipe Device

Courtesy Hypercom Corporation

- *Cash register/cash drawer,* which helps process the sale and houses money, checks, credit card receipts, and other funds
- *Receipt printer,* which prints receipts for customers
- *Pole display device,* which displays the purchase amount to customers
- *Card swipe terminal,* which processes credit cards
- *Check reader,* which authenticates checks
- *Computer,* which uses software and peripherals to integrate various sales functions such as ordering, billing, and inventory tracking; can produce informative and timely management reports

Exhibit 2   Sample Menu Keyboard for an Order-Entry Device

CARAFE WHITE WINE	CARAFE RED WINE	BOURBON	VODKA	DECAF COFFEE	COFFEE	SALAD	BAKED POTATO	HASH BROWNS	FRENCH FRIES	SOUR CREAM	TIME IN
CARAFE ROSE WINE	SCOTCH	SODA	WATER	BLOODY MARY	TEA	WITH	WITH-OUT	BREAD	STEWED TOMATO	VEGETAB	TIME OUT
RARE	GIN	TONIC	COLA	SCREW-DRIVER	MILK	HOUSE DRESS	FRENCH DRESS	VINEGAR & OIL	EXTRA BUTTER	MUSHRM SAUCE	ACCOUNT #
MEDIUM	WELL	SAUTEED MUSHRMS	SHRIMP COCKTAIL	FRENCH ONION SOUP	CRAB MEAT COCKTAIL	OYSTERS ON ½ SHELL	ITALIAN DRESS	BLEU CHEESE DRESS	COUPON 1	COUPON 2	COUPON 3
PRIME RIB	T-BONE	SHRIMP	LOBSTER	CIGARS	CASH BAR	CLEAR	ERROR CORRECT	CANCEL TRANS	CHECK TRANSFER	PAID OUT	TIPS PAID OUT
CHATEAU-BRIAND	FILET	CLAMS	TROUT	CANDY	SERVER #	TRAN CODE	SCREEN	NO SALE	CASHIER #	EMPL DISC	MGR DISC
TOP SIRLOIN 16 OZ	TOP SIRLOIN 12 OZ	SEA BASS	SCALLOPS	SNACKS	VOID ITEM	7	8	9	QUANTITY	ADD CHECK	CREDIT CARD 2
PORTER-HOUSE	CHOPPED SIRLOIN	OYSTERS	ALASKAN KING CRAB	# PERSONS ADD ON	REVERSE RECEIPT	4	5	6	VOID TRANS	CHARGE TIPS	CREDIT CARD 1
STEAK & CHICKEN	SURF & TURF	RED SNAPPER	SEA FOOD PLATTER	DINING ROOM SERVICE	PRICE LOOK UP	1	2	3	NEW CHECK	CASH BAR TOTAL	CHARGE
LEG OF LAMB	ROAST DUCK	PORK CHOPS	CHICKEN LIVERS	LOUNGE SERVICE	MODE SWITCH		0		MENU 1	PREVIOUS BALANCE	CHECK TOTAL	CASH TEND

Source: Validec, Inc., San Carlos, California.

Supermarkets and other retail stores use barcode technology in their POS systems; hospitality businesses can also use barcodes for inventory control of certain products. A **barcode** is a series of white spaces and bars (vertical lines) of varying thicknesses that is affixed to or printed on retail store items, identification cards, and postal mail to identify a particular product number, person, or location. The sequences of vertical bars and spaces represent numbers and other symbols that encode information such as product numbers, serial numbers, transaction codes, supplier numbers, and other types of data.

Barcoding increases accuracy by eliminating the human error that can occur when product information and prices are entered into POS and other systems manually.

Barcode systems require the following additional components:

- *Barcode label design software,* which designs barcode labels

- *Barcode printer,* which prints barcode labels

- *Barcode scanner,* which scans the barcodes affixed to products

Real-Time Credit Card Processing

Real-time credit card processing is a must for Internet and mail order/telephone order (MOTO) businesses. Real-time processing on the Internet works as follows:

- When customers are finished shopping, they click a *check out* link.
- Next, a secure page appears.
- The customer enters the credit card number, expiration date of the credit card, and other information, then clicks a *Pay Now* link.
- A message shows whether the card has been accepted or declined.
- Shortly thereafter, the funds are deposited in the merchant's account.

Real-time capability is a great convenience for credit card users, because their purchases are authorized and completed very quickly. Moreover, real-time credit card processing reduces the risk for the business, because a credit card purchase can immediately be denied for any of the following reasons:

- The credit card has been canceled.
- The spending limit on the credit card has been exceeded.
- The credit card has been reported stolen.
- The credit card number or expiration date has been incorrectly entered.

For customers, some of the advantages of real-time credit card processing are as follows:

- The customer can order the product or service immediately.
- The customer is immediately notified that the transaction is approved.
- Real-time credit card processing is fast, efficient, and secure.

Most merchants on the Internet use real-time credit card processing, even though an extra expense is involved. The merchant does not have to purchase additional hardware or software for real-time credit card processing, because a third party's computers handle the processing.

Real-time processing is not possible without a payment gateway.

Payment Gateways

A **payment gateway** links the online buyer's and online seller's respective banks/ financial institutions; it is a third-party network that processes transactions from an e-commerce portal and routes them through the banking or credit card system by linking the banking network with the Internet. It is a link into the banking network and is inaccessible to Internet users.

A payment gateway takes a transaction, then certifies it and routes it after securing it with **encryption**, which is the transformation of data into a form that makes it unreadable by anyone without a secret decryption key; only the intended recipient can read the encrypted messages. Almost all payment gateways are based on Secure Electronic Transaction technology, which ensures the security of financial transactions on the Internet.

When a customer attempts to buy goods using a credit or debit card, a payment gateway performs three vital functions:

- Authorization: it checks that the credit is acceptable.

- Clearing: it passes the transaction to the merchant's bank.

- Recording: it records the transaction and allows the merchant to view it (and all other transactions upon request).

Credit Card Fraud

Every business should assume that sooner or later it will be the victim of credit card fraud. Legislation generally exempts the cardholder from any liability for the unauthorized use of his or her card; therefore it is the merchant, not the customer, who suffers the financial loss when such fraud occurs.

The Internet makes credit card fraud easier, because the merchant has no face-to-face interaction with the customer. However, even in face-to-face transactions, the swiping of the card and a resulting authorization merely means the card has not expired and has not been reported as stolen; it doesn't mean that the user is valid. In a face-to-face transaction, the merchant can check the card's printed expiration date and see if the card is signed on the back. If it is, this signature can be compared with the customer's signature on the signed sales receipt. In face-to-face transactions, merchants can ask to see some photo ID if they suspect credit card fraud.

Authorization and Authentication

Authorization is a process in which a customer's credit card account is checked to make sure it is in good status. In a hospitality environment, the credit card is swiped through a terminal and, if the transaction is accepted, an approval message appears on the screen or is printed. Otherwise, the terminal will show that the transaction is declined. As part of the authorization process, the credit card number is checked to make sure it is a valid account number, the expiration date is checked to make sure it applies to the account number in question, and the credit limit is checked. Authorization does not confirm that the use of the credit card is not fraudulent. The credit card could have been stolen and its owner does not yet realize it, or the theft has not been reported at the time of the transaction.

Authentication is a process to verify that the user of the credit card is its legal owner. In retail and hospitality operations, a purchase is referred to as a *card present* transaction because both the customer and credit card are physically present. The merchant should compare the signature on the back of the credit card to the signature on the transaction document. If the signatures do not match, credit card fraud may be a possibility.

Internet transactions are *card not present* transactions, but these transactions are not unique to the Internet; they also occur in mail order and telephone order transactions. Since neither the physical card nor the cardholder's signature is available in these transactions, Internet, mail order, and telephone sales transactions expose merchants to a greater risk of credit card fraud.

Internet fraud detection software can check the IP (Internet Protocol) address with the computer network address. An IP address is a unique number that identifies a specific computer or other network device on the Internet. Simply stated, an IP address can be imagined as being similar to a street address or a phone number assigned to a computer or other network device on the Internet for identification purposes. A transaction originating in England with an IP address in the United States may be a red flag that a possibly fraudulent transaction is taking place.

Some credit card companies offer credit card holders a *Verified By* option, so that Internet credit card transactions by a *verified* customer can be authenticated; usually this is done by a password.

Cardholder Disputes and Chargebacks

A cardholder may dispute an entry on his or her credit card statement, claiming that it is fraudulent, that the product was never ordered, or that someone else used the credit card illegally. The bank that issued the credit card will either send a merchant inquiry, or take the sales funds from the merchant's account, called a **chargeback;** sometimes chargebacks are done immediately without the merchant's approval or rebuttal.

Excessive chargebacks due to credit card fraud can result in the loss of the privilege of a merchant account. Most merchant account providers accept a chargeback incidence rate of one to three percent before canceling the account.

Reserve or Holdback

Some merchant account service providers insist upon reserving or holding back a percentage of a merchant's sales each month, as security against any disputed charges that may arise from the month's credit card transactions; called a **reserve** or **holdback,** this charge is most often levied against high-risk businesses. If a business operates for several months without a problem, this requirement may be dropped, and the money held back released.

The holdback could also take the form of a cash deposit up front; a personal guarantee by company officers is also a possibility. Another condition sometimes imposed on high-risk merchant accounts is a limitation on the monthly sales volume that can be processed.

Merchant Account Fees and Charges

Choosing a merchant account service provider is not an easy task. Some businesses choose providers on the basis of the fees and charges that they impose. Sometimes low fees do not represent the great deal that they promise at first glance. For example, one provider may have a lower transaction fee than another, but compensate for this low fee by charging an additional monthly fee or requiring a long-term contract that cannot be broken without a financial penalty.

Many factors influence credit card processing fees, such as the type of business, the number of years the business has been in operation, the business's credit rating, the percentage of sales made over the phone or the Internet, the average dollar amount of each sales transaction, and the total dollar amount of sales per month. In some cases the rates and fees may be negotiable. Keep in mind that costs should not be the only consideration; a merchant must also evaluate the technical and administrative support services of the provider.

Many fees may be associated with a merchant account; some are applicable only to Internet transactions. The more common merchant account fees are the following:

- *Application/setup fee.* Some merchant account service providers charge an application fee, which is usually refundable if the merchant is not approved. After approval, there may be a charge for setting up the merchant account.

- *Discount rate.* A **discount rate** (also called a *commission*) is the percentage that the merchant account service provider takes from every transaction. For example, a $20 sales transaction with a discount rate of two percent results in the merchant's receiving only $19.60 on the sale; the service provider receives $0.40 as its commission. Discount rates vary among credit card companies; American Express's rate is different from Visa's or Discover's, for example. Generally, discount rates for Internet transactions are higher because of the inherent risk in these transactions. Retail processing rates can be below two percent, while real-time and online processing rates may range as high as three percent.

- *Transaction fee.* Generally, a **transaction fee** applies to Internet transactions in addition to the discount rate. It is a fixed amount regardless of the sales amount. If the contractual transaction fee is $0.25, any sale, regardless of the amount, incurs a transaction fee of $0.25.

- *Monthly fee.* While some merchant account service providers do not charge a monthly fee, others charge a fixed monthly fee or a minimum monthly fee if the discount rate and transaction fee levies are below a certain amount.

- *Secure gateway fee.* This Internet fee may be a flat monthly fee or be charged on a per-transaction basis.

- *Software fee.* This fee may be included in the setup charge or might be billed separately. Some providers only rent out their software, and therefore their software fees are a continuing expense.

- *Equipment rental fee.* Merchant accounts often include a fee for the rental of equipment; an option may be available to purchase the equipment. Generally it is more advantageous to purchase the equipment if the provider will allow it. Some companies offer buy-out provisions in their leases, allowing the merchant to buy the lease out (that is, purchase the equipment) during the term of the lease for a specified one-time payment.

- *Batch header fee.* Some merchant account service providers levy a **batch header fee** on Internet transactions processed through a gateway. The credit card transactions are batched at the end of each day and sent to the merchant's bank for deposit. If this fee is levied, it is usually nominal.

- *Address verification fee.* While address verification is usually a free service, some merchant account service providers charge a small **address verification**

fee for each transaction. Address verification helps prevent credit card fraud. The address verification service checks that the billing information the customer submitted is accurate.

* *Fraud screening fee.* Some merchant account service providers offer a fraud-checking service that checks each transaction for any signs of fraud or potential fraud. They may charge extra for this service.

Key Terms

address verification fee—A fee per transaction that some merchant account service providers charge to verify the billing address of a credit card user. Usually this is a free service.

authentication—A process undertaken to verify that the user of a credit card is its legal owner.

authorization—A process in which a customer's credit card account is checked to make sure that it is in good status; however, it does not confirm that the use of the credit card is not fraudulent.

barcode—A series of white spaces and bars (vertical lines) of varying thicknesses that is affixed to or printed on retail store items, identification cards, and postal mail to identify a particular product number, person, or location. The sequences of vertical bars and spaces represent numbers and other symbols.

batch header fee—A fee charged for a batch of transactions processed through a payment gateway.

chargeback—An amount a merchant's bank charges back to the merchant for a credit card transaction previously accepted but that is later in dispute.

discount rate—A percentage taken from every credit card transaction by the merchant account service provider.

e-commerce—Buying and selling transactions that occur over the Internet.

encryption—The transformation of data into a form that is unreadable for anyone without a secret decryption key.

holdback—A cash percentage of a merchant's credit card sales retained by the merchant account service provider as security against any disputed credit card transactions that might arise. It can also take the form of a cash deposit up front, or a personal guarantee by company officers. Also called a *reserve.*

independent sales organization—A company that acts as a go-between for a merchant and a bank that provides merchant accounts.

merchant account—A special account set up for a merchant to accept and process credit cards through a bank or other financial institution.

merchant account provider (MAP)—A bank that provides merchant accounts.

merchant service provider (MSP)—Any business that offers credit card processing services for merchants.

payment gateway—A third party network that processes transactions from an e-commerce portal and routes them through the banking or credit card system by linking the banking network with the Internet.

point-of-sale (POS) system—A network of personal computers or specialized terminals that are combined with cash registers, barcode readers, optical scanners, and magnetic stripe readers to accurately and instantly capture sales transactions.

reserve—A cash percentage of a merchant's credit card sales retained by the merchant account service provider as security against any disputed credit card transactions that might arise. It can also take the form of a cash deposit up front, or a personal guarantee by company officers. Also called a *holdback*.

transaction fee—A fixed amount charged per transaction to the merchant by the merchant account service provider, regardless of the sales amount.

Review Questions

1. What is the major disadvantage an Internet retail operation faces if it doesn't accept customer credit cards?

2. What is the definition of e-commerce? How is it conducted?

3. What two major factors influence the services and fees a merchant may expect to pay a merchant service provider?

4. What is the similarity and the difference between a MAP and an ISO?

5. What is the advantage of credit card swipe technology in a POS system?

6. How does real-time credit card processing work for an Internet store?

7. What is a payment gateway?

8. What is the difference between credit card authorization and authentication?

9. Why is credit card fraud more likely to occur in e-commerce?

10. What are holdbacks? Why are they used?

Internet Sites

For more information, visit the following Internet sites. Remember that Internet addresses can change without notice. If the site is no longer there, you can use a search engine to look for additional sites.

ATMs—How They Work
http://money.howstuffworks.com/per-
  sonal-finance/banking/atm.htm

Credit Cards—How They Work
http://money.howstuffworks.com/
  personal-finance/debt-management/
  credit-card.htm

Debit Cards—How They Work
http://science.howstuffworks.com/
  debit-cards.htm

Debit Cards vs. Credit Cards
http://banking.yahoo.com/ff010808.html

Point-of-Sale System
http://en.wikipedia.org/wiki/
  Point_of_sale

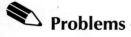

Problems

Problem 1

Which of the following is/are false?

a. A merchant account is a bank account.

b. A merchant account can process only Visa or MasterCard, not both.

c. The term *merchant service provider* (MSP) applies only to banks.

d. Getting authorization on a credit card detects fraud.

e. The term *discount rate* refers to a discount a merchant receives due to higher sales volume.

Problem 2

A merchant got authorization to process a credit card for the following purchase:

Food	$ 60.00
Liquor	20.00
Sales tax	5.60
Tip	16.00
	$101.60

The credit card holder disputes the charge after viewing the monthly credit card statement and claims fraudulent use. The merchant's service provider decides to charge back the merchant. What, if any, will be the amount of the chargeback?

Problem 3

A restaurant has entered into the following credit card agreement:

Discount rate:	2 percent
Monthly fee:	$25
Equipment rental fee:	$75

The credit card sales for a particular month are $100,000, and 1,600 credit cards were processed. How much is the credit card processing expense for that month?

Problem 4

An Internet retail store has entered into the following contract:

- Discount rate: 3 percent

- Transaction fee: $0.20

- Monthly fee: $50 minimum (charged if the discount and transaction fees do not equal $50; if the discount and transaction fees are less than $50, the difference is the monthly fee)

- Equipment rental fee: $75

- Batch header fee: $0.04 per batch

- Address verification fee: $0.03

The following credit card transactions occurred for a particular month:

Dollar sales volume	$ 150,000
Number of transactions	5,000
Number of batches	25

How much is the credit card processing expense for that month?

Problem 5

A merchant's contract calls for a holdback of 1 percent per month until $1,500 is in reserve. From the start of the contract, the merchant's credit card sales are as follows:

Month 1	$ 50,000
Month 2	$ 70,000
Month 3	$ 80,000
Month 4	$ 90,000

What is the holdback amount for each month?

Case Study:
Principles of Credit Card Processing and Credit Card Fraud

Your client is starting a retail Internet store operation and has been approved for a merchant account. A point-of-sale system is installed, but no contract for a merchant provider has been signed. Write a report to your client explaining the basic principles of real-time credit card processing and the critical issues your client should know about credit card fraud.

Chapter 15 Outline

What Is a Budget?
    The Budgeting Process
    Assembling a Budget
    Budgeting Guidelines
Sales Forecasting
    Forecasting Considerations for a New
        Business
    Forecasting Considerations for an
        Existing Business
    Percentage Method of Forecasting
        Sales
    Forecasting Rooms Sales
    Forecasting Food Sales
The Relationship of Expenses to Volume
    Total Cost Equation
Variable Expenses
    Budgeting a Variable Expense
Fixed Expenses
    Budgeting a Fixed Expense
Semi-Variable Expenses
    Budgeting a Semi-Variable Expense
Breakeven Point
    Breakeven Point Formula
    Profit Target

Competencies

1. Explain the importance of budgeting and forecasting, describe the budgeting process, and summarize general guidelines for creating a budget. (pp. 359–362)

2. Describe sales forecasting. (pp. 362–364)

3. Explain the relationship of expenses to volume, and describe variable, fixed, and semi-variable expenses. (pp. 364–370)

4. Discuss the breakeven point, and explain the breakeven point and profit target formulas. (pp. 370–372)

15

Introduction to Budgeting and Forecasting

Hospitality owners, executives, managers, department heads, and anyone else responsible for sales or expenses should know how to prepare budgets and forecasts. Budgeting plays a key role regardless of the size of a business. Any business is more susceptible to failure when budgeting is not put to use as a financial management tool.

While studies cannot agree on the failure rate of restaurants, it's generally true that new restaurants fail at a higher rate than many other types of small businesses. Two major reasons for this higher failure rate are lack of operations expertise and poor financial management. Many owners and managers of hospitality businesses incorrectly view budgeting as merely accounting or recordkeeping, and put more importance on operations. Application of all business skills, whether related to operations or finances, is an important ingredient for success in any type of business.

It's easy to look at budgeting as just more paperwork that takes time away from more exciting, immediate operational tasks such as managing staff members, greeting guests, or preparing food. However, budgeting should be looked on as an operations tool (even though financially related), because it helps managers prepare for the future and can reveal potential problems that lie ahead for the business. A budget is a written plan that authorizes and controls company spending. A budget helps managers control expenditures by providing them with a tool that allows them to analyze expenses compared to company goals.

It's not only good for a business if its managers are skilled at budgeting and forecasting; it's also good for the managers. On a personal career note, managers in the hospitality profession who can understand and use budgetary procedures and controls are generally more likely to be selected for promotion and will enjoy personal financial success more quickly than those managers for whom budgeting and forecasting are impenetrable mysteries.

Sophisticated statistical budgeting and forecasting models are beyond the scope of this introductory chapter. Instead, the chapter will concentrate on the budgeting of expenses and on simple, yet pragmatic, methods of forecasting sales. This chapter will answer such questions as the following:

1. What is a budget?

2. What information is required to develop a budget?

3. How can sales be forecasted accurately for new and existing businesses?

4. How do expenses react to changes in sales volume?

5. What are variable, fixed, and semi-variable expenses?

6. How are budgets developed for variable, fixed, and semi-variable expenses?

7. What is the breakeven point, and how is it computed?

What Is a Budget?

Simply stated, a **budget** is a financial plan. Budgets cover many areas of concern to managers, such as forecasting sales, controlling future expenses, and planning for capital expenditures (new buildings and equipment). A budget does the following:

*   Serves as a financial road map of the future
*   Provides benchmarks against which actual performance can be measured
*   Gives managers information to help them make correct financial decisions

A budget indicates where the funds to do business will come from and where funds will be spent. Of course, sales are a source of funds; loans are another source. A successful business with a budget plan can more easily secure bank loans it needs.

The main objective of any business is to operate so that sales exceed expenses and net income results; profitability is the key to staying in business.

The Budgeting Process

Budgeting requires that managers have access to appropriate and accurate information. Budgeting is based largely on the objectives of the business. Managers must be good at analyzing and thinking ahead if they want their budgets to be meaningful and useful financial tools. Good budgeting requires analyzing dependable sources of data, such as historical financial statements and ratios, rather than merely using guesswork. Inflation and increases in such costs as food costs, rent, and annual salaries must be taken into account when developing a budget. Managers of a new business lack historical information, but they don't have to start from scratch; to help them prepare their first budget, they have access to industry ratios and a uniform system of accounts.

Budgets are usually done separately for each month of the business year. Larger companies are known to develop five-year budgets and amend them annually, based on changing trends and circumstances.

After business objectives have been identified and the period of budgeting determined, information must be selected and gathered to compile the budget. This information includes historical reports such as income statements, balance sheets, cash flow statements, and departmental reports. Such information is helpful in analyzing sales and related costs. Sales are difficult to predict because many variables affect them, such as competitors, the economy, and changes in consumer habits and tastes.

Some companies ignore all previous history and instead prepare each budget from a starting point of zero; this process is called **zero-base budgeting**, which requires in-depth planning and budgetary expertise. It also requires much more time and planning than the usual budgeting processes. In theory, zero-base budgeting ensures a more well-thought-out budget, because managers are not simply building on last-year's budget numbers without thinking them through.

Assembling a Budget

To begin assembling a budget, managers should prepare a worksheet that includes a list of all personnel and business expenses related to the hospitality operation. New or out-of-the-ordinary costs that might be incurred during the budgetary period must also be considered, such as the costs for consultants, temporary employees, major repairs, and new equipment.

A budget may be a simple one-page statement of projected sales expenses, or a complicated spreadsheet explaining various items of expense or revenue. In any case, the budgeted items and the calculations of the dollar amounts for each item should be supported by working papers to show how the numbers were developed. Working papers are important to the budgeting process because they serve as support documentation that can be reviewed should questions arise as to how the budget was put together.

Budgeting Guidelines

Expense estimates should be neither too low nor too high, to avoid producing an unrealistic budget; a budget is supposed to be a reliable financial plan for the success of the business. If costs are greatly underestimated, the budget will certainly be exceeded; if they are greatly overestimated, the care with which the managers put the budget together may be questioned. In either case, the budget becomes less effective as a management tool.

The following are some general guidelines for creating a budget:

- *Remember that budgeting is not an exact science.* Budgets are never exact, but the philosophy behind going to the time and trouble to put them together anyway is this: it is better to take educated guesses at what might happen than to have no idea whatsoever. The longer hospitality managers prepare and use budgets, the better they get at putting them together.

- *Use last year's figures only as a guide.* While historical information on sales and costs is helpful, each year brings new challenges. The hospitality environment is dynamic and competitive. Not only must managers analyze the business's historical financial information, they must also consider factors beyond the business's control when putting new budget numbers together.

- *Create realistic budgets.* Managers should look at many sources of data — historical information, the business plan, proposed operational changes, expansion plans, information about the competition, general economic trends, and more — when putting together a realistic budget that will be a useful management tool.

- *Involve managers and staff members throughout the process.* Everyone at the business who has financial and planning responsibilities should be involved in the budgeting process, from the outset of the planning stage to the budget's completion, so that they fully understand the budget and feel comfortable working with it. Ultimately, they will be responsible for performing within the budget; therefore, they should be involved in the budgeting process from the beginning to ensure their best input and cooperation.

Sales Forecasting

Sales forecasting is the process of organizing and analyzing financial and other information to arrive at a future sales volume estimate expressed in units or dollars. If the forecasted sales volume is expressed in room units or meal covers, these figures are easily converted to sales dollars by using an average room rate or average meal price.

The inherent uncertainty of the business environment complicates the forecasting process. Business size and product mix (variety of products) are factors that can help determine whether sales forecasting methods will be simple or complex. The research phase of a good forecasting process usually consumes more time and is more difficult than the final process of calculating the sales forecast. Any assumptions used to forecast sales should be so noted in the working papers.

The budgeting of expenses is critically dependent on a realistic sales volume. Therefore, the accuracy of any budget is contingent on the forecasting of a rational and attainable level of sales volume. Forecasting sales for a new business is much more difficult than for an existing business that already has well-defined products, a loyal customer base, and historical information to analyze.

Forecasting Considerations for a New Business

A new business has neither historical information nor an established customer base. Nevertheless, sales forecasting for a new business, while more theoretical in nature, may still produce useful results that will aid management in making the business succeed financially. Sales forecasting should be done for each month of the business year, and adjustments should be made if actual results are materially different from forecasted expectations.

The following are some factors that a new business's managers should analyze and research before making any sales forecast calculations:

- Customer profile
- List and profile of competitors
- The product mix
- Product pricing

Developing a customer profile helps managers define their market. Customers may be profiled by their age and income; by whether they are tourists, singles, or families; and other criteria. Competitors should be identified and profiled by their locations, volumes, products, hours of operation, busy periods, prices, quality of goods and services, advertising, promotions, and other factors. The product mix for a restaurant depends primarily on the food items and dishes on its menu; the product mix for a lodging operation includes the types of rooms it offers, such as single rooms, double rooms, and suites. Product pricing is always a conundrum: prices must be competitive, draw in customers, render a profit margin so the business can remain in business, and reward the business's owner(s) for the risk undertaken.

Forecasting Considerations for an Existing Business

Managers of an existing business have the advantage of historical data and known markets, products, and prices when they forecast. However, just like the managers of a new business, they must take into account environmental factors beyond their control when forecasting, such as existing and potential new competitors. Additionally, the business's current customer base, products, and product pricing should be carefully reviewed each year during the budgeting process to help the business maintain its competitive edge and profitability.

Percentage Method of Forecasting Sales

Sales revenues from a given month this year provide a good base for predicting sales for the same month next year. For example, managers can use this year's January sales as the basis for forecasting next January's sales, adjusted by volume or price factors. The following table shows last year's sales for three months, and then the sales forecast for the same three months in the next year, adjusted by a 10 percent price increase:

Month	Last Year	Increase	Forecast for Next Year
1	$100,000	10%	$110,000 ($100,000 × 110%)
2	80,000	10%	88,000 ($80,000 × 110%)
3	90,000	10%	90,000 ($90,000 × 110%)

This is a very simple yet effective method of sales forecasting. Last year's sales amounts are multiplied by the percentage increase in price (in this case, 10 percent) plus 100 percent to arrive at the sales forecast. The results would have been the same with no price increase but with a 10 percent increase in volume. The calculations are identical.

Forecasting Rooms Sales

Instead of using a percentage method, a more refined approach to forecasting rooms revenue is to use an average room rate (ARR), which can be applied to the total rooms or to each type of room. An important component in lodging sales forecasting is occupancy percentage, because it is unlikely that all rooms will be sold for every day of the year. Historical analysis and research provides occupancy percentage information. One method of forecasting rooms revenue is to use the following statistical formula:

Rooms × Occupancy % × Average Room Rate × Days Open = Forecasted Sales $

The following is an example of the application of this formula:

Month	Rooms	× Occupancy % ×	Average Room Rate	× Days Open =	Forecasted Sales Dollars
A	200	60%	$50	30	$180,000
B	200	70%	$70	31	$303,800

These calculations would be performed for each month of the business year and totaled to arrive at the annual sales forecast. There are other, more refined methods of forecasting rooms revenue, but this basic formula is a good place to start.

Forecasting Food Sales

While the percentage method may be satisfactory for many food operations, management may prefer to use a more sophisticated method that considers seats, turnover, and average food check. One method of forecasting food revenue is to use the following statistical formula:

Seats $\times$ Turnover $\times$ Average Food Check $\times$ Days Open $=$ Forecasted Sales $

Historical information can provide the turnover and the average food check amounts, which can be modified for any price changes. A restaurant's average food check and turnover vary from meal period to meal period. For that reason, to produce a more exact forecast, these computations should be made for each meal period. The following is an example of the application of this formula for a particular month:

Meal Period	Seats $\times$	Turnover $\times$	Average Food Check $\times$	Days Open $=$	Forecasted Sales Dollars
Breakfast	100	4.0	$ 4	23	$ 36,800
Lunch	150	2.5	$ 8	23	69,000
Dinner	150	2.0	$14	31	130,200
Total for the month					$236,000

These calculations would be performed for each month of the business year and totaled to arrive at the annual sales forecast. There are other, more refined methods of forecasting food revenue but, again, this is a good basic formula with which to start.

The Relationship of Expenses to Volume ————————————

Different kinds of expenses react in different ways to sales volume. Some expenses rise or fall incrementally with sales volume, others do not. Meal covers, rooms, guests, and sales dollars are all measurements of volume. Any expense can be categorized by its relationship to volume, as follows:

- Variable
- Fixed
- Semi-variable

Exhibit 1 presents these expense categories in a diagram format for emphasis. This chapter will discuss the importance of the categories and how each of these three types of expenses reacts to volume changes.

Experienced financial managers know that it is not always practical to define expenses as being 100 percent true in their relationship to volume. Quite often, professional judgment is necessary to classify expenses as variable, fixed, or

Exhibit 1   Categorizing Expenses According to Action Traits

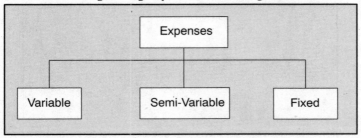

semi-variable. Sometimes, for expediency, managers will classify certain semi-variable expenses as variable, for example.

Total Cost Equation

A helpful equation that managers can use to determine cost is as follows:

$$\text{Total Cost} = \text{Variable Cost} + \text{Fixed Cost}$$

This is usually shown as:

$$\text{TC} = \text{VC} + \text{FC}$$

This equation is useful in determining cost components. If two components are known, the unknown component is easily determined. For example:

$$
\begin{aligned}
\text{TC} &= \text{VC} &+ &\text{FC} \\
\$50 &= \$30 &+ &\;?
\end{aligned}
$$

In this case, the fixed cost (FC) would be $20. Here is another example, in which the total cost (TC) is the unknown factor:

$$
\begin{aligned}
\text{TC} &= \text{VC} &+ &\text{C} \\
? &= \$80 &+ &\$15
\end{aligned}
$$

In this case, the total cost (TC) would be $95.

Variable Expenses

Variable expenses are the only expenses that act in a parallel pattern with volume. If volume goes up one unit, the variable expense also goes up one unit. (This direct relationship is shown in Exhibit 2.) The cost equation for a $100 variable cost would appear as follows:

$$
\begin{aligned}
\text{TC} &= \text{VC} &+ &\text{FC} \\
\$100 &= \$100 &+ &\;0
\end{aligned}
$$

How a variable expense relates to volume is also demonstrated in Exhibit 3, which shows that each sales unit of $10 creates an identical unit of $3 variable expense. This would be generally true regardless of the volume, because

Exhibit 2   Graphic Presentation of Variable Expense

Sales

Variable
Expense

Exhibit 3   Relationship of a Variable Expense to Volume

Unit Sales	Sales $	Variable Expense	% of Sales $
0	$ 0	$ 0	nm (not measurable)
1	10	3	30%
2	20	6	30%
3	30	9	30%
10	100	30	30%
50	500	150	30%

variable expenses are incremental: sell one more unit, incur one more unit of variable expense.

Notice that, while total variable dollar expense changes, the variable cost percentage remains the same (see Exhibit 3). There is no variable expense if there is no sales volume.

The following are some typical variable expenses in the hospitality industry:

- Cost of food sold
- Cost of beverage sold
- Any cost of sales

While not necessarily 100 percent true, for expediency and simplicity, the following are typically treated as variable expenses:

- Guest supplies
- Other supplies

Budgeting a Variable Expense

Variable expenses do not exist if sales volume is zero. Variable expenses are simple to budget because the variable expense percentage remains constant. If the food cost is 34 percent at one level of sales dollar volume, it is treated as being 34 percent at every level of sales dollar volume. This static percentage will be true as long as menu prices and purchase costs do not change.

Assume that an income statement shows the following:

Food Sales	$100,000	100%
Cost of Food Sales	34,000	34%

The food cost percentage is 34 percent, computed by dividing the $34,000 cost of sales by the $100,000 net sales volume. Since food cost is a variable expense, the percentage can be used at any volume within a relevant range.

If management forecasts that the next period's food sales will be $125,000, the food cost for that period is calculated as follows:

$125,000	Food Sales
× 34%	Food Cost %
$ 42,500	Forecasted Food Cost

Fixed Expenses

Fixed expenses are expenses that do not vary with sales. The cost equation for a $100 fixed expense would appear as follows:

$$TC = VC + FC$$
$$\$100 = 0 + \$100$$

Incorrectly, **fixed expenses** have been defined as those expenses that stay the same; the technical, more precise definition is that fixed expenses are those expenses that are not affected by sales volume, so that they stay relatively constant regardless of changes in sales volume. The relationship of a fixed expense to sales volume is shown in Exhibit 4. If volume goes up one or more units, the fixed expense is not affected.

The relationship of a fixed expense to volume is also demonstrated in Exhibit 5. Assuming a particular fixed expense is $50 per day, it remains at $50 per day regardless of the sales volume level. Notice that the percentage of a fixed cost to sales volume is not related and is meaningless in the development of budgets.

Examples of fixed expenses for a hospitality business are the following:

- Depreciation
- Amortization
- Rent
- Interest
- Property taxes
- Property insurance

Exhibit 4   Graphic Presentation of Fixed Expense

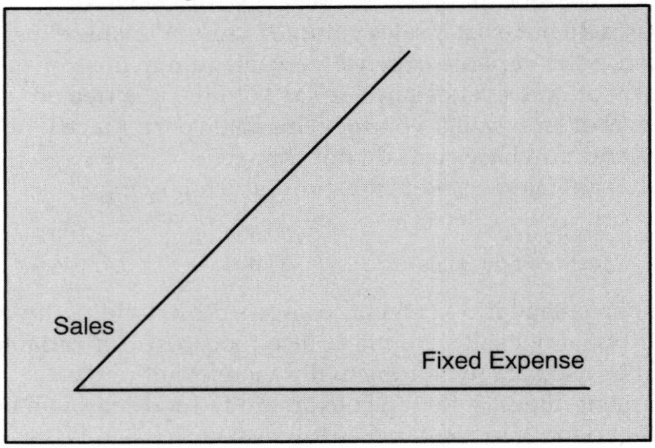

Exhibit 5   Relationship of a Fixed Expense to Volume

Unit Sales	Sales $	Fixed Expense	% to Sales $
0	$ 0	$50	nm (not measurable)
1	10	50	500%
2	20	50	250%
3	30	50	167%
10	100	50	50%
50	500	50	10%

Budgeting a Fixed Expense

Unlike variable expenses, fixed expenses are incurred even if sales volume is zero, and a fixed expense remains fairly constant as sales volume increases: sell one more unit, incur no additional expense.

Fixed expenses are simple to budget because the expense dollar remains relatively constant. If the daily fixed expense is $50, it will be $50 at any sales level; therefore, the percentage of a fixed cost cannot be used to calculate a fixed expense, because there is no relationship to sales volume.

Semi-Variable Expenses

Semi-variable expenses, unlike variable and fixed expenses, do *not* have a predictable relationship to sales volume. Semi-variable expenses have a random relationship to volume because they consist of mixed elements; one portion is variable and the other is fixed. The cost equation for a $100 semi-variable expense might appear as follows:

$$TC = VC + FC$$
$$\$100 = \$70 + \$30$$

Exhibit 6   Graphic Presentation of Semi-Variable Expense

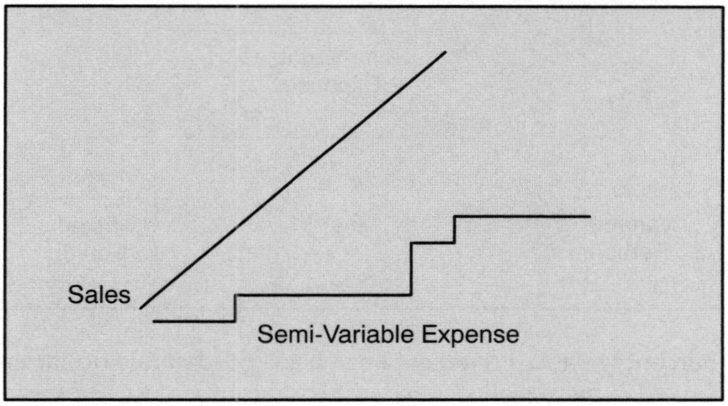

Exhibit 7   Relationship of Semi-Variable Expense to Volume

Unit Sales	Sales $	Semi-Variable Expense	% to Sales $
0	$ 0	$ 20	nm (not measurable)
1	10	20	200%
2	20	30	150%
3	30	40	133%
10	100	60	60%
50	500	100	20%

The pattern of a particular semi-variable expense might look like a series of steps, as shown in Exhibit 6. If volume goes up one or more units, the semi-variable expense has no direct relationship that can be stated in dollars or a percentage.

Exhibit 7 shows that a semi-variable expense has no relationship to volume (in this case, sales dollars are the volume basis). Note that the percentages of this semi-variable expense, as related to sales, provide no basis for making any judgment or principle. For this reason, semi-variable expenses require considerable examination, as shown later.

Payroll and related expenses rank with food cost as the largest operating expenses in the hospitality industry. Payroll-related expenses are costs such as employee fringe benefits, payroll taxes, and employee meals. Semi-variable expenses can be categorized as follows:

- Payroll and related expenses
- Any expense not variable or fixed

Budgeting a Semi-Variable Expense

A semi-variable expense cannot be precisely estimated unless it is separated into its fixed and variable components (see Exhibit 8). Since a variable expense has a

Exhibit 8   Separating a Semi-Variable Expense into Its Mixed Elements

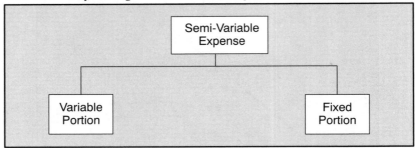

predictable percentage and a fixed expense has a predictable dollar amount, separating these mixed expenses allows accurate budgeting of a semi-variable expense.

Two methods used to separate a semi-variable cost into its variable and fixed components are the *high-low method* and *regression analysis*. These methods require historical data and mathematical formulas. Regression analysis is very time-consuming. Fortunately, a computer can perform the repetitive steps and extensive computations.

Because of the complexities and time involved in budgeting semi-variable expenses, they are often treated as variable. However, managers—especially those in large businesses—should use caution when they change semi-variable expenses to variable expenses for expediency's sake when creating budgets; the larger the business, the larger the margin of error in the budget calculations. Since labor is one of the largest costs in the hospitality industry, special care should be taken in treating it as a variable expense. However, if labor costs are not significantly large, using a variable approach may produce satisfactory results.

Breakeven Point

The **breakeven point** is the level of sales at which there is no profit and no loss **(breakeven)** before income taxes. The zero profit or loss is *not* the breakeven point. The following example clarifies this differentiation:

Sales	$100,000	← *Breakeven point*
Variable Costs	70,000	
Contribution Margin	30,000	
Fixed Costs	30,000	
Income (loss)	$ 0	← *Breakeven*

The computation of breakeven point requires that all expenses be listed on a working paper and grouped as variable or fixed, as shown in Exhibit 9. This analysis can be performed using last year's financial data or this year's budget. The semi-variable expenses require separation into their variable or fixed elements by use of the high-low method, regression analysis, or professional judgment. Once all expenses are grouped, a total is taken to arrive at variable costs and fixed costs. One calculates the variable cost percentage by dividing the total variable expenses by the sales dollars.

Exhibit 9   Worksheet for Grouping Costs

Forecasted Sales		$200,000			
Budgeted Expense	**Type**	**TC**	**VC**	**FC**	**Comments**
Cost of Food sold	V	$ 61,000	$ 61,000		
Payroll & related	SV	58,000	36,000	$ 22,000	Regression analysis
Guest supplies	V	3,000	3,000		
Operating supplies	V	8,000	8,000		
Utilities	SV	9,000	7,000	2,000	High-low method
Other variable cost	V	10,000	10,000		} In actual practice,
Other fixed costs	F	12,000		12,000	} each expense is
Other SV costs	SV	7,000	5,000	2,000	} listed individually.
Total expenses	SV	$168,000	$130,000	$ 38,000	
Income Before Income Tax		$ 32,000			

Variable Cost % $= \dfrac{VC}{Sales} = \dfrac{\$130,000}{\$200,000} = 65\%$

After the working paper is completed, the data can then be applied to the breakeven point formula.

Breakeven Point Formula

The formula to compute breakeven point (sales volume) is as follows:

$$\text{Breakeven point} = \frac{\text{Fixed Costs}}{100\% - \text{Variable Cost \%}}$$

The formula is often condensed as follows:

$$\text{BEP} = \frac{\text{FC}}{100\% - \text{VC\%}}$$

Applying the breakeven formula with the information in Exhibit 9 results in the following:

$$\text{BEP} = \frac{\text{FC}}{100\% - \text{VC\%}} = \frac{\$38,000}{100\% - 65\%} = \frac{\$38,000}{35\%} = \$108,571$$

The breakeven point formula indicates that the company in Exhibit 9 will incur no profit or loss at a sales volume of about $108,571. This breakeven point can be verified by the following procedure:

Sales	$108,571	← *Breakeven point*
VC ($108,571 × 65%)	70,571	
CM	38,000	
FC ($38,000 at any volume)	38,000	
Income Before Income Tax	$ 0	← *Breakeven*

It is a common custom to round the variable cost percentage to a whole percentage, and round the computed breakeven sales volume and all monetary calculations to whole dollars. This is done to condense the data and also not to deceive the reader that any planning formula produces exactness. While these formulas produce an approximate and very useful number, the result does not represent an explicit number.

Profit Target

A hospitality business does not set a goal of breaking even. Instead, a more useful management tool is one that answers: What sales volume is required to achieve a specific profit? Profit planning is a primary goal for any successful hospitality business. Planning for profits can be accomplished by using a modification of the breakeven formula, as follows:

$$\text{Sales \$} = \frac{\text{FC } + \text{ Profit Objective}}{100\% - \text{VC}\%}$$

Using the data in Exhibit 9, assume the company has a profit goal of $40,000 before income taxes. The solution is as follows:

$$\text{Sales \$} = \frac{\$38,000 + \$40,000}{100\% - 65\%}$$

$$\text{Sales \$} = \frac{\$78,000}{35\%}$$

$$\text{Sales \$} = \$222,857$$

The formula projects that this company will require sales of $222,857 to achieve its profit objective of $40,000, based on its projected cost structure. The $222,857 may not be the exact number, but it is a representative number that should help management achieve the stated profit objective. As is true with any formula of this kind, the result is a yardstick; the actual sales number that the business needs to achieve to hit its $40,000 profit goal may be slightly more or slightly less than the formula result.

 Key Terms ————————————————————————————————————

breakeven—No profit and no loss.

breakeven point—The level of sales volume at which there will be zero profit or loss.

budget—A financial plan covering areas such as sales and expenses.

fixed expenses—Expenses that have no relationship to volume and are not affected by volume changes. Typical examples are rent, interest, property taxes, depreciation, and amortization expenses.

sales forecasting—The process of organizing and analyzing information to arrive at an estimated future sales volume.

semi-variable expenses—Expenses that do not have a predictable relationship to volume because they consist of two expense components, one fixed and the other variable.

variable expenses—Expenses that act in a parallel relationship with sales volume. Cost of sales is one example.

zero-base budgeting—A budget-planning process in which managers ignore the financial history of the business and justify budget requests as if they were starting from a base of zero. In theory, this ensures a well-considered budget, since managers are not simply building on last-year's budget numbers without thinking them through.

 ## Review Questions

1. What is a budget? What advantages does budgeting offer?

2. Why can the predicting of sales be difficult?

3. If budgeting is not an exact science, why should it be done?

4. What is sales forecasting? What are its uncertainties and its importance?

5. What factors should be considered in forecasting sales for a new business?

6. What formula uses occupancy percentage and average room rate to forecast room sales?

7. What formula uses turnover and average check to forecast food sales?

8. What three kinds of expenses are closely related to sales?

9. What is the total cost equation?

10. What is a variable expense? A fixed expense? A semi-variable expense?

11. What is the difference between *breakeven* and *breakeven point*?

12. What is the breakeven point formula?

 ## Internet Sites

For more information, visit the following Internet sites. Remember that Internet addresses can change without notice. If the site is no longer there, you can use a search engine to look for additional sites.

Breakeven Point
www.accountingcoach.com/
  online-accounting-course/01Xpg01.html
www.fast4cast.com/
  break-even-calculator.aspx

Budgeting
www.investopedia.com/articles/pf/08/
  small-business-budget.asp
www.gaebler.com/
  Business-Budgeting.htm

Fixed and Variable Expenses
www.referenceforbusiness.com/small/
   Eq-Inc/Fixed-and-Variable-
   Expenses.html
http://bizfinance.about.com/od/
   pricingyourproduct/qt/
   Fixed_Variable_Costs.htm

Forecasting
http://communication.howstuffworks.com/
   sales-forecasting.htm
www.va-interactive.com/inbusiness/
   editorial/sales/ibt/sales_fo.html

 # Problems

Problem 1

A lodging operation had rooms sales of $100,000 in March of last year. Management estimates the same rooms volume for March of next year, but with a price increase of 6 percent. Forecast the room sales amount for March next year.

Problem 2

A restaurant had food sales of $100,000 in March of last year. Management estimates a 6 percent increase in volume for next March, but no price increase. Forecast the food sales amount for March of next year.

Problem 3

Management for a 300-room lodging operation predicts the following statistics for July next year: 75 percent occupancy, $70 average room rate, and the operation will be open 31 days. Forecast the room sales amount for July next year.

Problem 4

Forecast the food sales for the current (31-day) month. The restaurant serves lunch and dinner each day. The following statistics are available:

	Seats	Turnover	Average Check
Lunch	100	4.0	$ 8.00
Dinner	100	3.0	15.00

Problem 5

A semi-variable expense totaled $800 for a month. Its fixed component was $200. Compute its variable component.

Problem 6

Budget the food cost for a particular month if the sales volume is $150,000 and the food cost is 32 percent.

Problem 7

The rent expense is $3,000 per month. Sales levels for the next three months are $300,000, $400,000, and $600,000. Budget the rent expense per month for the next three months.

Problem 8

Compute the breakeven point using the following data, and verify that your answer is correct:

> Fixed costs total $140,000
> The percentage of all variable costs to sales is 60 percent

Problem 9

Using the following data, compute the sales level required to achieve a profit target of $200,000, and verify that your answer is correct:

> Fixed costs total $140,000
> The percentage of all variable costs to sales is 60 percent

Problem 10

The managers of a chain of restaurants are developing an annual budget for one of their smaller units. Labor will be treated as a variable expense for purposes of expediency. (Historical analysis reveals that this treatment will not materially affect the accuracy of the budget for this unit.)

Using the following information, prepare a budget for this unit, using an income statement format:

- Sales last year were $200,000. Menu prices will increase 5 percent. Sales volume is expected to remain the same.

- Cost of sales remains at 33 percent.

- Payroll and related expenses are estimated at 30 percent.

- Cost of supplies is estimated at 5 percent.

- Rent is $2,000 per month.

- All other expenses are estimated at 10 percent.

Problem 11

Management is planning to increase sales volume 2.5 percent and leave menu prices the same. Forecast food sales for months 1, 2, and 3 this year by using the following historical information:

Month	Sales Volume Last Year
Month 1	$120,000
Month 2	$160,000
Month 3	$180,000

Problem 12

Management is planning to increase menu prices 2.5 percent and does not expect any change in sales volume. Forecast food sales for months 1, 2, and 3 this year by using the following historical information:

Month	Sales Volume Last Year
Month 1	$120,000
Month 2	$160,000
Month 3	$180,000

Problem 13

Management is planning to increase menu prices 3 percent and also expects a 2 percent increase in sales volume. Forecast food sales for months 1, 2, and 3 this year by using the following historical information:

Month	Sales Volume Last Year
Month 1	$120,000
Month 2	$160,000
Month 3	$180,000

Problem 14

Management is planning to increase menu prices this year by 4 percent in Month 2 and another 2 percent in Month 4. Forecast food sales for months 1, 2, 3, 4, 5, and 6 this year by using the following historical information:

Month	Sales Volume Last Year
Month 1	$120,000
Month 2	$160,000
Month 3	$180,000
Month 4	$250,000
Month 5	$300,000
Month 6	$320,000

Problem 15

Using the following information, forecast the rooms sales for the next three months for a 600-room lodging operation:

Month	Days	Occupancy%	Average Room Rate
Month 1	31	55%	$120
Month 2	28	70%	$140
Month 3	31	85%	$150

Problem 16

Forecast food sales for a restaurant serving breakfast, lunch, and dinner for a 30-day month that has four Sundays and five Saturdays. Breakfast is not served on Saturday, and the restaurant is closed on Sunday. Use the following data:

	Seats	Turnover	Average	Check
Breakfast	100	4.0	$ 4.00
Lunch	200	3.5	7.00
Dinner	200	3.0	15.00

Case Study:
Budgeting—Planning, Preparation, and Implementation

The owners of a large restaurant have decided to implement an operating budget for the next business year. A hospitality consultant has been engaged to develop the budget. There is a three-week deadline. The consultant gathers the restaurant's historical data and brings it to his office to prepare the final budget. The consultant and his staff concentrate their full-time efforts to accomplish this task. The consultant then submits the budget to the owners for review and approval. Management approves the consultant's work. The monthly budget amounts are computed by dividing the annual budget amounts by 12. These monthly budgets are then forwarded to the department heads; these managers will be responsible for the budget's implementation and accountable for their department's performance within the budget plan.

Critique this budgetary process. Cite any positives and negatives in the budget's planning, preparation, and implementation.

Chapter 16 Outline

Definition and Objectives of Internal
    Control
        Limitations of Internal Control
Internal Control of Cash Receipts
        Cashier's Daily Report
Internal Control of Cash Disbursements
Bank Reconciliation
    Bank Statement
    Reconciling Items
    Bank Reconciliation Procedure
    Example of a Bank Reconciliation
    Journal Entries

Competencies

1. Define internal control and explain its
   objectives and limitations.
   (pp. 379–380)

2. Describe the principles of internal
   control for cash receipts and of
   preparing a cashier's daily report.
   (pp. 380–384)

3. Describe the principles of internal
   control for cash disbursements.
   (p. 384)

4. Describe bank reconciliations and
   why and how they are prepared, and
   explain reconciling items.
   (pp. 384–390)

16

Internal Control of Cash

THE HOSPITALITY INDUSTRY IS A RETAIL PROVIDER of goods and services. While many customers use credit cards, numerous cash sales still require special attention. *Cash* includes cash, personal checks, money orders, and traveler's checks. While cash is more vulnerable to theft, credit card transactions can also pose embezzlement problems.

Cash receipts are only one side of the internal control problem. The payment of cash (cash disbursements) requires specific internal control procedures to prevent misuse of house funds and wrongful issuance of checks. The cash transactions from the cash receipts journal and cash disbursements journal are posted in the cash general ledger account. The balance in the cash general ledger accounts should equal the cash balance in the checkbook.

Under the Foreign Corrupt Practices Act of 1977, all major U.S. corporations are required to have an internal control system. This act applies to all corporations falling under the jurisdiction of the Securities and Exchange Commission, whether or not they have any foreign operations. A company that fails to comply with this act is subject to fines, and its officers could face imprisonment.

Definition and Objectives of Internal Control

Internal control is a system designed to accomplish four major objectives:

1. *Safeguard assets.* Assets include cash, investments, inventory, furniture, equipment, vehicles, and property. The protection of these assets focuses on theft prevention as well as proper maintenance. Inventories also require systems to reduce waste and spoilage.

2. *Ensure compliance with company policies.* Many companies have written policies covering personnel and operational matters. Management expects adherence to these rules. Authorization is required for deviation from any standard policy.

3. *Facilitate operational efficiency.* A hospitality business requires suitable equipment and properly trained personnel to serve its guests at a satisfactory level. All businesses need profits to survive, and services should be achieved without incurring unnecessary costs.

4. *Ensure accurate financial information.* Management requires accurate financial information to properly manage profitable operations. Accurate and timely reporting to government agencies is necessary to avoid legal action.

Limitations of Internal Control

There is no perfect or universally applicable system of internal control. Any system can be defeated by acts of **collusion**. By definition, collusion occurs when two or more employees operate together to defraud the company.

The design of an internal control system should not be so complex that customer service or productivity is impaired. The design of a good internal control system must weigh that system's effect on operations and customers and evaluate the costs relative to the intended benefits.

Internal Control of Cash Receipts

It takes an extremely experienced accountant to design an effective all-inclusive internal system to control cash receipts. The most we can do here without being overly detailed is explain the academic theory. Therefore, the chapter presents only basic issues, emphasizing the critical points of a cash receipts internal control system.

At a minimum, a policy for the protection of cash receipts should include these fundamentals:

- *Bonding of employees.* An insurance company should bond employees who handle large amounts of cash. The insurance company screens employees before bonding them and will prosecute offenders. This insurance bond reimburses the hotel or restaurant if dishonest employees misappropriate assets.

- *Daily deposit of cash in a bank account.*

- *Proper accounting procedures for checks received.* Checks received by mail should not be forwarded directly to the accounts receivable department. The designated department or individual authorized to receive checks by mail should remove the remittance advices, prepare a list of all checks received (in duplicate), and stamp the reverse of the checks with a restrictive endorsement (*For Deposit Only*). A copy of the list and all checks should then be sent to the general cashier for deposit. The second copy of the list and the remittance advices should be forwarded to the accounts receivable department for posting to customer accounts.

- *Checks and balances in the food department.* Food service operations should implement controls such as duplicate checks or electronic systems that coordinate the production of meals and beverages with the service, collection, and recording of funds.

- *A control system for house banks and petty cash funds.* An **imprest system** is one in which funds are kept at a predetermined fixed amount. The imprest balance is maintained through reimbursement of the funds for any paid-outs. At unannounced intervals, surprise audits of these funds should be conducted. The cash and paid-out documents should total the imprest amount. Any shortages or IOUs should be investigated.

Exhibit 1   Cashier Reconciliation—Electronic Cash Register

```
Date: 12/15/X8 Saturday Weather: Rainy & cold
Cashier: Jim

Z

Food sales                        $ 1,350.67 +
Sales tax                              81.04 +
Tips due servers                       50.00 +
Customer collections                  185.00 +
Food purchases                          8.75 −
Tips paid out                          50.00 −
Customer charges                      200.00 −
Cash to account for               $ 1,407.96 =
Cash drop                           1,407.06 −
Cash shortage                            .90 =
-----------------------------------------------
Quantity of checks:            10
Quantity of credit cards:      15
-----------------------------------------------
Accounts Receivable Tenders
Account                   Amount
212                       200.00 +        Charge
855                       185.00 −        Collection
-----------------------------------------------
```

- *A cash registering system.* All sales should be recorded using a cash register or other electronic equipment. The cash register should have a display clearly visible to the customer or waitstaff.

- *Shared preparation of the cashier's report.* At the end of work shifts, supervisory personnel and cashiers should participate in preparation or analysis of the cashier's daily report.

Cashier's Daily Report

The **cashier's daily report** is an internal control document that reconciles the sales from the register readings with the cash drawer. (The report is also known as the *daily cashier's report,* the *cash drawer report,* the *daily cash drawer report,* or simply the *cashier's report.*) Today's electronic sales equipment generates the cashier's daily report. Exhibit 1 illustrates a reconciliation generated by an electronic cash register. In this restaurant, the cashier counts the drawer and makes what is known as a *blind drop* because the cashier does not know the register readings. Managers use a special key to get the register readings. Selecting the symbol Z prints the readings and indicates that the register counters are reset to zero. A symbol X indicates that a reading has been taken during a shift but register counters are not reset to zero.

All hospitality students and professionals should understand the mechanics of how this tally is performed. There is no better way to do this than by doing it manually.

Our example will look at a restaurant that uses a cash register, but manually prepares the final cashier's daily report. Before processing this report, it is important to be familiar with the following restaurant policies:

- The restaurant does not accept credit cards that do not offer cash treatment as provided by bank credit cards.

- Tips on charges and credit cards are paid out to waitstaff at the end of each shift.

- The shift supervisor is the only authorized individual with access to the cash register readings.

- An authorized individual must approve any voids.

Exhibit 2 shows a completed manual cashier's daily report for this restaurant. It is divided into two major sections: *Total to Be Accounted For* and *Total Accounted For.*

Contents of the Total to Be Accounted For Section. This section represents the *target*; its total is the *control* total. If everything was as intended, this control total would be the actual deposit. However, this is not always the case, because shortages and overages do occur for various reasons. The *Total to Be Accounted For* section includes the following:

- Sales calculated from register readings

- Sales taxes calculated from register readings

- Tips charged (entered on credit cards or charge accounts)

- Customer collections (payment of prior charge accounts)

- Amount of change fund at start of shift

Contents of the Total Accounted For Section. This section represents the *offer*. It consists of the following:

- Cash (including credit cards that are treated as cash)

- Purchases paid out (small COD deliveries or incidental purchases)

- Tips paid out (should be equal to the tips charged)

- Customer charges (new house charges by customers)

- Return of change fund

- Resulting cash shortage or overage

Preparing the Cashier's Daily Report. Preparing this report requires an orderly processing of the cash drawer and its contents. The shift supervisor (or other authorized individual) and cashier should be in attendance for this important tally. The following are the basic steps:

- Enter the readings of the previous shift and this shift. The differences—less any voids—are the results for this shift.

- Count the cash drawer and replenish the change fund.

Exhibit 2   Cashier's Daily Report

		Key A (Sales)			Key B (Sales Tax)		
Cashier's Daily Report							
DATE 12/8/X8 Day: Sat. Weather: Rainy + Cold							
Z Readings		1	350	67		81	04
TOTAL TO BE ACCOUNTED FOR:							
Food Sales		1	350	67			
Sales Tax			81	04			
Tips Charged			50	00			
Customer Collections			185	00			
Change Fund (Start)			150	00			
CONTROL TOTAL		1	816	71			
TOTAL ACCOUNTED FOR:							
Cash for Deposit		1	407	06			
Purchases Paid Out			8	75			
Tips Paid Out			50	00			
Customer Charges			200	00			
Change Fund (Return)			150	00			
Total Receipts and Paid-Outs		1	815	81			
Cash Short (+)				90			
Cash Over (−)							
TOTAL ACCOUNTED FOR		1	816	71			
EXPLANATION OF CUSTOMER COLLECTIONS & CHARGES:							
CUSTOMER	TAB	COLLECTION			CHARGE		
DEBCO, Inc.	1812				200	00	
J.R. Rickles		185	00				
TOTAL		185	00		200	00	
EXPLANATION OF PURCHASES PAID OUT:							
PAID TO	PURPOSE	AMOUNT					
Ted's Market	Food items for kitchen	8	75				
TOTAL		8	75				

- Calculate the *cash to be deposited*. This is the sum of cash, personal checks, traveler's checks, money orders, and credit cards treated as cash by the bank.

- Tally charges and paid-outs.

- Enter all information in the applicable sections of the report.

- Total each section as follows:

$$\text{To be accounted for} = \text{Control total (the target)}$$
$$\text{Accounted for} = \text{Total receipts and paid-outs (the offer)}$$

Cash Shortage or Cash Overage. A **cash shortage** occurs if the control total is *larger* than the total receipts and paid-outs. It results when the *offer* does not reach the *target*. A **cash overage** occurs when the control total is *smaller* than the total receipts and paid-outs. It results when the *offer* exceeds the *target*.

Many managers concentrate only on shortages. However, cash overages are also important; they could be due to an embezzler's processing errors. Another danger signal is when the tally is, for example, $20 short one day and $20 over on another. These swings might indicate that an employee is "borrowing" and "paying back," which, of course, is an unacceptable cash management practice.

Internal Control of Cash Disbursements

Cash disbursements include payments from checking accounts and house banks or petty cash funds. As with a cash receipts control system, the design of an effective all-inclusive internal control system for cash disbursements requires the skills of a highly experienced accountant. The internal control of cash payments should, at a minimum, include the following fundamental principles:

- Payments from house or petty cash funds should be supported by documentary evidence such as invoices. A stipulated maximum single payment amount should be part of the internal control policy.

- Unless the operation is very small, it is better to have two checking accounts, one for payroll and the other for all other types of payments.

- Checks should be prenumbered and signature policies established and enforced.

- Paid invoices should be canceled (that is, stamped *Paid*) or perforated with an invoice perforating device to indicate that they have been paid.

- Voided checks should be defaced or their signature portion removed.

- A check protection device that imprints the check amount should be used to prevent alteration.

Bank Reconciliation

A **bank reconciliation** is an internal control document that reconciles the cash balance on the bank statement with the cash balance on the accounting records (books). The reconciling process detects any bookkeeping or bank errors. Individuals who do *not* have a role in cash receipts or disbursement should prepare

Exhibit 3   Bank Statement

Hartman Savings and Trust

Harrisburg, PA   17112

Period Ending
May 31, 20X8

James Company
HACC Way
Harrisburg, PA   17112

Account Number 4092

Beginning balance	Checks/Debits	Number	Deposits/Credits	Number	NEW BALANCE
30402.90	13850.30	9	14760.00	4	30312.60

CHECKING ACCOUNT DETAIL OF TRANSACTIONS

Date	Check Number	CHECKS AND DEBITS Amount	Check Number	Amount	Deposits/Credits Amount	Daily Balance
4/30						29402.90
5/1					2860.00	32262.90
5/8	919	1500.00	910	1800.00	4900.00	33862.90
5/12	911	150.00				33712.91
5/14	912	1100.00			3000.00	35612.90
5/22	913	1200.00				34412.90
5/23					4000.00	38412.90
5/26	916	3300.00				35112.90
5/27	917	4700.00				30412.90
5/31	NSF	80.00	SC	20.30		30312.60

the bank reconciliation. This follows the internal control principle of *separation of duties*. Cash embezzlement can be concealed if the principle of separation of duties is ignored.

Bank Statement

A bank sends monthly bank statements to its checking account customers (or may make the statements accessible through its website if the customer wishes). The **bank statement** shows the customer's beginning and ending cash balances, deposits, checks cashed, and other transactions. Exhibit 3 presents a sample bank statement. Some banks return the **canceled checks** (checks cashed by the bank), others send a list of the canceled checks, and still others send nothing extra because all canceled check transactions appear on the bank statement.

The ending cash balance in the accounting records generally does not match the amount shown on the bank statement, even though both may be correct. To verify the accuracy of the accounting records, the accountant or bookkeeper prepares a bank reconciliation that explains the reasons for any differences.

Bank's Use of Debits and Credits. Confusion can result from attempting to interpret the bank's use of the terms *debit* and *credit*. A customer account represents a liability to the bank because the customer owns the cash in the account. Therefore, when a bank uses a debit, it is reducing that liability. The bank uses a credit for deposits because they increase the bank's liability to the customer.

Reconciling Items

The disparity between the ending cash balance per the bank statement and the ending cash balance per the accounting records is generally caused by timing differences in processing transactions and other events. These require special procedures called *reconciling items,* such as the following:

- Deposits in transit
- Outstanding checks
- Interest earned
- Bank service charges
- Credit card fees
- ATM withdrawals
- NSF checks
- Bookkeeping errors
- Bank errors

Deposits in Transit. A deposit entered in the cash receipts journal (or checkbook) at the end of a month but not appearing on the bank statement is a **deposit in transit**. These are detected through a comparison of the deposits in the business's accounting records with those on the bank statement.

Deposits in transit can occur when a bank does not date a deposit with the date shown on the business's deposit slip. For example, a bank's bookkeeping day may end at 2 p.m. Therefore, any deposit made on March 31 after 2 p.m. will be dated by the bank as April 1 and will appear on the April bank statement.

Credit card sales can also be affected by deposits in transit. The electronic credit card process involves the retailer, the credit card service provider, and the retailer's bank. The retailer transmits the credit card sales and depends on the credit card service provider to deposit funds into the retailer's bank account. If the service provider is slow in depositing the funds, the credit card sales may not be deposited by the end of the month and/or may not appear on the bank statement.

Interestingly, retailers using manual credit card vouchers under a direct bank deposit arrangement might receive funds for credit card deposits more quickly than if they were processed electronically. The retailer manually deposits the bank credit card vouchers along with cash at the retailer's bank, and the bank provides instant credit for that deposit; there is no waiting for a third party to transmit the credit card sales. The disadvantage of using credit card vouchers for manual direct deposit is that the credit card fee is generally higher.

Outstanding Checks. Issued checks not appearing on the bank statement are called **outstanding checks**, which are detected when entries on this month's cash payments journal (or checkbook) and last month's listing of outstanding checks are compared with the canceled checks, a listing of bank-processed checks, or the bank statement.

It sometimes occurs that a check outstanding in May, for example, is still outstanding in June (and even in subsequent months). An *outstanding checks listing* accompanies the internal bank reconciliation and, with the current month's cash payments journal, forms the basis for determining outstanding checks.

Interest Earned. Commercial checking accounts cannot earn interest because current bank regulations prohibit it. Some banks offer interest on personal checking accounts; in such cases, the interest becomes a reconciling item and its value is unknown until the customer receives the bank statement.

Bank Service Charges. These include the monthly checking account fee, printing of checks, and credit card fees. If these charges are not entered in the accounting records but are on the bank statement, they become a reconciling item.

Credit Card Fees. The gross amount of credit card sales deposited or transmitted is not the true cash deposit, because the credit card company deducts a fee for its services. Merchant credit card providers generally deduct this fee on each credit card batch electronically processed. The fee is located at the end of the batch process, therefore enabling the bookkeeper to journalize the fee on a current basis. A hospitality business that deposits its cards directly into its checking account might not know the fee until its monthly bank statement arrives. In any case, if these credit card fees are not entered in the current month, they become a reconciling item.

ATM Withdrawals. ATM transactions are associated with personal checking accounts. Withdrawals should be entered as they are made, though it is not unusual for account holders to neglect recording a withdrawal in their checkbooks. These unrecorded ATM withdrawals are detected upon examination of the bank statement.

NSF Checks. An **NSF check** is commonly called a *rubber check*. NSF stands for *nonsufficient funds*. An NSF check is a check included as part of a deposit, recorded, and subsequently rejected and returned by the bank. A journal entry is required to correct the original deposit; if such an entry is not made, the amount of the NSF check becomes a reconciling item.

Bookkeeping Errors. Transposition (the reversal of adjacent digits) often causes bookkeeping errors. For example, a check for $196 could be entered in the checkbook erroneously as $169, or a deposit for $578 could be incorrectly entered as $587. The differences between the entry and the actual amount are reconciling items. (A telltale sign that a transposition error has been made is that the difference between the entered amount and the correct amount is divisible by nine.)

Bookkeeping errors have been eliminated or significantly reduced through the use of computerized systems that, for example, print checks and update the cash payments journal in the same process.

Bank Errors. Bank errors should occur rarely, but they do occur. One common error is the processing of checks. These checks are manually encoded by the bank's processing center and then processed in the bank statement. It is possible that the

Exhibit 4   Working Format Bank Reconciliation

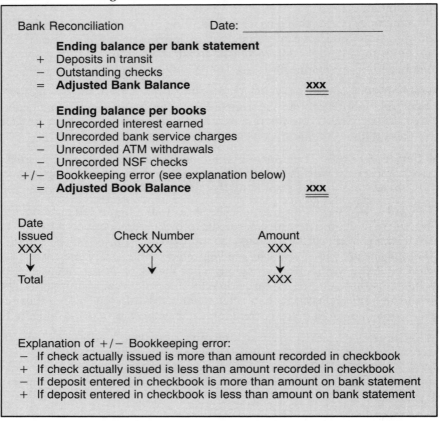

Bank Reconciliation   Date: _____

        Ending balance per bank statement
  +   Deposits in transit
  −   Outstanding checks
  =   **Adjusted Bank Balance**   **xxx**

        Ending balance per books
  +   Unrecorded interest earned
  −   Unrecorded bank service charges
  −   Unrecorded ATM withdrawals
  −   Unrecorded NSF checks
+/−   Bookkeeping error (see explanation below)
  =   **Adjusted Book Balance**   **xxx**

Date Issued	Check Number	Amount
XXX	XXX	XXX
↓	↓	↓
Total		XXX

Explanation of +/− Bookkeeping error:
−   If check actually issued is more than amount recorded in checkbook
+   If check actually issued is less than amount recorded in checkbook
−   If deposit entered in checkbook is more than amount on bank statement
+   If deposit entered in checkbook is less than amount on bank statement

person encoding the amount misread the check's written amount. Encoding errors can be detected through a comparison of the check amount magnetic coding at the bottom of the check with the original written check amount.

Bank Reconciliation Procedure

Exhibit 4 shows a working format for a bank reconciliation. Notice that it has two parts. Since the likelihood of a bank error is remote, the bank statement portion appears at the top and is prepared first. The steps for completing this portion are as follows:

•   Enter the ending balance from the bank statement amount.

•   Enter the applicable reconciling items.

•   Conclude with a total called *Adjusted Bank Balance*.

The bottom portion pertains to the accounting record. The steps for completing this portion are as follows:

- Enter the ending balance per books.
- Enter the applicable reconciling items.
- Conclude with a total called *Adjusted Book Balance.*

The bank reconciliation is successful when the adjusted bank balance equals the adjusted book balance. The top of the form (bank portion) is often assumed to be correct if the bank reconciliation is initially unsuccessful. If, after rechecking all steps, the bookkeeper still cannot detect an error in the books, he or she can investigate the possibility of a bank error by comparing each transaction amount on the bank statement with corresponding accounting records and canceled checks (or list).

Example of a Bank Reconciliation

The Edal Company has received its bank statement for the month ending May 31. The statement shows the following:

- Ending balance $30,312.60
- Service charge   20.30
- NSF check   80.00

After checking the accounting records, the accountant determines the following:

- The May 31 checking account book balance is $29,112.90.
- The bank service charge and NSF check were not entered by the bookkeeper.
- A $2,100 deposit made on May 31 is not on the bank statement.
- Outstanding checks total $3,400.

The outstanding checks are listed showing date, check number, and amount to supplement the bank reconciliation. Exhibit 5 shows the completed bank reconciliation prepared by the accountant. Notice that the adjusted bank balance equals the adjusted book balance.

Journal Entries

A completed bank reconciliation also serves as the source document for checkbook entries made to correct the cash balance and journal entries made to correct the general ledger cash account.

Any reconciling item in the *books* section of the reconciliation form requires corrective action in the checkbook and general ledger. For example, based on the reconciliation data in Exhibit 5, the following journal entry is required:

Bank Service Charge	20.30	
Accounts Receivable	80.00	
Cash—Checking Account		100.30

To record adjustments from the May 20X8 bank reconciliation for the following:
Monthly bank service charge $20.30
Return of NSF check issued by Horton, Inc. $80.00

Exhibit 5   Completed Bank Reconciliation

Bank Reconcilliation—May 31, 20X8		
Ending balance per bank statement	$	30,312.60
Deposits in transit (5/31)		2,100.00
Outstanding checks		(3,400.00)
Adjusted Bank Balance	$	29,012.60
Ending balance per books	$	29,112.90
Unrecorded bank service charge		(20.30)
Unrecorded NSF check		(80.00)
Adjusted Book Balance	$	29,012.60

Listing of Outstanding Checks:

Date Issued	Check Number	Amount
5/26	914	$ 1,200.00
5/26	915	800.00
5/27	918	1,400.00
Total		$ 3,400.00

🔑 Key Terms

bank reconciliation—An internal control document reconciling the cash balance per the bank statement with the cash balance per the books (accounting records).

bank statement—A statement from a bank that shows the customer's monthly beginning and ending cash balances as well as the month's transactions.

canceled checks—Checks that have been cashed by the bank.

cash overage—A situation in which the control total is smaller than the total receipts and paid-outs.

cash shortage—A situation resulting when the control total is larger than the total receipts and paid-outs.

cashier's daily report—An internal control document reconciling the cash register readings with the cash drawer. Also called a *daily cashier's report*, a *cash drawer report*, a *daily cash drawer report*, or simply a *cashier's report*.

collusion—Two or more employees operating together to defraud the company.

deposits in transit—End-of-month deposits that do not appear on the bank statement but appear on the account-holder's books.

imprest system—A system in which a house bank, petty cash fund, or other account is kept at a predetermined fixed amount.

internal control—A system with four major objectives: (1) safeguarding of assets, (2) ensuring compliance with company policies, (3) facilitating operational efficiency, and (4) ensuring accurate financial information.

NSF check—A check a business deposits in good faith but is returned by the bank because the issuer's account has non-sufficient funds.

outstanding checks—Checks that have been issued but not yet cashed by the bank.

Review Questions

1. What items are included in *cash*?
2. What is the definition of *internal control*? What are its objectives?
3. What assets are intended to be safeguarded?
4. What is collusion?
5. What is the advantage of bonding employees?
6. What is an internal control procedure for house banks?
7. What is the purpose of the cashier's daily report?
8. What is the purpose of a bank reconciliation?
9. What is the definition of the following terms?
    a. Canceled checks
    b. Deposit in transit
    c. Outstanding checks
    d. NSF check
10. Why does the balance shown on the bank statement generally not equal the balance shown in the checkbook or the accounting records?

Internet Sites

For more information, visit the following Internet sites. Remember that Internet addresses can change without notice. If the site is no longer there, you can use a search engine to look for additional sites.

Bank Reconciliation
www.investopedia.com/terms/b/bankreconciliation.asp
http://banking.about.com/od/businessbanking/a/bankreconciliat.htm

Bank Statement
www.ehow.com/facts_5516282_bank-statement.html
www.ehow.com/about_5375841_definition-bank-statement.html

Cashier's Daily Report
http://retail.about.com/library/bl_cash_drawer_report.htm

Operation of a Petty Cash Fund
www.googobits.com/articles/1282-keeping-a-petty-cash-fund-for-a-small-business.html

Problems

Problem 1

Indicate the correct section of the cashier's daily report in which the following activities will be entered.

	"Accounted For" Section	"To Be Accounted For" Section
Customer charges	_____	_____
Cash to be deposited	_____	_____
Sales	_____	_____
Customer collections	_____	_____
Initial change fund	_____	_____
Sales tax	_____	_____
Return of change fund	_____	_____
Control total	_____	_____

Problem 2

The cashier's daily report is being prepared. The total of the *To Be Accounted For* section is $2,080.20 and the total of the *Accounted For* section is $2,080.30. Is there an overage or a shortage for this shift?

Problem 3

The Ranger Inn has a $400 change fund for each shift. The following is the summary of the cashier's daily report:

To Be Accounted For		Accounted For	
Sales	$812.36	Cash for deposit	$1,300.90
Sales tax	40.60	Paid outs	10.56
Collections	100.50	Customer charges	42.00
Control total	$953.46	Accounted for	$1,353.46

What appears to be the reason for the discrepancy between the *Control total* and the *Accounted for* amounts?

Problem 4

Tom's Diner has a $100 change fund for each shift. The following is the summary of today's register activity: the cash drawer contains $685.25 cash, paid-out slips totaling $8.23, and a customer charge of $9.45. The register readings show sales of $607.58 and sales tax of $28.93. Determine the cash overage or shortage for the day.

Problem 5

As the food and beverage supervisor, your responsibility is to reconcile the transactions for the day with the cash register readings. The following are the results of your check-out procedures for the bar:

Register Readings:

	Sales	Sales Tax
This shift's close	$126,875.95	$6,343.80
Prior shift's close	126,195.45	6,309.77

There are no voids to consider for this shift. The change fund is on a $200 imprest system. The following are the contents of the cash drawer:

Return of change fund	$200.00
Cash for deposit	620.00
Bank credit cards	29.36
Traveler's checks	50.00

In addition to register funds, there is a paid-out voucher of $12.76 for supplies.

What is the cash shortage or overage for this shift?

Problem 6

The Dorco Company has received its bank statement for the month ending May 31, which showed the following:

Ending balance	$10,650.05
NSF check	63.40
Service charge	10.70

After checking the bank statement and accounting records, the accountant has determined the following:

- The May 31 cash balance per books is $10,781.76.
- The bank's service charge and an NSF check were not entered by the bookkeeper.
- A $354.60 deposit made on May 31 is not on the bank statement.
- Outstanding checks total $296.99.

Prepare a bank reconciliation in proper format.

Problem 7

Jim has received his bank statement for the month ending July 31, which shows the following:

Ending balance	$328.25
NSF check	55.00

Service charge	15.00
Interest earned	0.25

After reviewing the checkbook and bank statement, he determines the following:

- The July 31 checkbook balance is $808.00.
- Bank service charges, an NSF check, and interest have not been recorded.
- A $642.00 deposit made on July 31 is not on the bank statement.
- Outstanding checks total $232.00.

Prepare a bank reconciliation in proper format.

Problem 8

Sara has received her bank statement for the month ending November 30, which showed the following:

Ending balance	$641.50
Service charge	15.00
ATM withdrawal	70.00
Interest earned	0.50

After reviewing the checkbook and bank statement, she determines that:

- The November 30 checkbook balance is $1,136.00.
- Bank service charges, an ATM withdrawal, and interest had not been recorded.
- A $954.00 deposit made on November 30 is not on the bank statement.
- Outstanding checks total $544.00.

Prepare a bank reconciliation in proper format.

Problem 9

On July 31, Don's checkbook balance was $1,667.90, and the bank statement as of that date showed a balance of $1,828.80. A comparison of the bank statement and accounting records showed the following:

- Outstanding checks were:

Number	Amount
114	$79.50
117	96.42
118	17.48

- Check number 112 for $19.00 had been issued, processed by the bank, and charged on the bank statement, but was not recorded in the checkbook.
- A bank service charge of $4.50 was not recorded in the checkbook.
- Check number 116 was written for $121.00 and processed by the bank for $121.00. It was entered and deducted in the checkbook as $112.00.

Prepare a bank reconciliation in proper format. List and total the outstanding checks at the bottom of the bank reconciliation.

Problem 10

On March 31, Sigment Company had a $44,547.60 checkbook balance. The bank statement showed a balance on that date of $46,574.10, and the following information on the bank statement had not been entered in the checkbook:

$24.75 Service charge
$68.85 NSF check

A review of the company's bank statement and checkbook showed a deposit in transit of $3,919.44 and outstanding checks as follows:

- Number 234 for $281.34
- Number 236 for $445.12
- Number 237 for $2,901.60
- Number 238 for $2,411.48

Prepare a bank reconciliation in proper format. List and total the outstanding checks at the bottom of the bank reconciliation.

Problem 11

The following is a completed bank reconciliation for June 20X8. Prepare the necessary journal entry from the information provided.

Ending balance per bank statement	$44,002.00
Deposits in transit (5/31)	3,500.00
Outstanding checks	(6,850.00)
Adjusted Bank Balance	$40,652.00
Ending balance per books	$40,897.00
Unrecorded bank service charge	(45.00)
Unrecorded NSF check (Photo, Inc.)	(200.00)
Adjusted Book Balance	$40,652.00

Ethics Case

The Siesta Hotel is owned by several individuals who also manage its operations. These management team members are individuals of high integrity with a strong commitment to guest service. They realize that making a profit is necessary, but they also recognize the importance of product quality and customer satisfaction.

In the hospitality industry, ethics is a critical issue for top management, as are operational, financial, and promotional considerations. Any

(continued)

(continued)

hotel's business is to sell the occupancy of its rooms. Any room occupancy that is not sold for the night represents revenue that is lost forever. Overbooking occurs when a hotel sells more room occupancy than is actually available. Overbooking is very common among hotels because of no-shows and cancellations.

The managers of the Siesta Hotel do allow the hotel's front office staff to overbook. Overbooking does not necessarily result in the hotel's inability to honor reservations. However, when overbooking does result in the inability to honor a reservation, the procedure for *walking a guest* is most gracious and generous; the hotel will arrange and pay for accommodations at another hotel, arrange and pay for travel to that hotel, and pay for dinner for the walked party.

1. Ethics is composed of two attitudes: ideological and operational. (*Ideological* attitudes pertain to beliefs and convictions. *Operational* attitudes pertain to actual actions or practices.) Discuss the difference between these attitudes as related to this case.

2. Some hospitality managers are affected by ethical ignorance and professional cynicism. (*Ethical ignorance* refers to the state of not knowing or of being unaware. *Professional cynicism* refers to the state of having a pessimistic or distrustful attitude.) Discuss these factors as related to this case.

3. Discuss why hospitality managers may find that dealing with ethical issues on the job can be stressful.

Chapter 17 Outline

Interest Expense
    If Time Is Stated in Full Years
    If Time Is Stated in Full Months
    If Time Is Stated in Days
    Working with Fractional Interest Rates
Cash Discounts
    2/10,n/30 Discount Term
    2/10,n/30 ROG Discount Term
    2/10,n/30 EOM or 2/10,n/30 PROX
        Discount Terms
    Freight Charges
    Extended Cash Discount Terms
Compound Value
Present Value
Compound and Present Values with
    Annuities

Competencies

1. Describe the simple interest method of calculating interest expense, and explain how to calculate simple interest when the time period is stated in full years, in full months, and in days, and when working with fractional interest rates. (pp. 399–401)

2. Describe cash discounts, interpretation of various invoice discount terms, freight charges, and extended cash discount terms. (pp. 402–404)

3. Determine when compound and present value calculations are required, and perform those calculations. (pp. 404–408)

4. Apply compound and present value concepts to annuities, and perform those calculations. (pp. 408–410)

17

Business Math Topics for Hospitality Managers

AㄷㄷOUNTING AND BUSINESS are closely related. An accounting education must provide more than accounting principles for the hospitality student who is a specialized business major. A successful hospitality manager requires a great deal of knowledge and experience to reach targeted profit goals and other business objectives.[1] This chapter discusses topics that are important to the hospitality business major. These are as follows:

- Simple interest expense
- Cash discounts
- Compound and present values

This chapter provides valuable financial information while answering such questions as the following:

- What are principal and maturity value?
- What is simple interest? How is it calculated?
- What are cash discounts?
- How is an invoice payment amount calculated when cash discounts apply?
- What are extended cash discount terms?
- What are compound value, present value, and compound or present value with annuities? How are they calculated?

Interest Expense

Interest expense is a cost incurred when a person or entity borrows money from a lending source. A prevailing method of calculating interest expense is called the **simple interest method**, in which the interest charge is always calculated only on the principal. (Contrast this with **compound interest**, which is charged on the principal plus prior interest earned.) Simple interest computations involve time periods that may be stated in days, months, or one year or more. The numerator for any simple interest calculation is as follows:

$$\text{Principal} \times \text{Interest Rate} \times \text{Time Period}$$

The numerator is expressed mathematically as *PRT*. The denominator, explained later, depends on the period of time involved (days, months, and one year or more).

Definitions of the terms commonly used in interest calculations and abbreviations for them (shown in parentheses) are as follows:

- *Interest Expense (I):* The charge for the use of the principal.

- *Principal (P):* The amount borrowed.

- *Rate (R):* The interest charge is expressed as a percentage, which is usually stated as an *annual* rate.

- *Time (T):* The time period over which the amount is owed and payment is due.

- *Maturity Value (MV):* The total of principal plus interest.

If Time Is Stated in Full Years

The formula used to calculate simple interest if the time period is stated in full years is:

$$I = PRT \text{ (Interest} = P \times R \times T)$$

For example, suppose $3,000 is borrowed at 7 percent interest with payment due at the end of 2 years. The simple interest charge for this loan is calculated as follows:

$$
\begin{aligned}
I &= PRT \\
I &= 3{,}000 \times 7\% \times 2 \\
\text{Interest} &= \$420.00
\end{aligned}
$$

If Time Is Stated in Full Months

The formula used to calculate simple interest if the time period is stated in full months is as follows:

$$I = \frac{PRT}{12} \text{ (interpreted as Interest} = P \times R \times T; \text{ the result is divided by 12)}$$

For example, assume $3,000 is borrowed at 7 percent interest with payment due at the end of 2 months. The simple interest charge for this loan is calculated as follows:

$$I = \frac{PRT}{12}$$

$$I = \frac{3{,}000 \times 7\% \times 2}{12}$$

$$\text{Interest} = \$35.00$$

If Time Is Stated in Days

When the time period is stated in days, the basic formula used to calculate simple interest (I = PRT) still applies. However, the formula must be modified to represent days instead of years or months.

The question of how many days are in a year depends on what entity is doing the interest calculation.

If a bank is computing interest on a loan you owe, it may use what is called an **ordinary year**, which has 360 days. When a government agency calculates interest, it often uses what is called an **exact year**, which has 365 days.

The formula for an *ordinary year* computation is the following:

$$I = \frac{PRT}{360}$$

For example, $3,000 is borrowed at 7 percent interest with payment due at the end of 200 days.

The interest calculation for the loan based on an ordinary year is as follows:

$$I = \frac{PRT}{360}$$

$$I = \frac{3,000 \times 7\% \times 200}{360}$$

$$Interest = \$116.67$$

If the lender uses an exact year (365 days), the interest calculation is based on the same procedure used for an ordinary year, except that the denominator is 365 days.

The formula for an *exact year* calculation is as follows:

$$I = \frac{PRT}{365}$$

The interest for the loan based on an exact year is as follows:

$$I = \frac{PRT}{365}$$

$$I = \frac{3,000 \times 7\% \times 200}{365}$$

$$Interest = \$115.07$$

Working with Fractional Interest Rates

The easiest way to process fractions with a calculator is to convert the fraction to a decimal. A fraction takes the following form:

$$\frac{Numerator}{Denominator}$$

To convert a fraction to a decimal, divide the numerator by the denominator. For instance, the decimal equivalent of the fraction ¾ is .75 (3 divided by 4).

Assume that someone borrows $3,000 at 7⅜ percent with payment due at the end of 2 years. The interest charge for this loan is calculated as follows:

$$7\tfrac{3}{8}\% \text{ converted to a decimal} = 7 + (3 \div 8 = .375) = 7.375\%$$

$$I = PRT = \$3,000 \times 7.375\% \times 2 = \$442.50$$

Cash Discounts

Cash discounts are incentives that sellers offer to buyers to encourage payment of invoices within a shorter period of time than the customary full payment period allowed. The invoice amount owed is reduced by the stated cash discount. Cash discounts benefit each party involved: the seller gets the payment sooner, while the buyer pays a slightly lower purchase price.

For example, a seller might state invoice payment terms as follows:

2/10,n/30

The interpretation of 2/10,n/30 is as follows:

2 percent discount if invoice is paid within 10 days; otherwise, the invoice is due in full within 30 days.

However, the question is, "within 10 days" of when? The interpretation of the time period depends on whether any modifiers follow the terms. The discount terms might be stated as any of the following:

- 2/10,n/30
- 2/10,n/30 ROG
- 2/10,n/30 EOM
- 2/10,n/30 PROX

These discount terms are explained with selected examples in the following sections.

2/10,n/30 Discount Term

A 2/10,n/30 discount term means that the buyer will get a 2 percent discount if he or she pays the invoice within 10 days of the invoice date (the date stated on the invoice). Otherwise, full payment is due within 30 days following the invoice date.

Suppose an invoice is dated June 12, the amount due is $90, and the terms are 2/10,n/30.

This would be interpreted as follows: the discount is available if the invoice is paid anytime up to and including June 22 (10 days from the invoice date). The payment is calculated as follows:

Invoice amount	$90.00	
Discount amount	1.80	($90.00 × 2%)
Pay	$88.20	

However, if the invoice is paid June 23 or later, the full $90.00 invoice amount is due no later than 30 days following the invoice date.

2/10,n/30 ROG Discount Term

A 2/10,n/30 ROG discount term means that the buyer will get a 2 percent discount if the invoice is paid within 10 days following the date of *receipt of goods (ROG)*. Otherwise, the full amount of the invoice is due within 30 days of receipt of goods.

For example, assume an invoice is dated June 12, its amount is $90, its terms are 2/10,n/30 ROG, and the buyer received the goods on June 9.

The discount is available to the buyer if the invoice is paid anytime up to and including June 19 (10 days from the date the goods were received). The discounted payment is $88.20. The gross amount due after the discount period expires is $90.00, and is due no later than 30 days from receipt of goods.

2/10,n/30 EOM or 2/10,n/30 PROX Discount Terms

The term *EOM* means *end of the month*. The Latin term *PROX*, an abbreviation of *Proximo*, means *next month*. The time period for calculating discounts under EOM and PROX is the same.

The invoice date requires additional analysis. An invoice dated *on or before* the 25th day of the month has a discount good into the following month. However, an invoice dated *after* the 25th of the month has a discount that is good into the *second* following month.

For example, an invoice dated May 8 has terms of 2/10 EOM (or 2/10 PROX). This indicates that a 2 percent cash discount is available until June 10.

This is because the invoice date of May 8 is before May 25; therefore, June is the discount month, and 10 days into June is the discount end date.

In another example, an invoice dated May 26 has terms of 2/10 EOM (or 2/10 PROX).

This means that a 2 percent cash discount is available until July 10.

This is because the invoice date of May 26 falls after May 25; therefore, July (the second following month) is the discount month, and 10 days into July is the discount end date.

Freight Charges

Purchase discounts can be taken only on the merchandise charged on an invoice; no discounts are taken on freight charges.

For example, assume an invoice shows the following:

Textbooks	$100.00
Freight	10.00
Total	$110.00

This is because a qualifying 2 percent discount amounts to $2.00, calculated on the $100 merchandise portion. The amount due on this invoice, if paid within the discount period, is $108.00 ($110.00 billing – $2.00 discount).

Extended Cash Discount Terms

Some suppliers offer extended terms for discounts; if the buyer misses the first discount date, he or she can still take advantage of the second date the seller has provided, but at a lesser discount. For instance, a discount term expressed in this way—2 /10,1/15,n/30—means the following:

- A 2 percent discount is available if the buyer pays within 10 days of the invoice date.

- If the buyer misses the 10-day date, a 1 percent discount is available if payment is made within 15 days of the invoice date.

- If the buyer misses both discount periods, the full payment (with no discount taken) is due 30 days from the date of invoice.

For example, assume the invoice date is March 15 with terms 2/10,1/15,n/30. The discount and payment schedule is as follows:

- A 2 percent discount is available until March 25.

- If the payment is not made on or before March 25, a 1 percent discount is available if the buyer pays by March 30.

- If the buyer misses both discount periods, the full payment (with no discount) is due 30 days after March 15.

Compound Value

Compound value is the sum of the principal amount plus the compound interest amount. **Compound interest** is interest that is calculated both on the initial principal and on the accumulated interest of prior periods. Compound interest differs from simple interest, which is calculated as a percentage of the principal, ignoring interest earned. In compound interest calculations, the principal and interest of all prior periods become the new basis upon which new interest is calculated. The more frequently interest is compounded, the faster the principal grows. Yearly compounded interest is considered the norm unless specified otherwise.

The objective of the compound value calculation is to determine the future value of a known amount invested today.

It is common for banking institutions to pay interest more than once per year. Therefore, the stated annual interest rate must be converted to an effective period interest rate to calculate interest for a specific period. The formula is:

$$\text{Period interest rate} = \frac{\text{Annual interest rate}}{\text{Number of interest periods in the year}}$$

For example, an investment yielding 8 percent annually and paid four times in that 12-month period would have a quarterly (period) interest rate of 8 percent divided by 4 quarters, or 2 percent.

Using this example, if $1,000 is invested at the start of a year (and no other investments are added to it during the year), the value in the first year would grow as follows:

	Principal	Interest Earned	Compound Value
1st quarter	$1,000.00	$20.00	$1,020.00
2nd quarter	1,020.00	20.40	1,040.40
3rd quarter	1,040.40	20.81	1,061.21
4th quarter	1,061.21	21.22	1,082.43

When the period you wish to project is several years, the calculation of compound value can be tedious, time-consuming, and subject to error. Fortunately, the use of compound value tables, also called future value tables, greatly simplifies the calculation of compound value. Compound value tables are available for any number of periods and interest rates. Exhibit 1 presents a sample compound value table for a single investment made at the start of the first period. Note that the interest rates per period are listed at the top of the table and that the interest periods are listed down the left side of the table. The intersection of the per-period interest rates and the number of periods in the table provides a compound value factor to use in calculating the compound value at the end of the period.

Again using the example of $1,000 invested at 8 percent annually, with interest earned quarterly, the procedure is as follows:

1. The interest rate per period is 2 percent.
2. The number of periods is 4.
3. The factor at the intersection of 2 percent and 4 periods is 1.0824.
4. $1,000.00 × 1.0824 = $1,082.40.

The amount differs by three cents from the manual calculation because the values in Exhibit 1 extend to only four decimal points. The same factor carried to a more accurate seven decimal points is 1.0824322, which accounts for the last three cents.

The preceding example covered one year, but compound value tables can easily be used to forecast investments over many years. Using the same example but changing the investment period to five years, the procedure is as follows:

1. The interest rate per period is still 2 percent.
2. The number of periods is 20 (4 interest periods per year × 5 years).
3. The factor at the intersection of 2 percent and 20 periods is 1.4859.
4. $1,000.00 × 1.4859 = $1,485.90.

Present Value

Present value is the value today of a known future amount. It is essentially the reverse of compound value, where we know the investment amount and wish to determine what it will be worth at a later date. With present value, we know what the future value is or must be, and from that amount we calculate what must be invested today to equal that amount in the future. Present value calculations are typically used to determine what must be invested now to meet a specific future goal.

As was the case with compound value, the use of present value tables makes it quick and easy to compute the amount needed now to achieve a goal at the end of a future period for an investment yielding a known percentage. A sample present value table for a single investment made at the start of the first period is provided in Exhibit 2.

Suppose the goal is to achieve a total of $2,000 at the end of a five-year period with an investment yielding 8 percent annually, and with interest compounded quarterly. The procedure to calculate the present value is as follows:

Exhibit 1 Compound Value Factors for a Single Cash Flow

$$FV_{n,k} = (1 + k)^n$$

Number of Periods	1%	2%	3%	4%	5%	6%	7%	8%	9%	10%	12%	14%	15%	16%	18%	20%	22%	24%	26%	28%	30%	35%
1	1.0100	1.0200	1.0300	1.0400	1.0500	1.0600	1.0700	1.0800	1.0900	1.1000	1.1200	1.1400	1.1500	1.1600	1.1800	1.2000	1.2200	1.2400	1.2600	1.2800	1.3000	1.3500
2	1.0201	1.0404	1.0609	1.0816	1.1025	1.1236	1.1449	1.1664	1.1881	1.2100	1.2544	1.2996	1.3225	1.3456	1.3924	1.4400	1.4884	1.5376	1.5876	1.6384	1.6900	1.8225
3	1.0303	1.0612	1.0927	1.1249	1.1576	1.1910	1.2250	1.2597	1.2950	1.3310	1.4049	1.4815	1.5209	1.5609	1.6430	1.7280	1.8158	1.9066	2.0004	2.0972	2.1970	2.4604
4	1.0406	1.0824	1.1255	1.1699	1.2155	1.2625	1.3108	1.3605	1.4116	1.4641	1.5735	1.6890	1.7490	1.8106	1.9388	2.0736	2.2153	2.3642	2.5205	2.6844	2.8561	3.3215
5	1.0510	1.1041	1.1593	1.2167	1.2763	1.3382	1.4026	1.4693	1.5386	1.6105	1.7623	1.9254	2.0114	2.1003	2.2878	2.4883	2.7027	2.9316	3.1758	3.4360	3.7129	4.4840
6	1.0615	1.1262	1.1941	1.2653	1.3401	1.4185	1.5007	1.5869	1.6771	1.7716	1.9738	2.1950	2.3131	2.4364	2.6996	2.9860	3.2973	3.6352	4.0015	4.3980	4.8268	6.0534
7	1.0721	1.1487	1.2299	1.3159	1.4071	1.5036	1.6058	1.7138	1.8280	1.9487	2.2107	2.5023	2.6600	2.8262	3.1855	3.5832	4.0227	4.5077	5.0419	5.6295	6.2749	8.1722
8	1.0829	1.1717	1.2668	1.3686	1.4775	1.5938	1.7182	1.8509	1.9926	2.1436	2.4760	2.8526	3.0590	3.2784	3.7589	4.2998	4.9077	5.5895	6.3528	7.2058	8.1573	11.032
9	1.0937	1.1951	1.3048	1.4233	1.5513	1.6895	1.8385	1.9990	2.1719	2.3579	2.7731	3.2519	3.5179	3.8030	4.4355	5.1598	5.9874	6.9310	8.0045	9.2234	10.604	14.894
10	1.1046	1.2190	1.3439	1.4802	1.6289	1.7908	1.9672	2.1589	2.3674	2.5937	3.1058	3.7072	4.0456	4.4114	5.2338	6.1917	7.3046	8.5944	10.086	11.806	13.786	20.107
11	1.1157	1.2434	1.3842	1.5395	1.7103	1.8983	2.1049	2.3316	2.5804	2.8531	3.4785	4.2262	4.6524	5.1173	6.1759	7.4301	8.9117	10.657	12.708	15.112	17.922	27.144
12	1.1268	1.2682	1.4258	1.6010	1.7959	2.0122	2.2522	2.5182	2.8127	3.1384	3.8960	4.8179	5.3503	5.9360	7.2876	8.9161	10.872	13.215	16.012	19.343	23.298	36.644
13	1.1381	1.2936	1.4685	1.6651	1.8856	2.1329	2.4098	2.7196	3.0658	3.4523	4.3635	5.4924	6.1528	6.8858	8.5994	10.699	13.264	16.386	20.175	24.759	30.288	49.470
14	1.1495	1.3195	1.5126	1.7317	1.9799	2.2609	2.5785	2.9372	3.3417	3.7975	4.8871	6.2613	7.0757	7.9875	10.147	12.839	16.182	20.319	25.421	31.691	39.374	66.784
15	1.1610	1.3459	1.5580	1.8009	2.0789	2.3966	2.7590	3.1722	3.6425	4.1772	5.4736	7.1379	8.1371	9.2655	11.974	15.407	19.742	25.196	32.030	40.565	51.186	90.158
16	1.1726	1.3728	1.6047	1.8730	2.1829	2.5404	2.9522	3.4259	3.9703	4.5950	6.1304	8.1372	9.3576	10.748	14.129	18.488	24.086	31.243	40.358	51.923	66.542	121.71
17	1.1843	1.4002	1.6528	1.9479	2.2920	2.6928	3.1588	3.7000	4.3276	5.0545	6.8660	9.2765	10.761	12.468	16.672	22.186	29.384	38.741	50.851	66.461	86.504	164.31
18	1.1961	1.4282	1.7024	2.0258	2.4066	2.8543	3.3799	3.9960	4.7171	5.5599	7.6900	10.575	12.375	14.463	19.673	26.623	35.849	48.039	64.072	85.071	112.46	221.82
19	1.2081	1.4568	1.7535	2.1068	2.5270	3.0256	3.6165	4.3157	5.1417	6.1159	8.6128	12.056	14.232	16.777	23.214	31.948	43.736	59.568	80.731	108.89	146.19	299.46
20	1.2202	1.4859	1.8061	2.1911	2.6533	3.2071	3.8697	4.6610	5.6044	6.7275	9.6463	13.743	16.367	19.461	27.393	38.338	53.358	73.864	101.72	139.38	190.05	404.27
21	1.2324	1.5157	1.8603	2.2788	2.7860	3.3996	4.1406	5.0338	6.1088	7.4002	10.804	15.668	18.822	22.574	32.324	46.005	65.096	91.592	128.17	178.41	247.06	545.77
22	1.2447	1.5460	1.9161	2.3699	2.9253	3.6035	4.4304	5.4365	6.6586	8.1403	12.100	17.861	21.645	26.186	38.142	55.206	79.418	113.57	161.49	228.36	321.18	736.79
23	1.2572	1.5769	1.9736	2.4647	3.0715	3.8197	4.7405	5.8715	7.2579	8.9543	13.552	20.362	24.891	30.376	45.008	66.247	96.889	140.83	203.48	292.30	417.54	994.66
24	1.2697	1.6084	2.0328	2.5633	3.2251	4.0489	5.0724	6.3412	7.9111	9.8497	15.179	23.212	28.625	35.236	53.109	79.497	118.21	174.63	256.39	374.14	542.80	1342.80
25	1.2824	1.6406	2.0938	2.6658	3.3864	4.2919	5.4274	6.8485	8.6231	10.835	17.000	26.462	32.919	40.874	62.669	95.396	144.21	216.54	323.05	478.90	705.64	1812.78
26	1.2953	1.6734	2.1566	2.7725	3.5557	4.5494	5.8074	7.3964	9.3992	11.918	19.040	30.167	37.857	47.414	73.949	114.48	175.94	268.51	407.04	613.00	917.33	2447.25
27	1.3082	1.7069	2.2213	2.8834	3.7335	4.8223	6.2139	7.9881	10.245	13.110	21.325	34.390	43.535	55.000	87.260	137.37	214.64	332.95	512.87	784.64	1192.5	3303.78
28	1.3213	1.7410	2.2879	2.9987	3.9201	5.1117	6.6488	8.6271	11.167	14.421	23.884	39.204	50.066	63.800	102.97	164.84	261.86	412.86	646.21	1004.3	1550.3	4460.11
29	1.3345	1.7758	2.3566	3.1187	4.1161	5.4184	7.1143	9.3173	12.172	15.863	26.750	44.693	57.575	74.009	121.50	197.81	319.47	511.95	814.23	1285.6	2015.4	6021.15
30	1.3478	1.8114	2.4273	3.2434	4.3219	5.7435	7.6123	10.063	13.268	17.449	29.960	50.950	66.212	85.850	143.37	237.38	389.76	634.82	1025.9	1645.5	2620.0	8128.55
40	1.4889	2.2080	3.2620	4.8010	7.0400	10.286	14.974	21.725	31.409	45.259	93.051	188.88	267.86	378.72	750.38	1469.8	2847.0	5455.9	10347.	19427.	36118.9	*
50	1.6446	2.6916	4.3839	7.1067	11.467	18.420	29.457	46.902	74.358	117.39	289.00	700.23	1083.7	1670.7	3927.4	9100.4	20797.	46890.	*	*	*	*
60	1.8167	3.2810	5.8916	10.520	18.679	32.988	57.946	101.26	176.03	304.48	897.60	2595.9	4384.0	7370.2	20555.	56348.	*	*	*	*	*	*

*$FV_{n,k} > 99{,}999$

Exhibit 2   Present Value Factors for a Single Cash Flow

$$PV_{n,k} = 1/(1 + k)^n$$

Number of Periods	1%	2%	3%	4%	5%	6%	7%	8%	9%	10%	12%	14%	15%	16%	18%	20%	22%	24%	26%	28%	30%	35%
1	.9901	.9804	.9709	.9615	.9524	.9434	.9346	.9259	.9174	.9091	.8929	.8772	.8696	.8621	.8475	.8333	.8197	.8065	.7937	.7813	.7692	.7407
2	.9803	.9612	.9426	.9246	.9070	.8900	.8734	.8573	.8417	.8264	.7972	.7695	.7561	.7432	.7182	.6944	.6719	.6504	.6299	.6104	.5917	.5487
3	.9706	.9423	.9151	.8890	.8638	.8396	.8163	.7938	.7722	.7513	.7118	.6750	.6575	.6407	.6086	.5787	.5507	.5245	.4999	.4768	.4552	.4064
4	.9610	.9238	.8885	.8548	.8227	.7921	.7629	.7350	.7084	.6830	.6355	.5921	.5718	.5523	.5158	.4823	.4514	.4230	.3968	.3725	.3501	.3011
5	.9515	.9057	.8626	.8219	.7835	.7473	.7130	.6806	.6499	.6209	.5674	.5194	.4972	.4761	.4371	.4019	.3700	.3411	.3149	.2910	.2693	.2230
6	.9420	.8880	.8375	.7903	.7462	.7050	.6663	.6302	.5963	.5645	.5066	.4556	.4323	.4104	.3704	.3349	.3033	.2751	.2499	.2274	.2072	.1652
7	.9327	.8706	.8131	.7599	.7107	.6651	.6227	.5835	.5470	.5132	.4523	.3996	.3759	.3538	.3139	.2791	.2486	.2218	.1983	.1776	.1594	.1224
8	.9235	.8535	.7894	.7307	.6768	.6274	.5820	.5403	.5019	.4665	.4039	.3506	.3269	.3050	.2660	.2326	.2038	.1789	.1574	.1388	.1226	.0906
9	.9143	.8368	.7664	.7026	.6446	.5919	.5439	.5002	.4604	.4241	.3606	.3075	.2843	.2630	.2255	.1938	.1670	.1443	.1249	.1084	.0943	.0671
10	.9053	.8203	.7441	.6756	.6139	.5584	.5083	.4632	.4224	.3855	.3220	.2697	.2472	.2267	.1911	.1615	.1369	.1164	.0992	.0847	.0725	.0497
11	.8963	.8043	.7224	.6496	.5847	.5268	.4751	.4289	.3875	.3505	.2875	.2366	.2149	.1954	.1619	.1346	.1122	.0938	.0787	.0662	.0558	.0368
12	.8874	.7885	.7014	.6246	.5568	.4970	.4440	.3971	.3555	.3186	.2567	.2076	.1869	.1685	.1372	.1122	.0920	.0757	.0625	.0517	.0429	.0273
13	.8787	.7730	.6810	.6006	.5303	.4688	.4150	.3677	.3262	.2897	.2292	.1821	.1625	.1452	.1163	.0935	.0754	.0610	.0496	.0404	.0330	.0202
14	.8700	.7579	.6611	.5775	.5051	.4423	.3878	.3405	.2992	.2633	.2046	.1597	.1413	.1252	.0985	.0779	.0618	.0492	.0393	.0316	.0254	.0150
15	.8613	.7430	.6419	.5553	.4810	.4173	.3624	.3152	.2745	.2394	.1827	.1401	.1229	.1079	.0835	.0649	.0507	.0397	.0312	.0247	.0195	.0111
16	.8528	.7284	.6232	.5339	.4581	.3936	.3387	.2919	.2519	.2176	.1631	.1229	.1069	.0930	.0708	.0541	.0415	.0320	.0248	.0193	.0150	.0082
17	.8444	.7142	.6050	.5134	.4363	.3714	.3166	.2703	.2311	.1978	.1456	.1078	.0929	.0802	.0600	.0451	.0340	.0258	.0197	.0150	.0116	.0061
18	.8360	.7002	.5874	.4936	.4155	.3503	.2959	.2502	.2120	.1799	.1300	.0946	.0808	.0691	.0508	.0376	.0279	.0208	.0156	.0118	.0089	.0045
19	.8277	.6864	.5703	.4746	.3957	.3305	.2765	.2317	.1945	.1635	.1161	.0829	.0703	.0596	.0431	.0313	.0229	.0168	.0124	.0092	.0068	.0033
20	.8195	.6730	.5537	.4564	.3769	.3118	.2584	.2145	.1784	.1486	.1037	.0728	.0611	.0514	.0365	.0261	.0187	.0135	.0098	.0072	.0053	.0025
21	.8114	.6598	.5375	.4388	.3589	.2942	.2415	.1987	.1637	.1351	.0926	.0638	.0531	.0443	.0309	.0217	.0154	.0109	.0078	.0056	.0040	.0018
22	.8034	.6468	.5219	.4220	.3418	.2775	.2257	.1839	.1502	.1228	.0826	.0560	.0462	.0382	.0262	.0181	.0126	.0088	.0062	.0044	.0031	.0014
23	.7954	.6342	.5067	.4057	.3256	.2618	.2109	.1703	.1378	.1117	.0738	.0491	.0402	.0329	.0222	.0151	.0103	.0071	.0049	.0034	.0024	.0010
24	.7876	.6217	.4919	.3901	.3101	.2470	.1971	.1577	.1264	.1015	.0659	.0431	.0349	.0284	.0188	.0126	.0085	.0057	.0039	.0027	.0018	.0007
25	.7798	.6095	.4776	.3751	.2953	.2330	.1842	.1460	.1160	.0923	.0588	.0378	.0304	.0245	.0160	.0105	.0069	.0046	.0031	.0021	.0014	.0006
26	.7720	.5976	.4637	.3607	.2812	.2198	.1722	.1352	.1064	.0839	.0525	.0331	.0264	.0211	.0135	.0087	.0057	.0037	.0025	.0016	.0011	.0004
27	.7644	.5859	.4502	.3468	.2678	.2074	.1609	.1252	.0976	.0763	.0469	.0291	.0230	.0182	.0115	.0073	.0047	.0030	.0019	.0013	.0008	.0003
28	.7568	.5744	.4371	.3335	.2551	.1956	.1504	.1159	.0895	.0693	.0419	.0255	.0200	.0157	.0097	.0061	.0038	.0024	.0015	.0010	.0006	.0002
29	.7493	.5631	.4243	.3207	.2429	.1846	.1406	.1073	.0822	.0630	.0374	.0224	.0174	.0135	.0082	.0051	.0031	.0020	.0012	.0008	.0005	.0002
30	.7419	.5521	.4120	.3083	.2314	.1741	.1314	.0994	.0754	.0573	.0334	.0196	.0151	.0116	.0070	.0042	.0026	.0016	.0010	.0006	.0004	.0001
35	.7059	.5000	.3554	.2534	.1813	.1301	.0937	.0676	.0490	.0356	.0189	.0102	.0075	.0055	.0030	.0017	.0009	.0005	.0003	.0002	.0001	*
40	.6717	.4529	.3066	.2083	.1420	.0972	.0668	.0460	.0318	.0221	.0107	.0053	.0037	.0026	.0013	.0007	.0004	.0002	.0001	.0001	*	*
45	.6391	.4102	.2644	.1712	.1113	.0727	.0476	.0313	.0207	.0137	.0061	.0027	.0019	.0013	.0006	.0003	.0001	.0001	*	*	*	*
50	.6080	.3715	.2281	.1407	.0872	.0543	.0339	.0213	.0134	.0085	.0035	.0014	.0009	.0006	.0003	.0001	*	*	*	*	*	*
55	.5785	.3365	.1968	.1157	.0683	.0406	.0242	.0145	.0087	.0053	.0020	.0007	.0005	.0003	.0001	*	*	*	*	*	*	*
60	.5504	.3048	.1697	.0951	.0535	.0303	.0173	.0099	.0057	.0033	.0011	.0004	.0002	.0001	*	*	*	*	*	*	*	*

*Rounds to zero

1. The interest rate per period is 2 percent.
2. The number of periods is 20 (4 interest periods per year × 5 years).
3. The factor at the intersection of 2 percent and 20 periods is 0.6730.
4. Goal of $2,000 × 0.6730 = $1,346.

If $1,346 is invested today under the assumed conditions, it will grow to the desired total of $2,000 by the end of five years.

Compound and Present Values with Annuities

In the discussions of compound value and present value, the investment consisted of a lump-sum amount paid at the beginning of a period. In pragmatic investing programs, a *series* of investments is typically made over a period of time. At the other end of the spectrum, one could also receive a series of payments over a period of time. Various calculations may be necessary with regard to annuities.

An **annuity** is a cash flow stream for a finite number of periods where all of the cash flows are equal in amount. An **ordinary annuity** is a series of investments made at the *end* of a period. The period might consist of months, quarters, or years. An **annuity due** is a series of investments made at the *beginning* of a period. Note that the only difference between an ordinary annuity and an annuity due is *when* the investments are made in a period. For both of these types of annuity, it may be desirable to calculate the future value of the series of payments.

On the other hand, you may also wish to calculate the present value of an ordinary annuity. This calculation determines how much must be invested now to receive a known stream of payments for a stated number of years.

Calculations for any of the above may be performed manually or with the help of special present and future value tables. Manual calculations are very tedious, time-consuming, and prone to error. For pragmatic purposes, the use of tables is highly recommended. Tables may be purchased in booklet form or retrieved from the Internet. This discussion will focus on the use of tables.

The objective of an ordinary annuity calculation is to calculate the future value of a series of investments. In an ordinary annuity, a series of payments is made at the *end* of each period. Suppose $1,000 is invested at the end of each year over a five-year period at an annual interest rate of 6 percent. Using the ordinary annuity table shown in Exhibit 3, the calculation of future value is as follows:

1. The interest rate per period is 6 percent.
2. The number of periods is 5 (1 interest period per year × 5 years).
3. The factor at the intersection of 6 percent and 5 periods is 5.6371.
4. $1,000.00 × 5.6371 = $5,637.10.

An investment of $1,000 per year made at the end of each year for five years in an investment yielding 6 percent annually will grow to $5,637.10 at the end of the five-year period.

The objective of an annuity due calculation is identical to that of an ordinary annuity calculation. The major difference is *when* the series of payments is made. An annuity due investment is characterized by a series of payments made at the

Exhibit 3 Ordinary Annuity Table (Future Value Factors)

$$FVA_{n,k} = \frac{(1+k)^n - 1}{k}$$

Number of Periods	1%	2%	3%	4%	5%	6%	7%	8%	9%	10%	12%	14%	15%	16%	18%	20%	22%	24%	26%	28%	30%	35%
1	1.0000	1.0000	1.0000	1.0000	1.0000	1.0000	1.0000	1.0000	1.0000	1.0000	1.0000	1.0000	1.0000	1.0000	1.0000	1.0000	1.0000	1.0000	1.0000	1.0000	1.0000	1.0000
2	2.0100	2.0200	2.0300	2.0400	2.0500	2.0600	2.0700	2.0800	2.0900	2.1000	2.1200	2.1400	2.1500	2.1600	2.1800	2.2000	2.2200	2.2400	2.2600	2.2800	2.3000	2.3500
3	3.0301	3.0604	3.0909	3.1216	3.1525	3.1836	3.2149	3.2464	3.2781	3.3100	3.3744	3.4396	3.4725	3.5056	3.5724	3.6400	3.7084	3.7776	3.8476	3.9184	3.9900	4.1725
4	4.0604	4.1216	4.1836	4.2465	4.3101	4.3746	4.4399	4.5061	4.5731	4.6410	4.7793	4.9211	4.9934	5.0665	5.2154	5.3680	5.5242	5.6842	5.8480	6.0156	6.1870	6.6329
5	5.1010	5.2040	5.3091	5.4163	5.5256	5.6371	5.7507	5.8666	5.9847	6.1051	6.3528	6.6101	6.7424	6.8771	7.1542	7.4416	7.7396	8.0484	8.3684	8.6999	9.0431	9.9544
6	6.1520	6.3081	6.4684	6.6330	6.8019	6.9753	7.1533	7.3359	7.5233	7.7156	8.1152	8.5355	8.7537	8.9775	9.4420	9.9299	10.442	10.980	11.544	12.136	12.756	14.438
7	7.2135	7.4343	7.6625	7.8983	8.1420	8.3938	8.6540	8.9228	9.2004	9.4872	10.089	10.730	11.067	11.414	12.142	12.916	13.740	14.615	15.546	16.534	17.583	20.492
8	8.2857	8.5830	8.8923	9.2142	9.5491	9.8975	10.260	10.637	11.028	11.436	12.300	13.233	13.727	14.240	15.327	16.499	17.762	19.123	20.588	22.163	23.858	28.664
9	9.3685	9.7546	10.159	10.583	11.027	11.491	11.978	12.488	13.021	13.579	14.776	16.085	16.786	17.519	19.086	20.799	22.670	24.712	26.940	29.369	32.015	39.696
10	10.462	10.950	11.464	12.006	12.578	13.181	13.816	14.487	15.193	15.937	17.549	19.337	20.304	21.321	23.521	25.959	28.657	31.643	34.945	38.593	42.619	54.590
11	11.567	12.169	12.808	13.486	14.207	14.972	15.784	16.645	17.560	18.531	20.655	23.045	24.349	25.733	28.755	32.150	35.962	40.238	45.031	50.398	56.405	74.697
12	12.683	13.412	14.192	15.026	15.917	16.870	17.888	18.977	20.141	21.384	24.133	27.271	29.002	30.850	34.931	39.581	44.874	50.895	57.739	65.510	74.327	101.84
13	13.809	14.680	15.618	16.627	17.713	18.882	20.141	21.495	22.953	24.523	28.029	32.089	34.352	36.786	42.219	48.497	55.746	64.110	73.751	84.853	97.625	138.48
14	14.947	15.974	17.086	18.292	19.599	21.015	22.550	24.215	26.019	27.975	32.393	37.581	40.505	43.672	50.818	59.196	69.010	80.496	93.926	109.61	127.91	187.95
15	16.097	17.293	18.599	20.024	21.579	23.276	25.129	27.152	29.361	31.772	37.280	43.842	47.580	51.660	60.965	72.035	85.192	100.82	119.35	141.30	167.29	254.74
16	17.258	18.639	20.157	21.825	23.657	25.673	27.888	30.324	33.003	35.950	42.753	50.980	55.717	60.925	72.939	87.442	104.93	126.01	151.38	181.87	218.47	344.90
17	18.430	20.012	21.762	23.698	25.840	28.213	30.840	33.750	36.974	40.545	48.884	59.118	65.075	71.673	87.068	105.93	129.02	157.25	191.73	233.79	285.01	466.61
18	19.615	21.412	23.414	25.645	28.132	30.906	33.999	37.450	41.301	45.599	55.750	68.394	75.836	84.141	103.74	128.12	158.40	195.99	242.59	300.25	371.52	630.92
19	20.811	22.841	25.117	27.671	30.539	33.760	37.379	41.446	46.018	51.159	63.440	78.969	88.212	98.603	123.41	154.74	194.25	244.03	306.66	385.32	483.97	852.75
20	22.019	24.297	26.870	29.778	33.066	36.786	40.995	45.762	51.160	57.275	72.052	91.025	102.44	115.38	146.63	186.69	237.99	303.60	387.39	494.21	630.17	1152.2
21	23.239	25.783	28.676	31.969	35.719	39.993	44.865	50.423	56.765	64.002	81.699	104.77	118.81	134.84	174.02	225.03	291.35	377.46	489.11	633.59	820.22	1556.5
22	24.472	27.299	30.537	34.248	38.505	43.392	49.006	55.457	62.873	71.403	92.503	120.44	137.63	157.41	206.34	271.03	356.44	469.06	617.28	812.00	1067.3	2102.3
23	25.716	28.845	32.453	36.618	41.430	46.996	53.436	60.893	69.532	79.543	104.60	138.30	159.28	183.60	244.49	326.24	435.86	582.63	778.77	1040.4	1388.5	2839.0
24	26.973	30.422	34.426	39.083	44.502	50.816	58.177	66.765	76.790	88.497	118.16	158.66	184.17	213.98	289.49	392.48	532.75	723.46	982.25	1332.7	1806.0	3833.7
25	28.243	32.030	36.459	41.646	47.727	54.865	63.249	73.106	84.701	98.347	133.33	181.87	212.79	249.21	342.60	471.98	650.96	898.09	1238.6	1706.8	2348.8	5176.5
26	29.526	33.671	38.553	44.312	51.113	59.156	68.676	79.954	93.324	109.18	150.33	208.33	245.71	290.09	405.27	567.38	795.17	1114.6	1561.7	2185.7	3054.4	6989.3
27	30.821	35.344	40.710	47.084	54.669	63.706	74.484	87.351	102.72	121.10	169.37	238.50	283.57	337.50	479.22	681.85	971.10	1383.1	1968.7	2798.7	3971.8	9436.5
28	32.129	37.051	42.931	49.968	58.403	66.528	80.698	95.339	112.97	134.21	190.70	272.89	327.10	392.50	566.48	819.22	1185.7	1716.1	2481.6	3583.3	5164.3	12740.
29	33.450	38.792	45.219	52.966	62.323	73.640	87.347	103.97	124.14	148.63	214.58	312.09	377.17	456.30	669.45	984.07	1447.6	2129.0	3127.8	4587.7	6714.6	17200.
30	34.785	40.568	47.575	56.085	66.439	79.058	94.461	113.28	136.31	164.49	241.33	356.79	434.75	530.31	790.95	1181.9	1767.1	2640.9	3942.0	5873.2	8730.0	23222.
40	48.886	60.402	75.401	95.026	120.80	154.76	199.64	259.06	337.88	442.59	767.09	1342.0	1779.1	2360.8	4163.2	7343.9	12937.	22729.	39793.	69377.	*	*
50	64.463	84.579	112.80	152.67	209.35	290.34	406.53	573.77	815.08	1163.9	2400.0	4994.5	7217.7	10436.	21813.	45497.	94525.	*	*	*	*	*
60	81.670	114.05	163.05	237.99	353.58	533.13	813.52	1253.2	1944.8	3034.8	7471.6	18535.	29220.	46058.	*	*	*	*	*	*	*	*

*$FVA_{n,k} > 99{,}999$

beginning of a period (unlike at the end of a period for an ordinary annuity). We can again use the table in Exhibit 3, but we have to adjust a couple of factors to account for beginning-of-period investments. We do this by adding one period and then subtracting one payment from the result. Using the same example of an investment of $1,000 per year, but made at the beginning of each year for five years, and earning 6 percent annually, the calculation can be done as follows:

1. The number of periods is 6 (1 interest period per year × 5 years + 1 to convert to beginning-of-year investments).
2. The factor at the intersection of 6 percent and 6 periods is 6.9753.
3. $1,000 × 6.9753 = $6,975.30.
4. $6,975.30 − $1,000 = $5,975.30.

An alternate way to calculate this total is to take the result from the ordinary annuity calculation ($5,637.10) and add one more year's interest calculation:

$$\$5,637.10 \times 106\% = \$5,975.33$$

An entity investing $1,000 per year at the beginning of each year for five years in an investment yielding 6 percent annually will have $5,975.33 at the end of the five-year period. (The difference of 3 cents between these two calculations occurs because the factors in Exhibit 3 run to only four decimals.)

Investing in an annuity that *pays out* a stream of cash flows will require a present value calculation. The *present value of an ordinary annuity* calculation deals with how much must be invested now (at the present) to receive a stated stream of payments for a stated number of years. Exhibit 4 presents a present value annuity table. To determine how much must be invested now in an investment yielding 6 percent annually to receive a stream of $1,000 annual payments over a period of 5 years, the calculation is as follows:

1. The interest rate per period is 6 percent.
2. The number of periods is 5 (1 interest period per year × 5 years).
3. The factor at the intersection of 6 percent and 5 periods is 4.2124.
4. $1,000.00 × 4.2124 = $4,212.40.

Given an annual interest rate of 6 percent, one must invest $4,212.40 now to receive $1,000 per year for five years.

Endnote

1. Readers wanting information on more advanced subjects in financial management and hospitality accounting are referred to Raymond Cote, *Accounting for Hospitality Managers* (Lansing, Mich.: American Hotel & Lodging Educational Institute), 2007.

Key Terms

annuity—A cash flow stream for a finite number of periods in which all the cash flows are equal in amount.

Exhibit 4 Present Value Factors for an Annuity

$$PVA_{n,k} = \frac{1 - \dfrac{1}{(1+k)^n}}{k}$$

Number of Periods	1%	2%	3%	4%	5%	6%	7%	8%	9%	10%	12%	14%	15%	16%	18%	20%	22%	24%	26%	28%	30%	35%
1	0.9901	0.9804	0.9709	0.9615	0.9524	0.9434	0.9346	0.9259	0.9174	0.9091	0.8929	0.8772	0.8696	0.8621	0.8475	0.8333	0.8197	0.8065	0.7937	0.7813	0.7692	0.7407
2	1.9704	1.9416	1.9135	1.8861	1.8594	1.8334	1.8080	1.7833	1.7591	1.7355	1.6901	1.6467	1.6257	1.6052	1.5656	1.5278	1.4915	1.4568	1.4235	1.3916	1.3609	1.2894
3	2.9410	2.8839	2.8286	2.7751	2.7232	2.6730	2.6243	2.5771	2.5313	2.4869	2.4018	2.3216	2.2832	2.2459	2.1743	2.1065	2.0422	1.9813	1.9234	1.8684	1.8161	1.6959
4	3.9020	3.8077	3.7171	3.6299	3.5460	3.4651	3.3872	3.3121	3.2397	3.1699	3.0373	2.9137	2.8550	2.7982	2.6901	2.5887	2.4936	2.4043	2.3202	2.2410	2.1662	1.9969
5	4.8534	4.7135	4.5797	4.4518	4.3295	4.2124	4.1002	3.9927	3.8897	3.7908	3.6048	3.4331	3.3522	3.2743	3.1272	2.9906	2.8636	2.7454	2.6351	2.5320	2.4356	2.2200
6	5.7955	5.6014	5.4172	5.2421	5.0757	4.9173	4.7665	4.6229	4.4859	4.3553	4.1114	3.8887	3.7845	3.6847	3.4976	3.3255	3.1669	3.0205	2.8850	2.7594	2.6427	2.3852
7	6.7282	6.4720	6.2303	6.0021	5.7864	5.5824	5.3893	5.2064	5.0330	4.8684	4.5638	4.2883	4.1604	4.0386	3.8115	3.6046	3.4155	3.2423	3.0833	2.9370	2.8021	2.5075
8	7.6517	7.3255	7.0197	6.7327	6.4632	6.2098	5.9713	5.7466	5.5348	5.3349	4.9676	4.6389	4.4873	4.3436	4.0776	3.8372	3.6193	3.4212	3.2407	3.0758	2.9247	2.5982
9	8.5660	8.1622	7.7861	7.4353	7.1078	6.8017	6.5152	6.2469	5.9952	5.7590	5.3282	4.9464	4.7716	4.6065	4.3030	4.0310	3.7863	3.5655	3.3657	3.1842	3.0190	2.6653
10	9.4713	8.9826	8.5302	8.1109	7.7217	7.3601	7.0236	6.7101	6.4177	6.1446	5.6502	5.2161	5.0188	4.8332	4.4941	4.1925	3.9232	3.6819	3.4648	3.2689	3.0915	2.7150
11	10.3676	9.7868	9.2526	8.7605	8.3064	7.8869	7.4987	7.1390	6.8052	6.4951	5.9377	5.4527	5.2337	5.0286	4.6560	4.3271	4.0354	3.7757	3.5435	3.3351	3.1473	2.7519
12	11.2551	10.5753	9.9540	9.3851	8.8633	8.3838	7.9427	7.5361	7.1607	6.8137	6.1944	5.6603	5.4206	5.1971	4.7932	4.4392	4.1274	3.8514	3.6059	3.3868	3.1903	2.7792
13	12.1337	11.3484	10.6350	9.9856	9.3936	8.8527	8.3577	7.9038	7.4869	7.1034	6.4235	5.8424	5.5831	5.3423	4.9095	4.5327	4.2028	3.9124	3.6555	3.4272	3.2233	2.7994
14	13.0037	12.1062	11.2961	10.5631	9.8986	9.2950	8.7455	8.2442	7.7862	7.3667	6.6282	6.0021	5.7245	5.4675	5.0081	4.6106	4.2646	3.9616	3.6949	3.4587	3.2487	2.8144
15	13.8651	12.8493	11.9379	11.1184	10.3797	9.7122	9.1079	8.5595	8.0607	7.6061	6.8109	6.1422	5.8474	5.5755	5.0916	4.6755	4.3152	4.0013	3.7261	3.4834	3.2682	2.8255
16	14.7179	13.5777	12.5611	11.6523	10.8378	10.1059	9.4466	8.8514	8.3126	7.8237	6.9740	6.2651	5.9542	5.6685	5.1624	4.7296	4.3567	4.0333	3.7509	3.5026	3.2832	2.8337
17	15.5623	14.2919	13.1661	12.1657	11.2741	10.4773	9.7632	9.1216	8.5436	8.0216	7.1196	6.3729	6.0472	5.7487	5.2223	4.7746	4.3908	4.0591	3.7705	3.5177	3.2948	2.8398
18	16.3983	14.9920	13.7535	12.6593	11.6896	10.8276	10.0591	9.3719	8.7556	8.2014	7.2497	6.4674	6.1280	5.8178	5.2732	4.8122	4.4187	4.0799	3.7861	3.5294	3.3037	2.8443
19	17.2260	15.6785	14.3238	13.1339	12.0853	11.1581	10.3356	9.6036	8.9501	8.3649	7.3658	6.5504	6.1982	5.8775	5.3162	4.8435	4.4415	4.0967	3.7985	3.5386	3.3105	2.8476
20	18.0456	16.3514	14.8775	13.5903	12.4622	11.4699	10.5940	9.8181	9.1285	8.5136	7.4694	6.6231	6.2593	5.9288	5.3527	4.8696	4.4603	4.1103	3.8083	3.5458	3.3158	2.8501
21	18.8570	17.0112	15.4150	14.0292	12.8212	11.7641	10.8355	10.0168	9.2922	8.6487	7.5620	6.6870	6.3125	5.9731	5.3837	4.8913	4.4756	4.1212	3.8161	3.5514	3.3198	2.8519
22	19.6604	17.6580	15.9369	14.4511	13.1630	12.0416	11.0612	10.2007	9.4424	8.7715	7.6446	6.7429	6.3587	6.0113	5.4099	4.9094	4.4882	4.1300	3.8223	3.5558	3.3230	2.8533
23	20.4558	18.2922	16.4436	14.8568	13.4886	12.3034	11.2722	10.3711	9.5802	8.8832	7.7184	6.7921	6.3988	6.0442	5.4321	4.9245	4.4985	4.1371	3.8273	3.5592	3.3254	2.8543
24	21.2434	18.9139	16.9355	15.2470	13.7986	12.5504	11.4693	10.5288	9.7066	8.9847	7.7843	6.8351	6.4338	6.0726	5.4509	4.9371	4.5070	4.1428	3.8312	3.5619	3.3272	2.8550
25	22.0232	19.5235	17.4131	15.6221	14.0939	12.7834	11.6536	10.6748	9.8226	9.0770	7.8431	6.8729	6.4641	6.0971	5.4669	4.9476	4.5139	4.1474	3.8342	3.5640	3.3286	2.8556
26	22.7952	20.1210	17.8768	15.9828	14.3752	13.0032	11.8258	10.8100	9.9290	9.1609	7.8957	6.9061	6.4906	6.1182	5.4804	4.9563	4.5196	4.1511	3.8367	3.5656	3.3297	2.8560
27	23.5596	20.7069	18.3270	16.3296	14.6430	13.2105	11.9867	10.9352	10.0266	9.2372	7.9426	6.9352	6.5135	6.1364	5.4919	4.9636	4.5243	4.1542	3.8387	3.5669	3.3305	2.8563
28	24.3164	21.2813	18.7641	16.6631	14.8981	13.4062	12.1371	11.0511	10.1161	9.3066	7.9844	6.9607	6.5335	6.1520	5.5016	4.9697	4.5281	4.1566	3.8402	3.5679	3.3312	2.8565
29	25.0658	21.8444	19.1885	16.9837	15.1411	13.5907	12.2777	11.1584	10.1983	9.3696	8.0218	6.9830	6.5509	6.1656	5.5098	4.9747	4.5312	4.1585	3.8414	3.5687	3.3317	2.8567
30	25.8077	22.3965	19.6004	17.2920	15.3725	13.7648	12.4090	11.2578	10.2737	9.4269	8.0552	7.0027	6.5660	6.1772	5.5168	4.9789	4.5338	4.1601	3.8424	3.5693	3.3321	2.8568
35	29.4086	24.9986	21.4872	18.6646	16.3742	14.4982	12.9477	11.6546	10.5668	9.6442	8.1755	7.0700	6.6166	6.2153	5.5386	4.9915	4.5411	4.1644	3.8450	3.5708	3.3330	2.8571
40	32.8347	27.3555	23.1148	19.7928	17.1591	15.0463	13.3317	11.9246	10.7574	9.7791	8.2438	7.1050	6.6418	6.2335	5.5482	4.9966	4.5439	4.1659	3.8458	3.5712	3.3332	2.8571
45	36.0945	29.4902	24.5187	20.7200	17.7741	15.4558	13.6055	12.1084	10.8812	9.8628	8.2825	7.1232	6.6543	6.2421	5.5523	4.9986	4.5449	4.1664	3.8460	3.5714	3.3333	2.8571
50	39.1961	31.4236	25.7298	21.4822	18.2559	15.7619	13.8007	12.2335	10.9617	9.9148	8.3045	7.1327	6.6605	6.2463	5.5541	4.9995	4.5452	4.1666	3.8461	3.5714	3.3333	2.8571
55	42.1472	33.1748	26.7744	22.1086	18.6335	15.9905	13.9399	12.3186	11.0140	9.9471	8.3170	7.1376	6.6636	6.2482	5.5549	4.9998	4.5454	4.1666	3.8461	3.5714	3.3333	2.8571
60	44.9550	34.7609	27.6756	22.6235	18.9293	16.1614	14.0392	12.3766	11.0480	9.9672	8.3240	7.1401	6.6651	6.2492	5.5553	4.9999	4.5454	4.1667	3.8462	3.5714	3.3333	2.8571

annuity due—A series of investments made at the beginning of a year.

cash discounts—Incentives that sellers offer to buyers to encourage payment of invoices within a shorter period of time than the customary full payment period allowed.

compound interest—Interest that is charged on the combined amount of the loan principal and accumulated interest of prior periods.

compound value—The sum of the principal amount plus its compound interest.

exact year—A year based on 365 days.

interest expense—The cost incurred when a person or entity borrows money from a lending source.

ordinary annuity—A series of investments made at the end of a period.

ordinary year—A year based on 360 days.

present value—An amount that must be invested now to grow into a larger amount in the future.

simple interest method—A method of calculating interest expense in which the interest charge is based only on the principal of the loan.

 Review Questions ————————————————————————

1. What is the formula for calculating interest expense on a loan if the time period is stated in years?

2. What is the formula for calculating interest expense on a loan if the time period is stated in months?

3. What is the ordinary formula for calculating interest expense if the time period is stated in days?

4. What is the exact formula for calculating interest expense if the time period is stated in days?

5. How is the cash discount term 1/5,n/25 interpreted?

6. How is the cash discount term 1/5,n/25 ROG interpreted?

7. What does the cash discount term 1/5,n/25 EOM mean if the invoice date is August 10?

8. What does the cash discount term 1/5,n/25 EOM mean if the invoice date is September 25?

9. Which of these discount terms—1/5,n/25 EOM or 1/5,n/25 PROX—will provide the longer time period?

10. What is the difference between the calculation of simple interest and the calculation of compound interest?

11. What is the objective of compound value? of present value?

Internet Sites

For more information, visit the following Internet sites. Remember that Internet addresses can change without notice. If the site is no longer there, you can use a search engine to look for additional sites.

Cash Discounts
www.accountingtools.com/questions-
  and-answers/what-is-a-cash-
  discount.html
http://simplestudies.com/what-do-2-
  10-n-30-terms-mean.html

Converting Fractions to Decimals
www.cliffsnotes.com/Section/
  How-do-you-convert-a-fraction-to-
  a-decimal-or-change-a-decimal-to-a-
  fraction-.id-305405,articleId-7841.html

Present and Future Value of Annuities
www.accountingcoach.com/online-
  accounting-course/81Xpg01.html
www.investopedia.com/articles/
  03/101503.asp#axzz1RB5GGfox
www.principlesofaccounting.com/ART/
  fv.pv.tables/pvofordinaryannuity.htm

Problems

Problem 1

The invoice amount is $1,000 for all items below. Calculate the last allowable date for the discount and the amount paid.

Date of Invoice	Goods Received	Terms	Discount Good till	Date Paid	Amount Paid
9/16	9/25	4/10,n/30	_____	9/26	$ _____
9/16	9/20	4/10,n/30 ROG	_____	9/30	$ _____
9/16	9/12	2/10,n/30 ROG	_____	9/26	$ _____
9/16	9/25	2/10,n/30	_____	9/27	$ _____
9/16	9/25	3/10,n/30 EOM	_____	10/9	$ _____
9/16	9/25	3/15,n/30 EOM	_____	10/15	$ _____
9/26	9/25	3/10,n/30 EOM	_____	11/9	$ _____
9/16	9/25	3/15,n/30 EOM	_____	11/9	$ _____

Problem 2

Compute the interest expense for the following loans.

a. $8,000 borrowed at 9% for 5 years.

b. $5,400 borrowed at 15% for 3 years.

c. $12,000 borrowed at 9% for 5 months.

Problem 3

An investment yields 6 percent annually; the interest is earned semiannually. Calculate what the value of a $5,000 investment made today would be at the end of 10 years.

Problem 4

Calculate the lump sum that must be invested now to attain $5,000 at the end of 6 years in an investment yielding 4 percent annually, interest earned quarterly.

Problem 5

At the end of each year, $5,000 will be invested in an investment yielding 5 percent annually. Calculate what the value of the investment will be at the end of 15 years.

Problem 6

At the beginning of each year, $5,000 will be invested in an investment yielding 5 percent annually. Calculate what the value of the investment will be at the end of 15 years.

Problem 7

Calculate the amount that must be invested now to receive $2,000 per year for 10 years in an investment yielding 4 percent annually.

Case Study:
Purchase Discount and Vendor Selection

The owners of a new restaurant are in the process of selecting vendors. Some vendors offer cash discounts, others offer trade discounts, and still others offer no discounts at all. Discuss some issues buyers should consider when choosing among vendors that offer similar food products.

Index

C